JOHN
OF
GAUNT

JOHN
OF
GAUNT

SON OF ONE KING,
FATHER OF ANOTHER

KATHRYN WARNER

AMBERLEY

This edition published 2023

Amberley Publishing
The Hill, Stroud
Gloucestershire, GL5 4EP

www.amberley-books.com

British Library Cataloguing in Publication Data.
A catalogue record for this book is available from the British Library.

ISBN 978 1 3981 1725 9 (paperback)
ISBN 978 1 4456 7032 4 (ebook)

1 2 3 4 5 6 7 8 9 10

Typeset in 10pt on 13pt Sabon.
Typesetting by SJmagic DESIGN SERVICES, India.
Printed in India

Old John of Gaunt, time-honour'd Lancaster,
Hast thou, according to thy oath and band,
Brought hither Henry Herford thy bold son,
Here to make good the boisterous late appeal,
Which then our leisure would not let us hear,
Against the duke of Norfolk, Thomas Mowbray?

Shakespeare, *Richard II*, Act 1 Scene 1

Contents

Family Trees   9
Dramatis Personae   13
Introduction   22

1   Birth in St Bavo, Ghent   25
2   The Infant's Earldom   32
3   The Two Leonors   36
4   Spaniards on the Sea   41
5   No Pleasure in the Company of Ladies   45
6   A Damsel and a Daughter   49
7   Guileless, of Humble Manner   55
8   The Departure of Duke Henry's Soul   59
9   Great Wonders and Signs   63
10 Almost the King of Scotland   67
11 Defeating Enrique and Claiming Provence   72
12 Lady Blanche, Our Late Consort   76
13 My Very Honoured Mother, Whom God Absolve   80
14 Feasts and Celebrations in Aquitaine   83
15 My Lord of Spain   87
16 A Woman of Great Beauty   90
17 Dame Katherine de Roet, Lady Swynford   94
18 A Barrel of Relics and a Flying Dragon   100
19 The Midwife of Leicester   104
20 Victory over Your Enemies   109
21 To Resist and Withstand Malice   114
22 The King of Cambridge and Agnes Bonsergeant   117
23 Smelts, Bumbepiper and Frysh   122
24 The Lady of Woodstock   125
25 Floods and High Winds   128
26 Your Lusts Torture You   130
27 Making Merry with Anjou   134
28 A Great Need for Money   137

29	His Exact Image and True Likeness	139
30	The Heirs Male of His Body	142
31	Alice and the Rings	144
32	The Coronation and Curtana	148
33	Wasted and Ruinous	151
34	Abusive Words Touching the Duke	154
35	Elizabeth's Seven-year-old Bridegroom	158
36	Mutiny in Portugal	161
37	He Never after Loved the Duke	163
38	An Almost Infinite Variety of Objects	166
39	Of Very Noble and Royal Blood	169
40	A Wicked Life	172
41	Petitions and the Countess	175
42	The Commons in a Ferment	178
43	Corpus Christi and a Christening	181
44	A State of Decay	184
45	A Catalogue of Strange Names	188
46	Frightened Hares and Timid Mice	191
47	A Portuguese Son-in-law	194
48	Forty-seven Mules Carrying Money	198
49	Constanza and Catalina Grandly Received	202
50	The King and the Livery Collar	204
51	England Is in a Bad State	207
52	A Tablet of Jasper	210
53	Grievous Heaviness of Heart	214
54	I Know No Other News	219
55	Their Hearts Would Burst with Grief	223
56	The Extermination of Rebels	227
57	Caterpillars of the Commonwealth	231
58	Imprisoned in the Wardrobe	234
59	Severely Despondent	237
60	Aftermath	243

Appendix 1: John of Gaunt's Will	247
Appendix 2: John of Gaunt's Children	257
Appendix 3: John of Gaunt's Grandchildren	260
Endnotes	262
Bibliography	305
Index	312

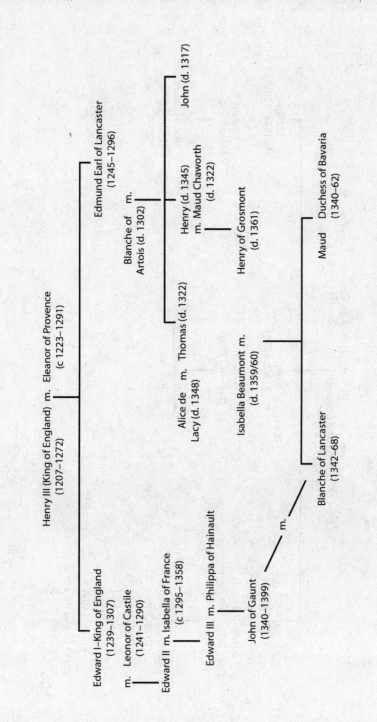

Henry III (King of England) m. Eleanor of Provence
(1207–1272)   (c 1223–1291)

Edward I–King of England
(1239–1307)
m. Leonor of Castile
(1241–1290)

Edward II m. Isabella of France
(c 1295–1358)

Edward III m. Philippa of Hainault

John of Gaunt
(1340–1399)

m.

Edmund Earl of Lancaster
(1245–1296)
Blanche of   m.
Artois (d. 1302)

John (d. 1317)

Henry (d. 1345)
m. Maud Chaworth
(d. 1322)

Alice de   m. Thomas (d. 1322)
Lacy (d. 1348)

Henry of Grosmont
(d. 1361)

Isabella Beaumont m.
(d. 1359/60)

Maud   Duchess of Bavaria
(1340–62)

Blanche of Lancaster
(1342–68)

Willem m. Jeanne de Valois
(Count of Hainault and Holland) (c 1294/5–1352)
(c 1286/7–1337)

Margaretha
(1310–1356)
m.
Ludwig of Bavaria
(Holy Roman Emperor)
(1282–1347)

Ludwig the Roman
(1328–1365)
Wilhelm
(1330–1388)
Albrecht
(1336–1404)

Otto Margaretha Anna
Elisabeth Beatrix

Johanna
(c 1311/2–1374)
m.
Wilhelm
Duke of Jülich

Gerhard Wilhelm Elisabeth
(others)

Philippa
(c 1314–1369)
m.
Edward III
King of England

John of Gaunt
(1340–1399)

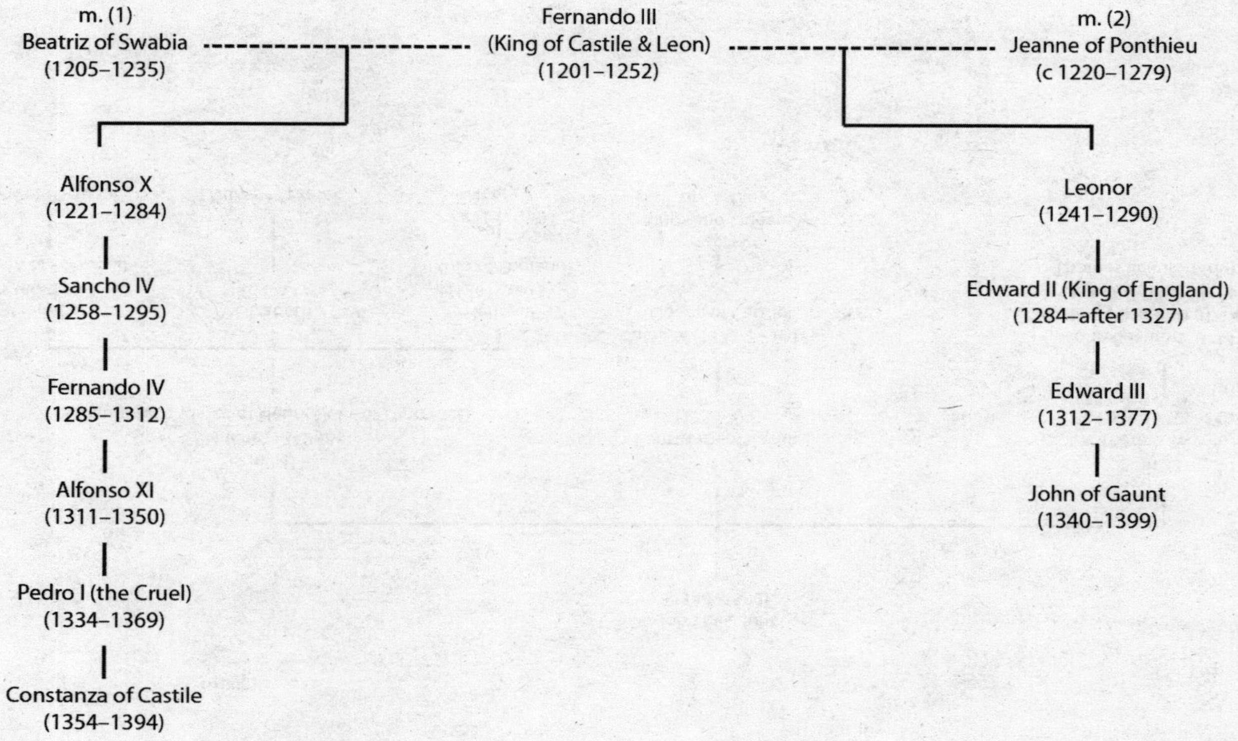

Fernando III
(King of Castile & Leon)
(1201–1252)

m. (1)
Beatriz of Swabia
(1205–1235)

m. (2)
Jeanne of Ponthieu
(c 1220–1279)

Alfonso X
(1221–1284)

Sancho IV
(1258–1295)

Fernando IV
(1285–1312)

Alfonso XI
(1311–1350)

Pedro I (the Cruel)
(1334–1369)

Constanza of Castile
(1354–1394)

Leonor
(1241–1290)

Edward II (King of England)
(1284–after 1327)

Edward III
(1312–1377)

John of Gaunt
(1340–1399)

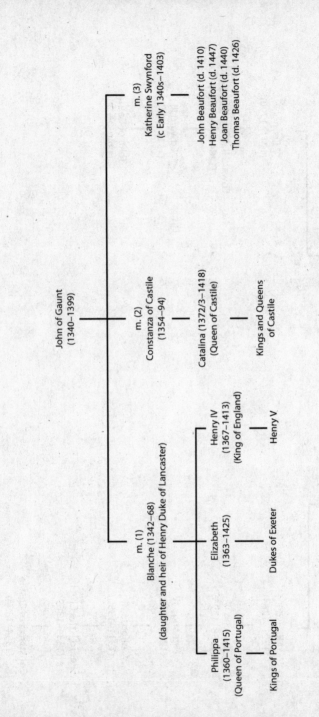

John of Gaunt
(1340–1399)

m. (1)
Blanche (1342–68)
(daughter and heir of Henry Duke of Lancaster)

m. (2)
Constanza of Castile
(1354–94)

m. (3)
Katherine Swynford
(c Early 1340s–1403)

Philippa
(1360–1415)
(Queen of Portugal)

Elizabeth
(1363–1425)

Henry IV
(1367–1413)
(King of England)

Catalina (1372/3–1418)
(Queen of Castile)

John Beaufort (d. 1410)
Henry Beaufort (d. 1447)
Joan Beaufort (d. 1440)
Thomas Beaufort (d. 1426)

Kings of Portugal

Dukes of Exeter

Henry V

Kings and Queens
of Castile

Dramatis Personae

John of Gaunt (b. 6 March 1340): titular king of Castile and Leon, second duke of Lancaster, duke of Aquitaine, earl of Richmond, Lincoln, Leicester and Derby, lord of Beaufort, Nogent, Bergerac and Roche-sur-Yon, and steward of England; fourth but third eldest surviving son of Edward III and Philippa of Hainault; born in Ghent in modern-day Belgium; uncle of Richard II and father of Henry IV

Blanche of Lancaster (b. 25 March 1342): duchess of Lancaster, countess of Richmond, Lincoln, Leicester and Derby; younger daughter, co-heir with her elder sister Maud, and ultimately the sole heir of Henry of Grosmont, first duke of Lancaster; marries John in May 1359

Blanche of the Tower (b. and d. 1342): John's younger sister, who dies soon after birth

Catalina (Katherine) of Lancaster (b. 1372/73): queen consort of Castile and Leon; only surviving child of John of Gaunt and his second wife Constanza of Castile, and her mother's heir; younger half-sister of Philippa, Elizabeth and Henry of Lancaster; marries her second cousin the future King Enrique III of Castile in 1389; mother of Juan II, king of Castile, and María, queen of Aragon

Charles V (b. 1338): king of France; eldest son of John II and Bonne of Bohemia; succeeds his father in 1364; marries Jeanne de Bourbon

Charles VI (b. 1368): king of France; elder son of Charles V and Jeanne de Bourbon; succeeds his father in 1380; marries Isabeau of Bavaria

Constanza of Castile (b. 1354): titular queen of Castile and Leon, duchess of Lancaster; second but eldest surviving daughter and heir of Pedro 'the Cruel', king of Castile and Leon (b. 1334, r. 1350–69) and his mistress María de Padilla; born illegitimate, later legitimised; marries John of Gaunt as his second wife in September 1371

David II (b. 1324): king of Scotland from 1329; only legitimate son and heir of King Robert I (Bruce); married to Edward III's sister Joan of the Tower and secondly to Margaret Drummond; John's uncle-in-law

Edmund Mortimer (b. 1352): third earl of March; married to Philippa of Clarence, and Gaunt's nephew-in-law; father of Roger (b. 1374) and Philippa (b. 1375)

Edmund of Langley (b. *c*. 5 June 1341): first duke of York, earl of Cambridge; John's younger brother, the fifth (though fourth eldest surviving) son of Edward III; marries Isabel of Castile, younger sister of John's second wife Constanza of Castile, in July 1372, and secondly Joan Holland in *c*. November 1393

Edward III (b. 13 November 1312): king of England from January 1327 to June 1377; eldest child of Edward II and Isabella of France; marries Philippa of Hainault in January 1328; John's father

Edward of Woodstock (b. 15 June 1330): prince of Wales and Aquitaine, duke of Cornwall, earl of Chester; eldest child of Edward III and Philippa of Hainault, and heir to the English throne; marries Joan of Kent in 1361, and father of Richard II; known to posterity as the 'Black Prince'; John's eldest brother

Edward of York (b. *c*. 1373/74): duke of Albemarle or Aumerle, earl of Rutland; son and heir of Edmund of Langley and Isabel of Castile; John of Gaunt's nephew; marries Philippa Mohun in the late 1390s

Eleanor de Bohun (b. *c*. 1366): duchess of Gloucester, countess of Buckingham and Essex; elder daughter and co-heir of Humphrey de Bohun, earl of Hereford, Essex and Northampton; marries Edward III's youngest son Thomas of Woodstock in *c*. 1374/76; Gaunt's sister-in-law; her younger sister Mary de Bohun marries Gaunt's son and heir Henry of Lancaster

Elizabeth de Burgh (b. July 1332): duchess of Clarence, countess of Ulster; heir of her father William de Burgh, earl of Ulster (1312–33), and her grandmother Elizabeth de Burgh née de Clare (1295–1360); marries Lionel of Antwerp in August 1342; John of Gaunt's sister-in-law

Elizabeth of Lancaster (b. *c*. February 1363): duchess of Exeter, countess of Pembroke and Huntingdon; second eldest surviving child of John of Gaunt and Blanche of Lancaster; marries 1) John Hastings, earl of Pembroke (b. November 1372, marriage annulled before consummation) in 1380; 2) John Holland, later earl of Huntingdon and duke of Exeter (b. *c*. 1353) in 1386; 3) John Cornwall, later Baron Fanhope, in 1400

Enrique II (b. 1334): king of Castile and Leon from 1369, called Enrique of Trastámara; son of Alfonso XI and his mistress Leonor Guzmán, half-brother and usurper of King Pedro 'the Cruel'; his son and successor **Juan I** (b. 1358); and Juan's son **Enrique III** (b. 1379), who marries John of Gaunt and Constanza of Castile's daughter Catalina of Lancaster

Galeazzo Visconti (b. *c.* 1320) and his brother **Bernabo** (b. *c.* 1323): lords of Milan and Pavia; Galeazzo's son **Gian Galeazzo Visconti** (b. 1351), first duke of Milan; Galeazzo's daughter **Violante** (b. 1353/54), who marries Gaunt's brother Lionel as his second wife in 1368; and Bernabo's daughter **Caterina** (b. 1361), proposed as a bride for Gaunt's nephew Richard II but marries her cousin Gian Galeazzo

Giovanna I (b. *c.* 1326): queen of Naples, countess of Provence; granddaughter and heir of Robert, king of Naples (d. 1343), and a first cousin of Philippa of Hainault, queen of England; in 1363, she marries her third husband, Jaime IV, titular king of Majorca

Henry Beaufort (b. *c.* 1375): bishop of Lincoln 1398, bishop of Winchester 1404, cardinal 1426; second son of Gaunt and Katherine Swynford

Henry of Lancaster (b. *c.* 1280/81): earl of Lancaster and Leicester; grandson of King Henry III (d. 1272); uncle of Isabella of France, queen of England, and John of Gaunt's great-great-uncle

Henry of Grosmont (b. *c.* 1310/12): only son and heir of Henry of Lancaster; earl and later the first duke of Lancaster, earl of Leicester, Lincoln and Derby; father of Blanche of Lancaster, and John of Gaunt's father-in-law

Henry of Lancaster, also sometimes known as Henry of Bolingbroke (b. April 1367): duke of Hereford, earl of Derby; only surviving son of John of Gaunt and Blanche of Lancaster, grandson of Henry of Grosmont, and the Lancastrian heir; marries Mary de Bohun (b. *c.* 1370) in 1381; third duke of Lancaster on John's death; King Henry IV of England from September 1399

Henry of Monmouth (b. 1386): eldest son of Henry of Lancaster (b. 1367) and Mary de Bohun; Gaunt's grandson, and the Lancastrian heir behind his father; later King Henry V

Henry Percy (b. 1341): made first earl of Northumberland in 1377; son of Mary of Lancaster (d. 1362), and a first cousin of Gaunt's first wife Blanche of Lancaster

Humphrey (b. 1382) and **Anne** (b. 1383) **of Gloucester**: children of Eleanor de Bohun and Thomas of Woodstock, earl of Buckingham and duke of Gloucester; Gaunt's nephew and niece

Isabel of Castile (b. 1355): duchess of York, countess of Cambridge; youngest daughter of Pedro, king of Castile, and younger sister of Gaunt's second wife Constanza of Castile; marries Gaunt's younger brother Edmund of Langley in 1372

Isabella of France (b. *c.* 1295): dowager queen of England; daughter of Philip IV of France and Jeanne I, queen of Navarre; sister of Louis X, Philip V and Charles IV, kings of France and Navarre; widow of Edward II (deposed January 1327) and mother of Edward III; John of Gaunt's paternal grandmother

Isabella of Woodstock (b. *c.* 16 June 1332): countess of Bedford and Lady Coucy; John's eldest sister; marries the French nobleman Enguerrand de Coucy (b. *c.* 1340), later earl of Bedford, in July 1365

Jan III (b. 1300): duke of Brabant; grandson of Edward I of England and first cousin of Edward III; his eldest child and ultimate heir Johanna (1322–1406) marries John of Gaunt's uncle Willem, count of Hainault and Holland; possibly John of Gaunt's godfather

Jeanne de Valois (b. *c.* 1294/95): widow of Willem (d. 1337), count of Hainault, Holland and Zeeland; sister of Philip VI, king of France, and first cousin of Isabella of France, queen of England; mother of Philippa of Hainault, queen of England; John of Gaunt's maternal grandmother

Joan Beaufort (probably b. *c.* 1376/7): countess of Westmorland, Lady Ferrers and Neville; only daughter of John of Gaunt and Katherine Swynford; marries firstly Robert Ferrers of Wem in the early 1390s and secondly Ralph Neville, later earl of Westmorland, in late 1396; grandmother of Edward IV and Richard III

Joan de Bohun née Fitzalan (b. 1345/6): countess of Hereford, Essex and Northampton; elder daughter of Richard, earl of Arundel (d. 1376); married to Humphrey de Bohun (1342–73) and mother of Eleanor and Mary de Bohun; mother-in-law of Gaunt's son Henry of Lancaster and Gaunt's youngest brother Thomas of Woodstock

Joan of Kent (b. September 1326 or September 1327): princess of Wales and Aquitaine, duchess of Cornwall, countess of Kent and Chester; daughter and ultimate heir of Edward III's uncle Edmund of Woodstock, earl of Kent (1301–30); widow of Sir Thomas Holland (d. 1360), and marries Edward of Woodstock, prince of Wales, in 1361; John of Gaunt's sister-in-law and mother of Richard II

Joan of the Tower (b. 1321): queen of Scotland as the wife of David II; Edward III's sister, and Gaunt's aunt

Joan of Woodstock (b. *c.* 21 January 1334): John of Gaunt's elder sister, the second daughter of Edward III; dies of plague in 1348 on her way to marry Pedro, heir to the throne of Castile and Leon, later King Pedro 'the Cruel'

João I (b. 1357): king of Portugal; marries Philippa of Lancaster in 1387, and Gaunt's son-in-law; son of King Pedro I of Portugal and his mistress Teresa, and later legitimised; half-brother and ultimate successor of Fernando I (d. 1383)

John II (b. 1319): king of France; son of Philip VI and Jeanne of Burgundy; duke of Normandy, succeeds his father as king in 1350; marries Bonne of Bohemia (1315–49); a first cousin of Philippa of Hainault, queen of England

John III (1286–1341): duke of Brittany; great-grandson of King Henry III of England

John Beaufort (b. *c.* 1373): eldest child of John of Gaunt and Katherine Swynford; earl of Somerset and marquis of Dorset; marries Margaret Holland in *c.* 1397; great-grandfather of King Henry VII

John Hastings (b. 1347): earl of Pembroke, son and heir of Laurence Hastings (1321–48); marries Gaunt's sister, Margaret of Windsor, in 1359 and secondly Anne Manny in 1368; and his son and heir **John Hastings** the younger (b. November 1372), from his second marriage, who marries Gaunt's daughter Elizabeth of Lancaster in 1380 and secondly Gaunt's great-niece Philippa Mortimer (b. 1375) after 1386

John Holland (probably b. 1353): younger son of Sir Thomas Holland and Joan of Kent, later princess of Wales; Richard II's older half-brother; earl of Huntingdon 1388 and duke of Exeter 1397; marries Elizabeth of Lancaster (b. 1363) in 1386; Gaunt's son-in-law

John of Kent (b. 1330): earl of Kent; grandson of Edward I and cousin of Edward III; marries Gaunt's first cousin Elisabeth von Jülich in 1348, but dies childless in 1352, and his elder sister Joan, later princess of Wales, is his heir

John de Montfort (b. 1339): Duke John IV of Brittany; half-nephew and ultimate heir of Duke John III; marries John of Gaunt's sister Mary of Waltham in 1361, Joan of Kent's daughter Joan Holland in 1366, and Juana of Navarre in 1386

John Mowbray (b. 1365): earl of Nottingham; John of Gaunt's ward; dies childless in 1383, and his heir is his brother Thomas Mowbray (b. 1367)

Karl IV (b. 1316): Holy Roman Emperor, king of Germany and Bohemia; son and heir of Johann 'the Blind' of Luxembourg and Eliška Přemyslovna, king and queen of Bohemia, and crowned emperor in 1355; his eldest child from his fourth marriage, **Anne of Bohemia** (b. 1366), marries Richard II of England in 1382 and becomes John of Gaunt's niece-in-law; his heirs are his sons Wenzel and Zikmund, and his sister Bonne (1315–49) is the mother of Charles V of France and his brothers

Katherine Swynford née Roet (probably b. *c.* early 1340s): daughter of Paon or Payn Roet of Hainault, sister-in-law of the poet Geoffrey Chaucer, and widow of Sir Hugh Swynford (d. November 1371); John of Gaunt's long-term mistress beginning *c.* 1372, and mother of his four Beaufort children; duchess of Lancaster from early 1396, when John marries her as his third wife

Lionel of Antwerp (b. 29 November 1338): first duke of Clarence, earl of Ulster; third, but second eldest surviving, son of Edward III and Philippa of Hainault; marries Elizabeth de Burgh in 1342 and Violante Visconti in 1368; John's elder brother

Louis, count of Flanders, Nevers and Rethel (b. 1330): betrothed to Isabella of Woodstock in 1347 but marries Margarethe of Brabant instead; his daughter and heir **Margarethe of Flanders** (b. 1350), marries Philip, duke of Burgundy

Louis, duke of Anjou (b. 1339), **John**, duke of Berry (b. 1340) and **Philip**, duke of Burgundy (b. 1342): the younger sons of John II, king of France, and Bonne of Bohemia; brothers of Charles V and uncles of Charles VI; John of Gaunt's second cousins

Margaret of Norfolk (b. *c.* 1322), also sometimes called Margaret Marshal: countess and later duchess of Norfolk in her own right; daughter and ultimate heir of Edward III's uncle Thomas of Brotherton, earl of Norfolk (1300–38); marries John, Lord Segrave (1315–53) and secondly Sir Walter Manny (d. 1372); grandmother of John and Thomas Mowbray, earls of Nottingham (b. 1365 and 1367) and John Hastings, earl of Pembroke (b. 1372)

Margaretha of Hainault (b. 1310): Holy Roman Empress, queen of Germany and Italy, duchess of Bavaria, countess of Hainault and Holland; eldest sister of Philippa of Hainault, queen of England, and John of Gaunt's aunt; married to Ludwig von Wittelsbach of Bavaria, Holy Roman Emperor (1282–1347); heir to her brother Willem, count of Hainault and Holland (*c.* 1317–45)

Marie de St Hilaire (first mentioned 1360, d. after 1413): damsel of Queen Philippa; according to one chronicler, the mother of an illegitimate daughter, Blanche, married name Morieux, whose father is supposedly John of Gaunt

Mary de Bohun (b. *c.* 1370): countess of Derby; younger daughter and co-heir of Humphrey de Bohun, earl of Hereford, Essex and Northampton (1342–73); marries Henry of Lancaster (b. 1367) in 1381; John of Gaunt's daughter-in-law and mother of his six Lancaster grandchildren

Mary of Waltham (b. 10 October 1344) and **Margaret of Windsor** (b. 20 July 1346): John of Gaunt's younger sisters; they marry John de Montfort, later duke of Brittany (b. 1339) and John Hastings, later earl of Pembroke (b. 1347) respectively, but die childless in their teens

Maud of Lancaster (b. 4 April 1340): duchess of Lower Bavaria, countess of Leicester, Hainault and Holland; elder daughter and co-heir of Henry of Grosmont, first duke of Lancaster; marries John of Gaunt's cousin Wilhelm von Wittelsbach of Bavaria, second son of Emperor Ludwig and Empress Margaretha, in 1352; John's sister-in-law

Pedro 'the Cruel' (b. 1334): king of Castile and Leon; succeeds his father Alfonso XI in 1350; betrothed to Gaunt's sister Joan of Woodstock (1334–48); marries Blanche de Bourbon (1337/39–61) in 1353, but his mistress María de Padilla is the mother of his daughters Constanza, duchess of Lancaster and Isabel, duchess of York

Philip VI (b. 1293): becomes king of France on the death of his cousin Charles IV in 1328, first king of the Valois dynasty, which ruled France until 1589; first cousin of Edward III's mother Queen Isabella and maternal uncle of Edward III's wife Philippa of Hainault; John of Gaunt's great-uncle; marries Jeanne of Burgundy (*c.* 1293–1349) and secondly Blanca of Navarre (*c.* 1330/31–98)

Philippa of Clarence (b. August 1355): countess of March and Ulster; only child and heir of Lionel of Antwerp and Elizabeth de Burgh; marries Edmund Mortimer (b. 1352), third earl of March, and mother of Roger Mortimer (b. 1374); John's niece

Philippa de Coucy (b. 1367): countess of Oxford, duchess of Ireland; younger daughter of Isabella of Woodstock, and John's niece; married to Robert de Vere (b. 1362), close friend of Richard II

Philippa of Hainault (b. *c.* February 1314): queen of England; marries Edward III in January 1328; third (or perhaps fourth) daughter of Willem, count of Hainault and Holland (d. 1337) and Jeanne de Valois (d. 1352); John's mother

Philippa of Lancaster (b. March 1360): queen of Portugal; eldest child of John of Gaunt and Blanche of Lancaster; marries João I, king of Portugal, in 1387; mother of Duarte I, king of Portugal, and the Illustrious Generation

Ralph Neville (b. *c.* 1364): made earl of Westmorland in 1397; marries the widowed Joan Beaufort, Lady Ferrers, as his second wife in late 1396; Gaunt's son-in-law

Ralph Stafford (b. 1301): earl of Stafford; his son and heir **Hugh Stafford** (b. *c.* early 1340s); Hugh's eldest son **Ralph** (b. mid-1360s), killed by Richard II's half-brother John Holland in 1385, and his second son **Thomas** (b. 1369), who marries Gaunt's niece Anne of Gloucester

Richard Fitzalan (b. *c.* 1313): earl of Arundel; marries his second wife Eleanor of Lancaster in 1345; heir of his uncle John de Warenne, earl of Surrey (1286–1347); grandfather of, among many others, Eleanor and Mary de Bohun

Richard Fitzalan (b. *c.* 1347): earl of Arundel; eldest son of Richard Fitzalan and Eleanor of Lancaster, and his father's heir; marries Elizabeth de Bohun (d. 1385), sister of Humphrey, earl of Hereford, and secondly Philipa Mortimer, countess of Pembroke (b. 1375); his heir is his son Thomas (b. 1381)

Richard of Bordeaux (b. January 1367): prince of Wales, duke of Cornwall and earl of Chester; second but only surviving son of Edward of Woodstock and Joan of Kent; succeeds his grandfather Edward III as King Richard II in 1377; John of Gaunt's nephew

Roger Mortimer (b. 1374): earl of March and Ulster; elder son and heir of Edmund Mortimer and Philippa of Clarence; grandson of Lionel of Antwerp, and John of Gaunt's great-nephew; possibly considered heir presumptive to the English throne in the 1390s

Thomas Beaufort (b. *c.* 1379): third and youngest son of Gaunt and Katherine Swynford; later duke of Exeter; marries Margaret Neville of Hornby, but has no surviving children

Thomas Holland (b. *c.* 1314/15): marries Edward III's cousin Joan of Kent; earl of Kent by right of his wife

Thomas Holland (b. 1350/51): earl of Kent; elder son of Thomas Holland and Joan of Kent, and heir to his mother; half-brother of King Richard II, and brother of Gaunt's son-in-law John Holland; marries Alice Fitzalan (b. *c.* 1348/49), younger daughter of Richard, earl of Arundel (b. *c.* 1313) and Eleanor of Lancaster, in 1364

Thomas Mowbray (b. 1367): earl of Nottingham, first duke of Norfolk; grandson and heir of Margaret, duchess of Norfolk; son-in-law of Richard Fitzalan (b. *c.* 1347), earl of Arundel

Thomas Percy (b. *c.* 1343/44): younger brother of Henry Percy, earl of Northumberland; made earl of Worcester in 1397

Thomas of Woodstock (b. 7 January 1355): first duke of Gloucester, earl of Buckingham; seventh but fifth surviving son of Edward III, and John of Gaunt's youngest sibling; marries the heiress Eleanor de Bohun in *c.* 1374/76

Thomas, John, Humphrey, Philippa and **Blanche of Lancaster** (b. 1387–94): the younger children of Henry of Lancaster (b. 1367) and Mary de Bohun; John of Gaunt's grandchildren

Wilhelm (b. *c.* 1300), duke of Jülich, earl of Cambridge: married to Queen Philippa's older sister Johanna of Hainault (b. *c.* 1311/12); John of Gaunt's uncle-in-law; father of Gerhard, count of Berg and Ravensberg, Wilhelm, duke of Jülich, Elisabeth, countess of Kent, and others

Wilhelm (b. 1330) and **Albrecht** (b. 1336) **von Wittelsbach**: dukes of Lower Bavaria, counts of Hainault and Holland; two of Empress Margaretha's sons, and John of Gaunt's first cousins; Wilhelm marries Maud of Lancaster in 1352, Albrecht marries Małgorzata of Brzeg in 1353 and his heir is their son Wilhelm of Ostrevant (b. 1365); Wilhelm von Wittelsbach becomes insane in 1357/58 and is incarcerated for thirty years

Willem (b. *c.* 1317), count of Hainault, Holland and Zeeland: Queen Philippa's younger brother, and their father's successor; marries Johanna of Brabant but has no children, and his heir is his eldest sister Empress Margaretha; John of Gaunt's uncle

William Montacute, earl of Salisbury (b. 1328) and his nephew and heir **John Montacute** (b. *c.* 1350); **Robert Ufford**, earl of Suffolk (b. 1298) and his son **William** (b. 1338); **John de Vere** (b. 1312), earl of Oxford, his son **Thomas** (b. *c.* 1337), and Thomas's son **Robert** (b. 1362), earl of Oxford, marquess of Dublin and duke of Ireland; **Thomas Beauchamp**, earl of Warwick (b. 1314) and his son **Thomas** (b. 1338/39): some of the English earls alive in the reigns of Edward III and Richard II

William of Hatfield (b. and d. January/February 1337): John of Gaunt's elder brother, the second son of Edward III; dies soon after his birth

William of Windsor (b. May 1348, d. August/September 1348): John's younger brother, the sixth son of Edward III; dies a few months after his birth

Introduction

Extensive preparations had taken place for a duel between two of the greatest noblemen in England, to be held near Coventry on Monday 16 September 1398. The two men were Thomas Mowbray, duke of Norfolk and earl of Nottingham, and Henry of Lancaster, duke of Hereford and earl of Derby. Each man had accused the other of treason, and King Richard II, kinsman to them both, ordered them to settle their differences by jousting. The impending duel aroused great interest throughout Europe. Gian Galeazzo Visconti, duke of Milan, sent armour to his friend Henry of Lancaster to use during the joust, as did Henry's brother-in-law King João of Portugal, while Thomas Mowbray probably ordered his armour from the kingdom of Bohemia, where King Richard's brother-in-law Wenzel ruled, and was attended by a Bohemian squire named Jacob Folin.[1]

Henry of Lancaster stayed at his father's castle of Kenilworth 8 miles away the night before the joust. Accompanied by six attendants all riding 'fine coursers', Henry courteously went to greet King Richard at the house in Baginton where he was staying before arriving at the tournament green at Gosford just outside Coventry at 9 a.m. Thomas Mowbray only arrived after King Richard himself had already done so. The joust was conducted under the command of the dukes of Albemarle and Surrey as constable and acting marshal of England. The two men dressed alike in magnificent houppelandes, a voluminous outer garment with trailing sleeves made of plain red sendal (a kind of silk material), with silver belts.[2] Watching in the stands was Henry of Lancaster's father John of Gaunt, duke of Lancaster and Aquitaine, earl of Richmond, Leicester and Lincoln and steward of England, the eldest surviving son of King Edward III and the uncle of Richard II.

King Richard dramatically stopped the joust at the last moment by standing and exclaiming, 'Ho, ho!' The onlookers, having looked forward to an exciting battle, were disgruntled, and they, along with Henry of Lancaster and Thomas Mowbray themselves, waited for two hours to see what would happen.[3] What came next shocked everyone. Richard's friend Sir John Bushy climbed onto the tribune and announced that Mowbray would be exiled from England for the rest of his life, and Henry for ten years.[4] For all his many years of loyalty to Richard II, John of Gaunt was unable to persuade his nephew not to exile his son. He never saw Henry again, and died only four and a half months later, his death perhaps hastened by his shock and grief. Soon afterwards, Richard made the fateful decision to confiscate the entire vast Lancastrian inheritance and to exile Henry permanently from his homeland, whereupon Henry returned to England to claim his rightful estate, raised an army, and forced Richard to abdicate. Under nine months after John of Gaunt's death, his son made himself the first of the three Lancastrian kings of England.

John of Gaunt is arguably one of the most well-known men of the English Middle Ages. His long-term relationship with Katherine Swynford, his mistress for many years and his third wife, was made famous worldwide with the publication of Anya Seton's perennially popular novel *Katherine* in the 1950s, which in 2003 was voted one of the UK's 100 best-loved books ever in the BBC's Big Read. John's life could hardly be more dramatic. He first experienced military action at the age of ten, claimed a throne in Spain (though never won it), had more than forty grandchildren, was the son of one king, uncle of another, father of yet another and grandfather of three more, and was married firstly to a great heiress, secondly to a queen, and thirdly (and scandalously) to his long-term mistress.

John's first marriage to the heiress Blanche of Lancaster brought him the dukedom of Lancaster and the earldoms of Leicester, Derby and Lincoln to add to the earldom of Richmond he had received from his father the king in 1342 at the age of just two, and the vast lands that Blanche brought him gave John an annual income estimated at around £12,000. To put this in perspective, the average wage for an English labourer in the fourteenth century was somewhere around £3 a year. John was, therefore, thousands of times richer than the average contemporary inhabitant of England, and in modern terms was a multimillionaire, perhaps even a billionaire. He was born as one of the sons of the reigning king of England, one of his German uncles-in-law was the Holy Roman Emperor and king of Germany and Italy, and another of his uncles-in-law was king of Scotland. Such wealth, privilege and illustrious connections were bound to – and did – cause great resentment, and John of Gaunt was the most unpopular man in England for many years. Should he have had the misfortune to be anywhere near London in June 1381 during the great social convulsion once known as the Peasants' Revolt and now more usually known as the Great Uprising, it is virtually certain that he would have ended up with his head on a spike.

John of Gaunt was a significant figure on the European stage, a rarity for an Englishman in the Middle Ages. His career is somewhat reminiscent of that of his great-great-great-uncle Richard, earl of Cornwall (1209–72), the younger son of King John (d. 1216) and the brother of Gaunt's great-great-grandfather Henry III (d. 1272). Richard was elected 'king of the Romans', i.e. king of Germany, in 1257 and, like Gaunt, he was also fabulously wealthy and was well known as far afield as Sicily, where the Holy Roman Emperor Frederick II, known to his contemporaries as Stupor Mundi or the Wonder of the World, honoured him by inviting him to stay for four months.[5] As well as being an important European figure, Gaunt was an ancestor of many of the major players in the series of conflicts in England in the fifteenth century later known as the Wars of the Roses: grandfather of Henry V, great-grandfather of Henry VI, Edward IV and Richard III, great-great-grandfather of the first Tudor monarch Henry VII, and the ancestor of the dukes of Norfolk and Buckingham and the earls of Northumberland, among many others.

In writing a book about John of Gaunt, one is very much standing on the shoulders of giants. A very thorough biography of John by Anthony Goodman was published in 1992, providing a great deal of brilliant analysis of the duke's political and military career in England, France and Spain, and the much earlier biography of him by Sydney Armitage-Smith, published in 1904, is still very much worth reading. Aspects of Gaunt's life and career have also been examined in numerous other books and academic articles, such as Jonathan Sumption's works on the Hundred Years' War, Simon Walker's analysis of the Lancastrian affinity, and David Nicolle on Gaunt's great *chevauchée*, his campaign across France in 1373. Ian Mortimer's and Chris Given-Wilson's biographies of Gaunt's son Henry IV, published in 2007 and 2016, also provide excellent accounts of John's career from the 1360s to the end of his life. And last but certainly not least, for many decades Chaucer scholars have done brilliant research and work on the poet, who knew John of Gaunt and his family extremely well, and have uncovered much useful information; it was, for example, a Chaucer scholar in the early 1970s who established the correct year of the death of Gaunt's first wife Blanche, duchess of Lancaster.

This book is intended to be a personal portrait of John of Gaunt and his relationships, especially with his long-term lover and third wife Katherine, using his letters and his extant registers as much as possible. I have also translated his long and detailed will in Appendix 1.

1

Birth in St Bavo, Ghent

In July 1338, Edward III, the twenty-five-year-old king of England, and his twenty-four-year-old queen, Philippa of Hainault, sailed from the River Orwell in Suffolk and embarked upon a long sojourn on the Continent. The year before, Edward had claimed the French throne, believing that as the only surviving grandson of King Philip IV of France (d. 1314) he had more right to it than the present incumbent, Philip IV's nephew Philip VI of the house of Valois, who was both the first cousin of Edward's mother and the uncle of his wife. Edward III travelled overseas to seek allies against Philip VI and the French among the princes and nobles of the Low Countries and Germany, and was to spend most of the period until late November 1340 outside his kingdom.

The king and queen's eight-year-old son Edward of Woodstock, duke of Cornwall and earl of Chester, heir to the English throne, was left behind in England as nominal 'keeper of the realm,' i.e. regent, in his father's absence. The royal couple took their two daughters, six-year-old Isabella of Woodstock and four-year-old Joan of Woodstock overseas with them – the three eldest royal children bore the name of their birthplace, a royal palace near Oxford. King Edward and Queen Philippa sailed up the River Scheldt into the city of Antwerp in the duchy of Brabant on 22 July 1338, where they were greeted by cheering crowds. Shortly after their arrival at Antwerp the house where the king and queen were staying caught fire, and they and their households had to flee to safety. Edward and Philippa, rather embarrassingly, had to seek shelter at the abbey of St Bernard in their nightclothes.[1] More happily, the royal couple received a visit during their stay in Antwerp from Edward's twenty-year-old sister Eleanor of Woodstock, her much older husband Reynald II, count of Guelders (a territory now in the Netherlands close to the German border), and Eleanor and Count Reynald's two young sons, Reynald and Eduard.[2] The English king had not seen his sister since she departed from England to marry Reynald II in May 1332.

Queen Philippa was a few months pregnant for the fifth time when she and her husband left England, and on 29 November 1338 at the abbey of St Michael in Antwerp, she gave birth to her third son, Lionel, known in his own lifetime and ever since as Lionel of Antwerp. (Philippa and Edward's fourth child and second son, William of Hatfield, died in January or early February 1337 shortly after his birth.) In 1334, Edward III had fought incognito at a jousting tournament in Dunstable, Bedfordshire, under the name 'Sir Lionel,' and once he and the queen had respectfully and conventionally named their first two sons after their fathers, King Edward II of England and Count Willem of Hainault and Holland, Edward III chose the Arthurian name he clearly loved for their third. In his own lifetime, Lionel of Antwerp was often called 'Leo,' the Flemish chronicler Jean Froissart called him 'Sir Lion,' and the *Brut* chronicle written in Middle English called him 'Sir Lyonell' or 'Sir Leonell'.[3] This latter spelling indicates how Lionel of Antwerp's name was pronounced in his own lifetime – as in Lionel Messi, not Lionel Ritchie.

A few months after Lionel of Antwerp's birth, in early or mid-June 1339, the royal English couple conceived another child while they were staying either in Antwerp or in Diest, 40 miles away. According to the chronicler Jean Froissart, Queen Philippa spent part of the winter of 1339/40, during her sixth pregnancy, at the castle of Louvain in the duchy of Brabant. She was visited at Louvain by her royal French mother Jeanne de Valois, sister of King Philip VI of France and now a nun at the abbey of Fontenelle near Valenciennes in Hainault; her younger brother Willem (born *c.* 1317), count of Hainault, Holland and Zeeland; and Willem's wife Johanna of Brabant, later duchess of Brabant in her own right.[4]

On 26 January 1340, in the marketplace of Ghent, Edward III of England was officially proclaimed king of France, an important moment early in the long series of struggles between England and France that took place from the 1330s to the 1450s and which later became known as the Hundred Years' War.[5] He and the heavily pregnant Queen Philippa had arrived in Ghent that same day, accompanied by Edward's kinsmen and allies Reynald II, count of Guelders, and Jan III, duke of Brabant. The royal couple took up residence in the abbey of St Bavo, and a special guard was posted around the building to ensure their safety.[6] Edward III returned to England for four months between February and June 1340, but Philippa's pregnancy was too advanced for her to be able to accompany him, so she remained on the Continent.

The queen gave birth for the sixth time on Monday 6 March 1340, in the abbey of St Bavo (now a cathedral called Sint-Baafskathedraal) in Ghent. It was a boy, the fourth she had borne and the third who would survive infancy, and she called him John. According to Jean Froissart, the latest royal son was named after his godfather, Duke Jan or John III of Brabant (b. 1300), ruler of a large territory in modern-day Belgium and the Netherlands with its capital at Brussels, who was Edward III's first cousin.[7] This is certainly possible, though there is no other evidence to confirm the story, and it is also possible that Edward and Philippa chose their son's name to honour the memory of the king of England's only brother, John of Eltham, earl of Cornwall, who had died in September 1336 at the age of just twenty. When Queen Philippa was purified and attended her first Mass after giving birth to her son John, she received a gift of three expensive cloths, one brown, one red and one particoloured.[8] The ceremony of purification, also sometimes called churching, took place forty days after birth and was intended to cleanse a woman spiritually after the birth.

Like the little boy's many siblings and his father (Edward III was known as Edward of Windsor before he became king), his paternal grandfather (Edward II was called Edward of Caernarfon), and his paternal uncle John of Eltham and aunts Eleanor of Woodstock and Joan of the Tower, John's birthplace became part of his name. In the Middle Ages, English people pronounced and spelt the name Ghent as 'Gaunt', and therefore John of Ghent has always been known as John of Gaunt. He appears by this name in the very first line of William Shakespeare's play about his nephew Richard II, 'Old John of Gaunt, time-honour'd Lancaster,' and in Act II Scene I of the play, John makes wordplay with his name: 'Old Gaunt indeed, and gaunt in being old … Gaunt am I for the grave, gaunt as a grave.' The English name John was almost always spelt 'Johan' in the fourteenth century, and this was the way it appeared in Gaunt's will of 1399 and in the many letters he wrote (or dictated, rather). In documents written in Latin in John's own lifetime, his name was Latinised as 'Johannes de Gandavo'.

John's parents were second cousins: both Edward III and Philippa of Hainault were great-grandchildren of Philip III, king of France (b. 1245, r. 1270–85) and his half-Spanish, half-Hungarian first wife Isabel of Aragon (*c.* 1247–71). Edward and Philippa most probably first met at the French court in Paris in December 1325, when Edward had recently turned thirteen and Philippa was coming up to twelve. She and her mother Jeanne de Valois, countess of Hainault and Holland, were then visiting Jeanne's dying father Charles, count of Valois, the second son of King Philip III of France and a man who was both Philippa's grandfather and her future husband's great-uncle.[9] The young couple were officially betrothed on 27 August 1326, and married in York on or around 25 January 1328. Edward, born at Windsor Castle on 13 November 1312, was fifteen at the time of their wedding, and according to the chronicler Jean Froissart, who knew her family well, Philippa was thirteen going on fourteen, and therefore was probably born in around February or March 1314.[10] Edward III's mother, Isabella of France, married to Edward II of England since early 1308, had arranged their marriage. In exchange for his daughter becoming the next queen of England, Philippa's father Willem, count of Hainault and Holland, agreed to provide money so that Isabella could invade England and bring down her husband's loathed favourite, chamberlain, co-ruler and probably lover, Hugh Despenser the younger, and Despenser's allies. Philippa of Hainault was, in effect, traded for her father Count Willem's ships and mercenaries in order for her mother-in-law to undertake an invasion of England and to have a nobleman and his father and other allies grotesquely executed – one of the most unromantic beginnings to a marriage imaginable. However, she and Edward III were to fall deeply in love and to enjoy a happy marriage for more than four decades.

Although they ultimately created one of the most successful royal marriages in English history, the early years of Edward III and Queen Philippa's life together were difficult ones. Edward's father, Edward II, was forced to abdicate his throne to his fourteen-year-old son in January 1327 four months after his wife's invasion of his kingdom and two after the downfall and execution of Hugh Despenser the younger, and the dowager queen Isabella ruled her son's, the teenage king's, realm during his minority. She and her chief counsellor Roger Mortimer, self-appointed first earl of March, treated the young king and queen in a way both Edward and Philippa found suffocating and infantilising. Their eldest child Edward of Woodstock was born on 15 June 1330, and four months later, at not quite eighteen years old, having secured the succession to his throne, Edward III launched a coup against Queen Isabella and Roger Mortimer at Nottingham Castle. Mortimer was captured and executed, and Isabella was placed under house arrest for a while, though her son soon allowed her to go free and restored her to the income and lands she had held during her husband's reign.

Isabella was the youngest child and only surviving daughter of King Philip IV of France and Jeanne I, queen regnant of Navarre, and her three older brothers ruled as kings of France and Navarre. All three men had daughters but no surviving sons, and when the youngest brother, Charles IV, died in 1328, their cousin Philip de Valois (b. 1293), brother of Queen Philippa's mother Jeanne de Valois, succeeded him as Philip VI of France. Isabella's son was to claim the French throne as Philip IV's grandson, and thus it was in Edward III's interests to treat his royal French mother well and honourably as he derived his claim to her family's throne from her, despite his fury with her for bankrupting his kingdom and for her generally disastrous rule during his minority.

John of Gaunt was descended from the royal family of France via both his parents, and was a grandson of King Edward II of England and great-grandson of Edward I (b. 1239, r. 1272–1307). Via his other grandfather, Willem (c. 1286/87–1337), count of Hainault and Holland, John came from a long line of counts of Hainault, Holland, Zeeland and Luxembourg, and via his maternal grandmother, Jeanne de Valois, was also descended from Erzsébet or Elizabeth the Cuman (d. 1290), queen of Hungary and Croatia. Queen Erzsébet was born into a nomadic, shamanistic people of the steppes in modern-day Kazakhstan, Russia and Ukraine who fled into Hungary in the 1230s and 1240s to escape the incursions of Genghis Khan's sons and grandsons into their territories, and John and his siblings carried her mitochondrial DNA.[11]

John's aunt Margaretha of Hainault (b. 1310), Queen Philippa's eldest sister, was married to a German of huge importance: Ludwig von Wittelsbach, duke of Bavaria, crowned king of Germany in 1322, king of Italy in 1327 and Holy Roman Emperor in Rome in 1328. Philippa's other older sister Johanna of Hainault (b. *c.* 1311/12) was also married to a German nobleman: Wilhelm, count and later duke of Jülich, a territory that nowadays lies partly in the German state of North Rhine-Westphalia and partly in the Dutch province of Limburg. John of Gaunt had a large number of German cousins from his mother's two older sisters, and was well acquainted with a few of them. Queen Philippa's only surviving brother, John's uncle Willem (b. *c.* 1317), succeeded their father as count of Hainault, Holland and Zeeland in 1337, though had no surviving legitimate children and was killed while putting down a rebellion in his own territories in 1345. Gaunt also had two cousins in the county of Guelders (a region that now lies mostly in the Dutch province of Gelderland, near the German border) via Edward III's sister Eleanor of Woodstock (b. 1318). Finally, King Edward's youngest sibling Joan of the Tower (b. 1321) was queen consort of Scotland as the wife of David II, who succeeded his father Robert the Bruce on the Scottish throne as a five-year-old in 1329. John of Gaunt knew this aunt particularly well, as she spent many years in England during his youth and attended his first wedding.

Edward III gave the large sum of £200 to be shared among the three women who brought him the news of little John of Gaunt's birth: Amice of Gloucester, Alice Betyngfield and Margery St Maur or Seymour, three of Queen Philippa's damsels or female attendants.[12] Edward did not see his sixth child until around 10 July 1340 when the boy was four months old, after the king's return to Ghent from England.[13] John's first nurse was the same Margery St Maur who had taken the news of his birth to the king, and she was replaced by Isolda Newman sometime before 22 February 1346, when Edward III gave Isolde an income of £10 a year for life.[14] His wet nurse was Margery Tilsthorpe; contrary to later stories told about Queen Philippa, she did not in fact breastfeed her children herself, though was certainly a devoted mother who created a happy and loving family environment for her many children.[15] It probably goes without saying that a rather spiteful story told many years later that John of Gaunt was not truly royal, but was born to a woman of Ghent and raised by Queen Philippa as her own son, is completely without foundation or any supporting evidence, and appears only in the chronicle of Thomas Walsingham, who loathed John and never missed an opportunity to vilify him.[16]

In addition to his nurse, wet nurse and 'rocker' (the girl or young woman who rocked his cradle), John of Gaunt had three female attendants, two male squires of the body, and six male chamber servants. He was provided with bright green and red bedding, and was dressed in silken robes. The eldest royal brother, Edward of Woodstock, duke of Cornwall and earl of Chester, had his own household, as befitted the heir to the throne, and in the summer of 1340, Edward III and Queen Philippa set up a household for their four younger children, Isabella of Woodstock,

Joan of Woodstock, Lionel of Antwerp and John of Gaunt (Isabella and Joan, born *c*. June 1332 and *c*. January 1334 respectively – eight and six years John's senior). The French noblewoman Isabelle, Lady de la Mote, was appointed as their *maistresce*, the woman in overall charge of the household. Isabella of Woodstock, as the eldest royal daughter, had three damsels and her younger sister Joan had two, while Lionel of Antwerp and John of Gaunt had one nurse and one wet nurse each as well as a joint *maistresce* for the two of them. Other senior staff of the royal children's household included a controller, two chaplains and a clerk of the chapel, and they had their own minstrel, Gerard le Gaeyt. One of the men who looked after John of Gaunt in the early 1340s was named John de Dryby. Queen Philippa remained on the Continent with her husband until November 1340, but their children were sent back to England at the beginning of August 1340 or a little earlier: evidently there were fears for their safety, especially that of the two little boys, who were potential targets for kidnap by French forces. John and Lionel were living in the Tower of London on 20 December 1340, perhaps in the company of their eldest brother Edward, when the mayor and aldermen of London sent 'the king's sons' a gift of four carcasses of beef, eight pigs, twelve swans, six calves, two dozen rabbits, four dozen capons and two tuns of wine (though John, well under a year old, was far too young to consume any of this).[17]

When the king and queen returned to England in late November 1340, Philippa of Hainault was already pregnant again. Lionel of Antwerp was just fifteen months older than John of Gaunt, and a fifth (though fourth surviving) royal son, Edmund, was born at the king's manor house of Langley in Hertfordshire on or soon before 5 June 1341, barely fifteen months after his brother John's birth. The middle three surviving sons of the king and queen of England were very close in age. Edmund of Langley's name in his own lifetime usually appeared as 'Esmon de Langele', and he was probably named in honour of his father's late uncle, Edward II's half-brother Edmund of Woodstock, earl of Kent (d. 1330). Three royal daughters and another royal son followed Edmund. Blanche of the Tower was born in March or June 1342 but died soon afterwards and was buried in Westminster Abbey in early 1343; Mary of Waltham was born in October 1344; Margaret of Windsor was born in July 1346; and William of Windsor was born in May 1348. John of Gaunt was the sixth of his parents' twelve children, and throughout his childhood his mother regularly gave birth to his younger siblings.[18]

John was still officially in his mother's 'wardship' in February 1352 when he was almost twelve, and his younger brother Edmund of Langley 'withdrew from her [Queen Philippa's] keeping' at the end of September 1354 when he was thirteen.[19] These were notably late ages for royal or noble boys to remain in their mother's care in the fourteenth century, an era when boys generally moved into other households or were set up in their own households at age seven or so. This reveals much about Philippa of Hainault's great affection for her children and her desire to oversee as much of their upbringing and education as possible; the queen was closely involved in her children's lives, and both she and Edward III created a loving family environment for their offspring. King Edward retained the loyalty of all his sons until the end of his life, a notable achievement in the Middle Ages when royal sons often rebelled against their fathers, and the king adored his daughters too, allowing his eldest daughter Isabella of Woodstock to choose her own husband and to remain unmarried until the unprecedented age of thirty-three. Isabella seems to have still lived in her mother Queen Phiippa's household in 1351 when she was nineteen, and perhaps later.[20]

2

The Infant's Earldom

John of Gaunt's father, the king, bestowed the earldom of Richmond on him on 21 January 1342, and officially created him earl on 20 September the same year.[1] Presumably by September 1342, now aged two and a half, John was considered old enough to take part in the ceremony that made him an earl, which involved him wearing a coronet or gold circlet, and was deemed able to speak whatever words the ceremony required. The earldom of Richmond had previously belonged to John III, duke of Brittany (b. 1286), a great-grandson of King Henry III of England (who died in 1272 and was also Edward III's great-grandfather). Duke John III died on 30 April 1341 and left no children, and the kingdoms of England and France subsequently battled over the War of the Breton Succession, a conflict that, as well as his father's wars to claim the throne of France, formed the backdrop to John of Gaunt's early life. The two people struggling for control of Brittany were the late Duke John III's niece, Jeanne de Penthièvre, supported by France, and the late duke's half-brother John de Montfort, the candidate favoured by the English and the person who ultimately won the struggle, later becoming Duke John IV. Montfort might perhaps have expected to receive the earldom of Richmond on his half-brother's death in 1341, but even though he was the English king's ally, Edward III wished to reclaim the honour of Richmond and to bring it back under English control. He therefore gave it to his third son.[2]

Although not much is known about the education of John of Gaunt and his siblings, John's mother's almoner founded Queen's College at the University of Oxford in her name the year after John was born, and Queen Philippa placed a high value on learning. She had grown up in Hainault and Holland (in modern-day Belgium and the Netherlands) with parents who enjoyed and often purchased books: Count Willem and Countess Jeanne de Valois sometimes sent men to Paris to buy books for them, and in 1311, some years before Philippa was born, her father owned nineteen books – a large number by the standards of an era when manuscripts were extremely costly – including two Arthurian tales and plenty of religious tomes.[3] As a wedding gift in 1328, Philippa bought Edward III an illuminated collection of texts for aspiring rulers, including the *Book of Julius Caesar* and the *Government of Kings*.[4] Edward III could read and write, and the Latin words *Pater Sancte* ('Holy Father'), which the teenage king wrote in his own hand in a letter to the pope in *c.* 1329 are one of the earliest, if not the earliest, extant examples of a king of England's handwriting. Edward III's grandson Richard II was also literate, and Richard's cousin Henry IV, John of Gaunt's son, could read and write in English, French and Latin. In 1406, when Henry was the reigning king of England, he spent much time in an abbey library reading, and gave all his children, including his daughters, an excellent education. The tomb of Henry's eldest sister, John of Gaunt's daughter Philippa, queen of Portugal, depicts her holding a book.

Gaunt's father-in-law, Henry of Grosmont, first duke of Lancaster, wrote a long and complex religious treatise in French in the 1350s, and there is every reason to suppose that the Lancasters prized literacy, books and education as much as their cousins, the royal family, did. It seems highly likely, therefore, that Gaunt himself was literate, perhaps in three languages, as his son certainly was. The chief written language of the English royal family and the English nobility for most of the fourteenth century was French (or rather Anglo-Norman, as the dialect of French used by the elite of medieval England is now known), but it may be that their first or primary spoken language was English, and of course they lived in a country where the vast majority knew no French and only spoke English.

Just over two years after John of Gaunt's birth, on 25 March 1342, his future first wife and kinswoman was born. Blanche of Lancaster was the younger daughter of Henry of Grosmont, earl of Derby (and later the first duke of Lancaster), himself the heir to his royal father Henry of Lancaster, earl of Lancaster and Leicester. The elder Henry was both a first cousin of Edward III's father Edward II, and the uncle of Edward III's mother, the dowager queen Isabella. Blanche's sister, Maud of Lancaster, was just a month younger than John of Gaunt, born on 4 April 1340.[5] Blanche may have been named after Blanche, Lady Wake, the eldest of her father's six sisters and perhaps her godmother. Her mother was Isabella Beaumont, second daughter of the Scottish heiress Alice Comyn and the influential nobleman Henry, Lord Beaumont, who spent his entire adult life in England but was French by birth and a grandson of the man who was the king of Jerusalem, the Latin emperor of Constantinople, and a claimant to the throne of Cilician Armenia. Henry Beaumont died on 10 March 1340, four days after John of Gaunt was born.[6]

Either in March or June 1342, Gaunt's sister Blanche of the Tower was born in the Tower of London, but died soon after her birth.[7] If she was born in March, it cannot have been a full-term pregnancy, as her brother Edmund of Langley was born at the end of May or beginning of June 1341, and the king and queen would not have been able to resume intimate relations until the queen went through the ceremony of purification forty days after giving birth. It is possible that Queen Philippa named her third daughter in honour of the recently born Blanche of Lancaster, as 'Blanche' was not a name found in her family and was not common in Edward III's either – the only exception being his great-grandmother Blanche of Artois (d. 1302), queen of Navarre and countess of Lancaster.[8] Gaunt's eldest brother, Edward of Woodstock, now aged twelve and the official (though nominal) regent of England while the king was away in the duchy of Brittany in 1342/43, sent letters on 30 January 1343 about the funerals of little Blanche of the Tower and their mother's uncle-in-law Robert of Artois, killed fighting on the English side in the duchy of Brittany in late 1342. Edward referred to 'Lady Blanche, our much loved sister' ('*dame Blaunche nostre tres amee soer*' in the French original) in his letters.[9] This reveals the love and affection the royal family felt for each other, and Edward of Woodstock, his siblings and their parents must have felt Blanche's loss keenly. She was the second of the king and queen's many offspring (after William of Hatfield in early 1337) who would die young, though sadly far from the last. Although John of Gaunt was only two years old when Blanche died and was therefore far too young to remember his sister, he would have been raised to be aware of her existence and of his family's loss, and in later years Queen Philippa would be buried alongside little Blanche of the Tower and several of her other children who had predeceased her.

Also at the Tower of London, on 15 August 1342 (the feast of the Assumption), Lionel of Antwerp married Elizabeth de Burgh, a great heiress who was set to inherit her late father William's (d. 1333) earldom of Ulster and her grandmother's third of the old earldom of Gloucester. Elizabeth, born on 6 July 1332 and a first cousin of Gaunt's future wife Blanche of Lancaster, was ten years old at the time of her wedding, and Lionel, almost six and a half years her junior, was only three. John of Gaunt must have been present at his brother's wedding, though of course he was too young to remember it, and even Lionel himself, still a few months away from his fourth birthday, must have been too little to recall much, if anything, of his own wedding. The celebrations, consisting of endless feasting and jousting, including a great banquet held at the Tower of London, lasted for fifteen days, and one of the guests was John of Gaunt and Lionel of Antwerp's twenty-five-year-old uncle Willem, count of Hainault, Holland and Zeeland. Gaunt's future father-in-law, Henry of Grosmont, earl of Derby, and Grosmont's elderly father, the earl of Lancaster and Leicester – respectively the uncle and the grandfather of the young bride Elizabeth de Burgh – also attended, and the Flemish chronicler Jean le Bel stated that the celebrations were the most magnificent events ever seen in England. A piper called Lubekin performed for the royal family on the eve of the wedding.[10]

In November 1342, Edward III gave Queen Philippa official custody of their five younger children: ten-year-old Isabella of Woodstock, eight-year-old Joan of Woodstock, four-year-old Lionel of Antwerp, two-year-old John of Gaunt and one-year-old Edmund of Langley, and Lionel's new wife Elizabeth de Burgh also lived with them. The entries on the Patent Roll granting Philippa custody of her children name John of Gaunt (his name appears as 'de Gandavo', the Latinised form) in first place, as he was earl of Richmond and hence outranked his elder brother Lionel (called 'Leo' here) and his younger brother Edmund, as well as his older sisters Isabella and Joan.[11] Lionel was married off to a great heiress in August 1342 and would one day become earl of Ulster, the title once held by his young wife's late father, and therefore Edward III bestowed the earldom of Richmond on his third son John in the same year, rather than on Lionel. The royal children spent much time with their mother for the next few years, though they and their household also frequently lived at Chertsey Abbey in Surrey. In November 1347, the abbot of Chertsey petitioned Edward III, pointing out that 'the abbey is very often burdened with diverse charges by frequent visits of the king's children and the lengthy stay of them and their households.'[12]

In early 1343, the toddler John of Gaunt was probably present at the funerals of his little sister Blanche of the Tower and his mother's uncle-in-law Robert of Artois, count of Beaumont-le-Roger. Still only three years old, John received a gift of the Yorkshire manor of Danby Wiske ('Daneby upon Wyske' as it appeared in the grant), north of Northallerton, from his father on 18 May 1343.[13] Later that year, John and his elder brothers Edward and Lionel were admitted to the fraternity of Lincoln Cathedral, along with John's great-great-uncle Henry of Lancaster, earl of Lancaster and Leicester, now in his early sixties.[14] Edward of Woodstock was already duke of Cornwall and earl of Chester, and at the Parliament that was held at Westminster in late April and May 1343, his father made him prince of Wales as well.[15] Queen Philippa became pregnant again in early 1344, and her ninth child and fourth daughter, Mary, was born at Bishop's Waltham in Hampshire on 10 October 1344, and hence was known as Mary of Waltham.

3

The Two Leonors

On 18 June 1345, Edward III wrote to Maria of Portugal, queen consort of Alfonso XI of Castile and Leon in Spain, regarding the possible future marriage of her sister and John of Gaunt.[1] Edward III did not specify which of Maria's sisters he was referring to, but he must have meant Leonor, the youngest and only unmarried daughter of King Afonso IV of Portugal. Leonor, probably born in 1328, was sixteen or seventeen years old in June 1345 to John of Gaunt's five. Perhaps realising that this age difference between the putative couple was too great, in 1347 Edward substituted his eldest son Edward of Woodstock, just a couple of years younger than Leonor, as her potential future husband in the negotiations with Portugal. On one occasion the negotiations came very close to fruition and the English envoys were instructed to travel to Portugal to arrange Leonor's journey to England and her wedding to the prince of Wales, but delays meant that the envoys did not arrive in Portugal until November 1347, whereupon they discovered that they were too late and that Leonor had just married King Pere IV of Aragon.[2]

Another Leonor, Leonor de Guzmán, was the beloved mistress of King Alfonso XI of Castile and Leon, and was highly influential at the Castilian court, far more so than Alfonso's wife and queen, Maria of Portugal. The eldest of Leonor de Guzmán's sons by Alfonso was Enrique of Trastámara (b. 1334), who many years later would loom large in John of Gaunt's life. Even in England, Leonor's powerful position was recognised, and Edward III wrote to her in August 1345 asking if she might be willing to send one of her sons to England to be a companion for his eldest son, the prince of Wales, though nothing came of it. The king also thanked Leonor for her efforts in promoting the potential future marriage of her lover Alfonso XI's only legitimate son and heir from his marriage to Queen Maria, Infante Don Pedro – also born in 1334 and seven months younger than his illegitimate half-brother Enrique of Trastámara – and Edward and Queen Philippa's second daughter Joan of Woodstock.[3]

Henry of Lancaster, earl of Lancaster and Leicester, died on 22 September 1345 at the age of about sixty-five. Henry was the greatest and wealthiest of English noblemen, a grandson of King Henry III via his father Edmund, earl of Lancaster and Leicester, and an uncle of John of Gaunt's grandmother Queen Isabella via his mother Blanche of Artois, queen of Navarre and countess of Lancaster. Earl Henry's heir to the vast Lancastrian lands across England and Wales was his only son Henry of Grosmont, now about thirty-five. Just four days after the earl of Lancaster's death, John of Gaunt's uncle Willem, count of Hainault and Holland, was killed near Staveren while attempting to put down a rebellion in his own territory of Friesland. He was about twenty-eight. Although Willem fathered several illegitimate children, he had no surviving legitimate children; his only child from his marriage to Johanna of Brabant, a son also called Willem, died young. In England, Edward III claimed a quarter of the late Count Willem's territories by right of Queen Philippa, third of Willem's four living sisters, but Philippa's eldest sister Empress Margaretha successfully claimed all the lands. She became countess of Hainault and Holland in her own right, and the territories later passed to her German sons, the Wittelsbachs of Bavaria. The Hainault sisters' uncle Philip VI of France promoted the empress's claims to her late brother's territories, probably because he thought that these wealthy and influential counties in the Low Countries would be safer in the hands of Margaretha's husband, the Holy Roman Emperor Ludwig of Bavaria, than in the hands of his deadliest enemy the king of England, the man who had begun claiming his throne in 1337.[4]

On 15 January 1346, the king, Queen Philippa and their children, and the king's mother, Edward II's widow Queen Isabella, attended the funeral of Henry, earl of Lancaster and Leicester, in the late earl's town of Leicester. John of Gaunt's eldest brother, Edward of Woodstock, placed three cloths on the old earl's coffin or tomb.[5] Lancaster's heir Henry of Grosmont was not present as he was currently leading a military campaign in France, but most of his six daughters attended with some of the earl's many grandchildren, who included John's sister-in-law Elizabeth de Burgh, countess of Ulster. After Henry of Grosmont, the late earl's heirs – assuming that Grosmont and his wife Isabella Beaumont did not have a son, which would disinherit them – were Grosmont's two surviving daughters Maud and Blanche of Lancaster, aged almost six and almost four in early 1346. The two little Lancaster girls were surely also present at their grandfather's funeral, and John of Gaunt must have known Blanche and her older sister for almost all their lives. All of them were members of the rarefied uppermost levels of English society, and all of them were born to great wealth and privilege.

Henry of Grosmont, who in 1345/46 was finding glory on French battlefields and proving his worth as one of Edward III's greatest military commanders, was now earl of Lancaster and Leicester as well as of Derby. In 1349, he added the earldom of Lincoln to his collection as well after his aunt-in-law Alice de Lacy, widow of his uncle Thomas of Lancaster (d. 1322), passed away in late 1348. It would be difficult to overestimate Grosmont's wealth; as well as the huge income he enjoyed from his four earldoms, he made tens of thousands of pounds – the equivalent of tens or perhaps even hundreds of millions in modern terms – from capturing French noblemen and knights during the many battles and military campaigns he fought in France and profiting from their ransoms (this was an accepted and usual part of medieval warfare). By 1347, Grosmont was acknowledged as lord of Bergerac, and also called himself lord of Beaufort, part of the territories in France formerly held by his uncle John of Lancaster (d. 1317) that passed to his father Henry on John's death and then to Grosmont. John of Gaunt and his first wife Blanche would, many years later, hold the lordship of Beaufort as part of Blanche's huge inheritance, and John would give the name 'Beaufort' to his four illegitimate children born to his mistress, Katherine Swynford, in the 1370s.

Six-year-old John of Gaunt was old enough to be aware of his father and his sixteen-year-old eldest brother leaving England for France in the summer of 1346 to take part in a military campaign in France, which would prove to be one of the most successful in English history. The heavily pregnant Queen Philippa remained in England and gave birth to her tenth child, her fifth and youngest daughter, Margaret of Windsor, at Windsor Castle on 20 July 1346. On 26 August, Edward III and Edward of Woodstock won a great victory over the French at the Battle of Crécy. Among the noblemen killed during the battle were Queen Philippa's uncle Charles, count of Álençon, her first cousin Louis de Châtillon, count of Blois, and her second cousin Johann 'the Blind', king of Bohemia. Another significant English military victory came on 17 October 1346, when Edward III's brother-in-law and John of Gaunt's uncle King David II of Scotland was defeated and captured at the Battle of Neville's Cross near Durham in the north-east of England. David was destined to spend the next eleven years in captivity in England.

Much of the English royal family would spend the next few months outside Calais when Edward III led a long siege of the port, though Lionel of Antwerp (who turned eight in late 1346) stayed in England as nominal 'keeper of the realm' in his father's absence, and some of the king's other children remained with him. Queen Philippa herself travelled to the Continent on or a little before 21 September 1346, after she had recovered from the birth of her daughter, Margaret of Windsor, and remained near Calais with her husband and some of her children until October 1347. While Lionel of Antwerp and some of his younger siblings were living at the castle of Beaumys in Berkshire in March 1347, the heiress Margery, widow of Nicholas de la Beche, was abducted from the castle. The abductors were a group of knights including John Dalton, the ringleader, Robert Holland, Thomas Arderne and William Trussell. The nobleman Michael Poynings was killed while trying to defend Margery de la Beche during the attack, and although Margery claimed that she was already married to Sir Gerald de Lisle, she was forced to wed Sir John Dalton. To make this horrible situation even worse, it took place on Good Friday, 'before the dawn ... to the terror of the said keeper [of the realm, i.e. Lionel of Antwerp] and the rest of the king's children then with him there'.[6] There is nothing to suggest that the young royal children were personally in any danger, but it must have been a distressing event for them, and especially for the abducted and forcibly married noblewoman Margery de la Beche.

John de Warenne, earl of Surrey and Sussex, died on 29 June 1347, the day before his sixty-first birthday. He had been married most unhappily to Joan of Bar (b. *c.* 1295/96), a granddaughter of Edward I and a much older first cousin of Edward III, for forty-one years, though they had no children. Surrey's primary heir was his late sister Alice's son Richard Fitzalan, earl of Arundel (b. *c.* 1313), but his lands in 'the parts beyond [the River] Trent', mostly in Yorkshire, were given to six-year-old Edmund of Langley, the king and queen's fourth surviving son and the late earl of Surrey's godson, on 6 August 1347. If Edmund failed to have male heirs, his brother John of Gaunt was then to hold the late earl's lands, followed by their elder brother Lionel of Antwerp if Gaunt failed to father children as well.[7] Another significant death occurred on 11 October 1347: Gaunt's uncle by marriage, sixty-five-year-old Ludwig von Wittelsbach, duke of Bavaria, collapsed and died while he was out hunting bears in Fürstenfeldbruck, in the Bavarian forest near Munich. Ludwig had been deposed as Holy Roman Emperor the year before, but was still a powerful political force to be reckoned with. He left six sons, of whom the younger four, Ludwig the Roman, Wilhelm, Albrecht and Otto von Wittelsbach, were also the sons of Margaretha of Hainault and hence were John of Gaunt's first cousins. Although there is little evidence to show that John was acquainted with either Ludwig the Roman or Otto, he knew Wilhelm and particularly Albrecht well. Another of John's German cousins, Elisabeth von Jülich, moved to England and married the earl of Kent not long after 3 April 1348, and Gaunt might have attended the wedding.[8]

At Windsor Castle sometime in the second half of May 1348, now aged about thirty-four, Philippa of Hainault gave birth to her eleventh child and sixth son, William, and was purified on 24 June 1348 – the feast of the Nativity of St John the Baptist. Edward III paid a massive £60 for twelve carpets for the rooms Queen Philippa lived in during her confinement, and for his baby son the king purchased a great bed of green taffeta decorated with red roses and (for some reason) serpents, and with curtains and cushions. Also in 1348, Philippa was given a set of wall hangings made of red sindon stamped with the letter S, and she owned a cloak 'powdered with gold roses of eight petals and bordered with white pearls, in the middle of each rose an S of large pearls.' Philippa's third son, John of Gaunt, and his Lancastrian descendants later made great use of the S symbol, and John's son and heir Henry of Lancaster was known to one contemporary poet as 'He who wears the S,' though the origin and meaning of it are unclear.[9]

The little boy born in 1348 was known as William of Windsor after his birthplace, and his given name must have been intended to honour Philippa's late father Count Willem or her late brother, also the count of Hainault and Holland. During the joust held at Windsor on 24 June 1348 to celebrate the birth of his latest son, Edward III bought two suits of clothes for Queen Philippa's purification. Edward of Woodstock bought his mother a courser – a horse often used for hunting – during the Windsor tournament of 1348, which bore the name of Bauzan ('Piebald') de Burgh, which perhaps indicates that the horse had been a gift to Edward in the first place from his sister-in-law Elizabeth de Burgh, countess of Ulster. At some point in around 1348, perhaps at the tournament held in June that year, Edward III devised a motto in Middle English that is still well known today: 'Hay, hay, the wythe [white] swan, by Godes soul I am thy man,' a motto which reveals that in the fourteenth century the words 'man' and 'swan' rhymed.

Philippa's other sons also attended the tournament of June 1348, and they were, like their mother, all dressed in velvet: Elizabeth de Burgh's husband Lionel of Antwerp (aged nine, going on ten) in azure blue, and John of Gaunt (aged eight) and Edmund of Langley (who had recently turned seven) in purple. The summer of 1348 was an unusually chilly and wet one; under normal circumstances, one imagines that the queen and her sons, wearing so much velvet in late June, would have been excessively hot.[10] Edward of Woodstock was always an affectionate and generous brother to his many younger siblings, and he was William of Windsor's godfather as well. The prince of Wales purchased a large number of expensive silver-gilt cups, dishes, jugs, bowls, pots and salt cellars for the little boy's household, and also bought a cup and a jug for William's nurse and a cup each for the three women or girls who looked after the little boy in his cradle. His brother is referred to in his accounts as 'Sir William of Wyndesore'; the children of kings, though no-one else, had the right to be called 'Lord' or 'Sir' and 'Lady' from birth. Except for the fact that Edward of Woodstock held the title of prince of Wales, the children of kings were not yet called 'prince' and 'princess', hence it would be inaccurate and anachronistic to refer to John of Gaunt as 'Prince John'.[11]

Tragically, William of Windsor died when he was only a few months old and was buried at Westminster Abbey in early September 1348.[12] King Edward and Queen Philippa had now lost two sons called William; it was an unlucky name for their children, although all their other five sons, Edward, Lionel, John, Edmund and Thomas, lived into adulthood. The little William of Windsor must have died at Brentford in Middlesex, a few miles outside London, as King Edward paid a shilling each to fifty 'poor persons' for 'carrying torches from Brentford to London with the body of William, the king's son'. The fifty people were dressed in black russet. The king also paid for cloth of gold to cover William's body, 170 wax candles and torches to burn around his tomb, and for sixty silk pennons with gold.[13] William was buried next to his older sister Blanche of the Tower. John of Gaunt was old enough to attend his little brother's funeral in Westminster Abbey and to remember it, and there were other good reasons why he would have remembered the terrible year of 1348 for the rest of his life. Around August, the Black Death, i.e. the bubonic plague, arrived in England, and by Christmas the dreaded disease was raging in and around London. By the summer of 1349, the deadly pandemic had reached the north of England and had already killed a huge percentage of Europe's population.

4

Spaniards on the Sea

John's fourteen-year-old sister Joan of Woodstock departed from England in June 1348; the eight-year-old John, and the rest of his family, would never see her again. Joan was to marry Infante Don Pedro, only son of Alfonso XI of Castile and Leon and his neglected queen Maria of Portugal, and the heir to his father's throne. Born in August 1334, Infante Pedro was about seven months Joan's junior, and was thirteen going on fourteen. He sent his minstrel Garcias to England to perform for his fiancée, a rather sweet gesture that shows that Pedro was thinking of Joan before their wedding and which perhaps somewhat belies his later atrocious reputation as Pedro 'the Cruel'. Garcias was to travel back to his native Castile in Joan's company, so would also be able to entertain her and her retinue, who included a company of 130 archers from Somerset, Dorset and Devon, during the long sea journey south.[1] Joan's eldest brother, Edward of Woodstock, gave her three tuns of Gascon wine 'when she left for parts beyond sea'.[2] Perhaps also on the occasion of her departure from England, Edward gave Joan a magnificent brooch with rubies, diamonds, emeralds and pearls.[3]

Joan of Woodstock never saw Spain, and never met her fiancé. She died of plague near her father's city of Bordeaux on or shortly before 1 July 1348, on her way to her wedding and her new home. The grieving Edward III sent moving letters on 15 September 1348 to King Alfonso, Queen Maria and Don Pedro, which makes his love for his daughter and his grief for her loss all too painfully apparent.[4] The royal English couple lost two children in the dreadful year of 1348. Despite Joan of Woodstock's sad and premature death, the English-Castilian connection endured. John of Gaunt and his brother Edmund of Langley would, in the distant future, marry Don Pedro's daughters, born to his mistress María de Padilla in 1354 and 1355, and later legitimised. When John was in Bordeaux in 1389, he endowed an obit for Joan of Woodstock in the cathedral of St André in the city.[5] More than forty years after her death, he still remembered his sister and honoured her memory. The terrifying and horrific experience of living through and surviving the Black Death, aged only eight, seeing so many of his countrymen die awful deaths and knowing that his sister was a victim of the same horrible disease and had died far away from her home and her loving family, surely made a strong impression on John.

The Black Death still raged in England and other European countries throughout 1349. In late February 1350, King Alfonso XI of Castile died in his late thirties during another wave of the great plague. His only legitimate son, Pedro, who was now fifteen and a half years old, succeeded him on the throne, and had Joan of Woodstock not died of the plague herself eighteen months earlier in the summer of 1348, she would have become queen consort of Castile at this point. John of Gaunt's great-uncle Philip VI, king of France since 1328, died on 22 August 1350 (probably of natural causes rather than plague) and was succeeded by his thirty-one-year-old son, John II. Philip was fifty-seven when he died, and had married his second wife, the teenage Blanca of Navarre, on 11 January 1350 not even a month after losing his wife of thirty-six years, Jeanne la Boiteuse ('the Lame') of Burgundy. Queen Blanca gave birth to her husband's posthumous daughter nine months after his death. The new king of France, Blanca's stepson John II, was a widower. His late wife Bonne (née Jutta) of Bohemia, who died in 1349, perhaps of plague, had been the daughter of Johann 'the Blind' king of Bohemia, who had fallen at the Battle of Crécy in 1346 fighting for Philip VI against Edward III, and they had four sons and five daughters.

On 29 August 1350, a week after King Philip's death, a sea battle known as the Battle of Winchelsea, or more colourfully as *Les Espagnols sur Mer* ('The Spaniards on the Sea'), was fought in the English Channel. Don Carlos de la Cerda, scion of a cadet branch of the Castilian royal family and of partly Spanish, partly French origin, was a notorious soldier of fortune who made a career out of capturing English trading ships, robbing them, and throwing their crews overboard to drown. The furious Edward III decided to deal with de la Cerda, and lay in wait for him as he returned from Flanders to Spain. Even though he was just ten years old, John of Gaunt did not stay on the shore with his mother and younger siblings at a safe distance from the sea battle, but was either with his twenty-year-old brother, the prince of Wales, on Edward's ship or with his father on his. (Chronicler Jean Froissart says that Edward III had his son John with him during the battle because 'he much loved him,' though from a modern perspective perhaps Edward might have done better to demonstrate his love for a ten-year-old child by allowing him to remain on shore without imminent danger to his life.[6]) The royal cousin Henry of Grosmont, earl of Lancaster, Leicester, Derby and Lincoln, saved the lives of the king's two sons just as their ship was about to sink during the fiercely fought battle.[7] Partly in gratitude and partly out of sincere affection for him, Edward III upgraded Grosmont's title a few months later, making him duke of Lancaster. He was only the second English duke in history (the kings of England were also dukes of Aquitaine in France) after the king's son Edward of Woodstock, duke of Cornwall, evidence of Edward III's high regard and great affection for his able, loyal kinsman.

Many Spanish ships were sunk during the Battle of Winchelsea and thus the English side was victorious, though also lost a few of their ships. Carlos de la Cerda survived the battle and soon afterwards would be made constable of France, though was later murdered in 1354. It is possible that John of Gaunt was knighted on the occasion of the sea battle in 1350, but this is uncertain, and it is also possible that he had to wait until 1355 when he was fifteen. After the stress and danger of the battle, the king and queen spent a pleasant evening – perhaps John and their other children were with them – 'in revelry with the ladies, conversing of arms and matters of love'.[8]

At the Parliament that was held in February 1351, Edward III changed the English law that had stated in order to inherit land within the territories ruled by the king of England (England itself, Wales, Ireland and Gascony), people had to be born within those same territories. It was the case of Henry Beaumont that forced the king to take action. Henry, a cousin of Gaunt's future wife Blanche, was born in the duchy of Brabant in late 1339 because King Edward and Queen Philippa, thoroughly enjoying the company of Henry's parents John Beaumont and Eleanor of Lancaster, persuaded the young couple to remain in Brabant with them rather than returning to England for the birth. John Beaumont died in the spring of 1342 when his son was only two years old, and when John's Scottish mother Alice Comyn died in July 1349, her heir was returned as John's younger brother Thomas rather than John's son as should have happened, because John had died 'without an heir of his body born within the realm of England or the allegiance of the king of England'.[9] Edward III abolished this requirement and Henry Beaumont duly inherited his father's and grandmother's lands when he came of age, and the king might have had it in mind that his sons Lionel and John, born in Antwerp and Ghent and thus also outside the lands he ruled, would be impacted by this law as well unless he changed it.[10]

According to the *Brut* chronicle, written in Middle English, there was a great drought in England in 1351, which lasted from March until July. 'There fell no rain into the earth,' says the chronicle, 'wherefore all fruits, seeds and herbs for the most part was lost; in default whereof there came so great disease of men and beasts, and dearth of victuals in England, so that this land, that ever before was plenteous, had need that time to seek his victuals and refreshing out of other countries.'[11] Along with the appalling events of 1348/49 when the Black Death killed a huge percentage of the English and European population, this drought and its consequent food shortages was another event that impacted the childhood of John of Gaunt. His father Edward III had spent part of his own childhood living through the tragedy of the Great Famine, which held northern Europe in its grip in the mid- and late 1310s; one contemporary chronicler made similar remarks to those made in the *Brut* some decades later, declaring 'Alas, poor England! You who once helped other lands from your abundance, now poor and needy are forced to beg.'[12]

As of 1350, John of Gaunt often appears in the accounts of his eldest brother, and seems to have lived in Edward of Woodstock's household.

(Gaunt's brothers Lionel of Antwerp and Edmund of Langley, fifteen months older and younger than he respectively, do not appear in Woodstock's accounts in the same way.) Despite an age difference of a decade, the two brothers were obviously very close. Edward of Woodstock's extant register, on 21 March 1351, reveals that John had a 'child of the chamber' called Wolfard Gistels and a henchman called Maak (the word 'henchman' simply meant an attendant in the fourteenth century, and had not acquired the sinister connotations of later eras). Rather intriguingly, two 'Saracen children' named Sigo and Nakok were living in the household of the prince of Wales at this time, and Edward purchased linen cloth, coats, hats, shoes, boots and cloaks for them and for Maak and Wolfard Gistels in March 1351.[13] 'Saracen' meant a person from Arabia or North Africa, or a Muslim more generally, and was a word used fairly often in fourteenth-century England. Gaunt's grandfather Edward II owned a belt with 'a purse hanging down from it, with a Saracen face' ('*od un visage de Saracyn*') and in May 1313, six 'Saracens' were said to be living at Dover Castle, and Edward II paid them rather generous expenses of 6*d* a day each.[14] Sigo and Nakok were perhaps among John of Gaunt's young companions.

In November 1351, again sometime before 5 September 1352, and on a third occasion in 1355, Edward of Woodstock spent £100 on saddles, bridles 'and other harness, both gilt and white' for himself and John of Gaunt, who usually appears as 'the earl of Richmond' in his brother's accounts. The man who made the saddles was called Lambekyn le Sadelere in the accounts, and lived and worked in London. The prince of Wales provided housings or caparisons (decorative cloths) for twelve-year-old John's three palfreys, or riding horses, in November 1352, and the horses were looked after by Edward's palfreyman, Rotelyn.[15] Woodstock's register states in June 1352 that he and John of Gaunt 'plan to stay a great deal' at the Surrey manor of Byfleet, which had been given to their grandfather Edward II in or before 1312 and passed to their father Edward III. This entry also makes it apparent that the king kept his stud farm, or rather, one of his stud farms, at nearby Guildford, and that Edward and John intended to utilise it.[16]

5

No Pleasure in the Company of Ladies

The royal cousin Henry of Grosmont, now duke of Lancaster, left England for a few months in 1352 and headed off on a crusade to Lithuania, though he was back in England by Christmas that year and spent the festive season with the king and queen and their children. His wife Isabella Beaumont and their younger daughter Blanche, now ten, were probably also present, and thus John of Gaunt might have spent time with his future first wife – whether their marriage was already on the cards as early as 1352 is not entirely clear. Usually the most courteous and affable of men, Henry of Grosmont managed to quarrel with the German duke of Brunswick while he was overseas, and came very close to duelling with him in Paris; only the tact of John II of France, who declared that Brunswick's words had been misreported to Henry and vice versa, prevented bloodshed.[1] Sometime early in 1352 before Grosmont's departure, though the date is not precisely recorded, the royal family attended a wedding in the royal chapel of Westminster. The bride was Maud of Lancaster, not quite twelve years old, Grosmont's elder daughter and co-heir, and the groom was John of Gaunt's first cousin Wilhelm von Wittelsbach of Bavaria, aged almost twenty-two and the second eldest son of Queen Philippa's eldest sister the dowager Holy Roman Empress, Margaretha of Hainault.

Wilhelm had been invited to England by Edward III on 12 November 1351, and his mother came with him; Margaretha was given safe conduct to depart from England on 16 March 1352. This might have been John of Gaunt's first opportunity to meet his aunt the empress, and probably also the last as she died in 1356.[2] Her son Wilhelm von Wittelsbach was born in Frankfurt-am-Main on 12 May 1330. His elder brother Ludwig the Roman, born in Rome in May 1328, was already married to Kunigunde, daughter of King Kazimierz of Poland, and his younger brother Albrecht, born in Munich in July 1336, also married a Polish woman, Małgorzata of Brzeg, in Passau in 1353. Via her marriage, Maud of Lancaster became duchess of Lower Bavaria and countess of Hainault, Holland and Zeeland, and to see his daughter married to the son of an emperor must have been a proud moment for Duke Henry of Lancaster.[3]

Chronicler Jean le Bel says of Maud's new husband that he was 'tall, strong, swarthy and agile, more fleet and dexterous than any man in his land ... but he was curiously distant and inscrutable: he wouldn't welcome or acknowledge people ... and took no pleasure in the company of ladies and damsels.'[4] Wilhelm evidently had a somewhat difficult relationship with Empress Margaretha, and feuded with his mother for years over the counties of Hainault and Holland, which she had inherited from her late brother Willem. Edward III sent Henry of Grosmont to negotiate between Margaretha and her son in October 1353.[5]

Despite his busy career as a military and political leader and mediator, Duke Henry of Lancaster found time to compose a long and remarkable text in French in 1354 and called it the *Livre de Seyntz Medicines* or *'Book of Holy Medicines'*. In it, Henry described at length the wounds of the soul caused by the seven deadly sins, and revealed much of himself in the process, including his love of fine cloth, his hounds, eating salmon, getting drunk, dancing, the smell of flowers, and 'kissing' (a euphemism) lowborn women.[6] Fourteenth-century noblemen are often shadowy figures whose personalities remain emphatically closed to us, and we are lucky to have the *Livre de Seyntz Medicines* to reveal so much of John of Gaunt's father-in-law.

As for the duke's other son-in-law Wilhelm von Wittelsbach, the unfortunate man became insane around 1357/58 and had to be incarcerated for his own safety and everyone else's. Edward III sometimes addressed letters to Wilhelm's younger brother and heir Albrecht (their elder brother Ludwig the Roman died childless in 1365) as the man in charge of looking after him. In Dutch, Wilhelm is still sometimes known, rather unkindly, as *'de dolle graaf'* or 'the mad count'.[7] Maud of Lancaster gave birth to a daughter, name unknown, in 1356 who died soon after birth and who would be her only child, though sometime before his incarceration and perhaps while waiting for his young wife to reach maturity, Wilhelm fathered two illegitimate children, who both lived into adulthood. Maud remained on the Continent near her husband, though was only seventeen when her marriage ended in all but name. She gained a reputation as a peacemaker and mediator – a talent she perhaps inherited from her father – during the long series of conflicts in the county of Holland known rather colourfully as the Hook and Cod Wars.[8]

On 7 March 1352, the day after John of Gaunt's twelfth birthday, his maternal grandmother Jeanne de Valois, dowager countess of Hainault, Holland and Zealand and the aunt of the reigning King John II of France, died at the age of about fifty-seven. Jeanne had become a nun at Fontenelle Abbey near Valenciennes soon after her husband Willem's death in June 1337. Given that she was cloistered as a nun before John of Gaunt was born, it is doubtful whether he ever had the chance to get to know her, though Jeanne did leave her abbey on occasion to visit her brother Philip VI and her son-in-law Edward III to try to persuade them to reconcile. She was buried in the middle of the so-called ladies' choir at the abbey of Fontenelle, where she had died, and her tomb was discovered there in 1977. On 7 September 2001, Countess Jeanne was reburied in the church of Saint-Géry in the town of Maing, near Fontenelle. Jeanne's youngest daughter Isabella of Hainault, and her granddaughter Anna von Wittelsbach of Bavaria, second daughter of Gaunt's aunt Empress Margaretha and one of Ludwig the Roman, Wilhelm and Albrecht's sisters, would also be buried at Fontenelle Abbey in 1361; Anna had followed in her grandmother's footsteps and become a nun there.

As John of Gaunt grew up in the 1350s, it is difficult to find out much about his life, other than a few references to him in his eldest brother's accounts. John and Edward of Woodstock spent much time at Byfleet in Surrey in 1352, and the references to the two 'Saracen children' named Sigo and Nakok in Edward's household accounts perhaps reveal that in childhood John was better acquainted with other cultures, and possibly other religions, than one might expect. John's youngest sibling was born on 7 January 1355 at the royal palace of Woodstock near Oxford. He was the seventh, though fifth surviving, son of the king and queen, and was named Thomas probably after his godfathers Thomas of Hatfield, bishop of Durham, and Thomas de la Mare, abbot of St Albans, and perhaps also in honour of his father's late uncle, Thomas of Brotherton, earl of Norfolk (1300–38).

Little Thomas of Woodstock was a quarter of a century younger than his eldest brother Edward of Woodstock, and fifteen years younger than Gaunt. After the royal sisters Mary of Waltham and Margaret of Windsor died in the early 1360s, Thomas of Woodstock's nearest surviving sibling was Edmund of Langley, who was thirteen and a half years older than he. Queen Philippa's twelfth pregnancy, many years after she had last borne a child (William of Windsor in May 1348, who died in infancy) and when she had passed forty, must have come as something of a surprise to herself, Edward III and their other children, and the king and queen's eldest legitimate grandchild was just seven months younger than her uncle Thomas. Philippa of Ulster, usually known to history as Philippa of Clarence as her father was made first duke of Clarence in 1362, was the first and, as it turned out, only child of Lionel of Antwerp and Elizabeth de Burgh, and was born at the royal palace of Eltham in Kent on 16 August 1355. She was named after her paternal grandmother Queen Philippa, who was also her godmother, and, as her parents' only child, was a great heiress who carried the earldom of Ulster and the lands of one third of the old earldom of Gloucester to the Mortimer family via her marriage.[9]

John of Gaunt had first experienced warfare during the naval Battle of Winchelsea as a ten-year-old in August 1350, and in the summer of 1355, now aged fifteen, he accompanied his father to France and experienced his first military campaign on land. Edward III, who also took sixteen-year-old Lionel of Antwerp and probably the fourteen-year-old Edmund of Langley with him, hoped to force a battle with John II of France, but King John refused to engage his forces, and Edward retreated to England, plundering the

French countryside before his departure. Subsequently, King Edward, with Lionel and John, rode north, as the important port of Berwick-on-Tweed on the far north-east coast had been captured by a Scottish force, though Berwick Castle still held out. In January 1356, Edward recaptured Berwick.[10]

Not yet sixteen, John carried out repairs to his bridges, houses, walls and other buildings at his manors of Cheshunt (Hertfordshire) and Bassingbourn (Cambridgeshire) in February 1356. He sent stonemasons and carpenters there. The following year, his father granted him the reversion of the important castle and lordship of Liddell in Cumberland, currently in the hands of Blanche, Lady Wake as part of her dower from her late husband Thomas Wake (1298–1349).[11] In October 1356, John appointed two 'guardians', Robert de Herle and Walter de Campeden, to 'sue and defend all pleas for and against him.' Although John was a landowner and an earl, he was still well underage, and was therefore not able to undertake legal actions himself.[12]

6

A Damsel and a Daughter

Edward of Woodstock left England in 1356 and won a startling victory over the French at the Battle of Poitiers on 19 September that year. King John II of France himself was captured during that battle in what was one of the most extraordinary events of the English Middle Ages, a historic, remarkable moment. Edward of Woodstock, with the captive John II in tow, arrived back in England on 5 May 1357, and on 24 May entered London.[1] Woodstock and John of Gaunt's grandmother, the dowager queen Isabella, now over sixty and thus rather advanced in age by the standards of the era but obviously still healthy and able to travel, was one of the many people who attended Woodstock's victory parade in London. King John II lived at various places in England during his long captivity, though mostly at the Savoy Palace in London, rebuilt on a magnificent scale by the almost impossibly wealthy Henry of Grosmont, which later passed to his younger daughter Blanche and her husband John of Gaunt. The captive king also spent some time at Somerton Castle in Lincolnshire, which had been given to Edward II by the bishop of Durham and passed into the possession of Edward III. Astonishingly, there was a period in the 1350s when the kings of both France and Scotland were held captive in England.

The dowager queen Isabella's accounts fortuitously survive for a few months in 1357/58, and demonstrate that her son the king, daughter-in-law Queen Philippa and grandsons Edward of Woodstock, Lionel of Antwerp and John of Gaunt visited her, sent gifts and kept in touch with her, as did Queen Isabella's first cousin Henry of Grosmont.[2] Isabella's youngest child, Joan of the Tower, queen of Scotland, estranged wife of the captive David II, lived with her mother near the end of Isabella's life. Isabella of France may have been the only one of his grandparents whom John of Gaunt ever met, depending on whether he had the chance to meet his other grandmother, Jeanne de Valois, who took the veil as a nun before he was born. Isabella was royal to her fingertips: her father was the king of France and her mother was the queen regnant of Navarre, all three of her older brothers reigned as kings of France and Navarre, she was crowned queen of England alongside her husband Edward II at the age of just twelve, and she gave birth to the future king of England when she was seventeen (or almost).

Queen Isabella died at her castle of Hertford on 22 August 1358, aged sixty-two or sixty-three. Her son paid fourteen 'poor persons' 2*d* a day each and also provided them with food until 23 November, as payment for their watching over the queen's body in the castle chapel. Edward III and his family met the funeral cortege when it arrived in London on 24 or 25 November, and one John Galeys was paid £10 for the use of his house at Mile End 'for the time the body of Isabella, late queen of England, remained there with the king and his household'. Isabella's funeral took place at the Greyfriars' (Franciscans') church in London on 27 November in the presence of her family.[3] It is not clear whether the choice of location was her own or her son's; her long-dead husband Edward II was buried at St Peter's Abbey in Gloucester, now Gloucester Cathedral, and perhaps, given Isabella's vital role in her husband's downfall and deposition in 1326/27, Edward III deemed it inappropriate to bury his parents together. Edward I's widow, Marguerite of France, Edward II's stepmother and Queen Isabella's aunt, had been buried in the London church of the Franciscans in 1318. In 1362 and 1382, John of Gaunt's aunt Joan of the Tower, queen of Scotland, and his sister Isabella of Woodstock, countess of Bedford, would be as well.

Shortly after the late queen's funeral, the royal family attended a wedding. The bride was King Edward and Queen Philippa's granddaughter Philippa of Ulster, child of Lionel of Antwerp and Elizabeth de Burgh, and she was only three years old. Her groom was Edmund Mortimer, and he was six.[4] Edmund was the son and heir of Roger Mortimer (b. 1328), second earl of March. This marriage would give the Mortimer family a strong claim to the English throne later in the century as well as giving them Elizabeth de Burgh's earldom of Ulster and the lands in England, Wales and Ireland which Elizabeth was set to inherit from her grandmother Elizabeth de Burgh the elder, Edward III's cousin (who was still alive in late 1358 when her great-granddaughter Philippa of Ulster married Edmund Mortimer, and lived for another two years). Lionel was only twenty when his daughter married, his wife Elizabeth de Burgh twenty-six, and Edward III must have expected them to produce more children and to leave a son as their heir. As it happened, they did not have more children and Philippa would be Lionel and Elizabeth's only child, and the Mortimer family thus benefited hugely both from the large payout the king gave them and the marriage of a great heiress, whose lands duly passed into Mortimer possession.[5] Philippa and Edmund Mortimer would have four children in the 1370s, and their elder son Roger, born in 1374, John of Gaunt's great-nephew, had a strong claim to the throne as the senior descendant of Edward III's second son.

Rather remarkably, Edward III had arranged and overseen the marriage of his only legitimate grandchild before he oversaw the marriages of any of his and Philippa of Hainault's children except Lionel, little Philippa's father (who, like his daughter, had married when he was only three years old). This was, of course, not entirely a deliberate choice: had Joan of Woodstock not died in southern France in 1348, she would now be the queen consort of Castile as the wife of King Pedro, and Edward of Woodstock would now probably be married to Leonor of Portugal had English envoys made better haste to the Iberian Peninsula in 1347 and arrived before Leonor married Pere IV of Aragon. Had Edward III put his foot down, as most royal medieval fathers surely would have done, his eldest daughter Isabella would have been married to one of her several fiancés eight years previously, but the king treated Isabella with remarkable indulgence and allowed her to turn down several suitable marriages and to remain unwed until the age of thirty-three.

In 1358/59, with eight living children (Edward of Woodstock, Isabella of Woodstock, Lionel of Antwerp, John of Gaunt, Edmund of Langley, Mary of Waltham, Margaret of Windsor and Thomas of Woodstock) yet only one married child and only one legitimate grandchild, the king decided it was high time to see to the marriages of several more of his offspring. For his and Philippa's third eldest surviving son, John of Gaunt, the king arranged a brilliant match with John's second cousin once removed: Blanche of Lancaster, younger daughter and co-heir of Henry of Grosmont.

Chronicler Jean Froissart claims that John of Gaunt fathered a daughter with Marie de St Hilaire, one of Queen Philippa's damsels, i.e. her female attendants. The girl was also named Blanche and was perhaps born before John married Blanche of Lancaster, though Froissart does not specify this.[6] It is certainly not impossible that John fathered an illegitimate child, and it seems most unlikely that he had not previously slept with a woman when he married Blanche of Lancaster in 1359 at age nineteen. As a man, he was not held to the same levels of chastity and fidelity that royal and noble women were, and had John been involved in a premarital or even extramarital relationship it would have been regarded indulgently by his family. For his sisters, sisters-in-law and daughters, the situation was, of course, entirely different. Elizabeth de Burgh, six and a half years older than her husband Lionel, had to wait and remain a virgin until her husband was at least fourteen, and more probably sixteen, when he was deemed mature enough and able to consummate their marriage. Their daughter Philippa was born thirty-seven weeks after Lionel's sixteenth birthday, which is probably not a coincidence, and Elizabeth was twenty-two years old when her husband of a dozen years became her husband in more than name only. John of Gaunt later arranged the marriage of his second daughter to a boy a decade her junior, and she was also expected to wait and preserve her virginity for many years until she was in her mid-twenties, when her husband would finally reach physical and emotional maturity (as it would turn out, she was unwilling and unable to wait that long).

Assuming Froissart's story is true, John of Gaunt might have named his illegitimate daughter in honour of his fiancée. Marie de St Hilaire, the child's alleged mother, certainly existed, and was named as one of the damsels of John's mother Queen Philippa in 1360 and again in 1368, on the latter occasion alongside Philippa Chaucer, wife of the poet Geoffrey Chaucer and the sister of Gaunt's future mistress Katherine Swynford. Both Marie de St Hilaire and Philippa Chaucer would attend the queen's funeral in early 1370.[7] Marie's name most probably signifies that she came from the port of Saint Helier in Jersey, in the Channel Islands, or at least that her father did, though otherwise nothing is known of her background. Froissart claims, however, that she came from Queen Philippa's native Hainault, and states further that Marie and John's daughter Blanche married Sir Thomas Morieux, who was the marshal of Gaunt's army in 1386. Sir Thomas Morieux did indeed marry a woman named Blanche who was known to John of Gaunt; in March 1381, John gave Thomas and Blanche Morieux rather lavish wedding gifts including a dozen silver spoons, saucers and two basins with matching ewers.[8] In June 1380 and March 1383, Gaunt granted Thomas and Blanche, for 'good services in times past' to him, a very generous income of a £100 a year from his manors of Snettisham and Fakenham in Norfolk.[9] The couple were certainly high in his favour.

We only have Jean Froissart's word for it, however, that Blanche Morieux was Gaunt's illegitimate daughter, or that he ever had an affair with Marie de St Hilaire, though the duke did give Marie a New Year gift in 1381, and on 22 March 1396 granted her an annuity of 20 marks for her previous good service to his mother Queen Philippa. His son Henry IV confirmed this grant on 5 November 1399, and his grandson Henry V on 27 June 1413.[10] As Marie was still alive as late as 1413, forty-four years after Queen Philippa died, she must have been much closer to John of Gaunt's age than his mother's, though the word 'damsel', Marie's job title, does not automatically imply youth as it does in more modern times. Later, Marie went on to serve in the household of one of John's sisters-in-law; if she ever was John's mistress, it certainly did her career no harm. It must be noted, though, that as well as the lack of supporting evidence for his affair with Marie and their daughter, Jean Froissart was somewhat confused about John of Gaunt's family. Although he correctly named Gaunt and his second wife Constanza's daughter as Katherine (or Catalina), he named Gaunt's two daughters from his first marriage as 'Ysabel [i.e. Elizabeth] and Philippe', in that order, though Philippa of Lancaster was older than her sister Elizabeth and should have been named first. Froissart also made some incorrect statements regarding Gaunt's illegitimate Beaufort children, as will be noted below.

It is possible, as suggested by the historical researcher and Swynford family expert Judy Perry, that the Blanche who married Sir Thomas Morieux was not an illegitimate daughter of John of Gaunt, but was in fact Blanche Swynford, daughter of Gaunt's mistress Katherine (mother of his four

Beaufort children) from her marriage to Sir Hugh Swynford.[11] Blanche Swynford, named as a damsel of Gaunt's daughters in 1369 and born in or before the early 1360s, was certainly of marriageable age in 1381, when Gaunt gave Thomas Morieux and his wife Blanche generous wedding gifts. It is not at all unlikely that Gaunt would have fathered an illegitimate child, as his father and his eldest brother (and even his grandfather Edward II, usually famed as a lover of men) did, but it is perhaps a little odd that no other evidence besides the statement by Jean Froissart exists to confirm that the duke was the father of Blanche Morieux. One researcher in the nineteenth century believed that Blanche Morieux was John of Gaunt's daughter with Katherine Swynford, but this is highly unlikely, as otherwise Blanche would have been given the name 'Beaufort' as the couple's four other children were, and would, like them, have been legitimised in the late 1390s after Gaunt married Katherine (assuming that she was still alive then).[12] Unless a hitherto undiscovered document is unearthed that sheds more light on Blanche's parentage, the matter remains unclear.

A papal 'dispensation to enable his [Edward III's] son John, earl of Richmond, and the lady Blanche, daughter of Henry, duke of Lancaster, to intermarry, they being related in the third and fourth degrees of kindred,' was issued on 6 January 1359.[13] John of Gaunt and Blanche of Lancaster married in Reading on Sunday, 19 May 1359, and the ceremony was performed by a clerk of Queen Philippa's chapel called Thomas Chynham.[14] The king's accounts talk of three marriages performed by Chynham in the royal chapel of Reading: John of Gaunt's, his sister Margaret of Windsor's, and 'the daughter of the earl of Ulster'. This is a reference to Lionel of Antwerp's daughter Philippa, who had married Edmund Mortimer the previous December.

John was nineteen at the time of his wedding, and Blanche was almost certainly seventeen. Edward III and Philippa of Hainault attended their son's wedding, as did, presumably, Blanche's parents Duke Henry and Duchess Isabella, née Beaumont. The king's sister Joan of the Tower, queen of Scotland, whose husband David II had until recently been a prisoner in England, was also there. Blanche and her father visited Duke Henry's town of Leicester before the wedding, and the sum of 3s 8d was spent on minstrels who performed at their arrival. The townspeople gave Blanche and her lady attendants a generous gift of £25.[15]

Edward III paid £30 for two silver buckles for his and the queen's eldest daughter Isabella of Woodstock to give to her new sister-in-law. A membrane still exists in the National Archives detailing other gifts given to the bride (referred to as '*dame Blaunch*', 'Lady Blanche') the day after her wedding. Those who gave Blanche gifts were her new husband, her father-in-law, aunt-in-law Joan of the Tower (called *la Roine Descoce*, 'the queen of Scotland,' though Edward III refused to acknowledge her husband as king and simply called him 'David Bruce of Scotland'), her brothers-in-law Lionel, Edmund and Thomas, her sisters-in-law Isabella of Woodstock, Mary of

Waltham and Margaret of Windsor, and Lionel's wife Elizabeth de Burgh, countess of Ulster. For some rather curious reason, Queen Philippa and her eldest son Edward of Woodstock are not mentioned on the list of gift-givers, though it would have been odd if they, alone of all the royal family, did not give Blanche wedding presents. John of Gaunt bought his new wife a gold brooch with a balas ruby and pearls and a gold and diamond ring, and Elizabeth de Burgh gave her cousin Blanche a silver cup and a ruby ring. Blanche also received three silver cups in the name of four-year-old Thomas of Woodstock and his sisters Mary and Margaret. [16]

7

Guileless, of Humble Manner

Both the poet Geoffrey Chaucer (b. *c.* 1340 or 1342 and thus exactly the same age as John and Blanche) and the chronicler Jean Froissart (b. *c.* 1337/38 and just slightly older) commented on Blanche of Lancaster's beauty. She was tall and lithe, had wide hips and round breasts – Chaucer was perhaps sharing rather too much information there – and was 'fattish and fleshy.' This was a definite positive in fourteenth-century England when few people enjoyed an abundance of food and deaths from starvation and malnutrition were not uncommon, and was a clear sign of wealth. Blanche was indeed born to virtually limitless wealth and privilege, yet despite this, did not grow up conceited, arrogant and unapproachable, but had a delightful personality. Froissart admired her enormously: she was 'light-hearted, happy, fresh, amusing, sweet, guileless, of humble manner,' and he jocularly requested a plaster to be placed over his heart at the memory of her many years later.

Geoffrey Chaucer knew the royal family extremely well and served in the retinues of Edward III, Queen Philippa, Lionel of Antwerp and Elizabeth de Burgh at various times, and after Blanche's death he composed his first great work *The Book of the Duchess*, which is almost certainly about her. The work contains the lines:

> And gode faire Whyte she hete [was called]
> That was my lady name right
> She was bothe fair and bright.[1]

Blanche's name means 'white' in French, and Chaucer commented on her appropriately white hands and 'faire shuldres'. Pale skin was another much-prized asset in the fourteenth century and also signified wealth and privilege, because most people worked outdoors all day and only the rich were able to remain indoors and to have skin that was not tanned or otherwise damaged by the sun.

Blanche was not only a great heiress but apparently beautiful, and was a kind, courteous, humble person who, like her father the duke, was widely liked and admired. It is certainly possible that love developed between her and John, though we have no way of knowing what happened between the couple in private or how John truly felt about his first wife. John and Blanche's relationship has been excessively romanticised by some later writers, who have sometimes assumed that Geoffrey Chaucer's poetry and the heartfelt emotions he has his characters expressing in the *Book of the Duchess* must represent John of Gaunt's own feelings. This is not necessarily the case. Their marriage has sometimes been described as a love match, and while it is of course possible that John and Blanche did grow to love each other and that they had liked or even loved each other for many years, the marriage was arranged by others and did not happen because they had fallen in love. John was certainly extremely lucky that the wealthy, partly royal heiress he married was also appealing and pleasant, and the description of her 'wide hips' referred to her fertility; Blanche would indeed spend much of the next few years pregnant with John's children. She became pregnant within weeks of marrying him: their first child was born ten months and twelve days after their wedding.

Assuming that Blanche's mother Isabella Beaumont attended the wedding, she would have spent time with the king and queen and with her new son-in-law in Reading during the great occasion, though Duchess Isabella is an oddly shadowy figure. In his long and remarkable *Book of Holy Medicines*, his religious treatise on the seven deadly sins, which Duke Henry completed in 1354, he admitted to having 'kissed', i.e. slept with, a number of low-born women and to have found them more responsive than noblewomen, though he stated that noblewomen smelt better. The duke is known to have fathered at least one illegitimate child, a daughter named Juliane who spent her life in Henry's town of Leicester and married there.[2] Henry did not, however, talk about his wife at all in his long work. Isabella and Henry's marriage seems not to have been a particularly happy or close one, and Isabella played no role whatsoever in her husband's public life; not only did Duke Henry not bother to mention her even once in his book, no fourteenth-century chronicler so much as mentioned her, either.[3]

Isabella, duchess of Lancaster, was apparently a shy, retiring figure, and sadly for posterity, it is impossible to say anything at all about John of Gaunt's relationship with his mother-in-law. She may have been dying at the time of her younger daughter's wedding to him in May 1359. That month, the pope granted Duke Henry, regarding an indult previously granted that his chaplains should give him and Isabella plenary remission at the time of their death, an extension 'to another wife, if he takes one after the death of Isabella.'[4] Certainly she died sometime between May 1359 and March 1361, and although Isabella Beaumont was the first duchess in English history (except that the queen consorts of England were duchesses of Aquitaine in France) and was a great-granddaughter of the man who was both emperor of Constantinople and king of Jerusalem, she is so obscure that we do not even know the year of her death for certain.

John of Gaunt, who was to benefit enormously as a result of his first marriage, which made him the richest man in the country for almost forty years, was lucky that Blanche was still available as a bride. On 4 May 1347,

Henry of Grosmont had arranged his five-year-old younger daughter's future marriage to John Segrave (b. *c.* 1340/41), a great-grandson of King Edward I, and heir to his parents Lord Segrave (1315–53) and Margaret, countess of Norfolk in her own right (*c.* 1322–99).[5] This did not work out because the Segrave boy died as a child sometime before April 1353, and left his older sister Elizabeth (b. October 1338), Lady Mowbray, as their parents' heir.[6] In November 1344, Duke Henry's four-year-old elder daughter Maud had married Ralph Stafford, heir to his parents Ralph, later the first earl of Stafford, and Margaret Audley, and heir also to his maternal grandparents Hugh Audley and Margaret de Clare, earl and countess of Gloucester. Little Ralph Stafford was around the same age as his wife, and, like young John Segrave, was a descendant of Edward I. The Stafford boy also died young, sometime before November 1347, and left Maud of Lancaster a widow at seven years old or even younger. The Stafford heir therefore was little Ralph's younger brother Hugh, later the second earl of Stafford.[7]

Both boys, John Segrave and Ralph Stafford, were of good noble birth, of partly royal descent, and heirs to their families, and would have made perfectly acceptable husbands for the daughters of the earl of Lancaster, Leicester, Derby and Lincoln. As the years wore on, however, Henry of Grosmont must have come to realise that he would not have a son, and that Maud and Blanche would be his heirs and would share the enormous Lancastrian inheritance. When he made the marital arrangements for his daughters with the Stafford and Segrave families in 1344 and 1347, he did not anticipate that the two girls would be his heirs, and must have assumed that as his wife Isabella Beaumont was only in her late twenties or early thirties in 1347, they had plenty of time to have a son, or indeed several. After Henry came to realise that in fact his two daughters would inherit his lands, he arranged greater matches for them, with Queen Philippa's nephew and the Holy Roman Emperor's son Wilhelm von Wittelsbach of Bavaria in 1352, and with Edward III and Queen Philippa's son John of Gaunt in 1359. Had the Segrave and Stafford boys not died young, they and their families would have enjoyed a great windfall and would have shared the entire Lancastrian inheritance; but their loss was John of Gaunt's gain.

John's youngest sister Margaret of Windsor married John Hastings, heir to the earldom of Pembroke, possibly in December 1358 around the same time that her niece Philippa of Ulster wed Edmund Mortimer, or possibly rather later. The king spent well over £200 on 2,000 pearls for his daughter's wedding.[8] Margaret, born in July 1346, was twelve when she wed, and her husband John was thirteen months younger than she was and only eleven years old at the time of their wedding. He was born on 29 August 1347, and lost his father Laurence Hastings, earl of Pembroke, on 30 August 1348 when he was one year and one day old.[9] The king and his four eldest sons Edward, Lionel, John and Edmund took part in a jousting tournament held in honour of John of Gaunt's new wife, at Smithfield in London from 27 to

29 May 1359, dressed as the mayor and aldermen of London, while John and his household knights are said to have jousted all the way from Reading to London 'fighting in the fields and towns' and offering combat to all comers. Thomas of Woodstock the youngest royal son, at only four, was of course far too young to compete though surely watched, and his new brother-in-law John Hastings at eleven was also too young to compete personally. Edward III paid £40 to William Volaunt, king of heralds, to distribute among the minstrels who had entertained the royal family and the watching crowds during the Smithfield tournament.[10]

John of Gaunt and Blanche of Lancaster conceived a child within five or six weeks of their wedding. Edward III demonstrated his anxiety for Blanche's well-being on 9 January 1360 by commenting that she was pregnant and 'because of the concern that we feel for her condition,' he wished her to stay with Queen Philippa for the last month or two before her delivery.[11] Perhaps Blanche's mother Isabella Beaumont, duchess of Lancaster, died while she was expecting her first child, increasing the king's concern for her, and if she had lost her mother this would explain why Edward wished his wife, a woman with strong maternal feelings, to look after her. The king's letter is yet more evidence of the affection the royal family felt for each other.

Blanche gave birth to her and John's first child, a daughter, on 31 March 1360, when she had just turned eighteen and John was twenty. The place of birth was not recorded. Inevitably, the little girl was named after her paternal grandmother the queen, who is likely to have been her godmother as well; Queen Philippa was certainly the godmother of her eldest granddaughter Philippa of Ulster, and gave her her name during her baptism in August 1355. Philippa was spelt Phelip, Phelippe, Philippe or Phellipe in the fourteenth century and was a unisex name, serving both for men called Philip and women called Philippa. In later years, John of Gaunt referred to his daughter as 'Phelippe de Lancastre'.[12] Little Philippa later became queen of Portugal and was the mother of six people known collectively to Portuguese historians as the Illustrious Generation, and is famous in her adopted land to this day as Filipa de Lencastre.

8

The Departure of Duke Henry's Soul

John of Gaunt was out of England from late October 1359 until the spring of 1360, so missed the last few months of his wife's first pregnancy and his daughter's birth. Edward III had extended a truce with France until 14 June 1359, then demanded greater territorial concessions from his foes, which the French, not surprisingly, rejected. The king therefore set off on yet another military campaign in France in October 1359, accompanied by his sons Edward, Lionel, John and Edmund, and John of Gaunt's father-in-law Henry of Grosmont. Queen Philippa remained in England with Blanche of Lancaster and the rest of her family, and the youngest royal son Thomas of Woodstock, still only four years old, was appointed as nominal keeper of the realm in his father's and his older brothers' absence.

John returned to England on 10 May 1360. On 20 May, his father gave him a generous gift: Hertford Castle, where John's grandmother, the dowager queen Isabella, had died in August 1358 and which had been one of her favourite residences (the often-repeated story that Edward III confined his mother to Castle Rising in Norfolk after overthrowing her in 1330 is a myth). John 'has not yet castles, houses or other buildings wherein he can lodge or stay as befits his estate, as the king has learned for certain,' Edward III announced as the reason for the grant.[1]

John must have seen his little daughter Philippa for the first time shortly after he returned to his homeland. It is possible that Philippa of Lancaster's maternal grandfather, Duke Henry, was rather disappointed that she was a girl; Henry had failed to father any sons, had six sisters but no brothers, and now his second, but currently his only living, grandchild was also female. Duke Henry of Lancaster, a towering figure in English public life for decades and certainly one of the great men of Europe in the fourteenth century, did not live long enough to see the births of his other grandchildren; he died in his town of Leicester on 23 March 1361, aged barely fifty.[2] His death came as a severe blow to the English royal family and to his kinsman the king, whom he had staunchly supported through thick and thin for many years.

John of Gaunt attended his father-in-law's funeral at the collegiate church of the Newarke in Leicester on 14 April 1361 twenty-two days after Henry of Grosmont passed away. In his will, dictated a few days before he died, the duke had requested that he should not be buried until three weeks 'after the departure of the soul'.[3] The funeral, in fact, followed unusually rapidly after the duke's death, given his high birth and status; his father's body had remained above ground for close to four months in 1345/46 before interment. Also present at the Newarke were John's wife Blanche of Lancaster, his parents the king and queen, his siblings, and the late duke's four surviving sisters: Blanche, Lady Wake; Maud, dowager countess of Ulster and now a canoness in Suffolk; Eleanor, Lady Beaumont and countess of Arundel; and Mary, Lady Percy. In his will, Duke Henry had made his eldest sister Lady Wake and his cousin Lady Walkington two of his ten executors. Gaunt's sister-in-law Maud, duchess of Lower Bavaria and countess of Hainault and Holland, almost certainly returned to England to attend her father's funeral.

Henry of Grosmont's inquisition post-mortem was held in the thirty-four English counties where he had held lands, and in Wales, in April and May 1361 (it would have been far easier for royal clerks to name the five English counties where he did not hold lands rather than those where he did).[4] No dower is recorded as being given to the dowager duchess, and it would have been considerable, so clearly Isabella had already died, probably when her younger daughter Blanche was pregnant in 1359/60. On 25 March, two days after the duke's death, John of Gaunt was assigned temporary custody of all Henry's lands and their revenues, and on 16 July 1361 the lands were divided between Henry's daughters, Maud and Blanche.[5]

Maud received the lands south of the River Trent and Blanche those in the north, which made good sense, as John was already earl of Richmond in Yorkshire. Maud took the earldom of Leicester, Blanche the earldoms of Lancaster, Lincoln and Derby. Among the castles assigned to Blanche and John were Pontefract in Yorkshire, where Blanche's great-uncle Thomas of Lancaster had been executed in 1322, and Kenilworth in Warwickshire, where John's grandfather Edward II was forced to abdicate his throne to his son Edward III in 1327 and where he was held in captivity for a while. Blanche and John also received Bolingbroke Castle in Lincolnshire, Pickering Castle in Yorkshire, Dunstanburgh Castle in Northumberland and Tutbury Castle in Staffordshire; Maud received, among numerous other properties, her father's castles in Newcastle-under-Lyme and Leicester, four castles in South Wales, and the Savoy Palace in London.

Another lordship assigned to Maud was Beaufort in France, which had passed to her and Blanche's grandfather Earl Henry on the death of his childless younger brother John of Lancaster in 1317. As well as the enormous Lancastrian patrimony from their father Duke Henry, grandfather Earl Henry, great-uncles Thomas and John of Lancaster and great-grandfather Edmund (d. 1296), Maud and Blanche inherited the lands and lordships in England and Wales that had once belonged to their paternal grandmother Maud Chaworth (d. 1322), including Kidwelly and Carmarthen in South Wales, and the large inheritance of their great-uncle Thomas's widow Alice de Lacy (d. 1348), countess of Lincoln in her own right and heiress of the wealthy de Lacy family.[6] Bolingbroke and Pickering were just two of the castles that passed to the Lancasters from the de Lacys.

Maud of Lancaster returned to England in 1361 for the first time, as far as is known, since she had married Duke Wilhelm in early 1352, and performed homage to Edward III for her share of her father's lands. She had been gone from England for so long that the jurors in Northumberland, Huntingdonshire and Lincolnshire who took part in her father's inquisition post-mortem admitted that they could not remember her name, and did not know if she was still alive or whether she had children. The Dorset jurors knew she was the wife of Duke Wilhelm and was alive, but could not remember her name either. The jurors of all counties realised, however, that either Maud herself, or any children she had if she had died, were co-heirs to Henry of Grosmont with her younger sister. Maud performed homage to the king in person; normally her husband would have done so, but the unfortunate Wilhelm, being incarcerated in a tower of Le Quesnoy Castle (Le Quesnoy is a town now in the Nord department of France near the Belgian border), was in no position to travel to England. John of Gaunt, 'by reason of his having offspring with Blanche,' paid homage to his father for his and his wife's extensive new lands, probably on the same occasion as Maud.[7] The date of John and Maud's homage is not known, but took place sometime before 16 July 1361. John was at Hertford Castle on 6 October 1361 when, as 'the king's son John, earl of Richmond, Lancaster, Derby and Lincoln, steward of England,' using his new titles, he issued letters patent granting land in Boston, Lincolnshire (Seint Bothulf, as the town was then known) to a couple named John and Maud le Ropere.[8]

An important royal wedding took place in Windsor on 10 October 1361, that of John's eldest brother Edward of Woodstock and his cousin Joan of Kent, widow of Sir Thomas Holland (d. late 1360). Edward turned thirty-one in June 1361, and his new wife was some years his senior, born either in September 1326 or September 1327. John, his parents, his aunt the queen of Scotland, his brother Edmund and his sister Isabella all attended.[9] The couple were first cousins once removed – Edward of Woodstock was a great-grandson of Edward I (d. 1307) by his first marriage and Joan was Edward I's granddaughter by his second – which meant that they needed a papal dispensation for consanguinity. In addition, Edward was the godson of Joan's two Holland sons, Thomas and John, which created a spiritual affinity between them that also required a papal dispensation. The dispensation was formulated incorrectly and had to be reissued a year later, and there is evidence that their son King Richard II fretted about the legality of their union, as in the 1390s he owned a box of documents relating to their marriage and to the dissolution of his mother's bigamous marriage to William Montacute (b. 1328), earl of Salisbury.[10] As was the case with John of Gaunt and Blanche of Lancaster, Edward of Woodstock and Joan of Kent must have known each other for almost all of their lives, and in the late 1340s Edward affectionately referred to Joan as Lady Jeannette.[11] One chronicler stated, however, that the marriage of the prince of Wales 'greatly surprised many people.'[12] Joan was the heir of her younger brother John, earl of Kent and Lord Wake, who had married Gaunt's cousin Elisabeth von Jülich in 1348 but died childless at the end of 1352, aged only twenty-two. She would be the mother of Edward's two legitimate sons, Edward of Angoulême and Richard of Bordeaux, born in early 1365 and early 1367 and heirs to the English throne behind their father.

Although the Savoy Palace had passed to Maud of Lancaster, John of Gaunt was staying there on 14 November 1361 when he made an indenture with the executors of the late Duke Henry's will. As any arrangements made regarding the duke's lands affected her as well, Maud may also have been present, and John and Blanche were guests at her palace. The indenture referred to Gaunt and Blanche as 'the very noble lord Johan, earl of Lancaster and Richmond, and my lady Blanche his consort'.[13] For John to be staying with his sister-in-law or at least in one of her many homes might imply that they got on well, though unfortunately it is impossible to say much about John's relationship with his wife's older sister – the evidence does not exist.

9

Great Wonders and Signs

John of Gaunt surely considered himself fortunate to own half of the Lancastrian lands, but little more than a year after his father-in-law's death, fate was to intervene and bring him and Blanche all of it. On 9 or 10 April 1362 (either on Palm Sunday or the day before), John's sister-in-law Maud, duchess of Lower Bavaria, countess of Leicester, Hainault, Holland and Zeeland, and lady of Monmouth, Beaufort and Nogent, died just a few days past her twenty-second birthday. Although Maud was born into endless wealth and privilege, her life was a short and sad one. Her first husband Ralph Stafford was dead by the time she was seven or even younger, she was married again before she turned twelve, her husband became insane and had to be confined for his own safety and hers, she lost her only child when she was sixteen, she probably never saw her mother again after she was twelve and her father only once, and now she was dead in her early twenties. According to a Continental chronicle, Maud was buried in the Benedictine abbey of Rijnsburg near Leiden, a city now in the South Holland province of the Netherlands, and if this is correct, she is unlikely to have passed away in England.[1] Perhaps, despite her ownership of lands across England and Wales, Maud felt that she rightfully belonged in Holland and Hainault, the counties her husband had inherited from his mother the empress. Flemish chronicler Jean le Bel states that after Wilhelm became insane, 'the two lands were governed by the lady, his wife'.[2] After Maud died, the counties passed into the governance of her brother-in-law Duke Albrecht.

The inquisition post-mortem of 'Maud, late the wife of William, duke of Bavaria' was held in numerous counties across the Midlands and southern England and in Wales in May 1362. 'The lady Blanche of Lancaster, her sister, aged twenty years and married to Sir John, earl of Richmond, is her heir,' said the Worcestershire jurors, correctly, though jurors in other counties across England estimated Blanche's age as anywhere between 'sixteen years and more' and twenty-four. In February 1365, the king pardoned his son and Blanche all the 'relief' – a sum of money that was basically inheritance tax – that was due on the lands they had inherited from Duke Henry and Duchess Maud. As the amount owing would have been considerable, this was a highly generous gesture on Edward III's part.[3]

Blanche and John now owned the town of Leicester and its castle, where Blanche and Maud's father had died the year before, and Grosmont Castle in Wales, where Duke Henry had been born in *c*. 1310/12. Another of the many residences which passed to Blanche and John from Maud in 1362 was the London palace now closely associated with John of Gaunt, which would be destroyed a few years later during the Great Uprising because it belonged to him – the Savoy, called 'the Saveye in Middlesex' in Maud's inquisition post-mortem and usually called the 'Sauvoye' in Gaunt's letters. The London jurors in 1362 referred to the Savoy simply as a messuage, i.e. a building with land around it and some outbuildings, as though it were merely a small hovel and not a great palace that had cost Duke Henry £35,000, or tens of millions in modern terms, to build on a massive and luxurious scale. A letter John of Gaunt sent in 1372 talks of 'houses within our manor of the Sauvoye' that needed to be repaired and restored, and there were gardens there as well, which ran down to the river. Fruits were grown there, and John hired Nichol Gardiner to tend his gardens. Two shops belonged to the Savoy which were rented out at 4*d* a week each, while seven other shops were rented out at 1 and a halfpenny a week each.[4] The Savoy was located on the Strand next to the River Thames, and had originally been built by Peter of Savoy, maternal uncle of John and Blanche's mutual great-great-grandmother Eleanor of Provence, Henry III's queen. Eleanor's son Edward I granted it to his brother Edmund of Lancaster in the early 1290s.[5] A famous hotel – still called the Savoy – now stands on, or very close to, the site.

Under normal circumstances Maud's widower, Wilhelm von Wittelsbach, would, because she had borne him a daughter in 1356, have been entitled to hold her entire estate until he died, by the 'courtesy of England'.[6] This was a medieval custom that entitled a man who married an heiress to hold all his wife's lands for the rest of his life if she died before him, as long as they had at least one child together who lived long enough to draw breath (as Maud's daughter apparently did). Wilhelm lived until April 1388 when he was in his late fifties, but because he was incapacitated and held under guard for thirty years, and was officially in the custody of his brother Albrecht, he was neither permitted nor able to hold and govern any lands.[7] If he had been, he would have held half the Lancastrian inheritance until his death and would have kept it out of John and Blanche's possession until the last eleven years of John's life. There was a medieval procedure called 'denization', where the king was able to grant a foreign subject what in modern times is called permanent residency, which permitted him or her to own, though not to inherit, lands. Despite being German, therefore, Wilhelm would legally have been able to own Maud's estate. In this case, the Savoy Palace would have belonged to the son of a German emperor at the time of the Great Uprising in June 1381, and therefore would surely not have been destroyed, as in fact it was because it belonged to the detested John of Gaunt. Wilhelm would also have held Maud's French lordship of Beaufort, almost certainly the inspiration for John's naming of his and Katherine Swynford's four children in the 1370s, as well as his late wife's many lands in South Wales and the south and midlands of England. Apart from Hertford Castle, Pevensey Castle and a few other places in the south granted to him by his father, John's ownership of lands, lordships and castles would have been restricted to the north of England until Wilhelm died in 1388, when John was forty-eight.

His unfortunate cousin's affliction, as well as his sister-in-law Maud's early demise and the deaths in childhood of Maud's first husband Ralph Stafford and Blanche's first fiancé John Segrave, was yet another twist of fate that unexpectedly brought John of Gaunt full possession of the enormous Lancastrian estate. Had Maud's little girl not died in infancy in 1356 and had grown up, she would have been named as her mother's heir in 1362 and would have inherited all of Maud's lands after her father's death; or had Wilhelm not become insane in 1357/58, he and Maud might well have had more children, who would have been Maud's heirs in 1362.

The cause of Maud of Lancaster's death at the age of twenty-two is unknown. Although the Leicester chronicler Henry Knighton reported rumours he had heard that John of Gaunt poisoned his sister-in-law, such rumours were probably inevitable given that John and Blanche benefited so greatly from her sister's passing, and there is no reason whatsoever to think that John was willing to poison a young kinswoman he had known for his entire life because he craved her lands.[8] Maud may in fact have died of the plague, although in the fourteenth century there were of course all kinds of diseases and infections that could carry off even young and seemingly healthy people. John's sisters Mary of Waltham and Margaret of Windsor, still in their teens, and his cousin Anna of Bavaria and their aunt Isabella of Hainault, Queen Philippa's youngest sister, both in their thirties, all died in 1361/62 as well.[9] There was an outbreak of plague in England and elsewhere in northern Europe in the early 1360s. The deaths of John's sisters Mary and Margaret, neither of whom left children from their marriages to the duke of Brittany and the young earl of Pembroke, must have come as a great shock to the royal family. Of the five daughters whom Queen Philippa had borne, only the eldest, Isabella of Woodstock, was now still alive.

The year 1362 was, in fact, a rather peculiar one. Apparently there was another drought in England that year, with 'great bareness of corn and fruit,' and around late May a strange rain 'almost like blood' fell. It was, a contemporary believed, a year of great wonders and signs: there was an eclipse of the sun, a cross that also looked like it was made out of blood was seen in the sky from dawn until dusk in northern France that summer, and numerous people in England, France and other countries supposedly witnessed a peculiar apparition. Two castles appeared out of thin air, and great armies rode out of each, one dressed all in white and the other in black, and engaged each other in battle. After the army dressed in black overcame the army in white, they all vanished and were never again.[10] The 'great and huge pestilence' that swept Europe in 1361/62, another terrible outbreak of the Black Death following the first catastrophic pandemic of 1348/50, supposedly affected men disproportionately, according to the author of the *Brut*, though, as noted, it might have killed as many as five of John of Gaunt's close female relatives.

John was at Kenilworth Castle in Warwickshire (a residence on which he was to lavish a great deal of money over the years) on 20 April 1362, ten or eleven days after Duchess Maud's death. By 14 May he had moved on to the Savoy, and, whatever he might have felt personally about the loss of Maud, he was surely delighted that he and Blanche now owned this large and sumptuous palace.[11] It seems likely that John and Blanche's second surviving daughter Elizabeth was born in February 1363 and therefore was conceived in about May 1362, and it is also likely that Blanche bore a son in 1361 or 1362 who died young; she and John, as will be discussed below, had two or perhaps even three sons who died in infancy.

10

Almost the King of Scotland

Edward of Woodstock and Joan of Kent travelled to Aquitaine in the summer of 1362 after Edward III made his eldest son prince of Aquitaine that June. John of Gaunt would see his brother again a few years later, but their mother, the queen, would never see her eldest child again. John lost his aunt Joan of the Tower in September 1362, when the queen of Scotland died at the age of forty-one. Joan had spent the last few years in England, her marriage to David II having fallen apart, and was buried with her mother Queen Isabella at the Greyfriars' church in London. King Edward had now lost all his siblings and marked the anniversary of Queen Joan's death every year.

The king celebrated his fiftieth birthday on 13 November 1362, a few weeks after losing his sister, by raising his middle three sons to higher titles – Thomas of Woodstock was still only seven, and would have to wait a few more years to receive an earldom. John of Gaunt was made the second duke of Lancaster, his elder brother Lionel became the first duke of Clarence, and his younger brother Edmund became the second earl of Cambridge (the first was their German uncle Duke Wilhelm of Jülich, husband of Queen Philippa's elder sister Johanna; Wilhelm died in 1361). Lionel of Antwerp's extant will reveals that the ceremony that made him and his brother John dukes involved the wearing of gold circlets. Gaunt first appears on record as duke of Lancaster in the chancery rolls on 15 November 1362, two days after his creation as such. He also inherited the Lancasters' right to act as steward of England.[1]

John's income has been estimated at around £12,000 a year gross and around £10,000 net, and he was certainly one of the richest English magnates in the entire fourteenth century, with an income twice as large as any of his contemporaries. He owned a sizeable part of England as well as castles and lands across South Wales, and employed an enormous retinue of many hundreds of people to emphasise his wealth and magnificence. In 1382, for example, John employed almost eighty knights and almost a hundred squires, numbers far in excess of his contemporaries.[2] The Lancasters, hugely rich and partly royal, were an important and influential family, which could cause difficulties for the English kings. Gaunt's grandfather, Edward II, had huge problems with his cousin Thomas of Lancaster in the 1310s and early 1320s, and Thomas's brother and heir Earl Henry played a vital role in Edward's downfall in 1326/27. Edward III, unlike his father, was able to retain the loyalty of Earl Henry and his son Duke Henry, but the Lancasters' wealth and influence would always mean that they were impossible to ignore, and in later years John of Gaunt's nephew the king would have his own problems with his uncle and with his Lancastrian cousin, John and Blanche's son and heir.

John of Gaunt's great-great-grandfather Henry III created the earldom of Lancaster for his younger son Edmund, Blanche of Lancaster's great-grandfather, in 1267; the earldom of Leicester had belonged to Henry III's brother-in-law and enemy Simon de Montfort, killed fighting against Henry and his elder son the future Edward I in 1265, and was subsequently given to Edmund of Lancaster; the earldom of Lincoln belonged to the de Lacy family and passed to the Lancasters via the marriage of Alice de Lacy and Thomas of Lancaster; and the earldom of Derby had belonged to the Ferrers family for generations but was confiscated from Robert de Ferrers (*c.* 1239–79) by Henry III and his elder son Edward in 1269, also to benefit Henry's younger son Edmund of Lancaster. The Ferrers family never regained their lost earldom and lands, which included the lordship and castle of Tutbury in Staffordshire, a place John and Blanche often visited. That John of Gaunt was well aware of the earldom of Derby's history and the Ferrers' ownership of Tutbury is revealed by a letter he sent after he and Blanche came into their inheritance, in which he mentioned the existence of a chaplain who sang divine services daily in the chapel of Tutbury Castle, a chapel John knew had been founded by William de Ferrers, earl of Derby (d. 1254).[3]

According to a chronicler, on 15 January 1363 and supposedly for a whole week afterwards, there was a hurricane in England that destroyed houses, churches and other buildings, and those that were not destroyed by the severe winds were badly shaken and weakened. Heavy rains and bad floods followed later in the year, and during Edward III's thirty-ninth regnal year, which ran from January 1365 to January 1366, a 'strong and huge frost' that lasted until mid-March made it impossible for anyone to till the hard, frozen ground.[4] Duchess Blanche was heavily pregnant at the time of the destructive hurricane, and probably in February 1363 gave birth to her and John's second eldest surviving child, Elizabeth of Lancaster. Gaunt's sister-in-law Elizabeth de Burgh, duchess of Clarence, may have been her niece's godmother, and perhaps Elizabeth of Lancaster was named after her; the name Elizabeth was still not particularly common in the royal family, and was not borne by any of John's sisters or any of Blanche of Lancaster's many aunts. Perhaps, however, it was intended as a variant name of Blanche's late mother, Isabella Beaumont.

Elizabeth, duchess of Clarence, died in Dublin a few months later at the age of only thirty-one, leaving her twenty-five-year-old widower Lionel of Antwerp and their eight-year-old daughter Philippa as her heir. Edward III paid to have Elizabeth's remains returned to England, and she was buried at Bruisyard Priory in Suffolk, which Lionel himself had founded and where

Elizabeth's much younger half-sister Maud de Vere née Ufford, countess of Oxford, would also be buried half a century later. Elizabeth's mother Maud of Lancaster the elder, dowager countess of Ulster and a canoness at Bruisyard, outlived her by a few years and died in 1377.

John was at the castle of Moor End ('Morende') in Northamptonshire on 30 September 1363 when he witnessed a grant of lands and the castle of Moor End itself to his father. His brother Edmund of Langley and their cousin Humphrey de Bohun, earl of Hereford, were also present.[5] In November 1363, David II of Scotland and his brother-in-law Edward III of England discussed the possibility of John of Gaunt succeeding his uncle as king of Scotland. David was now close to forty and still had no children, and as John held vast lands in the north of England, he had a vested interest in keeping the peace and ensuring cordial relations between England and its northern neighbour.[6] In the end, however, the idea was rejected. David married his second wife Margaret Drummond in early 1364, but had no children with her either, and on his death in 1371 the Scottish throne passed to his half-nephew Robert II, first king of the house of Stewart, rather than to his nephew-in-law John of Gaunt. Edward III gave Queen Margaret safe conduct to visit the shrine of St Thomas Becket in Canterbury on 20 February 1364, and one to King David on the same day to visit the shrine of Our Lady of Walsingham; perhaps the royal Scottish couple hoped that their pilgrimages would persuade God to give them children, and they visited Becket's shrine again in early 1368. John of Gaunt, meanwhile, was at Bolingbroke Castle in Lincolnshire on 12 December 1363, and perhaps spent the festive season there with Blanche.[7]

John was with his father at Westminster on 10 February and again on 12 April 1364, when he witnessed grants by the king to a Richard of Pembridge and to Canterbury Cathedral Priory.[8] Among the other witnesses to the grants were John's brother the earl of Cambridge, the archbishop of Canterbury (Simon Islip), Blanche of Lancaster's uncles the earl of Arundel and Lord Mowbray, and Lord Despenser. On 8 April 1364, John II, the captive king of France, died at John and Blanche's London palace of the Savoy. An English knight called Sir Nicholas Damory took charge of leading the king's funeral cortege to Dover. Edward III and the English royal family attended the late king's exequies in St Paul's, London, and Edward paid a rather less than munificent 6s and 8d in oblations.[9] John II's eldest son from his first marriage to the late Bonne of Bohemia, Charles V, succeeded him. John and Bonne's sons, born in January 1338, July 1339, November 1340 and January 1342, were remarkably close in age, and the four royal brothers were followed by five sisters born in June 1343, September 1344, December 1345, September 1347 and October 1348; Bonne gave birth to nine children in well under eleven years. Given the pattern of her childbearing, she might have died after giving birth to yet another infant in 1349, rather than of the plague.

John of Gaunt was at Westminster again with his father and his brothers Lionel and Edmund on 12 July 1364, when the king confirmed charters to the town of Faversham, Kent, issued by his grandfather Edward I in 1302 and his great-grandfather Henry III in 1252.[10] In May 1365, John and Blanche were taking legal action against William Montacute, the long-lived earl of Salisbury (b. 1328, d. 1397) to try to recover some manors in Wiltshire and Dorset that had belonged to Blanche's great-uncle Thomas of Lancaster but had subsequently been granted to Salisbury's father.[11]

John's eldest sister Isabella of Woodstock married at last on 27 July 1365, aged thirty-three.[12] The bridegroom was Enguerrand or Ingelram, Lord de Coucy, a dashing French nobleman who was about eight or ten years Isabella's junior and who had come to England in the retinue of the captive King John II. The marriage quickly produced two daughters: Marie, born about nine months after the wedding, who spent her life in France and became countess of Soissons, and Philippa, born in 1367, whose marriage to the earl of Oxford, Robert de Vere, was arranged in 1376. John of Gaunt travelled to the county of Flanders in or before November 1365 'respecting the nuptials between' his brother Edmund of Langley, earl of Cambridge, and fifteen-year-old Margarethe, daughter and heir of Louis, count of Flanders. He received £400 for his expenses. Margarethe would one day inherit the counties of Flanders, Nevers, Rethel, Artois and Burgundy. Her father Louis (b. 1330) had been betrothed to Isabella of Woodstock in 1347, but he was unwilling to marry the daughter of a man, Edward III, he believed had killed his father – Louis of Flanders the elder was killed at the Battle of Crécy in August 1346. Louis fled to the French court and married the duke of Brabant's daughter Margarethe instead; their only surviving child, named after her mother, was born in 1350. Unfortunately, Pope Urban V had other ideas, and refused to issue a dispensation for Edmund and Margarethe of Flanders to wed.[13] In later years, after John was widowed, he would also be put forward as a potential husband for the great heiress Margarethe, Edward III and Queen Philippa being determined to secure her inheritance for one of their children (though ultimately proved unsuccessful in all their efforts).

Both John of Gaunt and Blanche of Lancaster were descended from Eleanor of Provence (d. 1291), queen of Henry III. Queen Eleanor was the second of four daughters of Ramon-Berenger, count of Provence, and she and her sisters Marguerite and Sanchia were most disgruntled when their father left the county of Provence to their youngest sister Beatrice in its entirety on his death in 1245. Eleanor, refusing to accept what she believed was a grossly unfair situation, passed her claims to Provence to her Lancaster grandsons Thomas and Henry (then aged about eight and five) in 1286, five years before her death. Edward II, another of Eleanor's grandsons and the heir of her sister Sancha, tried unsuccessfully to claim a share of Provence in the 1320s, and in 1319 confirmed the rights of his Lancastrian cousins Thomas and Henry to

Queen Eleanor's claimed portion of the county.[14] As late as 1366, 121 years after the death of Ramon-Berenger, John of Gaunt thought that it might be a good idea to resurrect the Lancasters' claim to Provence. He asked his father to confirm his own father Edward II's letters patent in favour of Thomas and Henry of Lancaster in 1319, and the king did so on 30 October that year.[15]

The rightful owner of Provence in 1366 was Giovanna I (b. *c.* 1326), queen regnant of Naples and countess of Provence, a first cousin of John's mother Queen Philippa and the great-great-granddaughter and heir of Beatrice of Provence, who inherited the entire county from her father Ramon-Berenger as a teenager in 1245. In June 1365, the Holy Roman Emperor, Karl IV (1316–78), had been crowned king of Burgundy in Arles as part of his own attempts to gain control over the disputed territory of Provence. This might have been what triggered John of Gaunt's own interest in the county a few months later, at least in part. It is also possible that Gaunt claimed Provence as part of his father's attempts to put pressure on the pope over his ongoing refusal to permit the marriage of Edmund of Langley and the great heiress Margarethe of Flanders; from 1305 to 1378 the popes lived in Avignon, an enclave in Provence, and would certainly be threatened by an English invasion and attempted seizure of the county.[16]

Even though the powerful Emperor Karl made a formidable adversary, and even though Queen Giovanna of Naples and her third husband King Jaime IV of Majorca were hardly pushovers either, John of Gaunt took some kind of threatening action to try to claim his and Blanche's share of the county. On 26 July 1367, Pope Urban V sent letters to Edward III ordering him 'not to permit an invasion of the county of Provence by John, duke of Lancaster, the king's son.' In March 1371, Pope Gregory XI was still talking of the 'many cities and lands' in Provence 'asserted by John, duke of Lancaster, and supported by public instruments.' He asked the bishops of London and Worcester to look into the matter and report back to him.[17] Ultimately, however, nothing came of it, though it is interesting to speculate whether John genuinely thought that he might be entitled to a share of Provence after so many generations had passed and whether he thought he could win the territory by an invasion, despite other powerful people's interest in it. Although she was married four times, Queen Giovanna was to die childless in 1382, and left Provence to her adopted son Louis of Anjou, the brother closest in age to Charles V of France and a nephew of Emperor Karl.

11

Defeating Enrique and Claiming Provence

In mid-November 1366, John of Gaunt left England, leaving Blanche about four and a half months pregnant again. The couple had at least two sons who died in infancy and were buried at the collegiate church of the Newarke in Leicester, the burial place of Blanche's father in 1361 and grandfather in 1346. Blanche and John's only surviving son, yet another Henry of Lancaster, referred in 1404 to his brothers, plural, who were interred at the Newarke.[1] The *Complete Peerage* says that the Lancaster boys who died young were called John and Edward, and also states that Duchess Blanche may have given birth to a daughter named Isabella who died young.[2] In March 1378, John's then eleven-year-old nephew Richard of Bordeaux confirmed that £20 a year would be paid to Sir Walter de Ursewyk for the rest of his life. This was a grant originally made by his father Edward of Woodstock to Ursewyk, 'for bringing the news of his sister[-in-law] the duchess of Lancaster's safe delivery of an infant.' The confirmation of this annuity in 1377 dates Edward of Woodstock's original grant to Ursewyk to '18 November, 41 Edward III,' and supposedly the grant was made at Chester.[3] November in Edward III's forty-first regnal year was November 1367. The prince of Wales, however, was nowhere near Chester in November 1367, so either the place or date of the grant was recorded incorrectly. John and Blanche's son Henry was born in April 1367, so for Edward of Woodstock to grant an annuity to the knight who brought him the news of the birth seven months later seems a little delayed. Possibly this entry relates to another of John and Blanche's children, and was dated wrongly.

In the mid and late 1360s, King Pedro of Castile was embroiled in conflict against his illegitimate half-brother Enrique of Trastámara, eldest surviving son of Alfonso XI and his influential mistress Leonor de Guzmán. Pedro's mother Queen Maria had had Leonor imprisoned and then killed after she lost the protection of her lover King Alfonso in 1350, which made Pedro and Maria a mortal enemy in the person of Leonor's son Enrique. In 1366, Trastámara succeeded in defeating Pedro and had himself proclaimed king of Castile. The kingdom had long been an English ally, and Edward III and his sons, therefore, supported King Pedro against his half-brother. The prince of Wales made a treaty of mutual support against Enrique with Pedro and Carlos II, king of Navarre (a small kingdom in the north of Spain that bordered the vastly larger kingdom of Castile) on 23 September 1366. Pedro promised to hand over his three daughters to Edward of Woodstock as hostages to ensure that he would pay the wages of the English soldiers who fought for him.[4]

King Pedro, betrothed to John of Gaunt's sister Joan of Woodstock in 1348 before she died on her way to marry him, had imprisoned his unfortunate French wife Blanche de Bourbon within days of their 1353 wedding, and she died in 1361 having never regained her freedom. Her sister Jeanne de Bourbon was married to Charles V of France, and the French, understandably, therefore supported Pedro's half-brother and enemy against him. Pedro's children were born to his mistress, the Castilian noblewoman María de Padilla, and were legitimised after Queen Blanche's death, and three of them were alive in the autumn of 1366 when Pedro pledged them as hostages. Ultimately only two of them survived, Constanza and Isabel, born in the mid-1350s. Constanza, the second daughter, became her father's heir after her older sister Beatriz and her younger brother Alfonso died.

John of Gaunt began preparations to leave England on 20 October 1366 with the aim of taking part in Pedro's campaign against Enrique of Trastámara. John sailed probably from Plymouth to the duchy of Brittany, where he visited his brother-in-law Duke John IV (John de Montfort), and travelled overland through France. In Bordeaux, he also visited his sister-in-law Joan of Kent, princess of Wales, who had just given birth to her and Edward of Woodstock's second son Richard, and whose daughter Joan Holland had married Duke John IV of Brittany, widower of Gaunt's sister Mary of Waltham, in 1366.[5]

On 3 April 1367, John of Gaunt's, Edward of Woodstock's and King Pedro's forces met Enrique of Trastámara's army at the Battle of Nájera (in English records, the location of the battle was given as Nazare or Nazery). Just the day before, Enrique had informed Edward that he was the rightful king of Castile as a result of Pedro's appalling behaviour, and ordered the prince to withdraw his forces, but Edward took no notice.[6] Jaime IV, the titular king of Majorca and husband of Queen Giovanna of Naples, also fought with John, Edward and Pedro but was captured by Enrique of Trastámara, and during the victory of the English and Castilian forces, John, Lord Ferrers of Chartley was the only high-ranking Englishman killed. Enrique fled to France after his defeat, but returned to Castile in 1369, and on the latter occasion defeated King Pedro at the Battle of Montiel, stabbed him to death afterwards, and made himself king of Castile and Leon.

Gaunt knighted his squire Walter de Ursewyk, who took the news of the birth of one of Gaunt's children to the prince of Wales, on the day of the Battle of Nájera, and the prince himself sent a loving letter to his wife Joan of Kent telling her about the battle, referring to Trastámara as 'the Bastard of Castile'. After the victory, the English side set out for Burgos.[7] In the brutal heat of the Spanish summer that followed, the great prince of Wales came down with a serious recurring illness, and would suffer from it for the remaining years of his life.

While John of Gaunt was in Spain and the south of France in 1367, he made some kind of threat to invade Provence and claim a share of it on Blanche of Lancaster's behalf, and rumours regarding his planned invasion had come to the pope's ears by 26 July 1367, when Urban wrote to Edward III telling him to take steps to prevent it.[8] Either because of the pope's prohibition or for some other reason, John did not go ahead with the invasion, though nearly four years later was still making diplomatic efforts towards claiming parts of Provence. Perhaps John believed that the capture of Jaime IV of Majorca at Nájera left Jaime's wife Giovanna, queen of Naples and countess of Provence, more vulnerable, which gave him a new impetus to try to claim the territory. The other possible claimant to the county, the emperor Karl IV, was busy elsewhere in 1367 and took his eye off Provence: he attempted an invasion of Italy, and annexed the territory of Lower Lusatia (in modern-day Germany and Poland) to the kingdom of Bohemia which he had inherited from his father Johann 'the Blind' in 1346.

During John's absence from England, Blanche gave birth to his son Henry at Bolingbroke Castle in Lincolnshire on Maundy Thursday, 15 April 1367, twelve days after Nájera. The little boy was named after his maternal grandfather Duke Henry, and although he has often been called 'Henry of Bolingbroke' after his birthplace – not least by Shakespeare – in adulthood he always referred to himself as Henry de Lancastre, i.e. 'of Lancaster'.[9] Henry's sisters Philippa and Elizabeth were also always called 'of Lancaster', and unlike their father and his siblings, did not use their birthplaces as part of their names. Elizabeth in fact was often called 'Elizabeth Lancastre' not 'de Lancastre', as though it were her surname, and unusually, she retained that name throughout her marriages (she married three men all called John).

Henry became sole heir to the Lancastrian inheritance when his older brothers died young. His paternal grandfather King Edward paid £5 to Ingelram Falconer, Duchess Blanche's messenger, who brought him the news of the birth. This in fact was none too generous given that not long before, the king had paid 40 marks, or £26, 13s and 4d, to the messenger who informed him of the birth of a son born to the duke and duchess of Berry, brother and sister-in-law of Charles V of France.[10] The castle at Bolingbroke had passed to Blanche's father Duke Henry in 1349 as part of his inheritance from his aunt-in-law Alice de Lacy, countess of Lincoln. The unfortunate Alice had been abducted from Bolingbroke with the connivance of some of her own servants in late 1335 or early 1336 when she was in her mid-fifties, and was taken to Somerton Castle a few miles away and forcibly married to her third husband, Sir Hugh Frene. By May 1372, the buildings inside Bolingbroke Castle and a nearby bridge were in urgent need of repair, and Gaunt sent his master carpenter, Henry of Stafford, there to determine what needed to be done and to purchase the timber for the repairs.[11]

John of Gaunt left his brother the prince in the south of France and returned to England a few months after their victory at Nájera; he witnessed a royal charter at Westminster on 8 October 1367, and was at the Savoy on 8 and 22 November and at Hertford on 8 December 1367.[12] No doubt John was delighted to see his son Henry for the first time, and possibly he and Blanche conceived another child around Christmas 1367. The duke was with his father and his brother Edmund of Langley at the palace of Westminster on 15 February 1368, and witnessed a grant to the king by Henry, Lord Beaumont, who gave Edward his house and garden 'by the cross at Cherryng,' i.e. Charing Cross.[13]

Lionel of Antwerp, duke of Clarence, left England in early April 1368 and travelled to Italy with a large retinue including Lord Despenser, Lord Beaumont and John Holland, perhaps the young man or adolescent of this name who was the stepson of Lionel's elder brother Edward of Woodstock. Lionel was to marry his second wife, Violante Visconti, daughter of Galeazzo Visconti, lord of Milan and Pavia. Their marriage had been arranged a year previously, and was first discussed in 1366. Chronicler Jean Froissart gives a long account of Lionel's journey to Italy, calling him 'Monseigneur Lion, duc de Clarense'. The duke passed through Paris, where he dined with the queen consort, Charles V's wife Jeanne de Bourbon, his and John of Gaunt's brother-in-law Enguerrand, Lord Coucy, the dukes of Berry, Burgundy and Bourbon, and many others. He arrived in Milan in late May, and married Violante, who was about fourteen – she was born a year or two before Lionel's daughter Philippa, countess of March – in a magnificent ceremony.[14] John of Gaunt, who had had little opportunity to spend much time with Lionel for the previous few years as Lionel had lived in Ireland as their father's lieutenant there, would never see his brother again.

12

Lady Blanche, Our Late Consort

John of Gaunt was probably in Leicester on 22 July 1368, when Sir William Croiser granted him and Blanche some land in Higham Ferrers, Northamptonshire, which was one of the Lancastrian couple's many manors.[1] Blanche was possibly with him, and she may have been heavily pregnant.

On 12 September 1368, John was suddenly and shockingly bereaved when Duchess Blanche died at Tutbury Castle in Staffordshire. The cause of Blanche's death at such an early age is unknown, though it is likely that it was related to pregnancy or childbirth; she had certainly spent a good portion of her marriage to John of Gaunt pregnant. It was once believed that she was a victim of the plague, but the third great epidemic of the Black Death occurred in 1369, and the year of Blanche's death was proved to have been 1368, not 1369 as once commonly thought, by the Chaucer scholar J. J. N. Palmer in the early 1970s.[2] She was most probably twenty-six when she died, according to the evidence of her father's inquisition post-mortem of 1361, though Jean Froissart claims improbably that she was only in her early twenties.

It seems that Blanche's confessor John Bennington remained with her until the end, and apparently rendered her excellent service throughout her life, as just two days after the duchess's death John of Gaunt spoke of the 'complete trust' that Blanche had had in Bennington and granted him £10 a year for the rest of his life.[3] John had his wife buried in St Paul's Cathedral in London, spending £486 for her tomb and an altar beside it where two chaplains would 'sing for her soul'. The altar was made by Master Robert, a joiner of London. The duke was still ordering work to be done on Blanche's tomb and effigy in July 1374, when he paid for six cartloads of alabaster from Tutbury in Staffordshire to be taken to London for the sepulchre of 'Lady Blaunche, our late consort, whom God absolve'.[4] He punctiliously marked the anniversary of her death on 12 September every year for the remaining three decades of his life, and would be buried next to her in 1399. Blanche's surviving children Philippa, Elizabeth and Henry were eight, five and not yet eighteen months old when they lost their mother.

If Blanche ever made a will – John, as her husband, would have needed to give her his permission to do so – it has not survived. No inquisition post-mortem was held for the duchess, because John was entitled by the 'courtesy of England', as Blanche's widower and the father of her children, to hold all her lands until his own death, when they would pass to Henry as her only surviving son. If anything had happened to Henry before he became a father in 1386, when his firstborn son became the Lancastrian heir after him, Blanche's lands would eventually have been divided equally between her daughters Philippa and Elizabeth. This was in line with contemporary English inheritance law, which followed the system of primogeniture: the eldest surviving son inherited everything, while younger sons, and daughters wherever they came in the birth order, received nothing. In the absence of a male heir, female heirs inherited instead, but if there was more than one daughter or sister the women took equal portions of the inheritance – as Blanche and her elder sister Maud did on their father's death in 1361 – and being the eldest daughter conferred no advantage. If Blanche and John had had no children, if one of them had perhaps been infertile, John would have had no claim whatsoever to any of his wife's lands after her death, and in 1368 the Lancastrian estate would have been divided among Duke Henry's surviving sisters and the children and grandchildren of his other sisters. The beneficiaries would have been a number of the important noble families of the fourteenth century: the Mowbrays, the Percys, the Beaumonts, the Arundels, the Mortimers, and the Veres.

As though the awful loss of Duchess Blanche were not bad enough, more bad news soon arrived from Italy. Lionel of Antwerp, duke of Clarence, died in Alba on 17 October 1368, a few weeks before his thirtieth birthday and just months after his lavish Italian wedding. He was buried in the church of St Peter in the Sky of Gold (San Pietro in Ciel d'Oro) in Pavia, though his body was later returned to England and interred at Bruisyard, the Augustinian priory in Clare, Suffolk which Lionel himself founded some years before, and the duke was laid to rest there with his first wife Elizabeth de Burgh, as he had requested. He left his thirteen-year-old daughter Philippa of Clarence, countess of March, as his sole heir, and his widow Violante Visconti later married Secondotto, marquis of Montferrat and thirdly her cousin Ludovico Visconti. Lionel had, like John, benefited from the 'courtesy of England', because he married an heiress and because he and Elizabeth de Burgh had a child together, and he had held all Elizabeth's lands after her death in 1363 and would have had the right to keep them however long he lived. Although Philippa of Clarence and her husband Edmund Mortimer received all her late mother's lands after Philippa came of age (fourteen for a married woman) in August 1369, she did not inherit her father's dukedom of Clarence. It lay dormant until it was created again for John of Gaunt's grandson Thomas of Lancaster in 1412.

Pope Urban V and some of Lionel's kinsmen and followers, including Edward, Lord Despenser, came to believe that Lionel had been poisoned. Jean Froissart recorded their suspicions and pointed out how odd it was that such a young, healthy knight had died so suddenly. It seems far likelier, however, that Lionel died of an illness or infection. He wrote his will two weeks before he passed away, and as people in the fourteenth century tended only to make their wills when they thought they might be dying, it seems that he was already seriously ill. In fact, Lionel was apparently already ill in August 1368, two months before his death, when Pope Urban V wrote to Lionel's kinsman Sir Hugh Despenser, asking him to aid the papal chaplain Robert Stratton whom he had sent to Lionel to inquire after the royal duke's health.[5] In his will, the duke left two coursers called Maugeneleyn and Gerfaucon to two of his household knights, and three breviaries (books of prayers), two with musical notes, to his chaplains. Lionel also left valuable items – his gold coronets – to his wife Violante in his will and, despite her youth, appointed her as one of his executors.[6] This would seem to argue against the notion that he believed her family had had him killed, as would the fact that he was staying in the house of his father-in-law the lord of Milan in Alba when he made his will. Hugh Despenser and his brother Edward, Lord Despenser, however, joined Pope Urban V's ongoing war against the city of Milan and its Visconti rulers. John of Gaunt's other elder brother Edward of Woodstock had been seriously ill since their campaign in Spain the year before; Gaunt was now the eldest son of the king and queen of England still alive and in good health.

Only two and a half months after Blanche of Lancaster died, on 1 December 1368, John's mother Queen Philippa sent an envoy, Sir Richard de Stury, to Louis, count of Flanders. Stury returned to England with Louis's response on Christmas Day, and the count's letter reveals that Philippa had proposed a marriage between John of Gaunt, whom Louis called 'our dearest cousin, the duke of Lancaster, your son' and Louis's only surviving child, Margarethe of Flanders (b. 1350). Margarethe was heir to a vast inheritance, and both Queen Philippa and Edward III tried for decades to secure it for one of their children, either for Isabella of Woodstock in the 1340s via marriage to Louis of Flanders himself, or for Edmund of Langley or John of Gaunt in the 1360s via marriage to Louis's daughter and heir. The queen's proposal to Louis meant that John of Gaunt would be given little time to grieve for the recent loss of his wife of nine years, though one assumes that Philippa did not press ahead with a possible second marriage for her son against his will or without his knowledge. Louis replied to Philippa via Richard de Stury, however, that he had already consented to his daughter's marriage to Philip 'the Bold' (1342–1404), duke of Burgundy, youngest of the four sons of the late John II of France, and Charles V's brother. The couple duly wed in June 1369.[7] In the end, having missed out on the lucrative Flanders match, John of Gaunt would not marry again until September 1371, three years after losing Blanche.

John, his parents, his siblings and other members of the extended royal family spent the Christmas of 1368 at Windsor Castle.[8] It can hardly have been a happy festive season for the duke of Lancaster, given the sudden shocking losses of his wife and his brother Lionel, and Queen Philippa was also ailing. A clerk absent-mindedly wrote 'the duke of Clarence' just below the names of the king and queen and before John of Gaunt in the list of those for whom cloth was to be purchased for the festive season and had to strike the name out, remembering that in fact Lionel was dead. The royal family tried, however, to make the best of it. Although Edward of Woodstock was in Aquitaine with his wife Joan of Kent and their two infant sons, the king and queen's other four surviving children were there with them: Isabella of Woodstock, countess of Bedford, aged thirty-six, perhaps with her two infant Coucy daughters, though her husband Enguerrand is not mentioned as being present; John of Gaunt, aged twenty-eight; Edmund of Langley, earl of Cambridge, aged twenty-seven and still unmarried; and Thomas of Woodstock ('Lord Thomas de Wodestoke'), the baby of the family, not yet fourteen.

John Hastings, earl of Pembroke, widower of Gaunt's youngest sister Margaret of Windsor, was evidently still considered a member of the royal family – Edward III continued to refer to him as 'the king's son' for the rest of the young earl's life and even after his early death in 1375 – and was also at Windsor that Christmas. Earlier in 1368, Hastings, now twenty-one, had married his second wife Anne Manny, daughter and co-heir of the king's first cousin Margaret, countess of Norfolk and her second husband, the Hainaulter knight Walter Manny. Anne was only fourteen in 1368, and their only child, John Hastings the younger, who would become John of Gaunt's son-in-law, was not born until November 1372. Also present at Windsor during the festive season of 1368 were the young earl and countess of March and Ulster, Gaunt's niece and nephew-in-law, sixteen-year-old Edmund Mortimer and his thirteen-year-old wife Philippa of Clarence, and the earl of Oxford, Thomas de Vere (b. *c.* 1337).[9]

13

My Very Honoured Mother, Whom God Absolve

The Battle of Montiel took place in central Spain in mid-March 1369 between the forces of King Pedro of Castile and the half-brother who was just a few months his senior, Enrique of Trastámara. Pedro lost the battle and became trapped inside Montiel Castle afterwards, and apparently was tricked into surrendering to the French forces who had fought with his brother. The French commander Bertrand du Guesclin, instead of leading Pedro to safety as promised, handed him over to his half-brother, and a few days later Enrique stabbed him to death. Geoffrey Chaucer wrote an account of Pedro's death in his 'Monk's Tale', part of the *Canterbury Tales*, lamenting, 'O noble, o worthy Petro, glorie of Spayne ... wel oughten men thy pitous deeth complayne ... by subtiltee thou were bitrayed.'

Born in August 1334, Pedro was only thirty-four when he died, and left his daughters Constanza and Isabel, who in 1369 were fifteen and fourteen and had been handed over as hostages to the prince of Wales (and who had already lost their mother María de Padilla in 1361). Enrique of Trastámara was crowned king of Castile in his loathed half-brother's place, and over the next few years embarked on a series of wars against England's ally King Fernando of Portugal. From his marriage to Juana Manuel (d. 1381), heiress of Villena, Escalona, Peñafiel, Lara and Biscay and herself of royal Castilian descent via both her parents, King Enrique had a son named Juan, who was ten years old in March 1369 and became heir to the throne.

The king and queen of England's fourth son Edmund of Langley, earl of Cambridge, and their former son-in-law John Hastings, earl of Pembroke, left England in January 1369. They travelled to the duchy of Aquitaine with a sizeable army of men, intending to strengthen the forces of Edmund's eldest brother the prince of Wales and Aquitaine. John of Gaunt also left England in June 1369; Edward III appointed his son as his captain and lieutenant in Calais and Guisnes, and John set off for Picardy to forestall a French invasion of the south coast of England.[1] John was in Calais on 26 July 1369, and hired two carpenters called Master Otte and Master de la Sawe, though to what purpose is not stated.[2]

A tragic, though surely not entirely unexpected, loss for the royal family came on 15 August 1369, when Philippa of Hainault, queen of England, died at the age of about fifty-five. Queen Philippa passed away on the feast of the Assumption at Windsor Castle, her husband's birthplace in 1312, and the king and their adolescent son Thomas of Woodstock, the only one of the twelve children Philippa had borne who was alive and in England at the time of her death, remained with her until the end. She had been seriously ill and in pain for most of the 1360s, having fallen while hunting with her husband in the late 1350s and broken her shoulder blade. The queen spent much of the last decade or so of her life mostly immobile, and seems to have expected since 1362 that she might die at any moment.[3] It seems highly likely that the king and queen were unable to continue their intimate relations, and beginning around the early 1360s Edward III began a long relationship with a woman named Alice Perrers, who bore him a son, John de Southeray or de Surray, and two daughters, both named Joan. John de Southeray, at least, was certainly born in the queen's lifetime, and probably Edward and Alice's two daughters were as well. After the queen's death, the king's relationship with Alice Perrers became more public, and she was to remain his mistress for the next eight years until he died.

Jean Froissart states that Queen Philippa was mourned by everyone, but that her death was particularly hard on her son John of Gaunt.[4] Philippa's will, assuming she ever made one, does not survive, though Gaunt's own will written three decades later reveals that his mother left him 'a gold fastening of the old kind, with the name of God written in each part of the same fastening, which my very honoured lady and mother the queen, whom God absolve, gave to me, commanding me to keep it, with her blessing.' John in turn bequeathed it to his eldest son and heir, Henry of Lancaster, duke of Hereford and earl of Derby. John's surviving register also shows that at an unknown date, Philippa gave him a gold cup with foot and cover decorated with oak-trees and letters of the alphabet. Like his father King Edward, who broke up and gave away a book which Queen Philippa had given to him as a wedding gift in January 1328, John of Gaunt was not terribly sentimental about presents, even ones given to him by his late mother: at Christmas 1372, he gave the gold cup to the countess of Salisbury.[5] On the other hand, as he bequeathed the gold fastening to his own son in 1399 and had kept it for thirty years since Queen Philippa's demise, this particular gift from his mother must have meant a great deal to him.

A long delay between the death of a royal person and their funeral was normal in the fourteenth century, Edward III in 1377 being a notable exception. Gaunt's grandfather Edward II (reportedly) died on 21 September 1327 and was buried on 20 December; Edward II's widow Isabella died on 22 August 1358 and was buried on 27 November; and Isabella's uncle Henry, earl of Lancaster died on 22 September 1345 and was buried on 15 January 1346. Queen Philippa was not interred until 9 January 1370, almost five months after her death, and her tomb and effigy can still be seen in Westminster Abbey. The king paid for black cloth to make mourning clothes for the members of his family to wear during his wife's funeral, and for many of the members of Philippa's household (he also paid for fur for all the attendees; the queen's funeral took place in the dead of winter). One of those who attended was Gaunt's aunt Elisabeth of Holland, a nun of Stratford-le-Bow and the late queen's illegitimate half-sister.[6] Jeanne de Montfort, called the 'damsel of Brittany' and the sister of Duke John IV, who had grown up in England with some of the king and queen's children and was about Gaunt's age or a little younger, was also present. Edward III purchased thirteen ells of black cloth to provide mourning clothes for her rather than the twelve ells that the adult male members of the royal family, including John of Gaunt, received. This implies that Jeanne was of imposing stature. Gaunt's orphaned niece Philippa of Clarence, countess of March and Ulster, still only fourteen years old, and her husband Edmund Mortimer, were among the others for whom the king purchased black cloth and miniver fur on 1 September 1369 for the queen's funeral.[7]

John of Gaunt encountered a French army led by Philip, duke of Burgundy, at Tournehem-sur-la-Hem near Calais on 23 August, eight days after his mother's death. No battle took place as John managed to hold a strong defensive position, and after two weeks his kinsman Burgundy withdrew. John was still in Calais on 26 November and 1 December 1369, and returned to England in time for Christmas and for his mother's funeral at the start of 1370. He was already in England on 18 December, and on 24 December his father ordered him and others to fortify their castles in Wales.[8]

Philippa and Elizabeth, 'the two daughters of Lancaster' ('*les deux filles de Lancastre*'), attended their grandmother's funeral and were accompanied by three damsels. These women, or girls, were named as Agnes Falconer, Eleyne Gerberge and, interestingly, Blanche Swynford, whose mother Katherine Swynford would begin a famous long-term relationship with John of Gaunt several years later and would become his third wife and duchess in 1396. Philippa and Elizabeth of Lancaster also had no fewer than ten 'under-damsels' looking after them.[9] Philippa of Lancaster was now almost ten years old and Elizabeth was almost seven. Their two-year-old brother Henry of Lancaster is not recorded as attending the queen's funeral, though one of their little de Coucy cousins, either Marie or Philippa, who were the same age as Henry, did.

14

Feasts and Celebrations in Aquitaine

The 1360s and early 1370s were a sad time for King Edward III. As well as losing his wife of more than forty years, he lost a number of his long-term companions, friends and kinsmen. Robert Ufford, earl of Suffolk, Thomas Beauchamp, earl of Warwick, and Sir John Chandos all died in 1369, and Ralph Stafford, earl of Stafford, died in 1372. The king's cousins the earls of Northampton and Hereford and the duke of Lancaster had been dead since the beginning of the 1360s, and Edward III outlived most of his own generation. The king, whose reign for so many years had been so magnificent, slipped into a terminal decline, suffering from senility and general ill health. His eldest son the prince of Wales, ruling Aquitaine, also suffered long periods of bad health in the late 1360s and 1370s.

John of Gaunt was at his palace of the Savoy on 1 April 1370 when he made an indenture with Sir Gerard Usflete, and was 'about to go to Aquitaine' on 27 May; he appointed Godfrey Foljambe and Simon Simeon as his attorneys while he was away.[1] He departed from England at the beginning of July 1370, and was not to return until November 1371. While Gaunt was overseas in 1370/71, his children Philippa, Elizabeth and Henry stayed with their great-aunt Blanche, Lady Wake, eldest sister of their late grandfather Duke Henry, at Deeping in Lincolnshire and Ware in Hertfordshire. John courteously referred to Lady Wake as 'our very dear and beloved aunt'.[2]

Edward of Woodstock gave the castles and towns of Bergerac and Roche-sur-Yon to John of Gaunt on 8 October 1370, and John thereafter added 'lord of Bergerac and Roche-sur-Yon' to his many titles. John was in Libourne, a *bastide* or fortified town now in the Gironde department of France, founded in the thirteenth century by an English nobleman called Roger Leybourne, on 18 October 1370. He hired a clerk named Guyon, formerly in the household of the recently deceased Sir John Chandos.[3] The indenture Gaunt made with Guyon reveals that his clerks, i.e. the men who wrote out his dictated letters and other documents and were thus privy to all kinds of important and confidential information, swore a sacred oath 'on the Evangelists' not to reveal his secrets and to do everything in their power to avoid 'dishonour and damage' to the duke.

The prince of Wales, with his wife Joan of Kent and their second son Richard of Bordeaux, who had just turned four, sailed to England in early 1371, leaving the duchy of Aquitaine in John of Gaunt's hands. Edward of

Woodstock and Joan's elder son, Edward of Angoulême (b. January 1365), had died in Aquitaine not long before, though the little boy's brother Richard returned his body to England many years later and had him reburied at Langley Priory in Hertfordshire. Had he lived, little Edward of Angoulême would have succeeded his grandfather as King Edward IV of England in 1377. The prince of Wales was in such dire health and so exhausted, and the crossing from Bordeaux to Plymouth so rough, that he, Joan and Richard had to remain in Plymouth for a few weeks until the prince was well enough to continue their journey to London. John of Gaunt remained in the south of France, and was in Saintes on 7 May and in Pons on 13 May 1371 when he sent letters to Pope Urban V. He arranged the funeral of his nephew Edward of Angoulême in the cathedral of St André in Bordeaux.[4] On 21 July 1371, John gave up his lieutenancy in Aquitaine, though remained in the duchy for a while – he was in Bordeaux on 10 August.[5] While he was in Gascony in 1371, wealthy though he was, John borrowed 1,000 marks (£666) from the possibly even wealthier Richard Fitzalan (b. *c.* 1313), earl of Arundel and Surrey.[6]

The throne of Castile was still occupied by the late King Pedro's half-brother and usurper Enrique of Trastámara, but Pedro's rightful heirs were his daughters Constanza and Isabel. Jean Froissart records that John of Gaunt, whom he calls '*il dus Jehans de Lancastre*' or 'the Duke John of Lancaster', married Constanza of Castile in a village called 'Rocefort', i.e. Roquefort in Les Landes near Mont-de-Marsan, in early September 1371. There were great feasts and celebrations to mark this important royal wedding, and afterwards, John took his new wife to Bordeaux.[7] As hostages of the prince of Wales – albeit hostages doubtless treated with honour and consideration – Constanza and Isabel had been living in Aquitaine since 1366.

By his marriage to Pedro's elder daughter, John of Gaunt became rightful king of Castile and Leon, at least in name. John and Constanza were distantly related – third cousins twice removed – via common descent from Fernando III, king of Castile and Leon (d. 1252), whose daughter Leonor or Eleanor (d. 1290) married Edward I of England and was John's great-grandmother. Although Constanza was born in the north of her father's kingdom, she might have grown up in the Alcázar, the royal palace in her father's favourite city of Seville, southern Spain. Pedro himself had the Alcázar built, using many Muslim craftsmen; the words 'Only Allah is victorious' in Arabic can still be seen on the façade of Pedro's palace. Freshwater baths, which can also still be seen in the Alcázar, are called 'Los Baños de Doña María de Padilla' after Constanza's mother, the noblewoman who caught the eye of the king of Castile and Leon, and for whom Pedro abandoned and imprisoned his wife and queen Blanche de Bourbon.

Pedro and Doña María met during a series of peregrinations the seventeen-year-old king made through Castile in the spring and summer of 1352, which were, at least in part, a campaign against Enrique of Trastámara. Enrique, also a teenager himself, had already rebelled against his half-brother with his twin Fadrique (whom Pedro would execute in 1358) and their younger brother Tello, following the long imprisonment and vengeful execution of their mother Leonor de Guzmán by the king's Portuguese mother the dowager queen Maria.

King Pedro and Doña María de Padilla's first child was Beatriz, born in Córdoba in Andalusia, southern Spain in 1353, and their second child, Constanza, was born in Castrojeriz, near Burgos in the north, sometime in June or July 1354. Next came Isabel, born in 1355 in Tordesillas, central Spain, probably in the Royal Monastery of Santa Clara where her grandfather and father built a palace. Pedro and María also had a son whom they named Alfonso after Pedro's late father, much younger than his sisters and born also in Tordesillas in 1359. Alfonso died in Seville in October 1362, and his eldest sister Beatriz died as a teenager sometime after the autumn of 1366, when her father sent her as a hostage to Aquitaine with her sisters. If she had survived, she would have been the rightful heir to Castile, and John of Gaunt would have married her in 1371 rather than her younger sister Constanza.

King Pedro was to claim in 1362, almost certainly deceptively, that he had married his lover in Seville in 1352 before his official wedding to Blanche de Bourbon in Valladolid on 3 June 1353. In the interests of political expediency several biased witnesses confirmed his tale, including Doña María's brother Diego García de Padilla, master of the Order of Calatrava, and their uncle Juan Fernández de Henestrosa, and the Castilian *Cortes* duly legitimised Beatriz, Constanza and Isabel. For all his undoubted love for María de Padilla, however, Pedro was not faithful to her, and had an affair with her first cousin María González de Henestrosa. This relationship produced a son named Fernando, whom Pedro made lord of Niebla in Andalusia, who was alive in 1361 but must have died young. In *c.* 1355 Pedro fathered a son named Juan with his second cousin Juana de Castro, great-granddaughter of King Sancho IV of Castile (d. 1295) and the sister of Inês de Castro, mistress (and possibly wife) of Pedro's uncle King Pedro I of Portugal (1320–67). Pedro of Castile claimed in 1354, despite being involved with María de Padilla - their second daughter Constanza was born in June or July that year - to have divorced Blanche de Bourbon and to have married Juana instead.

Finally, Pedro's relationships with Isabel de Sandoval, Teresa de Ayala and Aldonza Coronel resulted in at least three more illegitimate children: María, prioress of Santo Domingo el Real in Toledo, and sons Sancho and Diego, who, with their half-brother Juan, were imprisoned by their uncle Enrique of Trastámara after their father's death, even though all three were children or adolescents at the time. Had Constanza and her sisters not been in Aquitaine beyond Enrique's reach when their father was killed, they might well have suffered the same fate.

María de Padilla died in July 1361, still only in her twenties. Pedro held a state funeral for her as though she were his wife and the queen of Castile, and buried her in the monastery of Santa Clara de Astudillo in the province of Palencia, which María herself had founded in the mid-1350s. The remains of John of Gaunt's mother-in-law were moved to the royal chapel in Seville Cathedral in 1362, and there is evidence that in the late 1380s her daughter Constanza had Pedro's body buried there as well. Blanche de Bourbon, meanwhile, the rightful queen of Castile, died in prison in Medina Sidonia probably in the same year as María de Padilla, and was buried in Jerez; she was about twenty-two or twenty-four when she passed away. Pedro had not set eyes on his French wife since he abandoned her for María two days after their wedding in 1353, and whether he had a hand in the death of this most unfortunate young woman, whom he had kept in captivity for eight years, is still debated.[8]

15

My Lord of Spain

John of Gaunt returned to England in a ship called the *Gaynpayn*, which usually transported salt, on or a little before 4 November 1371. The *Gaynpayn*'s captain was John Payn, and Gaunt commandeered Payn's ship and unloaded its cargo of salt to make space for himself, his horses and his possessions. Presumably with his new wife Constanza and her sister Isabel in his company (though they are not specifically mentioned as being on board the ship in his register), John sailed from La Rochelle and landed at Fowey in Cornwall, where he sent out various letters on behalf of his foresters and parkers. Travelling in a ship that usually carried salt was hardly the most glamorous mode of transport for three people, John, Constanza and Isabel, who were the children of kings, but they were so short of money that Constanza had to pawn some cloth of gold and a chalice to a group of men in Dartmouth.[1] John's council in London sent his squire Waryn de Eyrdale from the city in the direction of Salisbury to meet Gaunt on the road, and gave Waryn £100 in silver to give to Gaunt for the expenses of his return journey to England. (Two of the other squires serving John at this time were named Pieres Genlichshein and Kunze Trahe; presumably the men were German.)

While John was making his way through the south-west of England, he spent time with 'our dearest cousin the countess of Salisbury', Elizabeth Montacute née Mohun, and his household retainer Sir Hugh Swynford of Kettlethorpe and Coleby in Lincolnshire died on Thursday 13 November 1371, supposedly overseas. News of Hugh's death reached chancery clerks in Westminster, who ordered officials in his native Lincolnshire to take his lands into the king's hands (as always happened when a tenant in chief, a landowner who held lands directly from the king, passed away), only five days later on 18 November.[2] This seems an extraordinarily, even impossibly short time for the news to have reached them from a foreign country. By way of comparison, John of Gaunt's kinsman Sir Hugh Despenser, brother of Edward, Lord Despenser and Henry, bishop of Norwich, died in northern Italy on 2 or 11 March 1374, and chancery clerks in England only heard of his death on 1 September that year. It may be that the Lincolnshire jurors who stated in April 1372 that Hugh Swynford had died abroad were misinformed. Perhaps he returned to England with John of Gaunt and in fact died in Plympton Priory near Plymouth, Devon, where the duke was staying around 12 November 1371, but the jurors in Navenby, Lincolnshire – well over 300 miles from Plymouth – were unaware of the date when John and his retinue returned to his homeland and assumed they were still in Aquitaine when Hugh passed away. Gaunt could certainly have sent messengers to Westminster from the vicinity of Plymouth, who could have made that journey in five days. Wherever he died, Sir Hugh Swynford left two or, more probably, three children, and his widow, Katherine Swynford née Roet, who not long afterwards would become a hugely important person in John of Gaunt's life.

John stayed at Kingston Lacy in Dorset from just before Christmas 1371 until at least 6 January 1372. He ordered his warreners (the people in charge of the game and the rabbits in his parks, chases and warrens) in his manors of Aldbourne and Hungerford to send ten deer and six dozen 'fat rabbits' to Kingston Lacy to arrive on Christmas Eve, which fell on a Wednesday, and the same quantity to arrive the following Saturday and then again on the following Tuesday. One of the people John favoured with a gift of 40s while staying at Kingston Lacy during the festive season of 1371/72 was a sailor named Cok Wille, perhaps one of the men who sailed him back to England in the *Gaynpayn*.[3] John sent numerous other New Year gifts on 1 January 1372. In Constanza's name, but paid for by John himself, he ordered a clerk of his great wardrobe to send his father a pair of silver flasks, partly gilded and enamelled, and with a band of blue and white silk cloth. John sent his sister-in-law Joan of Kent, 'our very honoured and beloved sister the princess of Aquitaine and Wales,' an ornamental greyhound made of white gold with eight sapphires, and gave himself three of the same. Constanza's younger sister Isabel of Castile, who was now sixteen, was betrothed to John's younger brother Edmund of Langley, earl of Cambridge, to seal the English-Castilian alliance. John gave 'our dearest and beloved sister Isabelle, youngest daughter of the king Don Petre [Pedro], whom God absolve … a pair of gold beads with the paternosters decorated with little pearls with a gold pin with a balas ruby and a large pearl.' Isabel's future husband Edmund of Langley received a gold pin, Constanza a gold circlet with gemstones, and Constanza's *mestresse* (the woman in charge of her household) a silver cup.

One of the women who worked as Constanza's attendants after her arrival in England was the poet Geoffrey Chaucer's wife Philippa, whose name sometimes appears in John's register as 'Philippe Chause'. Constanza was so pleased with her service that John granted Philippa an annuity of £10 on 30 August 1372.[4] Another attendant serving Constanza was Eleyne or Alyne Gerberge, and Gaunt gave her, 'the damsel of our dearest consort,' no fewer than 626 pearls 'of the second sort' and another 1,673 pearls 'of the third sort' in early 1373. Eleyne had also worked in the household of John's eldest child Philippa of Lancaster, and was one of the three damsels who accompanied Philippa and her sister Elizabeth to the funeral of their grandmother Philippa of Hainault in early 1370. John was obviously very happy with Eleyne's service to his wife and daughter and talked of her as 'our beloved damsel', and it seems from the language John used in his grant to her that Eleyne had been particularly kind and helpful to Philippa after the girl lost her mother Duchess Blanche in 1368 when she was eight.[5]

Constanza of Castile's new family in England gave her splendid wedding gifts on her arrival in her new home in November 1371. She received a gold crown with emeralds, rubies and pearls from her father-in-law the king, and a gold circlet with diamonds, rubies, pearls, emeralds and sapphires, and two gold brooches with precious stones, one in the shape of a stag and one with an image of St George, from her brother-in-law the prince of Wales. John of Gaunt himself piled Constanza with presents: among much else, a gold mirror with sapphires, rubies, pearls and diamonds; a gold tablet with an image of Our Lady; a necklace or collar with more precious stones; almost 500 pearls for a 'fret', i.e. a headdress of interlaced wire; cloth of gold; and a gold brooch with rubies, sapphires, diamonds and pearls with a matching necklace.[6]

Constanza made a ceremonial entry into London on 9 February 1372 as the rightful queen of Castile and Leon, accompanied by numerous lords and knights and the city mayor. Her brother-in-law Edward of Woodstock hosted the ceremony, and Constanza's sister Isabel was also present. On their way to John's palace of the Savoy they passed along Cheapside, the central road and marketplace of medieval London, and numerous people, especially ladies and young ladies, braved the winter chill to watch them.[7] John of Gaunt was now generally called *monseigneur d'Espaigne*, 'my lord of Spain,' which in fourteenth-century usage almost always referred to the kingdom of Castile rather than the country of Spain more generally. John also always called himself 'king of Castile and Leon' after 1371, and received permission from his father the king to adapt his coat-of-arms to reflect his new titles. In a letter to one of his foresters dated 18 March 1372, Gaunt proudly used all his Spanish titles: 'Johan, by the grace of God, king of Castile, Leon, Toledo, Galicia, Seville, Cordoba, Murcia, Jaen, Algerbe and Algeciras, duke of Lancaster, lord of Molina.'[8] (Had he wished, he could have added 'earl of Richmond, Leicester, Lincoln and Derby, lord of Beaufort, Nogent, Bergerac and Roche-sur-Yon, steward of England.') In most of his subsequent letters which his clerk wrote down in his register, this long formulation was, unsurprisingly, recorded merely as 'Johan, by the grace of God etc' or 'From the king of Castile etc'.[9]

16

A Woman of Great Beauty

Constanza's father, King Pedro, was described by contemporaries as tall and muscular with very light blond hair, pale skin and blue eyes (and a lisp), and her grandfather Alfonso XI was also blond-haired, fair-skinned and blue-eyed. Constanza and John of Gaunt's daughter Catalina of Lancaster was described later in life as 'fair, rosy and blonde' as well as very tall and 'very heavy of body,' while Catalina's son Juan II of Castile was said to be 'fair-skinned and slightly ruddy' with hair 'of a very mature hazelnut' and eyes somewhere between green and blue.[1] Given the appearance of her father, grandfather, daughter and grandson, it seems highly likely that Constanza of Castile had blonde hair, fair skin and blue eyes, not dark eyes and black hair. It is often assumed that Constanza's daughter Queen Catalina and her descendants, including Catalina's namesake great-granddaughter Katherine of Aragon (1485–1536), Henry VIII's first queen, were fair-haired and fair-skinned because they were descended from John of Gaunt and the English royal family. The contemporary accounts of Constanza's father and grandfather, however, who were of entirely Spanish and Portuguese origin, reveal that this is not the case. The usual modern descriptions of Constanza of Castile owe far more to clichéd ideas of how Spanish people and other people from the south of Europe are 'supposed' to look than to historical reality, and we do not know for sure that John of Gaunt was fair-haired anyway; his hair colour and general appearance are not described in contemporary sources. When the remains of Gaunt's youngest son, Thomas Beaufort, were examined 346 years after his death in 1772, he was found to have had brown hair (see Appendix 1).

Constanza was almost certainly far more physically attractive than she has often been depicted in more recent times, and a contemporary Spanish chronicler described her mother María de Padilla as *'una doncella muy fermosa'* ('a very beautiful maiden'), as well as intelligent, kind, graceful and charming. The English writer of the *Anonimalle* chronicle was much taken with Constanza herself, calling her a 'beautiful young lady' (*'une tresbele damosel'*) in 1371, and a few years later 'a woman of great beauty.' Although her father has an atrocious reputation and is known to posterity as 'Pedro the Cruel,' it must be remembered that the Trastámara dynasty, who usurped his throne in 1369, had an interest in vilifying him as much as possible. Although Pedro certainly did do some appalling things, most notably his shocking treatment of his tragic wife Blanche de Bourbon, he was not as irredeemably awful as he was painted by his successors. In many respects, Pedro was arguably no worse than his father, whose shabby treatment of his own wife and infatuation with his mistress led directly to the tragedy that befell his sons after his death. Somewhat contradictorily, Pedro is known as 'the Just' as well as 'the Cruel,' and the depiction of him as a tyrant and unfit ruler owes much to the *Crónica del Rey Don Pedro y del Rey Don Enrique su Hermano, Hijos de Alfonso Onceno* ('Chronicle of the King Don Pedro and the King Don Enrique his Brother, Sons of Alfonso XI') by Pero López de Ayala (d. 1407), a work commissioned by Enrique of Trastámara himself.[2]

There is no reason at all to suppose that Constanza of Castile was a 'cold dark foreigner' and a religious zealot with a 'chill fanatic light' in her black eyes who worshipped her dead father and who failed to wash often enough and had an unpleasant body odour that offended John's nostrils.[3] Although we cannot know how he behaved towards his royal wife in private, John of Gaunt's references to Constanza in letters and grants were warm, respectful and courteous. In July 1373, for example, he spoke of the 'sincere love and affection which we have for our dearest and beloved consort the queen [of Castile], Lady Constanza.'[4] 'Dearest and beloved' was purely formulaic and says nothing whatsoever about John's feelings for his second wife, but 'sincere love and affection' ('*entier amour et affectione*') was not, and probably does.

Probably within a few months of Constanza's wedding to John of Gaunt, however, her husband began a relationship with a woman who was the great love of his life: Katherine Swynford, née Roet, the sister of Constanza's damsel Philippa Chaucer. Constanza's feelings on the matter are not recorded, but her marriage to John was, after all, a business arrangement at its core. Constanza could not, on her own, invade Castile and take possession of her late father's throne, now occupied by her illegitimate uncle, and needed a capable man who could help her win back her father's kingdom. John of Gaunt was the son of a king and of high royal birth, and was therefore of eminently suitable background to marry King Pedro's daughter. He had demonstrated his military capacity at the Battle of Nájera in 1367 and indeed, as early as 1350 at the age of only ten when he had insisted on accompanying his brother the prince of Wales on his ship during the naval battle of the Spaniards on the Sea.

Constanza would not have been raised to expect to fall in love with whomever she married or to have a great deal of choice (if any) on the matter of her husband, and she herself had been born to her father's chief mistress while Pedro's rightful queen languished in solitary confinement. Her grandfather had also been involved for many years in an intense extramarital relationship with his mistress, with whom he had ten children, and Leonor de Guzmán enjoyed far more influence at the Castilian court than Alfonso XI's queen Maria of Portugal, Constanza's grandmother. John of Gaunt at least treated his wife with respect, and Constanza had freedom of movement, unlike her father's unfortunate and imprisoned wife Blanche de Bourbon. Although it has sometimes been assumed that Constanza considered Katherine Swynford a 'rival' (and vice versa), we simply do not and cannot know if this was the case.[5]

Not only was Constanza herself born out of wedlock and fathered by a married man – she was conceived about three or four months after Pedro's wedding to Blanche – she must have been perfectly well aware that her father had at least five other lovers besides her mother, and had at least five illegitimate children with them as well as herself and her three full siblings Beatriz, Isabel and Alfonso. Constanza's half-brother Juan was born in *c.* January 1355, only about six months after her own birth and in the same year as her full sister Isabel. Her uncle Tello, one of the illegitimate sons of Alfonso XI and Leonor de Guzmán, fathered at least ten illegitimate children with seven different women, and Tello's brother King Enrique had seven or eight known mistresses and at least a dozen offspring with them as well as his four legitimate children born to Queen Juana Manuel. Given this background, it hardly seems likely that Constanza was the kind of person who would make a fuss over her husband having extramarital relations and illegitimate children. Although she is usually portrayed as entirely passive and helpless to do anything about her husband's passionate affair except to tolerate it whether she wished to or not, it is possible that John conducted his relationship with Katherine more openly than he might otherwise have done precisely because Constanza willingly accepted the presence of his lover and their four children in her life. As for John's feelings about Constanza, he might well have been fond of her and admired her even if he did not feel the enduring passion for her that he felt for Katherine Swynford, and certainly he respected her royal birth.

Constanza seems to have been a rather quiet and retiring person, and certainly she made little impact on English history and did not much resemble her larger-than-life father. She is, unfortunately, one of those fourteenth-century women who tends to fade somewhat into the background, another being John of Gaunt's mother-in-law from his first marriage, Isabella Beaumont. What little is known of Constanza reveals that she had a personality and interests of her own, however; she employed a Welsh jester named Yevan in her household, and once hired a 'wild knight' for her own and her attendants' entertainment.[6] Modern authors have not always written about Constanza of Castile with as much respect as they might have, and although there is no doubt that she was pious, depicting her as a smelly religious fanatic who prays to her dead father seems particularly unkind, even as a fictional portrayal. There was considerably more to her than being merely an uninteresting impediment to John of Gaunt and Katherine Swynford's glorious love affair who finally did the decent thing by dying and thus allowed them to fulfil their romantic destiny of marrying. Constanza was fourteen years John's junior, seventeen to his thirty-one when they married, and was (one assumes) an inexperienced virgin while he was a widower and a father. Katherine Swynford was much closer to John's own age and was a widow and a mother, and perhaps on those grounds alone, the couple had far more in common than John had with his new wife.[7]

The author of the *Anonimalle* chronicle, who admired Constanza of Castile enormously and called her a great beauty, viciously referred to Katherine Swynford as a 'she-devil' and 'enchantress', while John of Gaunt himself was called a 'great fornicator' (*'magnus fornicator'*) by a chronicler. Just as there was far more to Constanza than being merely a boring and coldly foreign impediment to someone else's wonderful relationship, however, there was far more to Katherine than being merely an immoral homewrecker who used her wiles to 'enchant' the duke of Lancaster. John and Katherine's relationship lasted for about twenty-seven years, and only John's death severed it. He took the extraordinary step of marrying Katherine twenty-three months after Constanza's death, legitimised their children, and made her duchess of Lancaster. Having a mistress was hardly uncommon for a nobleman – Edward III had Alice Perrers, Edward of Woodstock had Edith Willesford and probably others – but marrying one's mistress was unheard of. John and Katherine's relationship was no idle dalliance, but was arguably the most significant relationship of his life, and Katherine was perhaps extremely attractive physically as well as being a magnetic, charming and intelligent person for whom John felt considerable sexual and romantic attraction for many years. As well as her undoubted physical appeal to him, it is obvious that John respected and liked Katherine enormously, as did many others, and her charms went well beyond the merely carnal.

17

Dame Katherine de Roet, Lady Swynford

Katherine Swynford was the daughter of Paon (or Payn) Roet (or Roelt), a Hainaulter knight who, like many others, had come to England after Philippa of Hainault married Edward III in January 1328, though the identity of Katherine's mother is not known. Her sister Philippa, who married the poet Geoffrey Chaucer, was presumably named in honour of the Hainaulter queen of England. Philippa was the mother of Thomas Chaucer (d. 1434), Member of Parliament for Oxfordshire and Speaker of the Commons, and the grandmother of Alice Chaucer (d. 1475), who became duchess of Suffolk and countess of Salisbury by two of her three marriages, and was the mother-in-law of Elizabeth of York, sister of Edward IV and Richard III. Alice's grandson John de la Pole, earl of Lincoln, was heir presumptive to his uncle Richard III's throne in 1484/85. Katherine Roet – the great-grandmother of Edward IV, Richard III and Elizabeth of York – married the Lincolnshire knight Sir Hugh Swynford at an uncertain date probably in the early 1360s or thereabouts, perhaps before 1360. He was the son and heir of Sir Thomas Swynford, who died on 3 November 1361. Hugh was said to be aged 'twenty-one and more' in his father's inquisition post-mortem taken in late 1361, so was born in or before 1340, possibly several years before 1340, as 'twenty-one and more' is a rather vague estimate and might simply mean that Hugh was known to be of age, i.e. at least twenty-one, and therefore old enough to take possession of his late father's lands after Thomas's death. He was certainly born before 31 January 1341, as he performed homage to the king and received his lands on 31 January 1362.[1] If Hugh really was born in 1340, he was the same age as John of Gaunt, and only thirty-one when he died in November 1371.

From his father, Hugh Swynford inherited the Lincolnshire manors of Coleby and Kettlethorpe, which stand a few miles apart; Coleby is 7 miles south of the cathedral city of Lincoln and Kettlethorpe is 10 miles north-west of Lincoln. The village of Coleby stands 15 miles from the great royal stronghold of Newark Castle on the River Trent, and just 3 miles from Somerton Castle, in royal possession since 1309. Somerton was the location where Edward III temporarily imprisoned his cousin Margaret, countess of Norfolk, in 1354 after she married her second husband Walter Manny without his permission, and was also one of the prisons of the captive King John II of France for a while. Kettlethorpe, which is now strongly associated with Katherine Swynford, lies a couple of miles from the village of Torksey, where in medieval times there was a small Augustinian priory founded in the twelfth century; Edward II stayed in the priory on several occasions in the 1310s and 1320s. Nowadays Kettlethorpe seems a tiny and rather out of the way village, but it stood close to the route the royal court often took through Lincolnshire, along the River Trent, and hence was not quite as remote in the fourteenth century as it might appear in the twenty-first.

Katherine Swynford first appears on record on 24 January 1365 when she was named as an *ancille* or female servant in Duchess Blanche of Lancaster's household.[2] At an unknown date before 1376, she became the *maistresse* of Gaunt and Blanche's daughters Philippa and Elizabeth. *Maistresse* or *mestresce* – which has many other variant spellings as well – is a rather difficult word to translate; it is often rendered as 'governess' in modern English, though this gives it an oddly and unsuitably Victorian or Edwardian flavour. In the fourteenth century, the word *maistresse* meant a woman in overall charge of a royal or noble household, and did not always mean that tutoring children was involved, as 'governess' does. This is apparent from a couple of entries in John of Gaunt's register of the early 1370s: 'the *maistresse* of our beloved consort,' meaning Constanza of Castile, received gifts from him on several occasions. As Duchess Constanza, then in her late teens, married, and a mother or soon to become one, had a *maistresse*, the word cannot accurately be translated as 'governess', and cannot refer solely to a woman responsible for raising and teaching children or adolescents.[3]

Katherine and Hugh Swynford's daughter Blanche attended the two Lancaster daughters as one of their damsels when they went to their grandmother Queen Philippa's funeral in early 1370, which might indicate that Katherine was already in charge of the Lancaster girls' household at that stage, though if so, whether she was appointed by Duchess Blanche before her death in September 1368 or by John of Gaunt himself is not known.[4] As Katherine first appears on record as a member of Blanche of Lancaster's household in early 1365, perhaps it was Duchess Blanche who recognised that Katherine had the ability to run and take charge of her daughters' own household, rather than Gaunt. Gaunt and Blanche often stayed at Bolingbroke Castle in Lincolnshire, and it might have been this local county connection that led the ducal couple to make the Swynfords' acquaintance. On the other hand, it may be that the couple had known Katherine (via her father, the Hainaulter knight Sir Payn, and his connections to Gaunt's mother, Philippa of Hainault) since before she married Hugh, or perhaps Blanche had known the Swynford family for a long time via the Lincolnshire connection – her father had been earl of Lincoln since 1349 when she was seven years old.

Katherine gave birth to her son Thomas Swynford, Hugh's heir, in Lincoln, probably on 24 February in an uncertain year in the late 1360s. At his father's inquisition post-mortem in April/June 1372, Thomas was said to be four years old. Thomas's proof of age was taken in Lincoln sometime during the eighteenth year of Richard II's reign, which ran from 22 June 1394 to 21 June 1395, and states that Thomas was born 'on the feast of St Matthias, 47 Edward III' (i.e. in the forty-seventh year of Edward's reign).[5] This means 24 February 1373, a date of birth that is impossible, as it fell over fifteen months after Hugh Swynford's death on 13 November 1371. The jurors erred greatly on Thomas Swynford's year of birth, but were perhaps correct as to the date of 24 February, the feast of St Matthias. Given that Thomas was said to be four years old in April and June 1372, a date of birth on or around 24 February 1367 or 1368 seems about right.[6] (The jurors who took part in inquisitions post-mortem only estimated the approximate age of heirs, and had no documentation in front of them to confirm their exact age or date of birth. If the jurors of 1372 believed that Thomas Swynford was four years old, it is possible that he was indeed four, but also possible that he was three or five or six.)

Thomas Swynford was baptised the day after he was born in the church of St Margaret in the Close, Lincoln. He was probably named after his grandfather Sir Thomas Swynford (d. 1361), but perhaps also in honour of one of his godfathers, a clerk called Master Thomas de Sutton. His other godfather was another clerk, John de Worsop, i.e. from Wirksop in Nottinghamshire, and he had a godmother whose identity is not specified (it was usual for baby boys to have two godfathers and one godmother, and for baby girls to have two godmothers and one godfather). Nicholas Bolton was responsible for holding a basin and offering water to the three godparents for them to wash after Thomas Swynford's baptism, and William Middleton offered the godparents a towel to wipe their hands afterwards.

Hugh and Katherine Swynford's chamberlain, Gilbert de Beseby of Lincoln, who was aged 'fifty-four and more' in 1394/95 and therefore was in his late twenties in 1367/68, went to the church of St Margaret with various 'cloths of silk and gold' for Thomas during his baptism. Their steward, whose name is not recorded in Thomas's proof of age, ordered Richard Colville of Lincoln to 'bring home twenty-four bows' and to distribute them to 'diverse servants'. Master Thomas de Sutton, the clerk who was one of the little Swynford boy's two godfathers, had a servant called John Plaint, who 'brought fire to light the candle' during the baptism, and Sutton had another servant called John Baldon, who was sent with letters to the town of Louth 25 miles from Lincoln on the day of the baptism, and broke his leg when his horse stumbled and fell during the journey. John de Sereby of Lincoln provided the wine for the attendees, and sent his servant William Hamond to the church with two jars of wine; the unfortunate Hamond fell and spilt some wine out of one jar, and Sereby, unkindly, beat him for it.

In October 1411, John of Gaunt and Blanche of Lancaster's son, Henry IV, issued a notification that 'a doubt as to the legitimacy' of his stepbrother Thomas Swynford existed, and that therefore he had been kept out of some lands in Hainault that should have been his as Katherine's son and heir. The indignant Thomas pointed out that he was the son of 'Dame Katherine de Roelt, late duchess of Lancaster' and was 'born in lawful matrimony'.[7] This might simply have been vicious gossip after the deaths of Katherine, John of Gaunt and Hugh Swynford, and perhaps was a result of the Lincoln jurors' gross error in 1394/95 in stating that Thomas was born more than fifteen months after his father's death. Hugh Swynford is not mentioned as being personally present at his son's baptism (as Katherine herself certainly was), which is not in itself in any way suspicious given that he spent much of his career fighting outside England, but which might have added fuel to the fire of gossip, decades after his death. There is no reason to suppose that Thomas was not Hugh's son; the jurors in Lincoln and Navenby named him as Hugh's son and heir at Hugh's inquisition post-mortem in 1372 and stated that he was then four years old, so obviously Katherine cannot, as claimed in 1394/95, have given birth to Thomas in February 1373, months after the inquisition post-mortem was held.

Had there been any rumours that Thomas was not Hugh's real son, the Lincoln jurors of Hugh's inquisition post-mortem would have been in an excellent position to have heard them, as Katherine gave birth to her son in Lincoln, but evidently they had not heard such rumours or had not given them any credence. Thomas Swynford's godfather, John of Worksop, was a canon of Lincoln Cathedral, and hardly seems likely to have been willing to act as such if he believed that Katherine had committed adultery and that Thomas was not her husband's son. 'Hugo Swynford' received letters of protection to go to Aquitaine with John of Gaunt on 2 November 1366.[8] If Hugh's son was born and baptised in February 1367 when Hugh was in the south of France with Gaunt, this would certainly explain why he was not present at Thomas's baptism in Lincoln. Thomas Swynford presumably grew up in Lincolnshire, and was already a knight at only fifteen or sixteen years old when John of Gaunt spoke of 'the occasion of [his] marriage' to Joan Crophill on 1 March 1383.[9]

In addition to their son Thomas, Hugh and Katherine Swynford had at least one daughter, Blanche, and probably two. Many years later, a petition John of Gaunt and Katherine sent to the pope states that Gaunt was the godfather of a daughter of Katherine, and almost certainly this means Blanche Swynford.[10] She was most probably named after Blanche, duchess of Lancaster, and it seems plausible that Duchess Blanche was her godmother.[11] Blanche Swynford appears on record as one of the three damsels of Gaunt's daughters in a letter of Edward III's dated 1 September 1369, when the king ordered black cloth and fur for all the people expected to attend the funeral and interment of Queen Philippa, who had died seventeen days earlier. The Lancaster girls also had ten 'under-damsels' (*souzdamoiselles*). Blanche may therefore have been the same age as Philippa and Elizabeth of Lancaster, which would place her date of birth in the early 1360s, or she may have been older than they.[12]

Judy Perry, who has carried out extensive research on Katherine and her family, believes that Katherine and Hugh had another daughter, Margaret, born *c.* 1363/64.[13] A 'Margaret Swinford' appears on record on 27 July 1377 when she was placed as a nun in the wealthy abbey of Barking near London. Decades later she became its abbess; her appointment was ratified by King Henry V, John of Gaunt and Blanche of Lancaster's grandson, on 29 March 1419. On the same day as Margaret's nomination as a nun of Barking in 1377, an 'Elizabeth Chausier' was nominated as a nun of St Helen's Priory in London.[14] Elizabeth perhaps was Margaret's first cousin, a daughter of Geoffrey Chaucer and Katherine Swynford's sister Philippa. John of Gaunt paid for the dower of Elizabeth Chausier (or Chaucer) when she moved from St Helen's and entered Barking Abbey on 12 May 1381, and although it is not completely certain that Elizabeth was indeed Geoffrey and Philippa's daughter, and thus Katherine Swynford's niece, it seems likely that Elizabeth had a family connection to John's mistress, which would explain his willingness to pay for Katherine's niece to join the prestigious house of Barking.[15] Margaret Swynford's nomination as a nun of Barking Abbey in 1377 also strongly suggests Gaunt's influence. The house was an extremely wealthy and prestigious one, and the abbesses of Barking were almost always of noble birth and had precedence over all the other abbesses in England. The Crown had the right to nominate a nun of Barking at each accession of a new king, and Gaunt's nephew Richard II had just succeeded to the throne in the summer of 1377 when Margaret Swynford was the nun Richard nominated.[16] Richard was only ten years old in 1377, and his choice of Margaret Swynford is highly likely to have come about as a result of Gaunt's influence and his wish to promote Katherine's daughter.

It seems that Katherine gave birth to her two Swynford daughters around 1360/64, then to her son Thomas around 1367 or 1368. The gap might indicate that she had another child or children who died young, or that there was a stillbirth or a miscarriage, or it might simply mean that she and Hugh spent a long period apart in the 1360s owing to his military service overseas. Katherine Swynford's date of birth is usually estimated in modern writing as *c.* 1350, making her a decade or so younger than both John of Gaunt and her husband Hugh Swynford. This date is far too late. Katherine's biographer Jeannette Lucraft believes a date of birth closer to 1345 is more plausible, and states that it makes more sense of the fact that Katherine's last child was born in *c.* 1379 if she was then in her mid-thirties than if she was only in her late twenties.[17]

Assuming that she gave birth to Blanche Swynford around 1360/62 or earlier, Katherine might even have been born some years before 1345. As Lucraft points out, medieval people who were not of the highest social rank tended to marry and have children later than royal and noble people did. The evidence from proofs of age reveals that English people of common birth in the fourteenth century usually married in their twenties or thirties, and although those of knightly rank generally wed younger than that (Katherine and Hugh's son Thomas married at fifteen or sixteen), it is not automatically the case that very young couples began producing children immediately after marrying. Katherine Swynford is unlikely to have been as young as fifteen when she gave birth to her first child; she was much closer to Gaunt's own age than is usually claimed, and was certainly not ten years younger than he. It is impossible that Katherine could have given birth to a daughter old enough to be named as one of the three damsels of the royal duke of Lancaster's daughters (and important enough not to be one of their ten 'under-damsels') on 1 September 1369, and yet only have been about nineteen years old that year.[18] She was much closer to her late thirties than her late twenties when she gave birth to the youngest of her Beaufort children in *c.* 1379, and was around sixty when she died in May 1403, not fifty-two or fifty-three.

Contrary to popular modern belief, girls in the fourteenth and fifteenth centuries did not routinely give birth at age thirteen and fourteen. It was not unheard of – the example usually cited is that of John of Gaunt and Katherine Swynford's great-granddaughter Margaret Beaufort, who gave birth to Henry Tudor (King Henry VII) in January 1457 when she was most probably only thirteen years old – but it was very uncommon. Besides, Margaret Beaufort was an heiress of noble birth and was married to the half-brother of the reigning king of England, and was of vastly higher rank than her ancestor Katherine Swynford and Katherine's first husband Hugh had been.[19] The 'courtesy of England' gave Margaret's husband Edmund Tudor a strong incentive to produce a child with her as soon as possible, because according to this custom, if an heiress had no child, her husband would lose all rights to his wife's lands as soon as she died, when they would pass to her heir by blood, a nephew or uncle or cousin. (John of Gaunt himself, who held the entire Lancastrian inheritance for three decades, was a major beneficiary of the 'courtesy of England', perhaps the greatest beneficiary in the entire Middle Ages.) Hugh Swynford, by contrast, had no reason to make Katherine Roet pregnant at the beginning of her teens, and there are no grounds for supposing that he did.

18

A Barrel of Relics and a Flying Dragon

Katherine Swynford's life in Lincolnshire before she became John of Gaunt's mistress appears to have been more comfortable than is often supposed in the twenty-first century. She and Hugh Swynford employed a chamberlain and a steward, whose services would not have come cheaply, and the reference to their steward purchasing twenty-four bows to give to servants on the occasion of their son's baptism implies that they had twenty-four people looking after them. The 'cloths of silk and gold' purchased for Thomas Swynford's baptism must have been very costly. Possibly these cloths were provided by Duchess Blanche, but this is not stated, and therefore it seems likely that Hugh and Katherine had enough money to buy rich and expensive fabrics. Various fictional and even factual accounts of Katherine's life as Hugh Swynford's wife and widow depict her living in impoverished deprivation, even squalor, scratching out a living from the uncultivated, primitive manor she is forced to live on. The Swynfords held the manor of Kettlethorpe, and 90 acres of land, 15 acres of pasture and part of a dwelling in the village of Coleby as well. This latter dwelling was said to be 'ruinous.' The land Hugh Swynford owned at Coleby was said in 1361 to be 'hard and stony, and uncultivated because of its barrenness,' and eleven years later 'sandy and stony, and out of cultivation.' In 1361, the meadow of the manor of Kettlethorpe ('Ketilthorp') was said to be 'overflowed by the waters of [the River] Trent in ordinary years.'[1]

Although the village of Coleby sounds decidedly unpromising, the reference to the River Trent overflowing the meadow of Kettlethorpe hardly seems to indicate that the entire manor was necessarily regularly flooded, and therefore uncultivated and impoverished.[2] Hugh Swynford settled the manor of Kettlethorpe on himself and Katherine jointly, meaning that after his death she was the manor's sole owner and had the right to keep it for the rest of her life, when it would pass to her and Hugh's son and heir Thomas Swynford. Katherine was certainly a long way from being rich and living in splendid comfort, but the awfulness of her pre-Gaunt life has been exaggerated in the interests of creating a romantic 'rags to riches' fairy tale.

John of Gaunt and Katherine Swynford's relationship almost certainly began after the death of her husband, Sir Hugh, in November 1371. There are only two indications that it began when Hugh Swynford was alive. One dates to more than a century later, when Richard III claimed in 1484 that their eldest child, John Beaufort, was 'of their indouble avoutry gotten,' or 'begotten of their double adultery.'[3] As Richard stated this, however, in the interests of denying the claim to the throne of John Beaufort's great-grandson Henry Tudor, there is no reason to take the claim particularly seriously, to imagine that King Richard was merely a disinterested observer, or to suppose that a man born in 1452 had any special insights into a relationship that began eighty years before his birth. (Perhaps rather ironically, Richard III was himself a great-grandson of John of Gaunt and Katherine Swynford: their daughter Joan Beaufort, countess of Westmorland, was the mother of his own mother, Cecily Neville, duchess of York. This descent in the female line means that King Richard and his siblings carried the mitochondrial DNA of Katherine and her unknown mother.)

Chronicler Jean Froissart, however, who was certainly alive in the early 1370s and long afterwards, and who knew John of Gaunt and his family personally, also claims that Gaunt's relationship with Katherine began in Hugh Swynford's lifetime. He wrote that Katherine 'had been married to a knight of England. The knight alive and dead ['*Le chevalier vivant et mort*'], the Duke John ['*Jehan*'] of Lancaster loved and kept this lady Katherine, with whom he had three [*sic*] children.'[4] This might simply be malicious gossip that Froissart had picked up, and he made a serious error with their children: he thought they had two sons and a daughter, when in fact they had three sons and a daughter. Their second son, Henry Beaufort, became bishop of Lincoln in 1398, and their third son was Thomas Beaufort. Froissart knew that one of their sons had become bishop of Lincoln, but wrongly named this man as 'Thomas Beaufort'. Given that he made such a basic error, he might not be a particularly trustworthy or reliable source for John and Katherine's relationship. No-one else at the time seemed to think that John Beaufort might really have been Hugh Swynford's biological son, and certainly Gaunt himself did not (and he would seem to be in the best position to know). Additionally, Froissart wrote this statement in or after 1398, twenty-seven years or more after Hugh Swynford's death, and although his chronicles are full of well-told, entertaining and lively stories, he relied excessively on hearsay and his own – often faulty – memory.

In late 1371 and in the first four months of 1372, there are no references to Katherine Swynford in John of Gaunt's surviving register, and presumably his new wife Constanza was uppermost in John's mind, at least for the time being. On 30 April 1372, John was at the Savoy, and sent instructions to John de Yerdeburgh, one of the clerks of his great wardrobe: Yerdebergh was to send three gifts to the bishop of Carpentras, a town in the south-east of France, now in the Vaucluse department. The gifts were a tripod in the shape of a 'flying dragon with a crowned young lady seated on a green background,' a gilded silver ewer in the shape of 'a shepherd with two oak-trees standing on a green background,' and a silver cup with a cover. All these items had previously been given to John 'by our dearest cousin the earl of Hereford,' which probably means Edward I's great-grandson Humphrey de Bohun (1342–73) though might also mean his namesake uncle (*c.* 1307–61).

From her new husband, Duchess Constanza received 1,808 pearls 'of the largest sort' – one wonders why John specified such a precise number rather than rounding it down to 1,800 – as well as 2,000 pearls 'of the second sort,' a gold circlet with emeralds and balas rubies, and a gold fillet (i.e. a headband or a string of precious stones to be worn on the head) with gemstones, four balas rubies and twenty-one large pearls. John ordered the clerk of his wardrobe to send to Constanza's damsel Eleyne or Alyne Gerberge 'all manner of useful and necessary things to adorn the head of our said beloved consort,' as well as cloths and furs for her.

Finally, there is a reference to a barrel decorated with gold and gemstones, which John had specially made for Constanza so she could store her holy relics. That Constanza was able to fill a barrel with saints' relics implies that she owned many, and probably also indicates that she was an especially pious and devout Christian even by the standards of a notably pious and devout age. It is worth noting, however, that her father, as well as hiring Muslim craftsmen to work on his palace in Seville, hired a large number of Muslim and Jewish soldiers to fight in his armies. Whatever his numerous other faults, Pedro was famous for his tolerance and friendliness towards his non-Christian subjects, a fact used against him by various fourteenth-century writers and by Enrique of Trastámara. The latter allegedly sneered at his half-brother as 'the son of a Jewish whore, calling himself king of Castile,' affecting to believe that Pedro's mother was a Jewish servant, not Maria of Portugal, which would explain his cordial relations with his Jewish subjects.[5] Constanza grew up in an environment that was far more religiously tolerant than one might perhaps expect, especially given that she was the great-grandmother of Isabel the Catholic, queen regnant of Castile, who with her husband Fernando (or Ferdinand) of Aragon expelled the Jewish population of Spain or forced them to convert to Catholicism, brought down the Islamic emirate of Granada, and established the Spanish Inquisition.

For himself, John purchased an *Agnus Dei,* a devotional object usually made of wax and stamped with the figure of the 'Lamb of God,' decorated with gold. To the marshal of 'our Holy Father the pope,' Yerdebergh was to send a gilded silver cup 'with a minstrel standing on the cover' which the bishop of London had recently given to 'our beloved consort the queen'. John referred to Constanza's younger sister as 'Isabelle, countess of Cambridge, our dearest sister' (though Isabel of Castile had not yet married Edmund of Langley, legally she was his 'sister' because she was his wife's sister), and bought her a gilded silver tripod 'in the shape of a monster with three supports and three mace-bearers standing on a green background'. Isabel also received a silver cup that matched the tripod, and a silver ewer 'in parts enamelled with various grotesque figures'. John had previously given this last item to 'our beloved sister on the day of her marriage'. Although which of his married sisters – Isabella of Woodstock, Mary of Waltham or Margaret of Windsor – he was referring to was not clarified, another item given to Isabel of Castile was specified as having been previously given by Constanza to 'our beloved sister aforesaid,' and this can only mean Isabella of Woodstock, as all of John's other sisters were long dead by the early 1370s when Constanza arrived in England. Two final gifts that Gaunt gave to Isabel of Castile were another silver tripod 'with growing trees' and a silver ewer decorated with vines and roses. Almost certainly all these items purchased for Isabel were intended as John's wedding gifts to her, though she did not marry Edmund of Langley until July 1372.[6]

19

The Midwife of Leicester

On 6 June 1372, John of Gaunt told his receiver in Leicestershire, William Chiselden, to send 'the midwife' ('*la sage femme*', literally 'the wise woman') Ilote to Constanza of Castile at Hertford Castle as quickly as Chiselden possibly could. Ilote was to be given a cart or a horse to speed her journey to Hertford, and almost certainly is to be identified as the 'Elyot la middewyf de Leycestre' or 'Elyot, the midwife of Leicester' mentioned by John in August 1375. (On this second occasion in 1375, John asked his forester in Leicestershire to send Ilote, or Elyot, two carts full of firewood.) Ilote, the wise woman and midwife, had, John stated, previously served his late wife Blanche.

Ilote's speedy journey to Hertford suggests that Constanza may have been close to giving birth in June 1372, or that she was having a difficult first pregnancy. If Constanza did bear a child on or shortly after 6 June 1372, this was only thirty-seven weeks after her wedding to John on 21 September 1371, which would imply that she became pregnant on her wedding night or very soon afterwards. It is also possible that Constanza had recently discovered that she was expecting in early June 1372, and perhaps she and John were anxious about the progress of the pregnancy. Evidently John knew Ilote well, as she had aided Duchess Blanche during her own pregnancies and confinements, and he knew she would take good care of Constanza. He himself, meanwhile, was staying at the Savoy, though the palace lay close enough to Hertford Castle that he could easily ride there if necessary. On the other hand, John was intending to travel to either Kenilworth (in Warwickshire) or Tutbury (in Staffordshire) very soon: he sent letters to his staff in both castles on consecutive days, 6 and 7 June, announcing his impending arrival and ordering them to lay in casks of good wine ('*bon vin*') for himself and his retinue. This might imply that Constanza was not on the verge of giving birth at Hertford and that the visit of Ilote the wise woman had something to do with the duchess's pregnancy, not her confinement.[1]

At any rate, Constanza bore John of Gaunt a daughter whom they named Katherine, or Catalina as she will be called throughout the book to avoid possible confusion with Gaunt's mistress, sometime before the end of March 1373 and perhaps in 1372. In the fourteenth century, the name was spelt Kateryn, Kateryne, Katerin or Katerine (it never appeared with a H, and therefore apparently was not pronounced with the modern 'th' sound). Either Duchess Constanza herself or Gaunt sent Katherine Swynford to Edward III to give him the news of their daughter's birth in the full knowledge that the king would reward Katherine financially, and a payment of 20 marks (£13.33) to Katherine was recorded on 31 March 1373, a considerable increase on the £5 Edward had given for news of Catalina's half-brother Henry of Lancaster's birth six years earlier.[2] If it was Constanza who sent Katherine to the king, this hardly indicates that there was hostility between the two women, and Duchess Constanza may even have named her daughter after her husband's mistress, unless John of Gaunt himself chose his daughter's name. The feast day of St Katherine is 25 November, so perhaps Catalina of Lancaster was born on or close to this date in 1372 and her parents intended to honour St Katherine, and the little girl sharing a name with her father's lover was merely a coincidence.

John of Gaunt gave, or sent, Katherine Swynford the generous sum of £10 '*del doune monseignur*' ('of my lord's gift') at the Savoy on 1 May 1372, a few weeks before sending the wise woman Ilote to Constanza of Castile. It is not clear from the wording of the grant whether Katherine was present at the Savoy with John on that date or not.[3] This gift of cash is the equivalent of a few thousand pounds in modern terms, and would seem to be evidence that the duke's passionate relationship with Katherine had already, perhaps recently, begun. It was just under six months since Hugh Swynford's death, a period of time Katherine may have considered sufficiently lengthy to grieve, or at least to be seen to grieve, for her husband, though it should be noted that we have no possible way of knowing whether Hugh and Katherine had a happy and successful marriage or not. Exactly when and under what circumstances John of Gaunt and Katherine Swynford, a famous and beloved couple in the twentieth and twenty-first centuries, became lovers must remain a matter for speculation, though the sudden flurry of entries relating to Katherine in the duke's register in May and June 1372 strongly implies that their relationship had recently begun. Katherine had never been mentioned in the register before 1 May 1372, then in those two months, she appeared six times.

The entry in the *Oxford Dictionary of National Biography* for John Beaufort, eldest of Gaunt and Katherine's four children, gives his date of birth as *c.* 1371, as does the *Complete Peerage*.[4] As Beaufort's mother's first husband, Sir Hugh, was alive until November 1371, this is impossible; had John been born or conceived in Hugh's lifetime he would have been given Hugh's family name and would legally have been Hugh's son and recognised as such, even if he was John of Gaunt's biological child. There is evidence that in the fourteenth century a child was recognised as his or her father's posthumous child even if s/he was born as late as eleven months after the father's death. The *Vita Edwardi Secundi* states, in relation to the dowager countess of Gloucester claiming to be pregnant with her husband's heir well over a year after he was killed at the Battle of Bannockburn in 1314, that 'the law warns us that if a posthumous child is born after the eleventh month, it cannot claim the inheritance of the deceased'. John Beaufort was never claimed or recognised as Hugh Swynford's son, which, almost certainly, proves that he was born after August 1372 at the earliest, nine months after Hugh's death, and possibly after October 1372, taking fourteenth-century beliefs and practices into account. Jean Froissart called Beaufort 'my lord Biaufort of Lancastre' and stated that his father Gaunt 'loved him much' (*'moult l'aymoit'*).[5] Despite stating that Katherine became the duke of Lancaster's lover while her husband was alive, Froissart seemed in no doubt whatsoever that her son was the duke's son, not Hugh Swynford's.

John Beaufort was knighted sometime before 6 December 1391, and according to Jean Froissart, took part in the crusade of Louis, duke of Bourbon, to Barbary in May to September 1390. Froissart also named Beaufort as a knight during a jousting tournament held in France in March/April 1390, in which, Froissart says, Beaufort participated.[6] His knighting in or before 1390/91 does not necessarily mean that he must have been born earlier rather than later, i.e. in *c.* 1371. His half-brother Thomas Swynford, born 1367/68, was already a knight in early 1383, and if the story of John Beaufort's participation in the Barbary Crusade is true, it is not confirmed by any safe conduct issued to him before he supposedly travelled abroad in 1390; none is recorded in the chancery rolls. The *Complete Peerage* cites an entry on the Patent Roll that states John Beaufort was granted 100 marks a year to serve in the retinue of his cousin Richard II on 7 June 1392.[7] A later memorandum underneath this entry adds that the grant was cancelled because Richard II had granted Beaufort issues and profits from the royal castle and lordship of Wallingford instead, on '10 September in his twenty-first year'. This means the twenty-first year of Richard II's reign, which ran from 22 June 1397 to 21 June 1398, not the twenty-first year of John Beaufort's life as the *Complete Peerage* states, and does not mean that Beaufort was twenty or twenty-one years old at the time of the original grant in June 1392. It is certainly not evidence that Beaufort was born in 1371, as has sometimes been assumed.[8]

Although it seems virtually certain that John Beaufort was born after August 1372, it is impossible to ascertain his date of birth, except that it probably fell sometime in 1373. Katherine Swynford took news of the birth of Constanza and Gaunt's daughter Catalina of Lancaster to Edward III on or sometime before 31 March 1373 (the king spent the first three months of 1373 at several of his palaces a few miles outside London: Eltham, Langley and Sheen). Katherine obviously was able to travel at the time of her journey to Edward and cannot have been hugely pregnant, and it is most improbable that she had given birth in the few weeks before she travelled to the king. This is an assumption based both on the grounds of her own health and comfort, and on the fact that women were 'churched' or purified about thirty or forty days after birth and are unlikely to have ventured out in public much, if at all, during that period, let alone entered the presence of the most important person in the country. Whether John of Gaunt would have been brazen enough to send his obviously pregnant mistress to his father with news of his daughter born to his royal wife, and thus blatantly paraded his infidelity in front of the entire court and his relatives, seems highly doubtful, and it would have been a gross insult to Duchess Constanza. Katherine, therefore, was probably not visibly pregnant at the time, and John Beaufort was perhaps born later in 1373 rather than near the start of the year. As will be discussed below, Katherine may well have borne her second Beaufort child in January 1375, perhaps her third in February 1377 (though this date is a little tenuous, and Gaunt's register, which might give more hints on the matter, does not exist for the years 1376–78), and her fourth and youngest in November 1379.

On 12 March 1372 at the Savoy, Gaunt sent out letters that began: 'Johan by the grace of God etc [king of Castile and Leon, duke of Lancaster] to all those etc [who see or hear these letters]. Know that we have allowed our dearest consort the queen, for the necessary expenses of her chamber, £666, thirteen shillings and four pence in sterling per year.' This amount sounds oddly random, but it was not: it was the equivalent of 1,000 marks. A few weeks later, on 15 May, still at the Savoy, John sent more correspondence 'to all those who see or hear these letters'. John talked of 'our dearest damsel Katerine de Swynford' and of 'the good and agreeable service which she performed for our dearest consort, whom God absolve,' i.e. Blanche of Lancaster. He therefore granted Katherine an annuity of 50 marks, payable in two instalments at Easter and at the feast of St Michael, i.e. 29 September, for the rest of her life. This was to replace his previous grant to her of 20 marks a year, and Katherine sent John's letters granting her this amount to the Chancery to be annulled and cancelled.

Another letter from Gaunt, sent the following day, gives the amount of the annuity to be given to Katherine as £50, not 50 marks (which was the equivalent of £33.33). Either this was a clerical error, or John had once again increased the amount of Katherine's annuity. John also mentioned 'the very great affection which our said consort [Duchess Blanche] had for the said Katerine,' and added that he wished to do her greater favour than he had previously. Katherine, however, seems to have had problems accessing her money, as John sent another letter to his receiver in Lincolnshire a year later on 12 May 1373, ordering him to pay Katherine's annuity to her promptly and to ensure that future payments were not delayed.[9]

John dictated yet another letter on 20 June 1372, not addressed to anyone in particular, stating:

> Of our special grace, and for the good and agreeable service which our beloved lady Katerine who was the wife of Sir Hugh de Swynford, knight, formerly performed for our beloved consort [Blanche], the late duchess of Lancaster, whom God absolve, we have granted to the said lady Katerine the custody of the lands and tenements which belonged to the said Sir Hugh

in Lincolnshire on the day of his death, and which were held of us in chief as part of the honour of Richmond, and which are in our custody by reason of the nonage of Thomas, son and heir of the said Sir Hugh.[10]

John's letters always referred to Katherine as 'our beloved lady, Kateryne de Swynford' or 'our dearest and beloved lady, Katerine de Swynford' ('*nostre treschere e bien ame dame*'). Although there is no doubt whatsoever that Katherine was incredibly important and indeed beloved to John, this formulation was purely conventional in fourteenth-century letters, and John wrote to all his correspondents as his 'dearest and beloved', even his parkers, foresters, falconers and the workmen who laboured for him. Addressing people or referring to them in correspondence as 'Our dearest and beloved' was as formulaic and meaningless to John of Gaunt and his contemporaries as beginning letters or emails with 'Dear' is to us.

The late Sir Hugh Swynford's inquisition post-mortem was held in the Lincolnshire village of Navenby, a couple of miles from the Swynford manor of Coleby, on 27 April 1372 and in Lincoln, 7 miles from Coleby, on 24 June in the same year. Katherine Swynford was ordered on 8 June 1372 to take the customary oath not to marry again without the king's licence, which was a routine and entirely usual demand made of the widows of landowners in England and Wales before they received their rightful dower, and does not reveal anything about Katherine's relationship with John of Gaunt.[11] She was granted her dower, which by law was a third of her late husband's lands, in the manor of Coleby on 26 June 1372: 'A chamber called *le Westchambre* at the west end of the hall, with *le faux chambre* ['the false chamber'] and wardrobe, and with the cellars underneath those chambers; a kitchen; a building called *le Schepon* with a croft adjoining called *Belgarthes*; and the western part of the garden.' Katherine also received over a hundred acres of meadow and field, and her exact allocation was minutely specified: she received, for example, 9 acres 'in the south field towards the east,' 2 acres 'abutting Milnecroft,' 2 acres between 'Sty' and 'Litelgate' and 4 acres on 'Heywolde'.[12] Five days later, Edward III ordered the manor of Kettlethorpe to be given back to Katherine as she and Hugh Swynford had held it jointly and thus by right it was Katherine's to keep for the rest of her life, and was not to be held by the king until Katherine's son Thomas came of age at twenty-one, as would have been the case had Hugh held it alone. The escheator in Lincolnshire was told on 16 August 1372 to keep Hugh Swynford's lands in the king's hands as his son Thomas was underage, though on 12 September Katherine was given permission to keep the remaining two parts of the manor of Coleby during her son's minority in exchange for a payment of £20.[13]

20

Victory over Your Enemies

Henry of Lancaster, far too young to have any memories at all of the mother who died before he was even eighteen months old, was four when his father married Constanza of Castile, and seems to have been on good terms with her. Constanza and John gave Henry material for garments, lent him servants and craftsmen, and often paid for the presents and alms he gave out.[1] John's second daughter, Elizabeth of Lancaster, named two of her three daughters Constance, one of whom was born years after Constanza's death, and Constanza also spent much time with her eldest stepchild Philippa, who was only about six years her junior.[2] This implies that both of the late Blanche of Lancaster's daughters, as well as Blanche's son, felt considerable affection for their stepmother and that Constanza played a far more important role in John of Gaunt's family life than is sometimes assumed.

When Henry of Lancaster was king of England from 1399 to 1413, he always referred to Constanza as 'the king's mother,' as there was no contemporary word for stepmother or mother-in-law; your father's wife or your spouse's mother was almost always referred to as your own mother (the same applied to your mother's husband or your spouse's father, who was your 'father'). In a letter to Henry about the Newarke in Leicester, dated early 1401, Pope Boniface IX referred to 'the souls of John, sometime duke of Lancaster, and Constance his consort, the king's parents'.[3] Henry therefore also called his father's third wife Katherine Swynford his mother, but this does not, contrary to the claims sometimes made by modern writers, necessarily indicate his great affection for her or mean that their relationship was a close mother-son one. He might well have been extremely fond of her, and certainly he showed favour to her son Thomas Swynford, but the polite and entirely conventional formulation of 'the king's mother' does not reveal anything one way or another about his feelings, and Henry always referred to his mother-in-law Joan de Bohun as 'the king's mother' as well. Henry's son Henry V always called his stepmother Juana of Navarre his mother, even though their relations went badly awry and he imprisoned Juana for witchcraft. On one occasion in 1401 when the widowed Katherine petitioned Henry IV, she called herself, 'Katerine, formerly wife of your very honoured father, whom God absolve.'[4]

At an uncertain date, John of Gaunt received a letter from Maud, surname not given, the former nurse of his daughter Philippa (whom Maud called

'Dame Phelip' in the letter, which was written in French though Maud surely dictated it to a clerk in English). Maud addressed John merely as 'duke of Lancaster' and not as king of Castile and Leon, so it might date to the early 1370s before he married Constanza, or it might date to after 1389 when John had given up his and his wife's claims to her father's kingdom.[5] Maud's concern for John's well-being reveals that some of the duke's servants remained loyal and had his best interests at heart even after they left his service:

To the very dread and very puissant lord, my lord the duke of Lancaster. Very dread, very excellent and very puissant lord, I recommend myself to your very high lordship, desiring sincerely to hear good news of your very noble lordship, which I pray to our very sweet lord Jesus Christ that He may maintain, by His mercy. And because, very noble lord, the ancient proverb states that he who was warned beforehand is not shamed, it is for this reason, very dread lord, that I wish to warn you of some of your enemies, of whom I have learned by manifest experience, namely, the friars Hugh Bandon and John Drynkestor of the order of Friars Minor* of Cambridge, and the friars John Pykworth, John Robert and John Hill of the order of Friars Preacher** of Cambridge aforesaid, who have evilly and treacherously spoken of you, my very dread [*word 'lord' missing in the letter*], as I heard to the great sadness of my heart. Therefore I beseech you, my very puissant lord, that you watch out for them, and for all others, for the sake of God and the work of holy charity. Very dread and very puissant lord, may the Blessed Trinity keep your very high lordship for a long time, and give you victory over all your enemies. Your humble suppliant and servant Maud, former nurse of the very honourable lady, Lady Philippa, your dearest daughter.

The wish that John would have 'victory over all his enemies' was a fairly conventional closing salutation in fourteenth-century correspondence (it often appears as 'May God give you vengeance over your enemies'), and most probably does not refer to the five friars Maud spoke of in her letter. Nor does it reveal that Maud was of a particularly bloodthirsty nature or even necessarily that she thought John of Gaunt had more enemies than the average nobleman.

On 5 June 1372, at the Savoy, John sent a cask of wine each to Lady Poynings and Lady Ferrers. John acknowledged Lady Poynings, born Blanche Mowbray, as his 'dearest cousin', as she was a first cousin of the late Blanche of Lancaster. He sent Elizabeth, Lady Ferrers another cask of Gascon wine eleven months later, which cost him £9 and 13s. Yet another cask of wine

---

* The Franciscans or Greyfriars.
** The Dominicans or Blackfriars.

went to Lady Ferrers sometime in 1374, and on this occasion John also sent casks to his chamberlain, Sir Robert Swillington, the steward of his household, Sir William Croiser, and, rather surprisingly, to the prisoners incarcerated at the gaol of Newgate in London. Lady Ferrers was descended from Edward I via her mother Margaret Audley and was therefore a distant cousin of Gaunt, and was the widow of John, Lord Ferrers of Chartley, killed fighting with John and his brother the prince of Wales at the Battle of Nájera in 1367.[6]

John seems, given the regularity with which Elizabeth, Lady Ferrers appears in his register, to have been deeply fond of her. He was also very fond of Elizabeth Montacute, the countess of Salisbury; Countess Elizabeth's mother Joan, Lady Mohun; Margaret, countess of Norfolk and Lady Segrave, a granddaughter of Edward I and thus another of John's close kinswomen; and Lady Warre and her sister Lady Poynings, née Eleanor and Blanche Mowbray. There is no reason whatsoever to think that John's cordial relations with any of these women were intimate or romantic, and both the countess of Norfolk and Joan Mohun were old enough to be his mother, but his affection for them does reveal that he enjoyed female company and the friendship of women.

Gaunt sent a letter to his bailiff in Lincolnshire on 10 July at the Savoy, stating that some of the officials and tenants of his manor of North Cotes in that county had stolen items from a ship that had been wrecked 'at the sands of Tetney'.[7] Tetney was a village near North Cotes, and was held by Gaunt's brother the prince of Wales. The items the men had taken from the shipwreck were thirty pieces of iron, three anchors and two cables, and other 'goods and chattels' that were not specified, valued at 20 marks. John ordered the bailiff, William de Spaigne ('of Spain', or rather Castile) to investigate how the ship came to be wrecked and to whom it and the goods on it belonged, and where the goods were now and in what condition. John most probably attended the wedding of his brother Edmund of Langley and Constanza's sister Isabel of Castile at Wallingford Castle, about 50 miles from the Savoy, the following day, 11 July. Presumably Constanza was also there, assuming that her physical condition – if she was pregnant with her and Gaunt's daughter Catalina, or recovering from childbirth – permitted her to travel. John was back at the Savoy by 14 July 1372, so did not spend much time with his brother and sister-in-law, and was still there on the 16th.[8]

Edmund of Langley was now thirty-one, and Isabel of Castile was seventeen or almost. The couple are often assumed to have been rather incompatible on a personal level, though it is almost impossible to ascertain the true nature of people's private relationships so many centuries later. Chronicler Thomas Walsingham called Isabel a 'pampered and voluptuous lady,' and he described Constanza as an 'exceptionally innocent and pious lady,' a description surely confirmed by the duchess of Lancaster's possession of an entire barrel full of relics. The Spanish sisters were very different, and Isabel probably took after their mother María de Padilla far more than Constanza did. Isabel was rumoured to have had an affair with Sir John Holland, who was the second son of Gaunt's sister-in-law Joan of Kent, princess of Wales, and would become Gaunt's son-in-law in 1386. A note in a fifteenth-century manuscript of Geoffrey Chaucer's poem *Compleynt of Mars*, written by the manuscript copyist John Shirley, states that the work was inspired by John Holland's love for Isabel of Castile. It is probably significant in this context that John Shirley had a decades-long and successful career as the chief scribe of Richard Beauchamp, earl of Warwick, whose second wife Isabelle Despenser (1400–39) was the granddaughter of Edmund of Langley and Isabel of Castile via their only daughter, Constance, Lady Despenser. As John Shirley was born in *c.* 1366, he was only a few years younger than John Holland (*c.* 1353–1400) and Isabel of Castile (1355–92) and was an adult in their lifetimes.

Jean Froissart, meanwhile, calls Edmund of Langley 'indolent, guileless and peaceable,' and he seems not to have had the drive and ambition of his four brothers, though in fairness Edmund's comparatively very low income and his lack of landed wealth severely hampered the exercise of any abilities he might otherwise have demonstrated.[9] Edmund was the only one of Edward III's five sons not to marry an heiress (though his father had tried for years to marry him to the great heiress Margarethe of Flanders), and in fact his marriage into the deposed royal family of Castile brought him personally no benefits whatsoever; no lands or income or influential in-laws. He and Isabel also, apparently unwillingly, gave up any claims to the kingdom of Castile, and in *c.* 1385 they complained that John of Gaunt had unjustly set aside Isabel's rights to her late father's throne.[10]

In October 1376, Edmund's father granted him 1,000 marks (£666) a year from the Exchequer, and in June 1385 he was promised £500 annually also from the Exchequer 'to support his family becomingly'. However, the earl struggled to obtain even this small sum, while John of Gaunt, the brother who was just fifteen months his senior, enjoyed riches estimated at £12,000 a year from his first wife's lands and also looked forward to ruling the kingdoms of which his second wife was rightful queen. A memorandum appended to the October 1376 grant to Edmund, 'Vacated because nothing thereof was done,' and the fact that he had to sue the Exchequer at 'great expense' to himself in February 1380 as he had received no money at all, reveal how Edmund's financial needs were neglected and how he had fight even for a few crumbs from the royal table.[11]

One wonders whether Constanza of Castile, seemingly a quiet, serious and devout young woman, would have found greater personal happiness as the wife of the rather staid and steady Edmund of Langley than she did as John of Gaunt's wife. It may be that both John and Constanza, and Edmund and Isabel, did not find much in the way of contentment in their marriages, but Gaunt was the elder brother and Constanza was the elder sister and that was that; their personal compatibility or their likelihood of finding marital bliss together was not the issue. Edmund of Langley and Isabel of Castile's first child was born in 1373 or 1374, and was named Edward after his paternal grandfather the king of England. He is sometimes known to posterity as 'Edward of Norwich', but this seems to be a misunderstanding of 'Everwyk', the name for York in the variant of French used by the medieval English elite (now known as Anglo-Norman), which has been misread as 'Norwyk' or Norwich. There is no particular reason to suppose that Edward was born in Norwich, and it is more accurate to call him Edward of York, as his father received the dukedom of York a few years later, or Edward of Rutland, the earldom bestowed on him by his cousin Richard II in 1390.

Isabel of Castile and Edmund of Langley's only daughter was probably born sometime between 1374 and 1376, and was named Constance, which almost certainly means that Constanza of Castile was the little girl's godmother as well as her aunt. The second son and youngest child of Edmund and Isabel, Richard of Conisbrough – grandfather of two kings, Edward IV and Richard III, via his son Richard, duke of York – was a good few years younger than his siblings. The *Oxford Dictionary of National Biography* states that Richard was baptised in Conisbrough Castle, Yorkshire, around 20 July 1385, at a time when his eighteen-year-old godfather King Richard II was staying in York.[12]

Some writers have speculated that Richard of Conisbrough was fathered by Isabel of Castile's probable lover Sir John Holland rather than by Edmund of Langley, but although Edmund made no provisions for Richard financially – perhaps he could not afford to, given his small income – he never disavowed his son either. In the absence of any real evidence, it only seems fair to both Edmund and Isabel to assume that Edmund was the boy's biological father. On the other hand, Isabel left items to John Holland in her will of 1392, and other than her servants, Holland was the only person to whom she left bequests who was not a close member of her family. In the will, Isabel also left some very valuable things to her elder son Edward which Holland had given her, and although this might have been purely innocent - the English royalty and nobility of the late fourteenth century often did give each other costly presents, as John of Gaunt's register clearly shows – there was certainly a connection between the two, and Isabel did not mention any other gifts she had received from anyone else.[13]

21

To Resist and Withstand Malice

A letter that John of Gaunt sent on 21 April 1372 reveals there was something he called 'grammar schools' ('*les escoles de gramoire*', in the plural) in his Northamptonshire town of Higham Ferrers. The duke appointed Henry Barton of Billing Magna, who had 'great ability and competent knowledge of grammar,' to run them for the benefit of 'scholars and children wishing to study the subject of grammar.'[1] It is rather interesting to note that a small rural village in Northamptonshire had at least two such schools in the 1370s. Between April 1372 and early 1373, John contemplated the future marriage of his daughter Philippa of Lancaster, who had turned twelve at the end of March 1372. If he had a candidate in mind, however, he did not commit the man's identity to writing, but merely referenced the 'aid granted to us for marrying our eldest daughter' in various letters (in 1374, he contemplated a match for her with the count of Foix in southern France). He also wrote to his chief steward in Lancashire, William Nesfeld, in April 1372, regarding a tenement that the abbot of Sawley held from him in the Lancashire town of Grindleton and which bore the extraordinary name of 'Dobbestiddefuthianson'.[2]

Gaunt sent letters on 10 and 18 July 1372 to state that 'our very dread lord and father the king' intended to cross the sea in order to 'resist and withstand the malice of his enemies' in France and Castile, and that he himself would go with him, with his entire retinue. John told two of his receivers that he wished to raise a company of archers in Lancashire and Staffordshire.[3] King Edward appointed his five-year-old grandson Richard of Bordeaux as nominal keeper of the realm at the end of August 1372, when he left the kingdom to lead what would prove to be his last expedition to France. This campaign was a response to increasing French and Castilian hostilities in the Bay of Biscay, and King Enrique of Castile captured John Hastings, earl of Pembroke, widower of the king's youngest daughter Margaret of Windsor; the harsh treatment to which the young earl was subjected was to kill him in 1375. Edward of Woodstock, apparently enjoying a period of decent health for once, John of Gaunt and Edmund of Langley accompanied their father, but the royal men achieved absolutely nothing, merely bobbing about in a ship off the English coast, unable to go anywhere because of the winds. The short campaign was soon called off.[4]

John was still at the port of Sandwich in Kent on Monday 30 August 1372, having originally intended to cross the Channel three weeks earlier, and around noon on that date was with his father in the king's ship the *Grace Dieu* off Sandwich when Edward III handed over the great seal to the chancellor of England to use during his absence. Sometime on the same day, the duke of Lancaster granted an income of £10 a year to Katherine Swynford's sister, 'our beloved damsel Philippa Chaucer' ('Philippe Chause'), for the excellent service she had done in the past and would continue to do in the future for Gaunt's wife Constanza.[5] Gaunt was, like the king and his brothers, soon back in England. He had spent part of that summer prior to departure from Sandwich hunting in the park called the Frith near Leicester, and sent nineteen of his hunting dogs and nine huntsmen to his manor of Higham Ferrers as well. In the summer of 1372, the duke also expected trouble to break out in Wales, and put his castles on a war footing; this was a fairly regular occurrence.[6]

John was back at the Savoy, where he spent much time in the 1370s, by 29 September 1372, just weeks after the unsatisfactory campaign. He assigned 300 marks (i.e. £200) annually 'for the chamber of our dearest and beloved son Henry and of our dearest and beloved daughters Philippe and Elizabet.'[7] Henry was now five, and his sisters were twelve and nine. Shortly before 11 November 1372, John complained that a large group of men had broken into his park at Higham Ferrers and had hunted and carried away his deer, hares, rabbits, pheasants and partridges. Furthermore, the thieves had 'chased three oxen and 300 sheep at Rothwell [15 miles away] with dogs, inciting the dogs to bite them, so that the oxen and 200 sheep, worth £40, died, and the others were greatly deteriorated, and assaulted his men and servants there.' His father granted a commission of oyer and terminer to six men to investigate what had happened.[8]

On 24 December, Gaunt sent a letter to Johane Martyns, one of the 'young ladies of Castile' who attended Duchess Constanza. The following items were to be delivered to Constanza's damsel Eleyne or Alyne Gerberge: a gold crown with emeralds, balas rubies and pearls, which Edward III had given to Constanza; a gold circlet with a thousand diamonds, balas rubies, sapphires, emeralds and pearls 'with one pearl missing'; and a gold brooch with an image of St George and with balas rubies, sapphires, diamonds and pearls, a gift to Constanza from her brother-in-law the prince of Wales. John piled his wife with other gifts on this occasion, including forty small buttons decorated with (for a reason not explained) the letter T.[9]

A letter John sent from the Savoy on 26 November 1372 indicates that he was planning to provide a splendid feast for the noble people who lived in

Staffordshire at the coming Christmas, while he himself intended to spend the festive season at his castle of Hertford:

> Johan by the grace of God etc [king of Castile and Leon, duke of Lancaster] to our beloved Sir Avery Sulny, our chief forester of Needwood, or his deputy, greetings. Because we wish that many knights, ladies, young ladies, squires, and other persons of noble rank [*gentil estat*] who dwell in and around our lordship in those parts partake of our game and venison there at the feast of Christmas next coming, we wish and order you to hunt forty bucks and to give and deliver them to all the people aforenamed, according to the status and rank of each person.[10]

22

The King of Cambridge and Agnes Bonsergeant

At New Year 1373, John of Gaunt gave out a large number of presents, as was customary in the English royal family in the fourteenth century, which he paid for on 13 April 1373 and which are listed in order of the recipients' rank. For some reason, Edward III does not appear on the list, and neither does John's youngest brother, Thomas of Woodstock, who turned eighteen on 5 January 1373.[1] To 'our very honoured brother the prince [of Wales]', Edward of Woodstock, John gave a gold cup and a gold belt, and Edward's wife, Joan of Kent, received another gold cup.

Constanza came next, 'our beloved companion the queen [of Castile]', and received a *botoun*, a button or stud, 'in the shape of a wild boar' and made of gold with precious stones. Constanza also received a gold eagle, something called a '*bladekyn*' (most probably a clerical error for *baudekyn*, a kind of rich embroidered cloth) 'of double silk', and two gold brooches studded with precious stones, so she did particularly well out of John this year. Fourth on the list was Edmund of Langley, whom John's clerk rather amusingly referred to as the 'king of Cambridge' by mistake instead of 'earl of Cambridge', and who was given a silver cup with matching ewer. Next came John's heir, 'our beloved son Henre', who was given a silver cup, then John's daughters Philippa and Elizabeth, who each got ten buttons or studs of gold with precious stones. 'Our beloved sister the countess of Cambridge', Isabel of Castile, received a gold tablet.

Next came Lady Poynings, Blanche Mowbray, who received a silver cup; Lady Segrave, which presumably means Edward III's cousin Margaret, countess of Norfolk, widow of John Segrave (d. 1353), who received a pair of paternosters with a gold fastening; and the countess of March. Given her position in the list, this probably means Philippa Montacute, widow of Roger Mortimer the second earl of March (1328–60), rather than John's niece Philippa of Clarence the countess of March and Ulster, wife of Edmund Mortimer the third earl (b. 1352). The countess of March was also given a pair of paternosters with a gold fastening. Last on the list of ladies were Eleanor, Lady Warre, and Lady Courtenay, i.e. Maud Holland, one of Joan of Kent's two daughters from her previous marriage and the stepdaughter of the prince of Wales, who each also received a pair of paternosters with a gold fastening. John gave various cups and paternosters to Lord Latimer,

Sir Alan Buxhill, Sir Lewis Clifford, Sir Nicholas Sharnesfeld, Sir Simon Burley, Sir John of Ypres and Sir John Clanvowe.

The next two people on the list are named only as 'the *maistresse* of our beloved consort [Constanza]' and 'the *maistresse* of our dear children' ('*noz chers enfantz*'). Both the woman who headed Duchess Constanza's household and the woman who looked after the duke's children received yet another pair of paternosters with a gold fastening. Neither woman was named, but the person in charge of looking after the duke's children was presumably Katherine Swynford. Last on the long list of recipients came Joan Darcy, someone named only as 'Senche' (perhaps Sancho Ruche, a Spanish knight who came to England in 1371 with Gaunt and Constanza), four unnamed servants and eight unnamed squires of 'our very dread lord and father the king'; Montague the herald; and Gaunt's messenger John of Winchester, who was given a silver box stamped with the arms of Castile and England. Gaunt also bought himself a New Year present, his favourite item to gift this year: a pair of paternosters with a gold fastening, though in his case the fastening is specified as being 'small'. Gaunt and Constanza's daughter Catalina of Lancaster is not mentioned in the list of gift recipients at New Year 1373, which might mean that she had not been born yet, or perhaps that her father considered her too little to be given any.

Catalina's nurse was Agnes, widow of John Bonsergeant, who left this position sometime before 23 July 1375 when Catalina was two or perhaps had recently turned three years old. On that date, 'for her good and agreeable service ... to our dearest and beloved daughter Katerine,' John of Gaunt granted Agnes an annuity of 5 marks (the equivalent of approximately £3.30) for the rest of her life. Agnes Bonsergeant was not, contrary to the claim made in several modern works, the former nurse of Katherine Swynford. This entry in Gaunt's register has unfortunately been misread by one author, who missed the key word *fille*, 'daughter,' in John's reference to '*nostre tres chere e tres amee fille Katerine*'. Other writers have failed to check the original source and have subsequently perpetuated the error, and one of them has stated that it was 'virtually unheard of for a royal duke to remember the nurse of his mistress in this way.' Indeed, it was, and John did not do so.[2] The 5 marks were to be paid to Agnes from the issues of the duke's manor of King's Somborne in Hampshire, which had been part of the inheritance of Blanche of Lancaster's paternal grandmother Maud Chaworth, and passed to Maud's only son Duke Henry and then to Blanche and John of Gaunt.

Symond Templer was one of the valets of Catalina's chamber, and in January 1375 there is a reference to the little girl's household being based in Melbourne, near Derby, another manor of Maud Chaworth's inheritance that passed to Maud's son, granddaughter and grandson-in-law. 'Ingram, son of Henry, parker of Melbourne' was to hunt four deer in the park and hand the meat over to the officials of Catalina's household at this time, and she must have lived in the castle that stood in the village of Melbourne but was demolished in the seventeenth century. Within the manor of Melbourne lay fields and woods called Oxlesewe, Bencheparrok, Russhegrenes, Littelmedewebrok, Carreweye, Oldefisshepol and Hervestwellefeld.

A letter sent by Gaunt from Hertford Castle in late 1374 mentions five 'young ladies of Castile' who were former attendants of Duchess Constanza, and who were now living at his expense at Nuneaton Priory in Warwickshire (he paid the prioress 14s and 4d a week to feed, clothe and house them). Gaunt stated that one of them, Johane (or Juana) Martyns, was to join Catalina's household at Melbourne. In August 1375, he ordered repairs to be made to his own chamber at Melbourne Castle, which suggests that he was intending to visit his and Constanza's daughter there.[3] Somewhat later, John placed Catalina in the care of the widowed and very long-lived noblewoman Joan née Burghersh, Lady Mohun (b. *c.* early or mid-1320s, d. 1404), mother of Elizabeth Montacute, countess of Salisbury. In 1381, Catalina was referred to as 'Katerine d'Espaigne' or 'Catalina of Castile', suggesting that her father already foresaw a role for his half-Spanish daughter in his Iberian affairs.[4] As Catalina had no brothers, she was the prospective queen regnant of Castile, and surely learnt her mother's native language from Johane Martyns and other Castilians in England including Duchess Constanza herself, as well as English and French.

John marked the first anniversary of the death of Duchess Blanche's aunt Eleanor of Lancaster, Lady Beaumont and countess of Arundel, at the Savoy on 11 January 1373. He paid the bargemen – this word appears in English in his register, otherwise kept in French – of Lambeth 3s and 4d for taking him from Lambeth to the Savoy Palace on the occasion. Ralph Stafford, first earl of Stafford, died on 31 August 1372 at the age of almost seventy-one, and Gaunt's kinsman Humphrey de Bohun, earl of Hereford, died on 16 January 1373 at the young age of thirty; John paid £4, 3s and 4d to have a thousand Masses sung for the two men's souls sometime before 24 April 1373.[5] Stafford's heir was his only surviving son, Hugh Stafford, born sometime around the late 1330s or early 1340s; Hereford's heirs were his daughters Eleanor and Mary, probably born in 1366 and 1370 respectively, who in coming years would marry Gaunt's brother Thomas of Woodstock and his son Henry of Lancaster.

Gaunt spent the feast of the Purification, 2 February 1373, at Hertford Castle, and gave 26s and 8d to the preacher John of Paris, whose sermon he evidently enjoyed greatly. He was at the Savoy on 20 March when he made a reference to 'our dearest and beloved consort the queen', and appointed a clerk to receive the money assigned to Constanza's chamber.[6] A few days later, there is a reference to King Edward paying Katherine Swynford 20 marks for bringing the news of his granddaughter Catalina of Lancaster's birth to him.[7] It is possible that Catalina had recently been born, though also possible that she had been born a few weeks or months previously, and that the payment to Katherine was only now recorded by the king's clerks. Sir Richard Scrope visited Gaunt on 25 February with his squire George, and when he departed George presented the duke with a black courser (an expensive and fast horse used for hunting, in war, or as a general riding horse for knights) as a gift from Scrope.[8] Gaunt made an indenture with Sir William Beauchamp, one of the younger brothers of the earl of Warwick, to serve in his retinue in times of peace and war on 27 February 1373. Beauchamp would be paid 100 marks a year, and had the right to have his own chamberlain and squire who would be fed at Gaunt's expense, as well as stabling and feeding for six horses and four 'boys' looking after them. The duke also hired a physician and surgeon named Brother William de Appilton, who was to be paid 40 marks a year.[9]

At the Savoy on 1 May 1373, Gaunt sent a gift of a silver cup with foot and cover to 'the young son [*joesne filz*] of the earl of Pembroke'. This was John Hastings, born on or around 11 November 1372 as the son of Gaunt's former brother-in-law John Hastings the elder and his second wife Anne Manny, and was perhaps intended as a belated christening gift (or perhaps the gift was not belated and was only recorded in Gaunt's register a few months after he sent it). Young John Hastings was born ten months after the death of his maternal grandfather Walter, Lord Manny in January 1372, and was the heir of his father the earl of Pembroke and co-heir, with his cousin John Mowbray (b. 1365), of their grandmother Margaret, countess of Norfolk.[10]

Further gifts, perhaps belated New Year gifts, went from Gaunt to his father the king, who received a gold cup with cover and with an image of a white stag lying within a crown engraved on it. John of Gaunt, never sentimental about presents, had received the gold cup as a New Year gift from his sister-in-law Joan of Kent, and passed it onto Edward III shortly afterwards. Constanza gave an enamelled silver cup, recently given to her by the prince of Wales, to her father-in-law the king around the same time. John bought two fillets, i.e. headbands made of interlaced wire, for his daughters Philippa, who had just turned thirteen, and 'our other daughter, Lady Elizabeth', who was ten. Each head covering had three balas rubies and twenty-eight pearls.

A cup made of beryl with foot and cover, previously given to John by Margaret, countess of Norfolk, went to Joan, Lady Mohun, while another cup made of beryl with foot and cover, previously given to John by Lady Mohun, went to King Edward's mistress Alice Perrers, or 'Pirers' as John's clerk spelt her name (this gift is the only occasion when Alice appears in John's extant register of 1371–75). John also sent a gold cup in the shape of a swan, previously given to Constanza by her father-in-law Edward III, to Elizabeth, Lady Ferrers. It seems that the English royalty and nobility of the late fourteenth century endlessly recycled the presents they received among themselves and were very familiar with the concept of regifting. There are numerous examples in the duke's register, and as yet another example, in his will of 1399 John of Gaunt bequeathed to Katherine Swynford a gold goblet that William Scrope, earl of Wiltshire, had given to Richard II, then Richard gave it to John. A final gift John gave in May 1373 was a gilded cup with a silver cover and engraved with a bear to an unnamed 'clerk of the king of Portugal'.[11] King Edward of England and King Fernando of Portugal (r. 1367–83) signed the Treaty of Windsor, an alliance of perpetual friendship, on 16 June 1373, and a few years later Gaunt's eldest daughter would marry Fernando's half-brother and successor to seal the Anglo-Portuguese alliance.

23

Smelts, Bumbepiper and Frysh

John of Gaunt was still at the Savoy on 20 May 1373, when he confirmed a charter to the church of St John the Evangelist in Pontefract, Yorkshire. John's father-in-law, Duke Henry, had founded a chapel on the spot close to Pontefract Castle where his uncle Thomas of Lancaster, earl of Lancaster, Leicester and Lincoln, was executed by his cousin Edward II on 22 March 1322 (Gaunt's father and grandmother Queen Isabella also founded a chapel for Thomas of Lancaster in Pontefract). John granted a few acres of land to sustain a chaplain singing Mass daily in the chapel. Houses had been built next to the hill where Thomas was beheaded, though by the early 1370s they were ruinous and about to fall down, and a hermit called William of Bingham asked Gaunt's permission to live in them, promising to mend and restore the houses. Another chapel, dedicated to St Elaine, lay close to Pontefract Castle, and by the early 1380s a female recluse lived there; Gaunt gave her two oaks from his park in Pontefract to use as firewood.[1]

John took care of his musical needs on 13 June 1373, when he made indentures with four minstrels: Hans Gough, Henry Hultescrane and the oddly named Smelts (or Smeltes/Smelltes), all pipers, and James Sauthe (or Sanche), a trumpeter. All four were contracted to perform for John whenever he wished in times of peace and war, for the terms of their lives, in exchange for a fee of 100s a year, the right to eat in Gaunt's hall and at his expense, the right to stable and feed their horses, and the right to have a 'boy' ('garçon') looking after themselves and their horses on wages of a penny a day. Gaunt also employed other pipers called Jacobe Bumbepiper and Hankyn Frysh, and another trumpeter called, appropriately enough, 'Trumpet'.[2]

One of the many lordships Gaunt held by right of Blanche of Lancaster was Kidwelly in Wales, which had passed into the Lancaster family from Maud Chaworth. John was still at the Savoy on 19 June 1373 when he sent a letter to the 'keeper of our wood of Kevengorarth in our lordship of Kidwelly'. He wrote that 'the reverend father in God and our great friend the bishop of St David's has asked us to give him some timber' to build a chantry in the church of St David's, and ordered the keeper to let the bishop have twelve oaks for the purpose. John and Duchess Blanche had given financial assistance to Adam Houghton, who served as bishop of St David's from 1361 until 1389, in his foundation of a 'college of St Mary by the cathedral church of St David's'. The ordinances and statutes of the college, providing for a master and seven chaplains, were issued on 29 July 1368, just a few weeks before Blanche's death.[3]

On 27 June, John sent a letter to the keeper of his parks in Gringley in Nottinghamshire, a manor he would give to Katherine Swynford some years later. The keeper (whose name is not given in the letter) was to deliver three '*deymes de grece*' or 'fatted deer' to Katherine as a gift from Gaunt. Another letter went out on the same day to John Stafford, the duke's receiver in Lincolnshire, who was ordered to deliver six cartloads of firewood and three oak trees for use as timber to Katherine or her attorney.[4] The gift of timber surely means that she was having some building work done on one of her houses, perhaps either in Kettlethorpe or in the city of Lincoln a few miles away, given that this order was sent to one of Gaunt's officials in Lincolnshire. John was in 'Norbourne', i.e. Northbourne near Deal in Kent, prior to crossing the Channel to France by this time and Katherine had not travelled there with him, and in fact his letter indicates that she was in Gringley. The park-keeper was to deliver the deer to Katherine '*deinz*', an Anglo-Norman word that means 'within' or 'inside' (modern French: *dans* or *dedans*), the parks there. Gringley is only 15 miles from Kettlethorpe. Katherine was perhaps pregnant with John Beaufort at the time, or perhaps he had been born fairly recently.

Gaunt wrote another letter to his receiver in Lincolnshire from Northbourne on 4 July 1373. John Stafford and Simon Simeon, the duke's steward in the county, were to ensure that the wooden buildings within Bolingbroke Castle, which were on the verge of falling down, were repaired 'in case we [Gaunt] or our dearest and beloved consort the queen come there to stay'. Two days later, Gaunt decided that Duchess Constanza should instead stay at his castle of Tutbury in Staffordshire while he travelled overseas. (Tutbury is over 60 miles from Gringley, where Katherine Swynford was, so apparently John was tactfully keeping the two women in his life reasonably far apart.) His receiver in Tutbury, Robert atte More, was to transport 300 quarters of coal to the castle, as well as 'all the trees blown down by the wind ... for fuel.' This reference to a wind strong enough to blow down trees indicates that there had recently been a harsh summer storm, and in May 1373, October 1374 and February 1375 John made other references to 'great gales of wind', which had caused a lot of damage to Tutbury Castle and had blown down trees across the south of England.

His reference to large quantities of coal to be used as fuel probably reveals that the July of 1373 was an unusually cool one and that his wife would require fires throughout her stay at Tutbury – or perhaps Constanza, raised in southern Spain and only resident in England for twenty months, was struggling to cope with the harsher English climate and still found her new country chilly and damp even in the middle of summer. It certainly does seem, though, that something rather strange was going on in the summer of 1373, as on 13 July John told his forester in the Frith in Leicestershire that he had heard how 'a great part of our game in the parks of Toulawe and Bernepark has been destroyed by pestilence'. The forester was strictly ordered not to hunt any animals in the two parks until Gaunt returned to England, unless Constanza stayed in the area and desired meat.[5] The duke was still in Northbourne, Kent, on 16 July 1373 when he sent a letter as 'Johan by the grace of God king of Castile, Leon and Toledo'. 'Because of the sincere love and affection which we have for our dearest and beloved consort the queen, Lady Constanza,' John went on, he had given her permission and licence to pardon all crimes and trespasses committed by 'rebels' in the kingdoms of Castile and Leon.[6]

In early April 1373, John had bought thirty horses in Lancashire, forty in Lincolnshire, twenty in Staffordshire, thirty in Northamptonshire and thirty in Norfolk and Suffolk. All the animals were sent to his manor of Higham Ferrers, and then to the Savoy, until he needed them for the expedition to France he was planning. Finally, they were sent to Plymouth where they would be loaded onto ships to cross the Channel. John also sent six carpenters, two masons and two ironworkers to Lancashire to repair the siege engines and 'other such things' that he kept in the county.[7] He himself intended to arrive at Plymouth on 10 May 1373 and his knights, archers and men-at-arms were sent there, but on 20 May Gaunt declared that the port and date of departure would be either Dover or Sandwich, on 11 June. He sent his squire Wadekyn de Staynton to inform all his men of the new port and date, while his clerk Elys de Sutton was put in charge of all matters relating to the men's arrival in Kent and was to pay their wages.[8]

As pious as anyone else of the era, John took his chaplains with him to France, and numerous precious items for his chapel to be used while he was overseas, including a small silver container for holy water, a silver box for the Host, and a frontal for his altar embroidered with a scene of the Crucifixion. One of the clerks of Gaunt's chapel was called Perrot de Roynes ('Perot' or 'Perrot' was a nickname for men called Peres, the fourteenth-century spelling of the name Peter).[9] Gaunt travelled to France with a large army in August 1373 and led what is known as the 'Great Chevauchée', a word which meant riding through enemy country, burning and devastating it. It lasted for five months, and the duke was outside England for nine months.[10]

24

The Lady of Woodstock

Duchess Constanza was with Edward III and Joan of Kent, princess of Wales, on or a little before 7 January 1374, when the king granted pardons to two men for murder at the women's request. Edward referred to both women as 'the king's daughter.'[1] Constanza was in her father-in-law's company again at Westminster on 13 June and for a third time on 25 October 1374, when he pardoned other men for murder 'at the supplication of the king's daughter, the queen of Castile and Leon, duchess of Lancaster'.[2] Constanza would seem therefore to have spent at least part of the year 1374 at the royal court, though must have been in her husband's company in about August that year, as she seems to have given birth to a son in *c.* May 1375, according to Jean Froissart (see page 136). She was most probably with Gaunt at Higham Ferrers in Northamptonshire on 19 July 1374, when he spent £10 on a dun-coloured palfrey for her.[3]

John finally returned to England after his many months of raiding the French countryside in April 1374, and was at Dartmouth on the 26th of that month; for his journey to his homeland from the south of France, he had hired a ship of Bordeaux belonging to a Marcelline Albertson.[4] As well as the infant probably born to Constanza in the spring of 1375, it seems that Katherine Swynford also gave birth to their second child early in 1375. It is impossible to know for certain from the surviving documentation how much time John and Katherine spent in each other's company, though the couple were certainly not together in late June 1373 when John, in Kent, ordered gifts of timber and fatted deer to be given to his lover while she was in Nottinghamshire. Gaunt was at the Savoy on 24 and 31 May, 11, 13, 18, 19 and 22 June and 9 July 1374, and at Leicester by the beginning of August. If Katherine really did give birth in early 1375, she must have been with John around late April or early May 1374, and as noted above, the conception of John and Constanza's child apparently took place some months later as well.[5]

When John was staying at the Savoy in May and June, he was physically close to Westminster and to the royal court and his wife, and John and Constanza may have spent more time together than is apparent both from the documentation that we have and from the assumption that Gaunt's passionate affair with Katherine Swynford necessarily impeded his marital relationship. It is hard to say much, or indeed anything, about John and Constanza's private relations for sure. While at the Savoy in 1374, Gaunt granted the poet Geoffrey ('Geffray') Chaucer an annuity of £10 for the rest of his life, because of the excellent service Geoffrey himself and his wife Philippa, Katherine Swynford's sister, had given to 'our very honoured lady and mother the queen, whom God pardon, and our beloved consort the queen,' that is, the late Queen Philippa and Constanza of Castile.[6] Despite her sister's affair with the duke of Lancaster, Philippa Chaucer served the duchess well and faithfully for years.

John was often in touch with his ailing brother Edward of Woodstock and with Edward's wife Joan of Kent, and sometime before 8 May 1374 the princess of Wales sent eight minstrels to perform for her brother-in-law.[7] Although John of Gaunt, judging by the evidence of his register, was perhaps not particularly close to his youngest brother Thomas of Woodstock – Thomas rarely appears in the register, and John seems not to have sent him gifts even when he sent them to almost all the other members of his family – one entry in the register does refer to Thomas. On 1 June in an unstated year, perhaps 1374 given where it appears in John's register, John ordered a large silver cup and matching ewer to be 'delivered to our beloved sister the lady of Woodstock ['la dame de Wodstok'] on her wedding day.'[8]

This must mean Eleanor de Bohun, born probably not too long before 8 May 1366, who married Thomas of Woodstock sometime before 24 August 1376 when she first appeared on record as Thomas's wife. The title 'lady of Woodstock' cannot refer to Gaunt's eldest sister Isabella of Woodstock, as she was countess of Bedford and would have been described as such in his register, and Thomas of Woodstock had not yet been granted an earldom or another title (and indeed his father the king never did give him an earldom), so it makes sense for Gaunt to refer to his new sister-in-law courteously as the 'lady of Woodstock'.[9]

Eleanor was the elder daughter and co-heir of the late Humphrey de Bohun (d. 1373), earl of Hereford, Essex and Northampton, and via her mother was a granddaughter, though not an heir, of the wealthy earl of Arundel (c. 1313–76). Owing to her extreme youth – she cannot have been more than ten and was perhaps only eight when she married Thomas, who turned twenty in January 1375 – it would be several years before her marriage to the king's youngest son could be consummated, and their first child was born in April 1382 when Eleanor was sixteen or almost. In her own lifetime, her first name was spelt Alianor or Alianore, and her younger sister Mary's name usually appears as Marie.

Eleanor de Bohun was said to be 'now of age', i.e. fourteen for a married woman, on 8 May 1380, and she and Thomas were given her share of her late father's lands on 22 June 1380 after she proved that she had come of age; her proof of age was taken in Essex, meaning that she was born in that county, probably at her father's castle of Pleshey or at his manor of Rochford. Mary's proof of age was also taken in Essex, meaning that, like her elder sister, she was born in the county. Unfortunately, neither de Bohun sister's proof of age still exists, only references to them in instructions to royal officials. If they did still exist, we would know their exact dates of birth and the location, probably the identities of their godparents, and other interesting details.

25

Floods and High Winds

A group of Castilian men named by John of Gaunt's clerk as Sir Garsie Ferand, Johan Gutierz, Ruy Gonsals, Gonsal Ferondes and Alvar Rodrugues, came to visit John and presumably Constanza as well for forty days in the summer of 1374, and arrived on 15 July. The duke paid all their expenses. Sir Juan Fernandez of Castile also sometimes appears in John's register in the early and mid-1370s, and sometime before December 1379 Juan's wife – whose name appears in English records as 'Frances' – was held in Newgate prison in London for an unspecified long period 'upon suspicion of spying'. As well as spending time with his Castilian liegemen, John of Gaunt visited William, Lord Latimer at his home sometime before 20 July 1374, and lost the large sum of 66s 8d playing dice with him. The duke was evidently a fan of dice: in February 1375, he ordered the clerk of his great wardrobe to give him almost £300 'for our privy expenses and for playing at dice'.[1] Lord Latimer was royal chamberlain from 1371, and an important member of the faction which clustered around the influential Alice Perrers.

One of Constanza of Castile's letters still exists, in French, dated at Hertford on 7 August in an unstated year, possibly 1374:

> From the queen of Castile and Leon, duchess of Lancaster, to the honoured sire, chancellor of England. Honoured sire, we beseech you dearly that you may please grant by your letters for Brother Alvaro, bearer of this letter, to the prior of the Friars Preacher [Dominicans] of Oxford, that the said brother may be received there to be a student in the university of the said city, for love of us. And may our Lord, honoured sire, have you always in his sacred keeping. Written at Hertford on the 7th day of August.[2]

Constanza, if she did not already know French when she married Gaunt, must have learned it after her marriage, and surely came to know some English as well during the more than two decades she lived in England. The English nobility of John of Gaunt's era still often spoke French, and certainly they almost always wrote in that language (when they did not, they used Latin). Over the course of the fourteenth century, however, things gradually changed, and English became more and more frequently used as a written language and as the language spoken on formal occasions. William Courtenay, archbishop of Canterbury, a great-grandson of King Edward I and the son and nephew of earls, made a speech to Parliament in English in the early 1380s, and in 1394 the earl of Arundel (b. *c.* 1347) made a formal apology to John of Gaunt in English, also in Parliament. When John's son Henry took the English throne in 1399, his speech to Parliament was made in English.

On 26 August at Ravensdale in Derbyshire, John ordered his receiver in Tutbury to demolish all the rooms at his lodge of 'Belmote' except for two situated near the kitchen, and to take the lead and timber to his castle of Kenilworth and to use them to make any necessary repairs to it. A few weeks later, John had the hall of his castle at Castleton, Derbyshire (this must mean Peveril Castle) demolished, and the lead taken to Pontefract Castle, Yorkshire. John also had the castles of Pickering and Tickhill in Yorkshire, and the castle of Newcastle-under-Lyme in Staffordshire, repaired at this time, and had his garden at Kenilworth enclosed. In or soon before November 1374, the sea flooded parts of John's lordship of Pevensey in Sussex, and the duke told his steward there to ameliorate his tenants' hardship as soon as he possibly could, whatever the cost to John. It transpired that Pevensey Castle (one of the castles the duke had received from his father in compensation for giving up his earldom of Richmond in 1372) also required repair after the floods.[3] Kenilworth, an enormous castle, frequently required time-consuming work; Gaunt's grandfather Edward II hired nine carpenters to mend the beams and joists in one of the castle towers in 1326, and it took them nine months. In February 1375, Gaunt ordered his Welsh castles of Ogmore, Grosmont, Skenfrith and White Castle ('Blaunkchastel') to be repaired as well.[4] At an uncertain date sometime in the 1370s, perhaps in 1374, Hugh Bridewode, warden of the bridge over the River Severn at Gloucester, stated that 'by excessive rising of the river and great winds,' the bridge was weakened, ruinous and 'in several places about to be lost forever.' Bridewode petitioned John of Gaunt, requesting him to use his considerable influence to ensure that Bridewode received money to repair and maintain the bridge.[5]

John marked the sixth anniversary of Duchess Blanche's death on 12 September 1374 with considerable expense, as he doubtless did every year, but a roll of the 1374 expenses fortuitously happens to survive. Among the many other provisions the duke purchased for the 'magnates' who accompanied him during the vigil to remember Blanche at St Paul's Cathedral, he paid 7*s* 6*d* for ale, 7*s* 8*d* for wine, 4*s* 6*d* for beef, 11*s* 4*d* for mutton, 8*s* 3*d* for eleven geese, and 2*s* for four piglets. The meat was flavoured with ginger, pepper and saffron. As a gallon of ale in the fourteenth century usually cost a penny, or a penny and a half for a gallon of the superior kind, John's expenditure implies the provision of either 60 or 90 gallons of ale.[6] The duke had spent a few days in August 1374 at his castle of Tutbury, where Blanche had died, and perhaps she was much on his mind while he was there.

26

Your Lusts Torture You

John was at the Savoy on 1 January 1375, when he gave the marriage rights of Robert, the heir of his deceased father Sir Robert Deincourt (or Deyncourt), to Katherine Swynford, to use for her daughter Blanche Swynford, who was most probably Gaunt's goddaughter and had almost certainly been named in honour of the late Duchess Blanche. John wrote, 'We make known that we, of our special grace, have given and granted to our dearest and beloved lady Kateryn de Swynford the custody of the lands and heir of Sir Robert Deyncourt, knight, who has been commanded to God, and the marriage of the said heir for Blaunche, daughter of the said Lady Kateryn.'

The duke also stated that young Robert Deincourt would go and live with Katherine Swynford, and that Katherine would have custody of the Deincourt lands until Robert came of age at twenty-one (he seems to have been born around 1362/64, so was probably at or close to the start of his teens in January 1375). Gaunt's clerk used the wrong French grammar in this grant, and referred to Blanche Swynford as *'file du dit Kateryn'*, in the masculine form, meaning 'daughter of the said Katherine', when it should have been written in the feminine form, *'file de la dite Kateryn'*. The duke also remembered John Maudeleyn, whose mother Hawise was Katherine's damsel, and gave him a generous cash gift of 46s and 8d.[1]

A week later the duke of Lancaster had moved on to Hertford Castle, and sent rather belated New Year presents to Gaston Fébus, count of Foix, and his brother-in-law the duke of Brittany, widower of Gaunt's sister Mary of Waltham and now married to Joan of Kent's daughter Joan Holland. The count of Foix received a gold cup formerly given to John by his brother the prince of Wales, which was carved with ostrich feathers, the prince's emblem; the duke of Brittany was given another gold cup 'in the shape of a double rose'. Edward III, at the palace of Eltham in Kent, sent his heralds to Gaunt bearing (unspecified) New Year gifts for his son, and the duke gave £45 to the heralds and to the other squires and servants of 'many lords and ladies' who brought him presents from them.[2] John was at Hertford Castle on 11 January 1375 when he sent a letter declaring that some of his liegemen from Castile were due to arrive in his lordship of Ogmore in South Wales, 'in a ship,' as he helpfully clarified (one wonders how else anyone would travel from Spain to Wales or England in the 1370s). The Castilians were returning to John certain unspecified goods belonging to him, which had been transported in the ship on an earlier occasion and had been stolen from it.[3]

On 14 January 1375, still at Hertford Castle, John wrote to his receiver in Lincolnshire, John Stafford.[4] Stafford was to purchase a cask of Gascon wine and to 'have it carried at our expense to the town [*sic*] of Kettlethorpe, to the manor of our dearest and beloved lady Katerine de Swynford, as hastily as you can, which wine we have given to the said lady Katerine, of our gift.' If Stafford could not find a suitable supply of Gascon wine in Lincolnshire, he was to substitute '*vin del Ryne*', 'wine of the Rhine', and John specified that it must be the best Rhenish wine that Stafford could find available for purchase in the county.

Given that Katherine gave birth to John's four Beaufort children throughout the 1370s, and that their second son Henry Beaufort is often assumed to have been born in 1375, it may be that this gift of wine was sent to Katherine shortly before or after she gave birth to Henry. If it was only a general gift with no particular purpose, John would probably not have told his official to buy and send the wine to Katherine 'as hastily as you can.' It is surely also significant that there are only three entries relating to Katherine in the duke's register for the year 1373, only one in the whole of 1374, then suddenly four entries in one month, January 1375. This may, therefore, give some indication as to when Henry Beaufort, who would become a bishop, a cardinal, the chancellor of England, and the wealthiest and most powerful churchman in the realm, was born. If this assumption is correct, Cardinal Beaufort was born at his mother's manor of Kettlethorpe near the beginning of 1375 and would have been baptised in the small church of St Peter and St Paul in the village, and must have been conceived almost immediately after John returned to England in April 1374 after his long absence from his homeland and from his lover; John was in the port of Dartmouth on 26 April. The duke perhaps named his and Katherine's second son, as the Beauforts' biographer Nathen Amin has suggested, in honour of his late father-in-law Duke Henry, a man he admired and respected enormously.[5] It was also, of course, the name of his beloved Lancastrian son and heir.

Presumably, if Katherine had indeed borne Henry Beaufort, all was well with herself and the infant, as John did not rush north to Kettlethorpe, as he would do on a later occasion in 1379 when Katherine most probably gave birth to another of their children there. John was at Hertford Castle on 8, 12, 18 and 23 January 1375, at the Savoy on 8, 16, 19, 21, 26 and 28 January, back at Hertford Castle on 2, 3, and 4 February, and at the Savoy between the 6th and the 28th. (The Savoy and Hertford Castle stood only 25 miles apart, so it was possible for John to travel between the two places on the same day.)[6] Perhaps, though, John subsequently travelled to Lincolnshire to see Katherine and their child; neither his itinerary nor the chancery rolls give any hint as to his whereabouts from 28 February 1375 until 14 and 24/25 April that year, when he was at the Savoy again. He was also at his London palace on 9 and 19 May, and found time while there on 25 April to order the 1,000 marks he paid annually for the expenses of his wife Constanza's chamber to be handed over to the new treasurer he had recently hired for her, William Derwent.[7]

As for Katherine Swynford herself, she was still, or again, in Kettlethorpe on 24 July 1375, when John, staying at Warden Abbey in Bedfordshire, ordered his steward in Nottinghamshire to send forty oaks to provide timber from the parks at Gringley and Wheatley to Katherine in Kettlethorpe, for her to carry out repairs to her houses there ('houses' in the plural). On 25 February 1377, John gave Katherine the two manors of Gringley and Wheatley to hold for the rest of her life; Katherine must have known Gringley quite well already, as she was staying there in June 1373, and it lay only a few miles from Kettlethorpe.[8] Katherine was certainly in Kettlethorpe in January and July 1375, and almost certainly there again in November 1379, when Gaunt spent at least three days in the village (and it is hard to imagine that the duke of Lancaster would have wished to spend time in Kettlethorpe unless Katherine was there with him).

As is apparent from Gaunt's gift of timber to her in July 1375, Katherine cared enough about Kettlethorpe to wish to repair and improve her houses there and to spend quite a lot of her time in the village, and in 1383 she received permission to make a 300-acre park 'of lands and wood' at Kettlethorpe. If she was looking after the duke's recently born son Henry Beaufort, and probably their toddler son John Beaufort as well, in the village in the mid-1370s, it makes sense that Gaunt would have wished her and them to be as comfortable there as possible. It seems that Katherine thought of the village as her home. If she did indeed give birth to at least two of her four Beaufort children at her own manor of Kettlethorpe, and did live there a lot of the time, this perhaps reveals that her relationship with Gaunt was more discreet than is commonly assumed. After all, it would have been far more comfortable for Katherine to bear her and John's children at one of the duke's luxurious castles in the south of England or at his opulent palace of the Savoy, yet it appears that she retreated to her own properties in a tiny Lincolnshire village.

The St Albans chronicler Thomas Walsingham, a very useful source for England in the late fourteenth century but who tended to be vitriolic and spiteful, claims that John of Gaunt flaunted his affair with Katherine Swynford, and that he rode around the country with her at his side holding her horse's bridle, even though his wife was also present. The chronicler calls Katherine 'an abominable temptress' and states of Gaunt 'Most wretched of men, who think you are prosperous, and believe you are blessed, look how your troubles oppress you, and your lusts torture you.'[9] As Katherine's biographer Jeannette Lucraft points out, however, many of the important English chronicles of the day do not even mention Katherine, and, contrary to Edward III's powerful and detested mistress Alice Perrers, she generated comparatively little interest among them. The exceptions are Walsingham, Henry Knighton, writing in Gaunt's town of Leicester, and the *Anonimalle*, whose writer was a great fan of Duchess Constanza and disliked Katherine intensely.[10] The lurid details given by Walsingham about John of Gaunt and his intimate relationship with his mistress may represent his intense dislike of the duke, rather being an account that is in any way accurate.

Furthermore, in his *Chronicon Angliae* which tends to be excessively vitriolic towards John of Gaunt, Thomas Walsingham does not even mention Katherine Swynford until 1378, at which point the chronicler waxes lyrical at great length about the duke's immoral and indecent behaviour.[11] John and Katherine's relationship had already lasted for six years and they had three children together by that point, and it may well be significant that news of their affair does not seem to have reached Walsingham's ears until as late as 1378. The *Anonimalle* chronicle does not mention Katherine at all until 1381/82, when the writer expresses his satisfaction at John's supposed ending of their relationship and calls Katherine a 'she-devil', and Henry Knighton likewise first mentions her when John allegedly parted from her after the Great Uprising of 1381. The chroniclers' evident ignorance of John and Katherine's affair until a good few years after it had begun surely disproves their own claims that the duke of Lancaster flaunted his mistress and their affair in public and in front of his wife, and also reveals that John and Katherine conducted their relationship with discretion.

27

Making Merry with Anjou

While John was at the Savoy on 26 January 1375, he made a large number of purchases and cleared some of his debts. He spent £19 on a gilded silver cup and matching ewer, and a gold tablet, sent as a wedding gift to his kinswoman and friend Elizabeth, Lady Ferrers, sister of the earl of Stafford. The widowed Lady Ferrers married Sir Reynald Cobham, who was a few years her junior, as her second husband, but their marriage was a short one: she died on 7 August 1375.[1] John paid £35 to Piers of Preston for 'diverse pearls bought from him and delivered to ourselves, for our own use', and £6 and 10s to Edward Ferrour (this name means farrier or blacksmith in medieval French) for three hackney horses and three saddles for John's falconers to ride and use. £7 6s went to Hankyn Kanyng for a falcon John had purchased for himself on 14 October, and Florekyn, one of John's falconers, who had bought two lanners (another type of falcon) for the duke, received £14 6s and 8d for this purchase, which included a gift of 5 marks. Walter was another of John's falconers, and spent 66s 8d on a tercel for John's own use on 25 January. Louis, count of Flanders, who many years before had been betrothed to John's eldest sister Isabella of Woodstock and who discussed John's possible marriage to his daughter Margarethe with Queen Philippa in 1368, sent a group of minstrels to perform for the duke at the feast of Candlemas (also called the Purification) on 2 February.[2]

Henry Yevele, or Yeveley, a master mason whose name is still famous today because of his work on Westminster Hall and the Tower of London, received an instalment of the almost £500 John owed to him for making the tomb of 'our dearest and beloved consort Blaunche, whom God absolve' in St Paul's. John spent over £10 on a bay horse for himself, another £7 on a palfrey for his eldest child Philippa, and 35s on a hackney horse bought from someone called 'Trumpetter', which was to be given to an apprentice falconer John had hired who was named Adam Pope. Another £20 was spent on a courser, a horse often used for hunting, and from John's purchases and debts in early 1375, it appears that he spent a great deal of time in 1374/75 hunting and hawking, perhaps even more time than usual. Hawking was a pursuit he always enjoyed greatly, and in the early 1370s his chief falconer was called Hayne. Other falconers John employed were named Arde, Florekyn, Rombald, Antony or Antoyn, Wilkyn and Reynold.[3] Two large casks of wine were sent from London to Melbourne near Derby, where Catalina of

Lancaster lived with her household. Finally, the duke repaid a loan of 2,000 marks (£1,333, 6s and 8d) he had borrowed from the extraordinarily wealthy earl of Arundel, Richard Fitzalan (b. *c.* 1313), the late Duchess Blanche's uncle-in-law, in July 1372.[4]

John of Gaunt was very unpopular in the 1370s and early 1380s; he perhaps came across to the public as haughty, distant and cold, though he may well have been warm and loving in private with people he cared about, and was always courteous and well-mannered. Something of John's unpopularity is revealed by a letter he sent to his steward of Knaresborough in Yorkshire (a town and castle he owned that had formerly belonged to his mother Queen Philippa) on 18 November 1374. He declared in the letter that 'certain people' in Knaresborough were not well disposed towards his lordship and were inclined to try to undermine his officials in the area, and thereby were being disobedient towards Gaunt himself. In spite of this, the duke proved himself capable of compassion and forgiveness: after he heard in February 1375 that many of his tenants in Knaresborough were impoverished and unable to pay the rent they owed him, he agreed to reduce the rent due from the town by a total of £3 for the coming year. The duke sent his auditor Thomas Mapleton to Knaresborough to determine how best to divide this rebate among the inhabitants.[5]

In the spring of 1375, John travelled to the town of Bruges in Flanders to take part in peace negotiations with the kingdom of France. He expected the costs of his journey to reach at least 1,000 marks (£666).[6] The *Anonimalle* chronicle says that John went to Bruges with Simon Sudbury, bishop of London (who would be elected archbishop of Canterbury later in 1375), Simon Multon, bishop of Bangor (who was both a Dominican friar and a doctor of law), and 'other wise people,' which was meant sarcastically. The chronicler grumbled that the men's visit to Bruges was made 'at excessive cost without profit', and that they made a 'marvellous truce' – another sarcastic remark – intended to be kept until 24 June the following year. Gaunt, supposedly, spent large sums of money raising hell with 'the count of Anjou, son of the king of France'. This is a reference to Louis (born in July 1339 and just a few months Gaunt's senior), who was the duke and not the count of Anjou, and was the second son of the late John II and brother of Charles V. Louis of Anjou would become the count of Provence, the land Gaunt himself had tried unsuccessfully for several years to claim, as the adopted son of Queen Giovanna of Naples, after her murder in 1382. The two royals are said to have spent every day making merry and dancing.

Supposedly Gaunt and the other envoys' visit cost £20,000 but brought England nothing, though this amount must surely be a gross exaggeration. The *Anonimalle* adds, probably with rather less exaggeration, that the duke of Lancaster's antics in Bruges made him even more unpopular than he was already.[7] It also states that the year of Gaunt's visit to Bruges saw the 'fourth pestilence' in the north of England, a reference to a fourth mass outbreak of the bubonic plague following the ones of 1348/49, 1361/62 and 1369. The chronicler's statement that there was a pestilence in England in 1375 is confirmed by a letter John of Gaunt sent to his steward in Yorkshire on 12 October that year: the duke talked of the 'danger which might arise from this present pestilence'.[8]

John stayed in Bruges with a Sir Gerard de Roulbek, who, according to John himself, did his best to make his stay in those parts agreeable and comfortable, and the duke gave Roulbek a gilded silver cup worth 10 or 12 marks and containing fifty nobles in cash. John's first cousin Albrecht von Wittelsbach, duke of Bavaria-Straubing and count of Hainault and Holland (and guardian of his unfortunate older brother Wilhelm, Maud of Lancaster's widower, still held in captivity in the castle of Le Quesnoy owing to his insanity), and Albrecht's Polish wife Małgorzata of Brzeg, were also there. John gave Małgorzata a gold cup, and his clerk recorded her name as 'Duchess Albright'. John took some splendid items with him to Bruges that a few weeks later he gave to his clerk Lambert Trykyngham: a silver cruet and two gold cruets (small containers for salt, pepper or other condiments), a gilded silver chalice and a gold chalice, two new surplices for his chaplains, an embroidered velvet cushion (his clerk wrote this word in English in the middle of the French text, '*coshyn*'), two silver basins, a silver ship for carrying incense, a gilded silver cross, a gilded silver censer (a container in which incense was burnt) and a gold pax ('*paxbrede*', a board or tablet kissed by celebrants during Mass).[9]

When John was in Bruges in 1375, according to chronicler Jean Froissart, Duchess Constanza gave birth to his son in Ghent 25 miles from Bruges, after she returned to Ghent from a pilgrimage to the abbey of St Adrian in Grammont. The infant was named John after his father and was born in the same town, but died young.[10] Assuming Froissart was correct and John and Constanza did have a son who died, the little boy's death must have been shattering for both of them. The child's existence (again, assuming that Froissart was correct that he did exist) reveals that John and Constanza maintained their intimate marital relationship despite John's ongoing intense affair with Katherine Swynford and the likely conception of his and Katherine's second son Henry Beaufort also in 1374. The duchess of Lancaster did not, as far as is known, become pregnant again after 1375, though it is possible that Constanza had miscarriages or stillbirths which did not find their way onto record, or perhaps she even gave birth to other children who died young. Or perhaps the birth of the little John of Lancaster in Ghent in 1375 was a difficult one and made it impossible for her to conceive or to carry a child again. At any rate, Catalina of Lancaster would be John of Gaunt and Constanza of Castile's only child who survived infancy, and was her mother's heir.

28

A Great Need for Money

John of Gaunt was back in England and at the Savoy on 31 May 1375, when he settled some debts, including £33 and 6s to Fensalawe van Prage ('of Prague') for two horses, one black and one dun; about £20 to a jeweller of Paris called Jacobes for fourteen pieces of silver bought from him for John's use; and another sum in excess of £46 for John's 'private expenses'.[1] John spent most of August 1375 in Leicester, then went on to Kenilworth. While he was in Leicester that August, he arranged with his receiver in the town, William Chiselden, that 'new shopping stalls' would be constructed in the town centre 'in an area called Satirdaymarketh', i.e. 'Saturday market'. The word 'shop' also appeared in English in the middle of the French text of the duke's letter, *shoppe*, and a letter which Gaunt sent in February 1372 reveals that another area of fourteenth-century Leicester, near the eastern gate, was called Swynesmarket.

The duke's interest in trade and his permission for local people to profit from selling their goods at market might have increased his popularity; a letter John wrote to two of his officials in Staffordshire also in August 1375, strictly forbidding any of the residents in the town of Tutbury to own hounds as the dogs might imperil his game in the nearby forest of Needwood, surely did not.[2] On 22 August, Gaunt ordered a clerk of his great wardrobe to send him his collar made of gold, his belt made of gold, and a hundred pounds of gold, for unstated 'certain affairs' which he had to take care of.[3] Whatever the affairs were, the duke clearly wished to look as splendid as possible while dealing with them. At the Savoy on 30 September 1375, John leased 75 acres in Pevensey Marsh, Sussex to William Batesford for a period of thirty years. The acres were in two places called 'Cowhamme' and 'Ealdelond,' which means 'Old Land' in fourteenth-century English, and the duke specified that William was leasing 'all the salts belonging to them, both within the walls and without,' from him. On 10 October the duke was back at the Savoy, and dictated a letter which reveals that he had ordered a cask of wine to be sent from Kenilworth to the palace, but that the carter in charge of transporting it had somehow managed to lose the wine.[4]

Gaunt returned to Bruges in late 1375, and stayed there again from shortly after 24 October (when he was at the port of Dover, preparing to sail across the Channel) until at least 20 January 1376. On that date, he sent a letter from Bruges to the chancellor and treasurer of England and other members of the royal council, on behalf of four merchants from Aragon in Spain who traded in Bruges and whose goods had recently been impounded by some of Edward III's officials off the coast of Brittany.[5] John failed to take sufficient cash with him on this second visit, and had to order the clerk of his great wardrobe to send him 1,000 marks from London, which William 'Wilkoc' Oke, one of the clerks of John's wardrobe, brought to him in Bruges. He also borrowed £200 from Robert Holme of York, an English merchant who traded and worked in Bruges, and Holme received his money back from Gaunt's attorney Richard Nesse on 11 December 1375. The duke had made the same error during his previous visit to Bruges earlier in the year, and dictated a letter to his 'receiver in the parts of the south' in May, talking of the 'great need for money that we have at present' and ordering £100 to be sent to him.[6]

William Bacon, mayor of Southampton, sent a letter in French on 19 January 1376 to John of Gaunt, part of which is translated here as an example of how John was accustomed, as a king's son and as the king of Castile and Leon (in name, at least), to being addressed in correspondence:

> To the very noble, very reverend and very excellent lord, his [William Bacon's] lord, Johan, by the grace of God king of Castile and Leon, duke of Lancaster, his [John of Gaunt's] humble and simple servant, as one of the poor lieges and subjects of our very dread lord, your father the king of England and France, William Bacon, mayor of Southampton, recommends himself to your very excellent lordship with all manner of honours and reverences and with all manner of obeisances. Very reverend lord, may it please your highness to know that on the eighteenth day of January I received your very high command in letters regarding Johan Peres of Quexo, that the said Johan has a ship and certain goods in the custody of his host among us, and your orders regarding this are to put them in safe custody until such time as shall be ordained otherwise, for the profit and deliverance of the said Johan … Very honourable, very reverend and very excellent lord, may the Almighty grant you a good life of long duration and victory over all your enemies. Written at Southampton on the nineteenth day of January in the forty-ninth year [of Edward III's reign].[7]

29

His Exact Image and True Likeness

England in the mid-1370s was in a fairly pitiable state, faction-riven and bankrupt after the king's lavish expenditure on wars over the last few decades, wars which brought temporary glory but little if any long-term gain. Edward III, past sixty, had grown senile and was seemingly more interested in his mistress Alice Perrers than in governing. His eldest son the prince of Wales was an invalid, often in pain and discomfort. John of Gaunt, by virtue of being the eldest living son of the king still capable of leadership and because of his enormous wealth and his vast number of followers, came to dominate politics. In opposition to him stood his nephew-in-law Edmund Mortimer (b. 1352), the earl of March and Ulster. The so-called 'Good Parliament' was held in the chapter house of Westminster Abbey from 28 April to 10 July 1376, and was the first Parliament held since November 1373. John and his younger brother Edmund of Langley attended, and according to one contemporary, John was appointed as the 'lieutenant of the king to hold Parliament' and presided over the lords' sessions. King Edward himself was too ill to attend, and his eldest son the prince of Wales was also ailing and could not participate.[1]

The atmosphere at the Parliament was one of hostility on the part of the Commons, led by their speaker Peter de la Mare, towards the king and his government. They announced that they would not participate further in proceedings unless Edward III's 'evil counsellors' were banished, meaning Alice Perrers and her faction, chiefly her husband Sir William Windsor, William, Lord Latimer, and Richard Lyons. The *Anonimalle* chronicle says that Alice received a mighty sum of £2,000 or £3,000 in gold and silver from her lover the king every year. According to Thomas Walsingham – assuming he can be trusted on this point, given his overwhelming hostility towards John of Gaunt – the duke of Lancaster haughtily responded to the Commons' demands by announcing 'Do they think that they are kings and princes in this land? Have they forgotten how powerful I am?'[2]

Afterwards Gaunt supposedly tried to reassert his authority and sought revenge on the men who had incurred his wrath during the Parliament. Supposedly, he imprisoned Peter de la Mare, the speaker of the Commons and steward of the young earl of March, in Nottingham Castle, and according to the hostile Thomas Walsingham, the duke even intended to have his head cut off in the nearby woods. Fortunately, though, Henry, Lord Percy talked him out of it.[3] On 10 July 1376, the last day of Parliament, the knights of the shire who had participated held a splendid feast. King Edward sent two barrels of wine and eight deer, and more wine was provided by the lords. Although John of Gaunt's brothers Edmund and Thomas were present, and so were the earls of March, Warwick, Suffolk and Salisbury, the duke of Lancaster himself was conspicuous by his absence.[4]

On 8 June 1376, Trinity Sunday, Edward of Woodstock, prince of Wales, died, a week before his forty-sixth birthday and after almost a decade of ill health. In his long and detailed will, he appointed 'our dearest and beloved brother of Castile, duke of Lancaster' as one of his executors. From the moment of his birth in June 1330, Edward had been heir to his father's throne, and for the previous four and a half decades, both he and everyone else had expected that one day he would become king of England on Edward III's death. Now the great prince was dead, and left only one legitimate son, nine-year-old Richard of Bordeaux. The vital question of the succession to the aged Edward III's throne arose. In 1199, when King Richard I ('the Lionheart', b. 1157) died, he left no children, and his throne passed to his youngest and only surviving brother King John (b. 1166) rather than to his twelve-year-old nephew Arthur of Brittany, posthumous son of John's elder brother Geoffrey (1158–86). Using the same principle of a brother inheriting instead of an underage nephew, a case could be made that John of Gaunt, as the eldest surviving son of the king, might take the throne in preference to the young son of his late elder brother, who had never reigned as king. However, since King John's accession in 1199, the English throne had passed from father to eldest son without a break; from John to his elder son Henry III in 1216, from Henry to his elder son Edward I in 1272, from Edward to his fourth but eldest surviving son Edward II in 1307, and from Edward II to his elder son Edward III in 1327. The system of primogeniture had become normalised and entrenched.

During the long Parliament of April to July 1376, several weeks after Edward of Woodstock's death, the commons 'prayed humbly ... that it might please their lord the king, as a comfort to the whole realm, to cause the noble child Richard of Bordeaux, the son and heir of the lord Edward ... to come before Parliament so that the lords and Commons might see and honour Richard as true heir apparent to the realm'. They talked of their grief and dismay that Edward of Woodstock had left them, but added 'nevertheless the prince was as if present and not in any way absent, because he had left behind him such a noble and fine son, who is his exact image and true likeness.'[5]

Almost certainly, this desire to have nine-year-old Richard taken before Parliament as the heir to the kingdom, which he duly was on 25 June, was the result of suspicions that John of Gaunt would try to usurp his nephew's position and rights when King Edward died. Whether John ever had such intentions is impossible to know for certain without telepathy, though it is perhaps significant that his brother the prince of Wales trusted him enough to make him one of the executors of his will, while their other brothers Edmund of Langley and Thomas of Woodstock were not mentioned. John's biographer Anthony Goodman has commented on John's unending loyalty to his elder brother the prince, and how it reveals his 'basic steadfastness and decency' that he remained so faithful to the 'haughty and querulous invalid' Edward of Woodstock became in the 1370s.[6] On the other hand, there is evidence that Woodstock called his father and his brother John to his sickbed, commended his wife Joan and their son Richard to their protection, and asked all the lords present to take an oath 'to support his child and to maintain him in his right.'[7] This would certainly indicate that the prince felt there was a possibility of his son being set aside. Whether John ever truly considered attempting to usurp his nephew's rights, the son of the much-loved brother he had served so loyally for so long, is a difficult question to answer. Perhaps his contemporaries did him a disservice by assuming that he would; or perhaps, in his heart of hearts, John of Gaunt did yearn for the throne.

30

The Heirs Male of His Body

John of Gaunt was with his father at Westminster on 22 July 1376, at his castle of Hertford on 25 July when he sent a letter to the chancellor and treasurer of England, in Nuneaton, Warwickshire, on 7 August, at the royal manor of Havering-atte-Bower in Essex with his father on 17 August, and at the Savoy on 24 November.[1] King Edward was seriously ill in the early autumn of 1376, and dictated his will on 8 October. John of Gaunt was named as the first of the ten executors.[2] Sometime afterwards, in late 1376 or in the first quarter of 1377 – the likeliest date being shortly after the king made his will – Edward made a written declaration regarding the succession to the throne after his death.[3]

Edward III's document set out the order of succession as follows: Richard of Bordeaux, son of his eldest son; his third son John of Gaunt and 'the heirs male of his body'; his fourth son Edmund of Langley and his male issue; and his fifth son Thomas of Woodstock and his male issue. In short, he excluded his granddaughter Philippa of Clarence, daughter of his late second son Lionel of Antwerp, and her descendants. It seems possible that John of Gaunt put pressure on his father to exclude his niece Philippa because she was female, and to favour himself as the eldest surviving male heir of the king. If he did, it would appear to be somewhat hypocritical, given that he claimed the kingdoms of Castile and Leon via Constanza. It does seem to be the case, though, that John of Gaunt was heir presumptive to the English throne throughout his childless nephew Richard's reign, and he was certainly Richard's male heir.

Richard of Bordeaux was invested with all his late father's titles in November 1376, an indication that his grandfather recognised him as his heir. Perhaps as a result of his illness in the last few months of his life, however, Edward III made no formal arrangements for a regency government after his death. As Edward's biographer Mark Ormrod has pointed out, perhaps the king simply trusted his son John to do the right thing and to support Richard, and time would prove that Edward was correct to do so.[4]

The last Parliament of Edward III's reign was held at Westminster from late January until early March 1377, and Gaunt's youngest brother Thomas of Woodstock, who had recently turned twenty-two, was summoned for the first time. Richard of Bordeaux, who turned ten the day before his uncle Thomas's birthday, was given permission on 26 January to open the

Parliament. According to the hostile testimony of Thomas Walsingham in his *Chronicon Angliae*, John of Gaunt laboured the elections to make sure his own supporters were returned to the assembly, and his steward Sir Thomas Hungerford was appointed as speaker of the Commons. He received palatine powers in his duchy of Lancaster, as his father-in-law Henry of Grosmont had, on 28 February 1377.[5]

Also during this Parliament, on 18 March, Gaunt was granted custody of the lands of the late John, Lord Lestrange, who had died on 3 August 1375 in his early twenties.[6] Lestrange's heir was his daughter Elizabeth (b. *c.* 6 December 1373) and she would come into her lands when she turned fourteen in December 1387. Gaunt could, therefore, look forward to enjoying all the income from the Lestrange lands in Hampshire and Shropshire for a decade, though as it turned out, Elizabeth died as a child in 1383.[7]

John Wyclif or Wycliffe (b. *c.* mid-1320s), doctor of theology from Oxford and a religious reformer, was put on trial by the nobly born bishop of London, Gaunt's kinsman William Courtenay, in early 1377, charged with seditious preaching. Wycliffe was John of Gaunt's protégé, and John stormed into St Paul's on 19 February to rescue Wycliffe during the trial, accompanied by Henry, Lord Percy. The following day, an angry mob attacked the Savoy and then headed towards the house of Sir John of Ypres, where John was dining. The duke managed to flee and crossed the Thames to Kennington, the home of his sister-in-law Joan of Kent, dowager princess of Wales. She sent three knights to the Londoners begging them, for her sake, to reconcile with John of Gaunt.[8]

31

Alice and the Rings

Henry of Lancaster, just past his tenth birthday, and Richard of Bordeaux, three months older than Henry, were both knighted by their grandfather, the king, on 23 April 1377 during the annual St George's Day celebrations. Several other young noblemen had the honour of sharing this occasion: Henry and Richard's uncle, Thomas of Woodstock; Robert de Vere, aged fifteen, heir to the earldom of Oxford; three Percys; William Montacute, the earl of Salisbury's son and heir; and John Arundel, nephew of the earl of Arundel. All these young noblemen, with the exception of twenty-two-year-old Thomas of Woodstock, were born in the 1360s. Henry of Lancaster began to be known as the earl of Derby around this time, and Gaunt usually referred to Henry as 'our son of Derby' ('*nostre filz de Derby*') thereafter.[1]

Another new knight of April 1377 was Gaunt's decades-younger half-brother John de Southeray, illegitimate son of the king and Alice Perrers. Southeray, probably now at the start of his teens, had been married off earlier in the year to the young noblewoman Mary Percy, born in 1368, a half-sister of Henry, Lord Percy and heir to her late mother's family, the Orebys. Mary strongly objected to her marriage, complaining that John de Southeray was 'plebeian' and therefore unsuitable to be her husband, and after Edward III's death the marriage was annulled and Mary married John, Lord Ros instead. John of Gaunt had perhaps attended his half-brother's wedding on 7 January 1377, at the royal manor of Havering-atte-Bower in Essex. Whether John ever had much to do with the namesake half-brother who was young enough to be his own son is uncertain, though it is surely revealing that Southeray never appears in his extant registers. Edward III granted John de Southeray a generous income of £100 a year, to be paid to his mother Alice Perrers as his guardian.[2]

Sir John Deincourt, uncle of Robert Deincourt, whose wardship John of Gaunt had granted to Katherine Swynford in 1375, was the steward of Gaunt's household in January 1386 and possibly well before. Deincourt's son and heir Roger was born in Gaunt's castle of Kenilworth on 21 May 1377, and was baptised there. At Roger Deincourt's proof of age in 1400, one of the jurors stated that he was named after his French godfather Sir Roger Beaufort, who was the brother of Pope Gregory XI (born Pierre Roger Beaufort in the diocese of Limoges in *c.* 1330, d. March 1378) and was a prisoner of John of Gaunt, held at Kenilworth in John Deincourt's custody. Gaunt had been holding Roger Beaufort in captivity since before the election of Roger's brother as Pope Gregory at the beginning of 1371. Gregory XI wrote to the English nobleman Sir Hugh Despenser, a distant kinsman of Gaunt, on 19 January 1374, asking him to intercede with Gaunt on Beaufort's behalf. The pope wrote more letters on 27 March 1375, this time to Gaunt's sister Isabella of Woodstock, countess of Bedford, and Henry Wakefield, treasurer of King Edward's household. Any pleas the two might have made to John of Gaunt to free Roger Beaufort fell on deaf ears.[3] Although it is usually assumed that Gaunt named his four Beaufort children after his French lordship, it is interesting to note the presence of a man named Beaufort at one of the duke's castles in the 1370s, and Sir Roger was an honoured and well-connected captive of the duke, not a humble prisoner to be thrown into a dungeon and forgotten. He gave his first name to the son of one of Gaunt's retainers during the baptism held at Kenilworth Castle in May 1377, so evidently was well-respected among the duke's retinue.

The knighting of 23 April 1377 was the last great public event of Edward III's reign. Just under two months later on 21 June, the king finally passed away at the palace of Sheen west of London, at the age of sixty-four, six months into the fifty-first year of his reign. Thomas Walsingham claims that only Alice Perrers was with Edward when he died, and that she stripped the rings from his fingers and fled, leaving him to die alone. This seems extremely unlikely; it is hard to imagine that the king of England was abandoned by everyone in his last moments. Jean Froissart, by contrast, says that John of Gaunt, his brothers Edmund and Thomas and his sister Isabella of Woodstock (all the king's surviving children), Gaunt's nephew-in-law Edmund Mortimer, earl of March, and his brother-in-law the duke of Brittany, were with the king when he died.[4] This seems far more probable.

Although we do not know John's reaction to his father's death, it seems highly likely that he mourned Edward sincerely. John and all his brothers had always remained on excellent and affectionate terms with their father, and unusually for a medieval king and his adult sons, there was no rebellion nor even any hint of any discord even in the difficult last few years of Edward III's long (and mostly glorious) reign. The same applies to John and his elder brother the prince of Wales, and also to John's son and heir, Henry. In later years when Henry was an adult, the two men were always close, at least as far as the record shows, and always stood firmly on the same side. John does seem to have been a caring father to all his children and to have had warm relations with them, and certainly he promoted all his sons' interests.[5] If he perhaps treated his daughters as though they existed to benefit his own interests and to marry where it suited him, he was very far from being alone in this, and by the standards of the fourteenth century, arranging excellent marriages for his daughters and making two of them queens made him an exemplar of a good father.

There is much evidence that the Lancasters of the fourteenth century were a remarkably close-knit, affectionate family who enjoyed spending time together. For example, the five married daughters of Henry, earl of Lancaster (d. 1345) continued living with their father long after their marriages, and Henry's other daughter Isabella, a nun at Amesbury Priory in Wiltshire and later its abbess, often left her convent to spend time with her father and siblings. Henry of Grosmont and his fifth sister Eleanor visited their eldest sister Blanche, Lady Wake, Eleanor also often visited the fourth sister Joan, Lady Mowbray, and Isabella the nun of Amesbury sent presents to the sixth sister Mary when she married Henry Percy. There are numerous other examples, and the next generations of Lancasters carried on the tradition of family closeness. Edward III and Queen Philippa had also been affectionate parents to all their offspring, and both John of Gaunt and Blanche of Lancaster had benefited from growing up in loving families. Constanza of Castile, with her turbulent childhood in Spain, had been rather less fortunate.

The young King Richard was probably at the manor of Kennington with his mother Joan of Kent when his grandfather died, and travelled the few miles to Sheen on 22 June.[6] At Vespers or sunset that evening, an important ceremony took place in Richard's chamber at Sheen. The keepers of Edward III's great seal formally handed it over to Richard in a purse of white leather, in the presence of, among others, John of Gaunt, the archbishop of Canterbury, the duke of Brittany, and the earls of March and Warwick.[7] If John of Gaunt ever had intended to claim the throne, and there is no evidence that he did, nothing came of it.

Within days of the old king's death, a two-year peace settlement between France and England expired (on the Nativity of St John the Baptist, 24 June), and the French, with their Castilian allies, attacked the south coast of England. The town of Rye was burnt, other towns were attacked, and the French and Castilian forces temporarily occupied the Isle of Wight. They demanded a ransom of 1,000 marks from the populace to withdraw. Over five years later in November 1382, John of Gaunt sent a letter referring to the burning and destruction of the 'hospital of Our Lady of Nazareth and Saint Bartholomew the Apostle' in Winchelsea 'by the French enemies.'[8]

Edward III's funeral cortege left Sheen on 3 July and crossed London Bridge on the same day, and the king's body lay for one night at St Paul's Cathedral - where his daughter-in-law Blanche of Lancaster had been buried nine years earlier - before being taken to Westminster Abbey on Saturday 4 July for his funeral on the 5th. Although a long delay between the death of a royal person and their interment was common in the fourteenth century, such as Queen Philippa dying on 15 August 1369 and being buried on 9 January 1370, Edward III was interred very soon after death. A huge procession accompanied the king's body through London, led by John of

Gaunt, his brothers Edmund of Langley and Thomas of Woodstock, and their nephew-in-law the earl of March. John was almost certainly the senior male member of the royal family present at the public ceremonies as it seems that Richard II did not attend them, in order to cede precedence to his late grandfather. In Westminster Abbey, black cloths were hung on the walls, and King Edward's embalmed body was lowered into the ground wrapped in red samite (a kind of rick silk cloth) with a cross of white silk placed over it.[9] His and Queen Philippa's tomb still exists in Westminster Abbey, and Philippa's lifelike effigy shows what John of Gaunt's mother looked like near the end of her life in 1369.

32

The Coronation and Curtana

Richard II's coronation was held on Thursday 16 July 1377, only eleven days after the old king's funeral. It was the first coronation in England for half a century, Edward III's having been held on 1 February 1327 – beyond living memory for most people, and thirteen years before John of Gaunt was even born. Understandably, therefore, the event generated a great deal of excitement and enthusiasm. John himself, as steward of England, was in charge of the organisation of the massive and significant event. Numerous people worked hard to ensure that everything was ready in time: tentmakers in London and Middlesex set up pavilions around the great palace of Westminster for the guests and as venues for the festivities; stonemasons, carpenters, labourers and plumbers were hired 'wherever found' (and were liable to be arrested and imprisoned if they refused to work); stone and timber were ordered; and 1,000 barrels of ale were purchased in Hull and Grimsby and transported by ship to London.[1] Sometime before the ceremony, Gaunt appeared before his nephew and the royal council, and 'as earl of Leycestre claimed the office of steward of England, as duke of Lancastre claimed to bear the king's first sword called 'Curtana' on the coronation day, and as earl of Lincoln claimed to cut and carve that day before the king sitting at table. Judgement in his favour, as tenant by the courtesy [of England] after the death of Blanche his wife, to exercise those offices by himself or by deputies'. Other members of the English nobility petitioned for their own rights to perform certain ritual duties during the coronation, and zealously performed them.[2]

The day before the coronation, 15 July, all the lords of the realm present in the capital, with the mayor and aldermen of the city, rode to the Tower of London where Richard II was staying. He came out dressed in white, with his household knights, and a great procession accompanied him from the Tower to Westminster. First came the Commons of London, then squires, then knights, then the aldermen, the mayor and the two city sheriffs. Next, rode John of Gaunt with Edmund of Langley and Thomas of Woodstock, then a long way behind them, riding on his own in solitary splendour, came the ten-year-old king. After another long interval came all the earls, barons and lords. A tower had been constructed at Cheapside, with a framework of timber covered with painted canvas, and featuring four turrets. Inside the turrets stood four 'very beautiful' girls the same age as the young king who scattered coins over Richard as he passed, and there was also a small bell tower on which was displayed an angel wearing a gold crown. The *Anonimalle* chronicle makes a point of remarking how hot the day was, and also at Cheapside, a brightly painted conduit had been built to provide red and white wine for the huge number of spectators to refresh themselves in the heat. The crowds were so enormous, especially along Cheapside in the heart of the city, that John of Gaunt and Henry, Lord Percy, riding 'tall, noble steeds,' had to cut a swathe through them for the procession to pass. The two men, however, garnered praise from the usually hostile Thomas Walsingham for their skill and 'good-tempered eloquence' in doing so. Walsingham even states that John won the favour of almost all people who had previously regarded him with 'hateful suspicion'.[3]

On the morning of the coronation, a procession of the most important people in the realm accompanied Richard into Westminster Abbey. John of Gaunt carried Curtana, the first sword, while the earl of March carried the second sword and Thomas Beauchamp, earl of Warwick, the third. Edmund of Langley and Thomas of Woodstock carried the golden sceptre and the royal rod, and the earls of Arundel and Suffolk carried the young king on their shoulders while the barons of the Cinque Ports bore a cloth of gold above him. After the ceremony that made the ten-year-old the crowned and anointed king of England, a banquet was held in Westminster Hall, and Richard knighted eleven boys and men, including his cousin Edward of York, son of Edmund of Langley and Isabel of Castile, who was just three or four years old. He also created four earls. Thomas of Woodstock finally received a title and became the first earl of Buckingham; thirty-five-year-old Henry, Lord Percy, from a proud noble family of northern England, became first earl of Northumberland; John Mowbray, also of Lancastrian descent, and not quite twelve years old, became the first earl of Nottingham; and Richard II's former tutor Guichard d'Angle became earl of Huntingdon, though as he died in 1380 he did not have long to enjoy the honour. During the banquet, ten-year-old Henry of Lancaster stood in front of his cousin Richard as the king ate, carrying the sword Curtana 'naked and drawn', a responsibility delegated to him by his father.[4]

John was at the Savoy on 20 July 1377, a few days after his nephew's coronation, when he appointed a constable and a porter of his Yorkshire castle of Knaresborough, which he had inherited from his mother Queen Philippa.[5] John and Katherine Swynford's third Beaufort child is generally assumed to have been born sometime in or around 1377, though direct evidence for this assumption is lacking. It may be that Gaunt granted Katherine the manors of Gringley and Wheatley in February 1377 because she was pregnant again or because she had recently given birth, though the timing of this grant may simply be coincidental. The couple's third child is usually assumed to have been their third son, Thomas, though in fact their only daughter, Joan, may have been the third child and may have been the infant born in or *c.* 1377. There seems to be no real evidence that Joan was the fourth and youngest child, as will be discussed in more detail below. Whenever he was born, Thomas the third Beaufort son received the name of his older half-brother Thomas Swynford, just as his older full brother Henry Beaufort received the name of Henry of Lancaster, their other older half-brother.[6]

On 23 September, still, or again, at the Savoy, Gaunt sent a letter to the chancellor, Adam Houghton, which was endorsed 'From the king and Castile and Leon, duke of Lancaster, to the honourable father in God and our great friend, the bishop of St David's, chancellor of England.' The letter makes clear that John's 'beloved cousin Duke Albrecht' had sent him a gift of two horses which had arrived at the port of London, and were currently being looked after by two men called Hugh Blok and Gilmyn until John took possession of them. John began the letter by addressing Houghton again as 'Reverend father in God and our great friend.' He told Houghton that customs officials in the city were demanding payment for the horses in the belief that the animals belonged to merchants, and added somewhat haughtily that they in fact belonged 'to us ourselves and to none other' and that he was, of course, not liable to pay duties.[7]

33

Wasted and Ruinous

John had already arrived in London in time for the first Parliament of his nephew's reign in early October 1377, or perhaps had never left the city since the coronation in July. He was one of the noblemen and bishops who set his seal to letters patent regarding a huge loan of £10,000 made to the young king by four merchants of the city, Nicholas Brembre, William Walworth, John Philpot and John Hadley.[1]

Parliament was held at Westminster, beginning, as was customary, on 13 October, the feast of St Edward the Confessor (the king of England who died in early 1066 and was later canonised). John was addressed as '*monseignour d'Espaigne, duc de Lancastre*', 'my lord of Spain, duke of Lancaster', and made a heartfelt plea to his young nephew regarding the persistent rumours of his designs on the throne:

> ...the said duke immediately rose in Parliament, and kneeling before our said lord the king, requested most humbly that he listen to him a while, concerning an important matter which touched the king himself and his own person. And he said that although the Commons had thus elected him as one of the lords to consult with them over the said matters, he would not by any means so act, if it pleased the king, until he had been exonerated of that which the Commons had wickedly said of him. For he said that although he was unworthy, he was a king's son, and one of the great lords of the realm after the king: and his person had been spoken of so malevolently, and accused of something which should rightfully be considered open treason, if it were true, which God forbid, that he had no desire to do anything until the truth was made publicly known. And further, he said that none of his ancestors, on either side, had ever been a traitor, but true and loyal. And a marvellous thing it would have been, if he were to have strayed from the tradition of his ancestors, as well by nature as for other reason; for he had more to lose than anyone else within the kingdom.[2]

Gaunt had come to an agreement with his father in June 1372 whereby he exchanged his earldom of Richmond for the castles and manors of Tickhill in Yorkshire and High Peak in Derbyshire, and in early November 1377, Richard II granted the earldom of Richmond to John IV (de Montfort), duke of Brittany, and his second wife Joan Holland, King Richard's older half-sister.[3] At some point early in his nephew's reign, perhaps as a response to the grant to Montfort, John of Gaunt petitioned Richard II requesting to be granted either his earldom back, or lands to the same value. He stated that the estates and castles he had been granted in exchange for his earldom were wasted and ruinous, and that the costs of repairing them all were 'outrageous' (though surely he, of all people, could afford it).[4]

On 19 January 1378, John received a grant of a 'new inn' that had formerly belonged to his father's now disgraced mistress Alice Perrers, which stood near the River Thames in London. He was also granted 'all the new houses also built by her adjoining the great gate of the said inn, in the parish of All Hallows the Less, in the Ropery, between the lanes called Westonlane and Woleylane.' A few months later, he gave the inn and the adjoining houses to the brother who was so close to him in age yet so much less wealthy, the earl of Cambridge.[5]

Sometime between 29 September 1377 and 29 September 1378, probably in mid-April 1378, Gaunt and Duchess Constanza visited his town of Leicester, and the mayor gave Gaunt's minstrels 6s and 8d for their performance. Another 1s and 6d was given to 'a certain minstrel of the lady duchess, by name Yevan,' who evidently was Welsh. That same year, the mayor of Leicester claimed back £3, 6s and 8d which he had spent on a horse given as a gift to Katherine Swynford, and another two £ 2 and 6d which he had paid for a 'pan of iron' also given to Katherine. This item was specified as a gift to Katherine 'for expediting the business touching the tenement in Stretton, and for other business for which a certain lord [unnamed] besought the aforesaid Katherine with good effect for the said business and besought so successfully that the aforesaid town was pardoned the lending of silver to the king in that year.' This is an example of Katherine Swynford's influence over the duke of Lancaster. A couple of years earlier, there had been another reference to Katherine in the Leicester records: the town mayor and aldermen paid 16s for wine to send to 'Lady Katherine of the duke of Lancaster' (a word is obviously missing between 'Katherine' and 'of', probably deliberately).[6]

In 1377/78, Richard II's council tried to make an alliance with Aragon, second-largest of the Spanish kingdoms and ruled by Pere IV from 1336 to 1387. The council therefore dealt with the ongoing imprisonment of Alfonso, the Aragonese count of Denia, a cousin of King Pere, who had been captured at the Battle of Nájera in 1367 by two English squires named Robert Hawley and John Shakell. These two were demanding a very high ransom for the count, as was their right, and refused all requests to set it at a lower level or to release their hostage into John of Gaunt's custody. They were imprisoned in the Tower of London in October 1377, but a few months later dramatically escaped and sought refuge in Westminster Abbey. On 11 August 1378, the constable of the Tower, Sir Alan Buxhull, shockingly broke sanctuary and entered the abbey with a group of armed men. They managed to grab John Shakell, but in the ensuing fight Robert Hawley was killed on the steps of the high altar, and a sacristan who tried to help him also lost his life. Westminster Abbey had been desecrated, and all of those involved were excommunicated by William Courtenay, bishop of London, except Richard II, his mother the princess of Wales, and John of Gaunt.[7]

34

Abusive Words Touching the Duke

Sometime before July 1378, John of Gaunt purchased the marriage rights of the young earl of Nottingham, John Mowbray, then at the beginning of his teens, from Mowbray's maternal grandmother the countess of Norfolk. Gaunt also purchased Mowbray's wardship from Henry Percy, earl of Northumberland. John Mowbray seems to have lived in Gaunt's household from 1380 to 1382, but died in early 1383 at the age of seventeen, still unmarried and childless, leaving his younger brother Thomas (probably born in March 1367) as his and their parents' heir.[1] Thomas Mowbray, later the first duke of Norfolk, would loom large in the lives of Gaunt and his son Henry in the late 1390s. Another young nobleman in Gaunt's wardship in the 1370s was Sir Hugh Hastings of Elsing and Gressenhall in Norfolk, who attained his majority (twenty-one) shortly before 2 February 1375. Gaunt politely addressed Hastings as his 'dearest cousin' in 1386 when the younger man accompanied him to Spain and Portugal.[2]

The year 1378 saw the start of a period of European history known as the Great Schism, when two popes were elected in strict opposition to each other, one in Rome and the other in Avignon. Each was convinced that the other was an antipope and even the Antichrist. The pope in Rome was Urban VI, born Bartolomeo Prignano; the pope in Avignon was Robert of Geneva, who took the name Clement VII. The Schism divided Europe along pre-existing political lines: England and its allies supported the Rome pope, while France and its allies supported the Avignon pope. A letter John of Gaunt wrote in early March 1380 reveals the English attitude, as he referred to the Rome pope as 'our very holy father the pope, Urban VI.'[3] The English always referred to Clement as the antipope, and the official position nowadays of the Catholic Church is that the Avignon popes, Clement VII and his successor Benedict XII, born Pedro Martínez de Luna y Pérez de Gotor, were indeed antipopes.

This unusual situation of two popes was to bring the young King Richard a bride, Anne of Bohemia. Anne's half-brother Wenzel, king of Germany and Bohemia, stood on the same side of the papal divide as King Richard and his council and subjects, and thus envoys were sent to Wenzel in Prague to discuss his sister's marriage into England. Anne and Wenzel were two of the children of the Holy Roman Emperor, Karl IV, who died in November 1378 and who had always taken the side of France. Karl was a godson of

Charles IV (d. 1328), his father King Johann 'the Blind' of Bohemia was killed at the Battle of Crécy in 1346 fighting with Philip VI against Edward III and Edward of Woodstock, his first wife Blanche de Valois was a half-sister of Philip VI, and his sister Bonne (née Jutta) married Philip VI's son and was the mother of Charles V and his siblings. Had the Great Schism not happened and had the young King Wenzel not supported the Rome pope, a daughter of Karl IV would probably never have been considered as Richard II's queen.

At Leicester Castle on 4 October 1378, John gave his mistress Katherine Swynford permission to 'cut down woods belonging to the duke's manor of Enderby in Leicester chase, and to sell and carry this wood wherever she wishes and to use the profits for her own use, without hindrance of the duke or his heirs'.[4] Parliament was, most unusually, held in Gloucester in the autumn of 1378, from 20 October until 16 November; this was the first time it had been held outside London or Westminster for decades. Thomas Walsingham in the *Chronicon Angliae* claims that John of Gaunt insisted on the session taking place far from London because he believed the citizens of the city would interfere with proceedings.[5] While in Gloucester, Gaunt might have taken the opportunity to visit the magnificent tomb and alabaster effigy of his grandfather Edward II in the Benedictine abbey of St Peter, which became Gloucester Cathedral after the Dissolution, and was where the sessions of Parliament were held on this occasion. Throughout Richard II's reign, the young king made strenuous, though ultimately unsuccessful, efforts to have Edward II canonised as a saint; he was all too aware that he took after his great-grandfather far more than he did his father and his grandfather, and the canonisation of the deposed and disgraced king as a saint would work in his political interests. Gaunt petitioned the 1378 Parliament for 'the right to have for life an exchequer in his county palatine of Lancaster, with the same customs and usages as the king's exchequer,' and on 10 November this was granted.[6]

A number of petitions were presented against the late king's mistress Alice Perrers at the October 1378 Parliament, one of them by John of Gaunt's servant Peter Peterwych, who claimed that Alice had intruded into several of his properties in Middlesex. Alice had even taken lands which rightfully belonged to Gaunt's eldest sister Isabella of Woodstock, countess of Bedford, and Isabella, on the grounds that her husband Enguerrand de Coucy had left England and that she was now in effect a single woman, requested her powerful brother the duke of Lancaster's aid as well as that of the young king's council in recovering her manors.[7] On 8 November 1378 while Parliament was taking place in distant Gloucester, Thomas Knapet, a clerk who worked in the church of St Peter the Less near St Paul's Wharf ('Pouleswharf') in London, was arrested by the mayor of London and John Boseham, one of the two city sheriffs, for 'having used abusive words touching the duke of Lancaster in the house of John Shepeye and in the presence of Thomas Hiltone and other servants of the said John.' Knapet was sent to Newgate prison in London 'until he could purchase the duke's favour and that of the City.' He was afterwards released on surety.[8]

Parliament was held again from 24 April to 27 May 1379 at Westminster, and John's brother Thomas of Woodstock, earl of Buckingham, was appointed constable of England. Enrique of Trastámara, king of Castile, died on 29 May 1379 at the age of forty-five. The throne which John of Gaunt and Constanza of Castile considered rightfully theirs passed to Enrique's son, twenty-year-old Juan. On 25 July 1379, John was at Pontefract in Yorkshire, and it was almost certainly on this date that he granted custody of the lands belonging to the late Bertram de Sauneby to Katherine Swynford. He also gave her the wardship of Sauneby's son and heir, and stated that the grant was owing to the 'good and agreeable service' Katherine had performed, or was still performing, in her role as *maistresse* to Gaunt's daughters Philippa and Elizabeth.[9] As Simon Walker has pointed out, John gave Katherine the most lucrative wardships he had available, and the Sauneby grant came on top of the Deincourt wardship he had already given her in 1375.[10] In 1381, he was to give her custody of the lands and the marriage rights of Sir Elys de Thoresby's heir as well.

It seems likely that Katherine was pregnant again in 1379 with her and John's youngest Beaufort child. John was at his Warwickshire castle of Kenilworth from 1 November that year or earlier until 8 November or later.[11] On 14, 15 and 16 November, however, he dated several letters and orders at Kettlethorpe ('Keteltorp'), 100 miles away.[12] This implies that John rushed to Kettlethorpe with some haste, most probably because Katherine Swynford had borne one of their children there. This was perhaps Thomas, their fourth child and third Beaufort son. It seems unlikely to have been Joan, their only daughter, who is often stated to have been born in 1379 (albeit on no evidence), as Joan married in or around March 1392 and gave birth to her first child sometime between December 1392 and August 1393, and is most unlikely to have become a mother at the age of only thirteen. It is far likelier that Joan was born *c.* 1376/77. Assuming that Thomas Beaufort was indeed born in Kettlethorpe in November 1379, he must have been baptised in the small church dedicated to St Peter and St Paul which still stands in the village, and where his elder brother Henry Beaufort, if he was born in January 1375, would also have been baptised. It might have been a difficult birth, perhaps another factor in John of Gaunt's hasty journey to Kettlethorpe; Katherine was now in or approaching her late thirties, and she would have no more children.

The duke of Lancaster gave a wedding gift to a child couple in early November 1379 a little while before he dashed off to rural Lincolnshire: Edmund of Langley and Isabel of Castile's only daughter Constance of Cambridge, who was the niece both of Gaunt himself and of his wife Constanza, married Thomas, heir of the Despenser family.[13] Constance was no more than about five years old and was perhaps only three, while Thomas, born in September 1373, was six. He was a descendant of Edward I, and was heir to his wealthy and popular late father, Edward, Lord Despenser (d. November 1375), who had attended Lionel of Antwerp's wedding in Italy in 1368 and had spent much time with Gaunt in the 1360s and early 1370s. Thomas's uncle Henry Despenser was bishop of Norwich from 1370 until 1406, and would fall out with John of Gaunt in 1383 (and would also fall out with John's son Henry IV on several occasions at the end of the 1300s and the beginning of the 1400s). After his visit to Kettlethorpe, Gaunt returned to Kenilworth and spent the New Year of 1379/80 there, and while staying in the castle, granted his confessor Brother Walter Dysse an annuity of £10 for the rest of his life in gratitude for his good service, on top of another annuity of £10 he had previously granted Dysse. Gaunt requested that Dysse continue to act as his confessor for as long as he was able to work.[14]

35

Elizabeth's Seven-year-old Bridegroom

On 19 January, almost certainly in 1380, though his clerk wrongly dated the entry to 1379, the duke of Lancaster was at the Savoy, and acknowledged that he owed seven thousand florins to his cousin Albrecht von Wittelsbach, duke of Bavaria ('le duc Albert de Bayuere'). This money was for the ransom and deliverance of Sir Michael de la Pole, Sir Simon Burley (whom Gaunt's clerk, having a bad day, mistakenly named as 'Sir John Burley') and Sir Gerard del Isle or Lisle.[1] These men were the envoys sent to Wenzel, king of Germany and Bohemia, to negotiate Richard II's marriage to Wenzel's younger half-sister Anne of Bohemia, and they had been captured in Dordrecht and were being held for ransom. In their acknowledgement of the money, £2,100, they in turn owed John of Gaunt for their liberation, the men referred to his palace as 'his manor of Sauvoye in the suburbs ['*suburbes*'] of London.'[2]

A week later, on 26 January 1380, Duchess Constanza was with Richard II or with the royal council at Westminster, when a man was pardoned for murder at her request.[3] Whether she had spent the festive season at Kenilworth with her husband is unclear, though apparently Constanza was with John in January 1380, as he also was at Westminster, attending the Parliament which was held there from 16 January to 3 March 1380. Bad winter weather and torrential rain prevented some of the men summoned to Parliament from reaching Westminster on time, though in the end proceedings began only a day late.[4] If Katherine Swynford had indeed borne one of John's children around mid-November 1379, she may have preferred to remain at home in Kettlethorpe with the infant rather than travel the 150 miles south to London/Westminster in the depths of a hard winter. She would have been off limits to John until she was purified forty days after giving birth, so they could not have resumed their intimate relations until Christmas or thereabouts. John stayed at the Savoy during at least some of the long but uneventful Parliament held at Westminster in early 1380. While at the palace in February, he acknowledged a debt of 500 marks to Richard Fitzalan, earl of Arundel (the younger, born *c.* 1347) and John Philpot of London. A few weeks later, the duke borrowed another 1,000 marks from William Wykeham, the long-serving bishop of Winchester (Wykeham held the position from 1366 to 1404).[5]

The duke turned forty on 6 March 1380, and the following day, his nephew the king (or rather, the royal council) gave him permission to mint his own coins in Bayonne, Dax or anywhere else in Les Landes from the coming 1st of August for two years.[6] Easter Sunday fell on 25 March in 1380, which was the late Blanche of Lancaster's birthday and was also the feast of the Annunciation. On 1 May, Gaunt hired carpenters to construct a new chamber, several houses, a chapel, and various unspecified 'enclosed areas' within Hertford Castle. His master carpenter William de Wyntringham from Southwark was hired to take charge of the work, and promised that it would all be finished at the feast of the Nativity of St John the Baptist in three years, i.e. by 24 June 1383. William would receive £440 for the work, and as a bonus he would also be allowed to keep the timber of the houses already standing in the castle keep, which were to be demolished.[7]

As is often the case in John of Gaunt's register, some of the words relating to the work Wyntringham and his men would have to do were written in English in the middle of the French text in which the rest of the entry was written: *esteyres* (stairs), *lathying* (making and fitting laths, i.e. planes or boards of wood), *tyling* (tiling), and *daubyng* (daubing, i.e. plastering). Also in the early 1380s, Gaunt was having a new outer wall and a new gatehouse with a vaulted roof, a portcullis and a staircase built at his remote castle of Dunstanburgh on the coast of Northumberland, by masons named Henry de Holme and John Lewyn. Additionally, Holme was to build six houses, each with its own chimney, inside the castle keep. The word 'gatehouse' also appears in English (with the same spelling as in modern English) in the duke's register, as do *frestone* and *freeston* for 'free-stone'.[8]

The wedding of the duke's second daughter Elizabeth of Lancaster and John Hastings, heir to the earldom of Pembroke, took place at Kenilworth Castle on 24 June 1380. Gaunt gave his daughter a gold ring as a wedding gift, and had perhaps been planning young John's marriage to Elizabeth for a while – his father had granted him the rights to the boy's marriage on 16 September 1376.[9] The advantages of the marriage to Gaunt and his family were obvious. John Hastings was not only heir to an earldom and a wealthy inheritance from his late father (d. 1375), he was the maternal grandson and co-heir, with his cousin John Mowbray, earl of Nottingham, of Margaret, countess of Norfolk. As a great-great-grandson of Edward I, John was of royal descent and well-connected to most of the English nobility.[10] Unfortunately for Elizabeth of Lancaster, however, John Hastings was born on around 11 November 1372 and was a decade younger than she was. He was just seven years old when he married Elizabeth; she was seventeen.[11] That the duke of Lancaster arranged Hastings' marriage to Elizabeth rather than to Catalina, who was exactly the same age as the boy, surely confirms that Gaunt foresaw a possible marriage into Castile for his half-Castilian third daughter.

Gaunt's need for allies in England and his desire to hold his third daughter in reserve to benefit his Iberian affairs had condemned his second daughter to remain a virgin until she was at least twenty-four, perhaps twenty-six years old. Time would reveal that Elizabeth was unwilling and unable to wait this long, and it was indeed unusual for a fourteenth-century noblewoman to be married to someone this many years her junior. It was also unusual for the duke of Lancaster's eldest child Philippa to be still unmarried at the age of twenty, but the age gap between Philippa and John Hastings was almost thirteen years, so she was even more unsuitable than her younger sister to be the boy's bride. Gaunt was presumably also intending to use the marriage of his eldest daughter to further his interests in the Iberian Peninsula or elsewhere. After the June 1380 wedding, Gaunt referred to Elizabeth as 'our daughter of Pembroke,' and continued to pay £100 annually for the 'expenses of her chamber and wardrobe'. He also paid 40 marks a year to stable and feed Elizabeth's horses.[12] Her little husband, meanwhile, almost certainly remained in the care of his mother Anne Manny, dowager countess of Pembroke, for the time being. Anne and her mother Countess Margaret of Norfolk had been granted joint custody of John in early 1376, a few months after his father's death. On 8 July 1384, a few weeks after Anne died, Margaret was granted sole custody of her grandson 'for five years after he attains the age of twelve,' which he did in November 1384.[13]

1. Sint-Baafskathedraal or St Bavo's Cathedral, Ghent, Belgium, where John of Gaunt was born on 6 March 1340 when it was still the abbey of St Bavo. (Bvi4092 on Flickr under Creative Commons 2.0)

2. Portrait of John from the late sixteenth century, often attributed to the artist Lucas
Corneliz and possibly a copy of an earlier portrait. (Public domain)

3. Kenilworth Castle, Warwickshire, one of the places most strongly associated with John of Gaunt. (Tony Hisgett on Flickr under Creative Commons 2.0)

4. Part of Hertford Castle, which John received as a gift from his father in 1360 and where he spent much time in the 1380s and 1390s. His grandmother Queen Isabella died here in 1358. (Peter O'Connor on Flickr under Creative Commons 2.0)

5. The Alcázar or Royal Palace in Seville, southern Spain, built by King Pedro 'the Cruel', and most probably where his daughter and heir, Gaunt's second wife Constanza of Castile, spent most of her childhood. (Author's collection)

6. Windsor Castle, birthplace of John's father Edward III in November 1312, and where his mother Queen Philippa died in August 1369. (Tony Hisgett on Flickr under Creative Commons 2.0)

Above: 7. Ruins of Bolingbroke Castle, Lincolnshire, birthplace of John's son and heir Henry IV in April 1367. (Author's collection)

Right: 8. John of Gaunt and Blanche of Lancaster's tomb in Old St Paul's Cathedral, destroyed in the Great Fire of London in 1666. (Public domain)

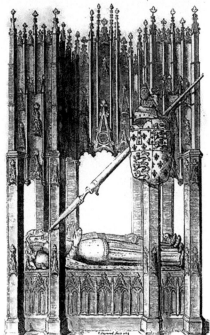

9. St Paul's Cathedral today. (Author's collection)

10. 'John of Gaunt's Gateway' at Tutbury Castle, Staffordshire, where Duchess Blanche died in September 1368. (Stevep2008 on Flickr under Creative Commons 2.0)

11. Roquefort, Les Landes, France, where John married his second wife Constanza in September 1371. (Wikimedia Commons)

12. An oriel window in the east gate of Lincoln Castle, removed and replaced here in 1849 during the reconstruction of a building called John of Gaunt's Palace, a fourteenth-century merchant's house and possibly where John stayed during his visit to Lincoln in 1386. (Author's collection)

13. Lincoln Cathedral, where John married his third wife Katherine Swynford in 1396, and where she and their daughter Joan Beaufort, countess of Westmorland, were buried. (Author's collection)

14. The church of St Peter and St Paul in Kettlethorpe, Lincolnshire, where some of Gaunt's Beaufort children may have been baptised in the 1370s. (Author's collection)

15. A fourteenth-century archway in Kettlethorpe that John and Katherine would have known. (Author's collection)

Above: 16. The Lincolnshire village of Coleby, a Swynford manor held by Katherine in dower from 1372 to her death, with the spire of All Saints church; in the fourteenth century Coleby was 'stony and out of cultivation'. (Author's collection)

Left: 17. John's elder brother Lionel of Antwerp, duke of Clarence and earl of Ulster (1338-68). (Public domain; nineteenth-century drawing of his statuette on his father's tomb)

ſch̃mmẽ ſde ꝟallozi̇ · fẽmme ſde Ǵmielamɑ Cõnte ſde Hꝛꝛnꝛ

18. John's maternal grandmother Jeanne de Valois, countess of Hainault and Holland (d. 1352), granddaughter of Philip III of France and sister of Philip VI. (Public domain)

19. Lancaster Castle, the great fortification which still stands in the county town of Lancashire, the town which gave John his chief title. (Andrew on Flickr under Creative Commons 2.0)

20. The gatehouse of Lancaster Castle, called John O'Gaunt Gate. (Stephen Gidley on Flickr under Creative Commons 2.0)

21. The monastery of Santa Clara de Astudillo, founded in 1354/56 by Constanza of Castile's mother Maria de Padilla. (Rubén Ojeda on Wikimedia Commons)

22. The Royal Chapel of Seville Cathedral, burial place of Constanza's parents Maria de Padilla and King Pedro, with the Giralda Tower behind. (Author's collection)

Mutiny in Portugal

King Fernando and Queen Leonor of Portugal promised on 15 July 1380 to assist John of Gaunt's brother the earl of Cambridge during the earl's forthcoming campaign against King Juan of Castile in Portugal on John's behalf. They agreed that their daughter Infanta Beatriz, who was Fernando's only surviving legitimate child, should marry Edmund of Langley's son Edward.[1] Both children were born c. 1373/74. Edmund of Langley departed for Portugal in May 1381 and remained outside England until late 1382, but unfortunately, his expedition to Portugal was an embarrassing failure, and in John of Gaunt's will written in early 1399, John refused any financial liability for it whatsoever (revealing that almost twenty years later, the expedition had not yet been fully paid for). By June 1382 Edmund's army was reduced to just a thousand men, none of whom had been paid since the previous autumn. Many died of malnutrition and there was widespread discontent with the earl of Cambridge's leadership.[2]

In May 1382, the soldiers mutinied, and their leader was none other than Edmund of Langley and John of Gaunt's much younger half-brother John de Southeray, illegitimate son of Edward III and Alice Perrers, who was barely out of his teens at the time and was the rejected husband of the earl of Northumberland's half-sister Mary Percy, Lady Ros and Oreby.[3] John de Southeray disappeared from the English record after 1384 and perhaps died young, or perhaps he made a new life for himself away from England. Jean Froissart incorrectly called him the 'bastard brother of the king of England,' meaning Richard II, rather than Richard's uncle, as Southeray in fact was. Probably, Froissart confused John with Sir Roger de Clarendon, who was an illegitimate son of the late prince of Wales and really was King Richard's half-brother.[4] Perhaps Froissart was also confused on this point because Southeray was much closer in age to his nephew Richard II than he was to his half-brothers John of Gaunt and Edmund of Langley, and because none of Edward III's many sons became king of England.

In France, meanwhile, King Charles V died on 16 September 1380 in his early forties, leaving his elder son Charles VI, born in December 1368 and not yet twelve, to succeed him. As was the case with his near-contemporary Richard II, the young French king had plenty of uncles: his father's younger brothers the dukes of Anjou, Berry and Burgundy, and his mother's brother the duke of Bourbon, who was also the brother of the late King Pedro's tragic wife Blanche de Bourbon. In the summer of 1385, Charles married the half-German and half-Italian Isabeau of Bavaria.

Sometime after 29 September 1380, the feast of Michaelmas, John of Gaunt was sent to Scotland to treat with the Scots, and made a truce between the two kingdoms to last until 'the day of the Trinity' the following year, i.e. 9 June 1381. On 18 October 1380 at Newcastle-upon-Tyne ('Noef Chastelle sur Tyne'), John called himself 'lieutenant of our very dread lord the king in the parts of the Marches towards Scotland,' having been appointed as such on 6 September 1380.[5] The duke was at the mighty castle of Bamburgh, Northumberland, a dozen miles north of his own castle at Dunstanburgh, on 25 October. On the 28th, still at Bamburgh, John granted safe conduct for four important Scottish lords and bishops to travel to Berwick-on-Tweed with a retinue of 200 people to meet him. The men were the bishop of Glasgow, the chancellor of Scotland, the earl of Mar and the lord of Galway, and they were to stay in Berwick until 4 November 1380. John received instructions for the Scottish meeting on 1 October, and was empowered to defend the realm in case the negotiations failed and the Scots invaded England.[6] John missed the Parliament held at Westminster in November 1380, which was, like the one held earlier that year, uneventful, except that those present unwittingly set off a chain of events which would lead in a few months to the Great Uprising when they decided to levy the unfair and grossly unpopular poll tax for the third time.

Whatever the nature of John of Gaunt's personal relationship with his wife, and whether they spent much time together or not, Constanza of Castile continued to play at least some role in English political life: she was in the company of Richard II or his council at Oakham Castle in Rutland on or a little before 2 November 1380, when her husband was far to the north in Berwick-on-Tweed. The duchess successfully requested a pardon for a man accused of murder.[7] Gaunt's extramarital relationship with Katherine Swynford also continued. On 20 January 1381, at his castle of Leicester, he gave custody of all the lands and tenements of the late Sir Elys or Elias de Thoresby, with the marriage rights of John de Thoresby, Elys's son and heir, to Katherine.[8] John made a rare visit to the county of Lancashire in early 1381, and dated a letter to the 'surveyors and controllers of the poll tax' in the county at Lancaster on 17 January.[9]

37

He Never after Loved the Duke

By early February 1381, John was back in the south-east of England, and on or about 5 February, attended the wedding of his son and heir Henry of Lancaster. Henry married his second cousin Mary de Bohun at Rochford in Essex, a manor belonging to Mary's mother Joan, dowager countess of Hereford, Essex and Northampton, who had helped to arrange the match. Richard II had granted Mary's marriage to Gaunt on 27 July 1380 in exchange for a due payment of 5,000 marks, of which John did not have to pay a penny as the king owed far more to him in war wages.[1] Henry's cousin King Richard and their uncle Edmund of Langley, earl of Cambridge, both sent minstrels to perform for the young couple; Richard sent ten and Edmund sent four, a couple of months before he departed on his disastrous expedition to Portugal. The bridegroom's older sisters Philippa and Elizabeth both attended the wedding and each gave their new sister-in-law a goblet and ewer. Gaunt himself gave Mary a ruby, and paid for the wedding and all the festivities.[2]

Born in April 1367, Henry was thirteen going on fourteen years old, and almost certainly, Mary de Bohun was only ten at the time of their wedding. It is highly likely that she was born not too long before 22 December 1370, as on 22 December 1384 she and Henry were given her share of her late father's lands after she proved that she had come of age, i.e. fourteen for a married woman.[3] She was thus about three years and eight months younger than her new husband, and about four years and eight months younger than her sister Eleanor, countess of Buckingham. Owing to her extreme youth, Mary would remain with her mother for several more years: Richard II granted Countess Joan £40 annually for her daughter's upkeep while Mary remained with her, and John of Gaunt also promised to pay 'our very dear and very well-beloved cousin Lady Johanne Boun [Bohun]' an annuity of 100 marks until Mary turned fourteen. This payment was supposedly due to begin on 5 February 1382, though this is most probably a scribal error by one of Gaunt's clerks for 5 February 1381.[4]

John of Gaunt's brother Thomas of Woodstock was already married to Mary's elder sister Eleanor de Bohun, and according to Jean Froissart, Gaunt abducted Mary against Thomas and Eleanor's wishes while Thomas was absent in Brittany, i.e. sometime between July 1380 and May 1381. Supposedly, the couple had wished her to enter a convent of the order of Poor Clares so that they could enjoy all of the large de Bohun inheritance rather than merely half of it (or rather a third of it, for the time being, as the dowager countess was entitled to hold a third as dower until her death, and Countess Joan ended up outliving both her daughters by many years).[5] Froissart states that as a result of losing a half of the large de Bohun inheritance to his nephew Henry and sister-in-law Mary, Thomas of Woodstock 'became melancholy, and never after loved the duke of Lancaster as he had done hitherto'.[6] It is possible that John and Thomas had never been particularly close anyway, perhaps owing to the large age difference between them; Thomas only rarely appears in John's register, and it is interesting to note that John does not seem to have purchased presents for his youngest sibling even on the occasions when he purchased them for the rest of his family.

Although it is sometimes stated that Mary gave birth to a child in 1382 when she was little more than a child herself, this is based on a misunderstanding. The child born in April 1382, assumed to be Mary's son, was in fact her nephew Humphrey of Buckingham, eldest child of Eleanor de Bohun and Thomas of Woodstock. Humphrey was John of Gaunt's nephew, not his grandson.[7] Henry of Lancaster and Mary de Bohun's first child Henry of Monmouth, later King Henry V, was born in September 1386 when Henry was nineteen and Mary most probably fifteen years and nine months old. Given that it seems highly likely that Mary was born in late 1370, she was eleven years old when her nephew Humphrey was born in April 1382, and would have been only ten when he was conceived in or around July 1381; it is therefore physically impossible that she could have been his mother.

John of Gaunt seems to have been in the company of his nephew the king, or at least with other members of the royal council, on or a little before 8 February 1381 a few days after his son's wedding, when two grants made by his late brother the prince of Wales to a knight named Thomas de Felton, a former seneschal of Aquitaine, were inspected and confirmed. Felton's widow Joan had petitioned Gaunt requesting that she should be given the lands she and Felton had jointly owned, on the grounds of the 'great oppressions and hardships Thomas de Felton endured' in Gaunt's service.[8]

Thomas of Woodstock, earl of Buckingham, had been sent to Brittany on the king's business in July 1380, and as he was the constable of England, he gave John of Gaunt the power to appoint a deputy to act for him during his absence. John was at the Savoy on 9 February 1381 when he finally did so, appointing Sir Robert de Asschton or Ashton.[9] The duke had travelled on to Hertford Castle by 16 February, when he gave his servant William de Thorneby a house and market stall in the town of Hertford 'which a certain Maude called "Godegibbewyk" used to hold from the duke [of Lancaster], but which now belongs to him because Maude died and was a bastard.' Easter Sunday fell on 14 April in 1381, and on that day John spent just under £30 on two dappled-grey coursers for his own use at his Yorkshire castle of Pontefract.[10]

On 4 May 1381, at the Savoy, Gaunt acknowledged receipt of the sum of £50 from Katherine Swynford, who had spent that amount on pearls for herself and the duke's daughter Philippa of Lancaster, now twenty-one. Gaunt's barber, Godefrey, delivered the money to him from Katherine, which suggests that the couple were not in each other's company at the time.[11] In the early 1380s, Gaunt negotiated a possible future marriage for Philippa with Wilhelm, count of Ostrevant, son and heir of Gaunt's cousin Albrecht von Wittelsbach, duke of Bavaria. Born in 1365, Wilhelm was five years Philippa's junior. In the end, the marriage never took place, and Wilhelm of Ostrevant married Marguerite of Burgundy, daughter of Duke Philip of Burgundy and Margarethe of Flanders, in Le Quesnoy in April 1385. John of Gaunt, on hearing of this, became 'thoughtful and melancholic,' according to Froissart, and sent a delegation to Le Quesnoy to register his displeasure. However, John received a sharp reply from the cousin with whom he usually enjoyed excellent relations (and who had sent him a gift of two horses in 1377). A clearly annoyed Duke Albrecht informed John that just as he would not presume to concern himself with the marriages of John's children, neither was it John's place to poke his nose into the marriages of Albrecht's children.[12]

38

An Almost Infinite Variety of Objects

John was at Hertford Castle on 6 May 1381, travelled to Scotland sometime that June, and on 28 and 29 June met John Stewart, earl of Carrick, eldest son of the long-lived King Robert II (who died in 1390 at the age of seventy-four).[1] Although Gaunt could not have known it, this journey to the north and his absence from the south-east of England was almost certainly to save his life. Fourteenth-century England was not an ideal place to be alive. Endless rain in the first half of the second decade led to the Great Famine of 1315 to 1317, then three decades later came the catastrophic first outbreak of the Black Death, followed by smaller, yet still horrible and deadly, outbreaks every few years. At the beginning of the 1350s, Edward III's government capped post-plague wages at pre-plague levels, meaning that workers were not able to benefit from the sudden and drastic shortage of labourers, which understandably caused much discontent. The endless wars in France meant that England was full of wounded or maimed former soldiers who, given that social welfare of course did not yet exist, had little choice but to beg for food and shelter. Throughout the fourteenth century, rates of violent crime and murder rose inexorably and reached levels barely seen in the modern world except perhaps in warzones.[2] Richard II's government unwittingly set a match to the powder keg in 1380 by levying, for the third time, the ludicrously unfair poll tax, which charged everyone, rich and poor, at the same rate and thus fell hardest on the poor. John of Gaunt, with an annual income of around £12,000 gross, would pay the same amount as a labourer trying to support his family on barely £3 a year. It was absurd, and resentment grew.

Throughout the first few months of 1381, tax collectors had extraordinary difficulties gathering the due payments, and in London did not even try for fear of inciting mass unrest. The widespread though as yet unfocused rage found a leader in Wat Tyler, and another famous leader of what became known as the Peasants' Revolt, or the Great Uprising, was the firebrand preacher John Ball. Bands of protestors in Kent and Essex began committing acts of civil disobedience and protest, and also burned legal documents, court rolls and even property belonging to hated tax collectors and local office holders. While the duke of Lancaster was travelling north towards Scotland, large groups of people assembled and marched towards London. On or about 9 June 1381, the Essex rebels gathered at Mile End and others at Blackheath outside the city. The advisers of the young king deemed it prudent for him to seek refuge in the fortified Tower of London on 11 June, and during the night of 12/13 June, rebels poured into the city. Three aldermen were later charged with allowing rebels to enter London over London Bridge and via Aldgate, one of the seven gates into the walled city.

Thursday, 13 June 1381 was the feast of Corpus Christi. St Albans chronicler Thomas Walsingham says that as the day grew warmer, the rebels who had entered London took to drinking wine they had looted from the wine cellars of the wealthy, in expensive goblets. As they grew more and more drunk, or not so much drunk as mad, he says, they began to discuss their next move, against the hated duke of Lancaster. Unable to lay their hands on John of Gaunt in person, the rebels took out their rage on his palace of the Savoy.

The palace was left a smoking ruin. The rebels poured through it, smashing gold and silver vessels into pieces with their axes or throwing them into the river or into sewers, tearing or trampling Gaunt's luxurious clothes, and grinding precious stones and jewels into dust with mortars. One of the duke's tunics was set up as a dummy on a spear and used as target practice by archers, and when that amusement palled, it was cut to pieces. Finally, fires were set all round the building, and it was deliberately destroyed. The Kirkstall chronicle also states that the Savoy was razed to the ground and that all of Gaunt's possessions inside, including money, jewels, bed hangings and tapestries, were either thrown into the Thames and lost or were consumed by fire. The *Historia Vitae et Regni Ricardi Secundi* says that the rebels 'found an almost infinite variety of objects' within the palace and that after looting it they left hardly one stone on top of another, and the *Anonimalle* adds the detail that as well as drinking Gaunt's wine, the rebels gorged themselves on his food.[3] According to a letter sent by John of Gaunt himself in September 1382, he had also kept twenty-three carts of hay and 427 pounds of wax at the Savoy – one wonders how he was able to be so precise about the amounts fifteen months later – which vanished during the 'horrible uprising' ('*horrible romour*'), as he called it.[4]

One of the men named as responsible for burning the Savoy was a draper from London called Stephen Hulle, and he was incarcerated in the prison of the king's household then sent to the sheriff of Surrey on 19 August 1381. In 1383, John of Gaunt brought a case in the Court of Common Pleas against the men he and his advisers believed had sacked his residence, and claimed that they had stolen and destroyed goods worth £10,000. The case was dropped, but the very long list of men's names, many dozens, reveals them to have been tailors, mercers, skinners, fullers, tanners, drapers, shipmen, taverners, cordwainers, brewers, carpenters, masons and many others.[5]

As early as 15 June 1381, Richard II granted a commission of oyer and terminer ('to hear and to determine') to the mayor of London, William Walworth, and six other men, 'on information that great crowds of labourers and others have collected together, especially in the counties of Essex, Kent,

Surrey, Sussex and Middlesex, compelled their betters to go with them, killed many of the king's lieges, and burned many houses, entered the city of London, and burned the house of the king's uncle, John, duke of Lancaster, called the Sauveye [Savoy].' One Roger Gailer of Holborn was described as 'a leader of the rioters and rode with a great rabble to the Savoy' and to the house of the order of the Knights Hospitaller of St John of Jerusalem at Clerkenwell. Allegedly, he stole £100 from the Savoy and the Hospitallers' house. Gaunt himself was appointed justiciar to oversee the inquisitions to be held to determine and punish the rebels' misdeeds on 18 August 1381.[6]

Although Gaunt was safely distant from London in June 1381 and from the rebels who would have loved to see him dead, his fourteen-year-old son Henry of Lancaster was in the capital, and stayed in the Tower with his cousin the king. Richard II's departure from the great fortification on 14 June, when he rode out to meet and to attempt to negotiate with the rebels at Mile End, was the cue for a large invasion of the Tower. Simon Sudbury, archbishop of Canterbury and chancellor, and Robert Hales, treasurer of England, were dragged out of the Tower and beheaded on Tower Hill; these men were held chiefly responsible for the loathed poll tax, and their heads were set on spikes and gleefully paraded around, then placed on London Bridge. The life of Henry of Lancaster, as son and heir of the loathed John of Gaunt, was also in severe danger. Luckily for him, a man named John Ferrour saved him 'in a wonderful and kind manner', though we do not know how; perhaps he hid Henry somewhere, or persuaded the rebels not to harm the boy, or fought them off.[7]

At any rate, Henry never forgot Ferrour's brave action. In early 1400, after Henry had become king, Ferrour joined the Epiphany Rising, intended to restore the deposed and imprisoned Richard II to the throne Henry had taken. Henry forgave him and pardoned him, referencing his brave action at the Tower almost twenty years earlier which had saved his life. On 15 June 1381, the day after Ferrour rescued his son from the murderous rebels in the Tower, John of Gaunt was in the port of Berwick-on-Tweed, certainly as yet unaware of the tumult in London and the danger Henry was in, as it would have taken messengers a good few days to ride the 350 miles north to inform him. The oblivious duke ordered his receiver at his castle of Dunstanburgh to purchase salmon for his and his retinue's impending arrival there.[8]

Richard II met the rebels again at Smithfield on Saturday 15 June, on which occasion he met Wat Tyler, the rebels' leader. William Walworth, the mayor, killed Tyler in some way during this meeting, probably by stabbing him, whereupon the young king, who like his cousin Henry was still only fourteen, rode bravely towards the mass of rebels, crying out 'I will be your king, your captain and your leader.' He managed to disperse the crowds and to lead them away from the city, and within weeks order had been restored and the danger was over.

39

Of Very Noble and Royal Blood

In the summer and autumn of 1381, John of Gaunt became embroiled in a huge and furious row with Henry Percy, first earl of Northumberland. Supposedly, Gaunt blamed the earl for refusing to shelter him during the uprising, and the ensuing quarrel came to the attention of several chroniclers, who wrote extensively about it, claiming that the two powerful noblemen's row threatened to destroy England. Both men brought large retinues to London and almost came to blows on Wednesday 6 November in the Painted Chamber in the palace of Westminster, where Parliament was about to begin. At first, Northumberland refused to back down, but in the end, he had to, and was forced to make a grovelling apology to John on his knees on 9 November. Addressing Lancaster as *'monseigneur d'Espaigne'* and speaking in French, Northumberland admitted that in his ignorance he had addressed Gaunt far less courteously than he should have, given that Gaunt was the 'son of my very dread liege lord the king, whom God absolve, and uncle of my very dread liege lord the present king, and of such high person and of very noble and royal blood as you are, my lord'.

Percy also addressed part of his apology to Richard II, admitting that he had displeased the king by addressing his uncle less than politely in his presence. It seems that John of Gaunt was genuinely hurt by Henry Percy's actions in 1381, and that he felt betrayed by a man he had always considered a good friend, kinsman, and ally. In May 1372, John had spoken of the 'very great and sincere affection and perfect love which we have and bear towards our dearest and beloved cousin, Sir Henry, Lord Percy.' A few years later, Gaunt sent Percy a gift of a tun of wine, and in September 1377, the duke of Lancaster was appointed as a mediator to settle Percy's ongoing dispute with the Scottish earl of Douglas.[1] According to the *Alnwick Chronicle*, Henry Percy had been brought up in the household of his uncle Henry of Grosmont, first duke of Lancaster (which seems very likely to be true, given that several of Grosmont's other nephews joined his retinue), and therefore might have known Gaunt well for a very long time.[2]

John of Gaunt was in Fulham on 8 and 18 November 1381 during Parliament when he granted safe conduct to the abbot of Holyrood in Edinburgh to travel to Canterbury on pilgrimage with a dozen attendants, and was still there on the 29th, when he ordered his servant Symond (or Simon) de Bygrave to bring 'partridges and other birds' for the consumption of his household in Higham Ferrers, Hertford, London and elsewhere. He was still in Fulham on 10 December when he wrote to his steward in Norfolk, Sir Edmund Gurney, making reference to the recent 'horrible uprising' and to any malefactors who might be living in the county. Gurney and Adam Pope, John's receiver in Norfolk, were told to discover the identities of the 'malefactors' who had done harm to the duke, and to discuss with them or with their associates to establish what possible compensation might be given to John for what they had taken from him. The two men were to present their findings to John and his council in London at 'the quinzaine of Saint Hilary,' i.e. at the end of January 1382.[3]

Parliament was prorogued on 13 December, and it was arranged that it would sit again in the New Year. Since the murder of Archbishop Simon Sudbury in June 1381, the archbishop-elect of Canterbury was William Courtenay, who had been bishop of London until his promotion to archbishop. Courtenay also managed to get on his kinsman King Richard's bad side, to the point where Richard threatened to run him through with a sword during a quarrel on the River Thames when their barges passed in late 1384; two royal knights who stopped Richard from attacking Courtenay had to leap into the archbishop's barge to save themselves. Again at Lent 1385, Richard reacted furiously when the archbishop reprimanded him for his arrogance, and only the intervention of his uncle Thomas of Woodstock prevented the king from striking Courtenay. Richard contented himself with shouting 'foul words' at the offended archbishop instead. At the November 1381 Parliament, Courtenay gave 'a good sermon in English' (*une bone collacioun en Engleys*), and stated that England could not long endure or survive if its inhabitants were wicked. It is interesting to note that Courtenay, a great-grandson of King Edward I, son of the earl of Devon (d. 1377) and nephew of the earls of Hereford (d. 1361) and Northampton (d. 1360), and thus a member of the English elite who for centuries had liked to talk French to set themselves apart from the masses, gave a sermon in English rather than in French or Latin, as would usually have been the case even a few years earlier.

The Commons presented a petition to 'their most honoured lord of Lancaster' and other lords, asking them to reform the king's household and its officials and to oust 'the evil ones', and to reduce the expenses of the royal household as much as possible. This was always an important issue in the fourteenth century, and was far from being unique to Richard II's reign. Finally, Gaunt himself requested a loan of £60,000 to lead a campaign with 2,000 men-at-arms and 2,000 archers to Spain and Portugal, 'for the safekeeping of the sea and and of the kingdom of England'. Although he promised to pay the sum back within three years, either with money or in service, his proposal caused a 'great argument and altercation'. Some were in favour because otherwise England's allies in Portugal would be 'destroyed'; others were opposed, arguing that if another rebellion broke out in England, 'there would be much more to fear' if the mighty duke of Lancaster were absent. The money was not forthcoming.

Gaunt and part of his family spent at least some of the festive season of 1381/82 in Leicester. That New Year, Duchess Constanza gave her stepson Henry of Lancaster a gift of pricy furred damask cloth, while for his part, Gaunt sent a minstrel (which kind of minstrel was not specified), to his son. Henry spent most of that winter and spring with his father as they attended various court events.[4] Gaunt's nephew-in-law Edmund Mortimer, earl of March and Ulster, died on 27 December 1381 at not yet thirty years old, leaving his seven-year-old son Roger as the heir of himself, his late wife Philippa of Clarence, and Gaunt's brother Lionel of Antwerp.

On 20 January 1382, Richard II married Anne of Bohemia, and two days later she was crowned queen of England in Westminster Abbey. Anne was the daughter of the late Holy Roman Emperor Karl IV, who had tried to gain control of the county of Provence in 1365 and probably triggered Gaunt's own attempts to gain part of the county, from Karl's fourth marriage to the Polish noblewoman Elżbieta of Pomerania. Karl and Elżbieta married in the Polish city of Krakow in May 1363, and Anne, their eldest child, was born in Prague in May 1366, so was eight months older than her husband. She and Richard were to form a very close and loving marriage, albeit a childless one. The chronicler Thomas Walsingham, snidely as ever, referred to Anne as 'the imperial girl' and the Westminster chronicler as a 'tiny bit of flesh' who had come to England as a purchase who had cost too much. Anne's marriage was not popular in England as she brought no dowry, and the union brought England little if anything in the way of political benefits either (though Anne herself, thanks to her quiet, pleasant personality and her kindness, made herself liked among the English people over the years). Two years earlier, Richard's marriage to Caterina, daughter of Bernabo Visconti, lord of Milan, had been under consideration, which, given Bernabo's wealth, might have proved a lot more popular among the king's subjects.[5]

40

A Wicked Life

The terror of the Great Uprising of 1381, when both he and his beloved son Henry might easily have been killed, seems to have affected John of Gaunt profoundly and to have caused him to make some great changes in his life, or at least to act in public as though he had done so. Perhaps he realised just how unpopular he was and how much the widespread loathing for him endangered not only himself, but his family. Katherine Swynford was evidently still high in John's favour and affection on 7 September 1381, when he granted her an annuity of 200 marks a year, supposedly in gratitude for her excellent service to his daughters Philippa and Elizabeth. Presumably this was to be paid on top of the annuity of 50 marks, or perhaps £50, which he had awarded her some years before. The fact that on 22 July 1381 Gaunt ordered a chapel to be built in his Yorkshire town of Roecliffe that was to be dedicated to the Virgin Mary and to St Katherine, may also be significant, unless perhaps the duke had his daughter Catalina in mind with that particular saint, rather than his mistress.[1]

On 14 February 1382 in London, however, Gaunt called Katherine Swynford the 'former governess' ('*nuper magistrisse*') of his eldest two daughters, and issued a quitclaim releasing himself and his heirs 'from all manner of actions concerning [Katherine]'. According to several chroniclers, John publicly renounced his relationship with Katherine around this time, although on 20 February 1382, just six days after the quitclaim, he sent her two tuns of Gascon wine.[2]

The author of the *Anonimalle* chronicle, always an admirer of Duchess Constanza, puts a speech in Gaunt's mouth. Allegedly, he admitted that he had committed the sin of lechery against God's will and the law of Holy Church, and especially with 'Lady Katherine Swynford, a female devil and enchantress' ('*dame Kateryne de Swynforth, une deblesce et enchauntresce*'). John also stated that he had committed the same sin of adultery with 'many others near his wife,' so presumably he admitted to having slept with some of Constanza's attendants, assuming that the *Anonimalle*'s account of his speech bears any resemblance to reality. He stated further that he had lived a 'wicked life' for a long time. Chronicler Thomas Walsingham, always eager to heap as much opprobrium on the duke of Lancaster as possible (though he became much more amicable towards him after 1381), calls John a fornicator and adulterer, and narrates the salacious tale that he 'took the most shameless prostitutes' to the beds of his wives Blanche of Lancaster and Constanza of Castile. The *Anonimalle* chronicle adds that Constanza herself, whom at this point the writer calls 'a woman of great beauty,' was staying at Pontefract Castle with her retinue at the time of John's confession, when she heard of John's 'disease' and fled to Knaresborough because she felt threatened; the chronicler appears to be mixing up the duchess's reaction to Gaunt's confessions of lechery with the Great Uprising of a few months earlier. Finally, the chronicle states with some satisfaction that Katherine Swynford went into hiding and that no-one could find her for a long time, while the duke and duchess of Lancaster enjoyed a joyous and tender reconciliation.[3]

Whether Gaunt really ended his relationship with Katherine is debatable, as there is considerable evidence that she remained in close contact with him and his family over the next few years. In 1382, the duke was seriously planning an expedition to Castile and genuinely thought the time had finally come to undertake one, so it is possible that his public ending of his extramarital relationship with Katherine was done for political reasons and to make it seem that he was entirely committed to Constanza of Castile and to winning their Spanish kingdoms, rather than because he truly stopped seeing her.[4]

Almost certainly John and Katherine met in Lincoln in February 1386, and in February 1387 John ordered a payment of £100 to be made to Katherine in part payment of a loan of 500 marks (£333) she had made to him 'in his great necessity.' He asked his receiver in Yorkshire, Robert Morton, to give or send the money to Katherine, which may indicate that she was residing in Yorkshire rather than Lincolnshire at the time.[5] Sometime between May 1391 and May 1392, John's son Henry purchased a 'diamond in a gold ring' for 'dne [*domine*, i.e. Lady] K. Swynford'. Probably in early 1394, Henry spent the huge sum of £14 14s for pieces of white damask cloth given to 'the countess of Derby and dne Kath' Swynford.' John of Gaunt, meanwhile, kept a stable of a dozen horses for Katherine's use at his court.[6] These generous gifts from John's son and the horses for her use strongly suggest that Katherine kept in close touch with her lover at the very least, and perhaps that she and John continued their intimate relationship, though it may be significant that Katherine bore Gaunt no more children after *c.* 1379. This may also, however, mean that Katherine passed beyond childbearing age not long after 1380; as noted above, she was certainly not born as late as *c.* 1350 as usually stated, and may have turned forty in the early 1380s or thereabouts.

The countess of Derby who received damask cloth was John of Gaunt's daughter-in-law Mary de Bohun, and Henry of Lancaster's joint gift to his wife and to Katherine strongly implies that the two women were together at the time and perhaps living in the same household (Mary was pregnant with her sixth and youngest child at the time of the gift). Katherine Swynford was, after all, the mother of four of Henry of Lancaster's half-siblings and was therefore a member of his and his wife's family, albeit rather unconventionally. There is also much evidence throughout the 1380s and 1390s that Mary de Bohun remained close to both Duchess Constanza and to Katherine, while Henry was close to Katherine's son Sir Thomas Swynford from her marriage to Hugh (Thomas and Henry were almost exactly the same age). When Henry was admitted to the fraternity of Lincoln Cathedral in 1386, as his father had been many years earlier, one of the two knights attending John of Gaunt during the event was Thomas Swynford, and Katherine's sister Philippa Chaucer was admitted to the fraternity on the same occasion.[7]

Katherine returned to live, or continued living, in her beloved Lincolnshire, and seems to have divided her time between Kettlethorpe, Grantham (30 miles south of Kettlethorpe) and Lincoln (25 miles from Grantham), a city that was one of the earldoms John of Gaunt held by right of the late Blanche of Lancaster. In October 1383, Katherine received permission to make and enclose a park of 300 acres at Kettlethorpe; in August 1384, eight named men and unnamed others 'broke her close' at Grantham and assaulted her servants; and in September 1384, another twelve men, including Robert de Saltby, the mayor of Lincoln, and the city bailiffs, 'broke her close' in Lincoln.[8] Such attacks and robberies were exceedingly common in fourteenth-century England, which could often be a violent and lawless place, and Katherine's unfortunate experiences do not necessarily indicate that she was being specifically targeted because of her long and intimate association with the unpopular duke of Lancaster.

In 1387, Katherine was made a Lady of the Garter, a great honour.[9] The Order of the Garter was founded by Edward III, and John of Gaunt became a Knight of the Garter in 1361. John's niece Philippa de Coucy, countess of Oxford, was also made a Lady in 1387, while Duchess Constanza, her daughter Catalina and her stepdaughter Philippa were honoured in 1385. Although Katherine's elevation to the Order might not have been a direct result of Gaunt's influence, as he was outside England for the whole of the year 1387, it does demonstrate that Katherine was still in favour and fondly remembered at the royal court, even though she might have spent most or all of her time in Lincolnshire. Unlike the wildly unpopular Alice Perrers, Edward III's long-term mistress, Katherine did not abuse her position to enrich herself, and seems to have had a gift of charming people and conducting herself with grace and dignity.

41

Petitions and the Countess

Henry of Lancaster turned fifteen in April 1382, and spent his birthday, Maundy Thursday (a moveable feast, which fell on 23 April that year), at his father's castle of Hertford. He washed the feet of fifteen paupers, and gave another twenty-five paupers a penny each. A few days before, he had given a bottle of Romney wine to his sister Philippa, who was now twenty-two.[1] On 16 April 1382 at Rochford in Essex, Eleanor de Bohun, countess of Buckingham, gave birth to her first child, Humphrey of Buckingham, often known to history as Humphrey of Gloucester as his father Thomas of Woodstock later became duke of Gloucester. John of Gaunt and his son Henry heard the news of Humphrey's birth two days later on 18 April, and John gave gifts of cash to his brother Thomas's squire, Westcombe, who brought him the news, and to little Humphrey's nurse.[2]

On 8 September 1382, while John of Gaunt was at his castle of Pontefract in Yorkshire, he sent messengers called John and Richard Barton with his letters to 'the parts of Zeeland and Holland'. Almost certainly this means he was corresponding again with his German cousin Albrecht, duke of Lower Bavaria and count of Hainault, Holland and Zeeland.[3] Gaunt spent most of the rest of September 1382 in Yorkshire, and took the house of the Carmelite friars in Doncaster, established in 1350, under his protection on the grounds that the house's founders John Nicbrothere and Richard Euwere and their descendants were all dead. Thereafter, the duke was regarded as one of the founders as well.[4] Between 17 and 23 September in York, Gaunt headed a commission of oyer and terminer, working with the archbishop of York, the earl of Northumberland and almost twenty other men, regarding the 'treasonable hostile rising of diverse evildoers ... and their perpetration of treasons, homicides, arsons, etc.' Those found guilty would be imprisoned and their goods seized, and their meetings 'suppressed'.[5]

Gaunt returned to the south of England and attended Parliament at Westminster from 6 to 24 October 1382. His great palace of the Savoy being now a ruin, he stayed at 'Neate' or 'La Neyte', a manor of the abbot of Westminster located roughly where Hyde Park stands now, throughout. His parker of Aldbourne was ordered to deliver twelve dozen rabbits to John's *pulter* or poulterer to be consumed during the Parliament, then another twelve dozen weekly from 1 December until 2 February 1383, the feast of the Purification.[6] As the most powerful lord in the realm, John was specifically named in a petition presented to this Parliament by Sir Thomas and Alice West. The couple stated that the previous July, Nicholas Clifton and a gang of armed men ambushed Alice and their children Thomas the younger and Eleanor at Malwood in the New Forest, and raped the unfortunate Eleanor West, who, her distressed parents said, was now seriously ill and likely to die as a result of her ordeal. The Wests presented another petition to the next Parliament, held also in Westminster in February 1383, which makes it apparent that 'because of their suit, a statute of rapes was made to punish such rapes in future.'

The problem for the Wests was that Nicholas Clifton, who attacked and raped their daughter, was not included in the statute, and they asked in their subsequent petition of early 1383 that he should be. A commission of oyer and terminer had been issued on 19 August 1382 naming Nicholas Clifton as the man responsible for raping Eleanor at 'Mallewod', while eight of Clifton's accomplices were accused of stealing a horse, a saddle, pearls and other precious stones, and linen and woollen cloths belonging to the Wests. The nine men were to be arrested and imprisoned in Winchester. Evidently, however, Thomas and Alice West were unhappy with the result of this investigation, and were determined to see justice done for the suffering inflicted on their daughter. They therefore called upon the powerful duke of Lancaster, and Gaunt apparently did see to it that a statute was issued to punish such rapes. However, Nicholas Clifton was pardoned 'for all felonies and rapes with which he is charged' on 14 March 1383, at the request of the teenage queen, Anne of Bohemia.[7]

Another petition was presented to John of Gaunt almost certainly during the October 1382 Parliament, and the petitioner was a widow named Margaret Tany. Margaret claimed that a royal clerk named Walter Almaly was, as a result of 'his great malice,' falsely accusing her and her son John Thorp of being present at the Tower of London when Simon Sudbury was killed there in June 1381. She stated that Thorp had been arrested on this account and had been beaten by one John Church. Thorp died of his injuries in Newgate prison in London, and his mother asked Gaunt to have Church brought before the royal council to confess to the truth of her accusations. Unfortunately, the outcome of Margaret's petition is not recorded.[8] John's possible expedition to Portugal and Spain was raised again at the Parliament of October 1382, and this time John stated that it would cost £43,000, £17,000 less than his estimate of a few months before. The 'prelates, earls, barons and bannerets' attending the Parliament were questioned on the matter, both in groups and individually, and stated their belief that the expedition would be profitable and honourable to King Richard and his kingdom. They added, however, that the number of men John planned to take, 2,000 men-at-arms and 2,000 archers, seemed 'too small to wage war against so strong a kingdom,' i.e. Castile. Although John dearly wished his expedition to go ahead and made a strong case for it, and although he was supported by many people, the money was still not forthcoming.

John's eldest and last remaining sister Isabella of Woodstock, countess of Bedford and Lady Coucy, died in London on 5 October 1382 at the age of fifty, just before the opening of Parliament. She was buried at the church of the Greyfriars in London, where her aunt Joan of the Tower and grandmother Isabella of France, queens of Scotland and England, were also buried. Countess Isabella left her two daughters from her marriage to the much younger Enguerrand de Coucy, who outlived her and was to marry again and have another daughter a few years later. Her daughters were Marie, future countess of Soissons, who was sixteen in 1382 and spent most or all of her life in her father's native France, and Philippa, countess of Oxford, who was fourteen or fifteen and married to Richard II's close friend Robert de Vere.[9] John of Gaunt and his younger brothers Edmund of Langley and Thomas of Woodstock were now the only survivors of King Edward and Queen Philippa's twelve children. John and Thomas, though apparently not Edmund who is not mentioned, were appointed as the supervisors of their late sister's will, and Isabella's executors requested their permission to sell a house of hers on Ludgate in London, called 'Pembrokesyn' or 'Pembroke's Inn'. The money raised from the sale was intended to pay off the countess's large debts, to pay the outstanding wages due to her servants, and to distribute 'alms for her soul' under the royal brothers' supervision.[10]

42

The Commons in a Ferment

Shortly after his sister's death, John ordered his 'receiver in the south', William Everle, to pay 200 marks to a mercer of London called Roger Canon for 'various wares and other things,' almost certainly fabrics, purchased from him for 'our beloved consort' Constanza. On 26 October, the duke wrote to John Hagh, the deputy of his steward of Bolingbroke in Lincolnshire; the steward himself was Simon 'Simkyn' Simeon.[1] Simon Simeon was a long-term Lancastrian retainer who had served Gaunt's father-in-law Duke Henry and Henry's father Earl Henry as well. Simon wrote his will in March 1386 and died not long before 23 December 1387 when he must have been a ripe old age; he is mentioned in the chancery rolls as one of the garrison who held out against Gaunt's grandmother Queen Isabella at Caerphilly Castle in South Wales between November 1326 and March 1327, so he can hardly have been born later than *c.* 1310, and was perhaps born quite a bit earlier than that. In September 1329, Simon was named as a member of the retinue of Henry, earl of Lancaster and Leicester, when the earl travelled overseas.[2] As a long-term faithful Lancastrian who served the family for six decades, Simon Simeon requested burial in 'St Mary's Collegiate Church' in Leicester, i.e. the Newarke, founded by Henry, earl of Lancaster in 1330 and much extended by his son Duke Henry. He was still obviously in good health and able to serve as Gaunt's steward of Bolingbroke in the early 1380s, when he must have been over seventy. That John greatly valued Simon's long service is revealed by the fact that the Savoy Palace had a tower called the Simeon Tower.[3]

In November 1382, John of Gaunt was still planning to go to Spain as soon as possible, 'with God's aid'. On 12 December at Westminster, however, he decided to travel to France instead, and therefore stated that he required a cart to carry his armour from Kenilworth Castle, where he obviously stored it, to London.[4] The winter of 1382/83 was a very wet one, and in January 1383 Gaunt had to pay for the mill, bridge and stank in his manor of Hertford to be repaired after they were badly damaged in floods (*'grantz eawes'*, 'great waters', as John's letters called them). At the same time and probably also as a result of the harsh winter weather, the duke hired Piers Clete, a *plummer*, i.e. a person who worked with lead, to reroof the chambers and battlements at Hertford Castle. Another letter Gaunt wrote on the same day reveals that a ship transporting herring from 'Skone' (probably Skåne in

Denmark) had been wrecked at Sutton on the coast of Lincolnshire during a storm just before Christmas 1382; yet more evidence of the high winds and bad weather of the season.[5]

Sutton, nowadays called Sutton-on-Sea, was one of John's many lordships, and his officials there had tried to seize the Danish ship in the belief that it belonged by right to the duke, as it had come ashore in one of his manors. John's letter on the matter to his bailiff in Lincolnshire, William of Spain, states that the ship was undamaged when it came ashore, and the sailors were unharmed by the probably rather frightening experience. After they had safely disembarked and his officials had arrived in Sutton, however, the storm once more tossed the ship back into 'the deeps', '*les depes*' as John called it, in a mixture of French and English. John ordered William of Spain to release the sailors, and, if any of the provisions carried on the ship had been saved from the sea, to let the men have all of them.

Parliament was held at Westminster in late February and early March 1383, and John of Gaunt walked out in disgust when a crusade to Flanders, to be led by the nobly born bishop of Norwich, Henry Despenser, was approved. The previous two Parliaments had approved John's campaign to the Iberian Peninsula, though no money had appeared; now it was to be given to Despenser instead. Bishop Henry was the youngest brother of the late Lord Despenser (d. 1375), and, as a descendant of Edward I, was a distant kinsman of John of Gaunt.[6] His 'crusade' to Flanders was to aid the inhabitants against the French armies overrunning most of Flanders, with the city of Ghent, where John had been born forty-three years earlier, desperately holding out against the French. John of Gaunt was less interested in aiding the inhabitants of his birthplace than in gaining control of Constanza's kingdoms, but this would have to wait a while. Many of the lords present agreed with the duke and spoke out vociferously against Henry Despenser, but two sons of the earl of Devon debated fiercely with them on Despenser's behalf, and Gaunt was so furious with them that he uttered insults which 'set the Commons in a ferment' and promptly stalked out. This hardly improved his already difficult and mutually hostile relations with the Commons. The records of this Parliament, written in French, refer repeatedly to '*la ville de Gaunt*', 'the town of Ghent,' with the usual fourteenth-century spelling of the place that is still always used as part of John of Gaunt's name.[7]

John was in London on 1 March 1383 during this disastrous Parliament when he granted an income of 100 marks a year to Katherine Swynford's son Thomas Swynford, now about fifteen or sixteen and already a knight, and Joan Crophill, 'on the occasion of their marriage.' The wording of the grant makes it sound as though their wedding was about to take place or recently had, though Joan's father Sir John Crophill (b. *c.* 1320) left 100 marks each to Joan and her sister Matilda 'for their marriage[s]' in his will of 3 July 1383, which would seem to indicate that Joan had not yet married Thomas. The Crophills were landowners in Lincolnshire, Leicestershire,

Nottinghamshire and Herefordshire, though Joan was not the Crophill heir; her brother Thomas, who died in November 1381, left a daughter Agnes, born on 27 March 1371, who was named as heir to all the lands when Joan's father Sir John died in July 1383 shortly after making his will.[8] Presumably Katherine Swynford was also present at her son's wedding to Joan that year or whenever it finally did take place, and as John Crophill held 60s rent and a wood in the Lincolnshire village of Navenby, which was where Sir Hugh Swynford's inquisition post-mortem was held in April 1372 and lay only a couple of miles from the Swynford manor of Coleby, it was surely Katherine herself who arranged her son's Crophill marriage.[9] John of Gaunt's grant of a generous annual income to her son and his interest in Thomas's welfare and in his marriage is yet more evidence that she and the duke kept in close touch after their long-term intimate relationship had supposedly ended the previous year.

The duke sent a servant to Leicester to buy thirty cows and 300 sheep for his household on 4 March. His improvements to Hertford Castle were ongoing, and he had 'our old great chamber ... moved from one place to another'. He made large payments of £66 and 10s to nineteen fishmongers of London on 13 March, and over £93 to one other fishmonger called John Trygg, payments that probably refer to some of the fish and seafood the duke purchased for himself and his household during Lent when the consumption of meat was forbidden.[10] Pope Urban VI issued a 'grant at the petition of John, duke of Lancaster' on 21 March 1383: as John 'intends to set out with a great force against John [Juan], king of Castile and Leon,' Urban granted that everyone in his company who 'die truly penitent and confessed' would have 'plenary pardon of sins.'[11] This was part of John's ongoing wish to go on campaign to Spain, but as Parliament refused to give him the money and gave it to Bishop Despenser instead, there was little he could do but wait.

43

Corpus Christi and a Christening

In 1352, when John was twelve years old, a gild in Cambridge had founded a college at the University of Cambridge, which became known as Corpus Christi College, to remember and say Masses for the souls of the many townspeople who had died during the first massive outbreak of the Black Death in 1348/49. In the fourteenth century it was often called the college of St Benet, i.e. Benedict, as it lay close to the church of St Benet in the town. Gaunt was patron of the college, and on 9 April 1383 sent a letter to William Oke, one of the clerks of his great wardrobe, regarding a 'little clerk' (i.e. a boy or very young man) named Thomas de Asshebourne. John was sponsoring Thomas through his studies at the 'schools in the University of Cambridge' ('escoles deinz lunnyversitee de Cantebrug'), and Thomas was to attend St Benet's College, which the duke proudly called 'our college of Seint Benett'. The college master, John Kynne, was told to inform Gaunt of the cost of feeding, clothing and educating Thomas de Asshebourne during his studies there.[1]

A petition that had been presented to the Parliament held in November 1381 after the Great Uprising makes it apparent that Gaunt's association with the college of St Benet led to the college also being attacked on 15 June 1381 by none other than the mayor, bailiffs and other elected officials of the town of Cambridge. The petitioners claimed that the college was 'of the foundation of our most excellent lord of Lancaster,' which in fact it was not, and interestingly, given that it was usually called the College of St Benet in the fourteenth century, they referred to it as Corpus Christi College ('collage de corps Crist' in the French original of the petition). Books, documents, charters and other goods 'of great value' including jewels were stolen from the college, and even doors, windows and timber were stolen.[2] Duke John's letter of April 1383 indicates that, despite the awful damage inflicted on the college twenty-two months previously by officials of the town, things had more or less gone back to normal, and that the college was accepting scholars again.

On 15 April, John borrowed 400 marks from the bishop of Lincoln (John Bokyngham or Buckingham) and another 400 marks from the bishop of Salisbury (Ralph Ergham, formerly Gaunt's chancellor).[3] The duke could not have realised it as early as 1383, when his son Henry Beaufort was probably only eight years old, but Henry would himself be consecrated as bishop of Lincoln fifteen years later. The annual Knight of the Garter celebrations took place at Windsor Castle on St George's Day, 23 April, as they always did. John paid £10 for the heralds who worked at Windsor on the day, and another 10 marks went to the minstrels who performed on the same occasion.

Sometime a little before 6 May 1383, John's niece Anne, second child and first daughter of the earl and countess of Buckingham, was born at Thomas of Woodstock's castle of Pleshey in Essex; she was just over a year younger than her brother Humphrey. Anne later became countess of Stafford and Eu, and was an ancestor of the Stafford dukes of Buckingham and the Bourchier earls of Essex. Although she had an older brother and several younger sisters, Anne would be the only child of Eleanor de Bohun and Thomas of Woodstock who lived past her teens, and was the only one of their children who married and had children of her own. A petition presented to the Parliament that had been held in February 1383 reveals that the earl of Buckingham was currently involved in a dispute with Hugh Stafford, earl of Stafford, and his daughter Anne married Stafford's son and heir Thomas Stafford in June 1391 when she was still only eight and he twenty-two, perhaps as a means of resolving the quarrel between the families.[4]

One of the earl of Buckingham's squires, name not stated, travelled to bring John of Gaunt the news of Anne's birth, and was rewarded with 40s. Gaunt subsequently rode to Pleshey to attend his little niece's baptism, and paid £46, 8s and 2d to Herman the goldsmith for a pair of gilded silver basins engraved with swans and the arms of 'our brother of Bukyngham, given to the daughter of our said brother on the day of her baptism at Pleshey.' John also gave Anne a gilded silver ewer, a 'great tripod' and a silver cup with cover, for which he paid a total of £44, as further christening gifts. A payment of eight £5 went to 'a damsel of our sister of Bukyngham, the day of the baptism of Anne her daughter,' and £5 to another of Eleanor de Bohun's damsels assigned to be the '*maistresse*' of the little girl. Finally, John gave 20s to Eleanor's '*middewyk*', which must be a clerical error in his register for *middewyf* or midwife, and 30s and 4d to Anne of Buckingham's '*rokestare*', the girl or young woman who rocked her cradle. On the same day, John also bought a silver basin and ewer for the chamber of 'our daughter of Pembroke' from John Botesham, goldsmith of London.[5] This perhaps indicates that his second daughter Elizabeth of Lancaster went to the baptism of her cousin Anne, two decades her junior, with him.

John paid 10 marks to minstrels and 10 marks to heralds at jousts he held at his castle of Hertford in May 1383, and he took part in other jousting tournaments at Smithfield and Chelmsford that spring, as well as at Windsor in April during the annual celebrations of the feast of St George. The duke did not neglect his charitable obligations, and ordered on several occasions that alms were to be distributed to poor people, 'as much money as is wagered on us [Gaunt] and our destrier [war-horse]' at the tournaments in which he competed at Smithfield, Chelmsford, Windsor and Hertford. 'Sir Poto, knight of Germany' visited John in England sometime in 1383 (or had perhaps been there since early 1382, having accompanied Anne of Bohemia to England from her half-brother Wenzel in Germany), and one of Poto's servants brought John a gift of a destrier when Poto departed for his homeland. John gave the servant a gift of 14s and 4d in return, and spent 10 marks on a new saddle and tackle, all covered with cloth of gold, from William of Lincoln, saddler of London. These items were perhaps intended for the new destrier he had received from Sir Poto. Lady Mohun was in charge of the household of Gaunt and Duchess Constanza's daughter Catalina, and Gaunt sent £50 to the lady for Catalina's recent expenses.[6] The record of this grant to Lady Mohun refers to Catalina of Lancaster as 'our daughter of Katerine' ('*nostre fille de Katerine*'), another careless error by one of Gaunt's clerks. Gaunt also spent 14s 4d on a pair of paternosters with large corals and jet from William atte Mille, which were to be 'delivered to our own hands', and also bought a primer with 'morning prayers of Our Lady, the Seven Psalms and Dirige with other devotions' for his own use.

Gaunt purchased two packhorses for his daughter Elizabeth at £8 and £6, 7s and 2d, which seems an inordinately large amount of money to pay for packhorses. Another £11 was spent on Elizabeth's expenses travelling from Hertford to Henley-on-Thames to visit her cousin the king for nine days. This visit is not dated, but Elizabeth of Lancaster was obviously in King Richard's presence on or a little before 24 September 1383 at Westminster, as on that date Richard granted a pardon to a Nicholas Parker of Brampton who had killed Thomas Dyke, at the request of 'the king's kinswoman, Elizabeth, countess of Pembroke.'[7] Elizabeth's twentieth birthday had passed in *c.* February 1383, and although in the summer of that year she had been married for three years, she had no immediate prospect of being able to live with her husband; John Hastings turned eleven in November 1383 and would not reach maturity for at least another three years and probably five. Elizabeth's elder sister Philippa, meanwhile, was with their stepmother Constanza on 11 September 1383, when John of Gaunt, in London, sent 'certain vessels of gold and silver' to 'our beloved consort the queen and our beloved daughter Phellipe'.[8]

Duchess Constanza departed from Kenilworth with her retinue on Saturday, 25 July 1383, and went to Tutbury. The earl and countess of Warwick, Thomas Beauchamp and Margaret Ferrers, and the earl's brother William Beauchamp, had dined with her at Kenilworth on 20 July. Constanza's daughter Catalina of Lancaster, now ten or eleven years old, stayed at Kenilworth between 30 August and 6 September that year, and John of Gaunt's household, or part of it at least, travelled between Banbury, Henley-on-Thames, Maidenhead and Westminster in this period.[9] Gaunt himself, meanwhile, was in Yorkshire, Derbyshire and Staffordshire in July and August 1383, with the rest of his retinue. On 23 July at his castle of Knaresborough, he sent his squire Robert Roos to Scotland with letters for the earl of Carrick, John Stewart, and 'other lords of Scotland.'[10] The truce between England and Scotland was due to expire on 2 February 1384, and therefore 'it pleased our lord the king to send to the March of Scotland the most exalted and noble lord, his most beloved uncle of Spain, duke of Lancaster.'[11]

44

A State of Decay

John was back in London from his trip to the north by early September 1383, and delivered to his almoner Elys de Sutton a number of valuable items including 'a salt-cellar of gold made in the shape of a turtle-dove, crowned with pearls, standing on a green background,' another salt cellar made of gold with an ornamental border featuring the letter S (the Lancastrian motto), and four gilded dishes for spices.[1] Gaunt was in the sixteen-year-old Richard II's company on 2 October 1383 when he witnessed a grant by the king to Canterbury Cathedral Priory: Richard allowed the prior and convent to hold four fairs annually within the precinct of their convent, in memory of his late father the prince of Wales, who was buried there. Both of Gaunt's brothers witnessed the grant as well, as did the earls of Arundel, Stafford and Northumberland, the latter perhaps back on speaking terms with the duke of Lancaster after their quarrel of two years earlier.[2] The duke was staying again at 'Neate' on 14 October, when he sent a letter in French to John de Yerdebergh, his long-term chief clerk of the great wardrobe and his chancellor:

> Dearest and well-beloved, we greet you very sincerely. And because we have been made aware of the very great illnesses and the hardship from which you suffer daily because of your infirmities, as a result of which you are no longer able to work nor ride nor serve us in the position of our chancellor, which troubles us greatly, and we have tenderly requested you to unburden yourself of your position as our chancellor; having regard and consideration for your illnesses mentioned above, considering the great illnesses and the hardship from which you suffer daily as a result of your infirmities, we command you to deliver our privy seal into our own hands. And may our Lord God have you always in his very sacred keeping.[3]

Parliament was held at Westminster between 26 October and 26 November 1383, and Gaunt's kinsman Henry Despenser, bishop of Norwich, was impeached following the humiliating failure of his campaign in Flanders that year. Gaunt, who had strongly opposed it and who spoke out for an expedition to the Iberian Peninsula instead, perhaps felt vindicated. The charges against Despenser were specifically said in the records of this Parliament to have been 'put to him by the chancellor of England, in the presence of the king himself and my lord of Lancaster ['*monsire de Lancastre*'], in full Parliament,' though Richard did his best to console the bishop and assured him that he was still well-disposed towards him. Among the first-time attendees at this Parliament were sixteen-year-old Thomas Mowbray, who now held his late brother John's earldom of Nottingham, and twenty-one-year-old Robert de Vere, earl of Oxford and the king's closest friend and companion, perhaps his lover.[4] Oxford, married to Philippa de Coucy, was the duke of Lancaster's nephew-in-law.

The young King Charles VI of France (who turned fourteen in late 1382) wrote to Richard II during this Parliament, suggesting a meeting of high-ranking ambassadors of England and France in Calais to discuss a peace settlement between the two kingdoms. In early November 1383, therefore, John of Gaunt travelled to Leulinghem between Calais and Boulogne and met his kinsman John, duke of Berry, and on 26 January 1384 the men made another temporary truce between England and France which was intended to last until the following 1st of May. John returned to England and reported on the summit to his nephew at the palace of Eltham in early February. Among the men who accompanied him were his son Henry, earl of Derby, and John Holland, younger of the king's two older half-brothers and Gaunt's future son-in-law. Curiously, the envoys were given permission to discuss with King Charles the possibility of settling the differences between the kingdoms by single combat between the two young kings, or between the kings and their uncles, or in a more general fight.[5]

Charles VI sent a polite letter to Gaunt at an uncertain date, addressing him as 'the very high and puissant prince the duke of Lancaster, our dearest and beloved cousin'. Charles had sent his squire Jehan Lisac to England as a messenger, and after his return to France, Jehan enthusiastically praised John of Gaunt to the young French king and told him how kind the duke of Lancaster had been to him. Charles thanked John profusely for this kindness and ended his letter by telling him that if John wished for anything, he only had to ask and Charles would happily help him accomplish it. While this was merely a conventional ending to a letter, it does show that the English and French royal families were not always at each other's throats during the endless wars between the two kingdoms in the fourteenth and fifteenth centuries. Richard II sometimes sent amicable letters to Charles VI's uncle Philip, duke of Burgundy, and indeed to Charles himself as well, who in 1396 would become his father-in-law (even though Charles was nearly two years his junior).[6]

By early 1384, John of Gaunt and others in England had heard important news from Portugal. King Fernando died on 22 October 1383 – Thomas Walsingham repeats a rumour that his wife Leonor poisoned him with the aid of her lover, Juan Fernandez Andeiro, count of Olum – leaving his young daughter, Beatriz, only nine or ten years old, as his heir. Although Beatriz had been betrothed to Gaunt's nephew Edward, Edmund of Langley's son, she married Enrique of Trastámara's son King Juan of Castile as his second wife not long before her father's death instead. Juan subsequently battled with Fernando's illegitimate half-brother João of Aviz for the Portuguese throne. For almost two years after Fernando's death, there was an interregnum in Portugal.

Another Parliament was held in Salisbury from late April to late May 1384, though John of Gaunt and other lords, including his two brothers, arrived a few days late as they had been 'waging war in the kingdom of Scotland,' and had a long way to travel from there to Wiltshire. The Salisbury Parliament became the scene of the latest dramatic event of Richard II's reign when the king threatened to have his uncle John put to death, after a Carmelite friar named John Latimer made accusations against the duke. While celebrating Mass in the king's presence, in the chambers of Richard's friend the earl of Oxford, Latimer suddenly began ranting that Gaunt was planning to have Richard killed and that he would thereafter attempt to seize the throne himself. Without waiting to ascertain the truth of the matter or even to have Gaunt summoned to him to be questioned on the matter, in a fit of passionate rage Richard ordered that the duke would be put to death (at least, according to one chronicler, though others do not give this story). On hearing of this, Thomas of Woodstock rushed into the king's chamber and furiously declared that he would attack and kill anyone, even Richard himself, who claimed that his brother was a traitor.

Some people in attendance on the king rather bravely pointed out to Richard that he was acting rather rashly and that it was unjust for anyone, especially his own uncle, to be put to death without being heard. Fortunately, Richard calmed down and conceded the point. John of Gaunt came to hear what had happened, and understandably demanded an immediate audience with Richard to set matters straight. The friar John Latimer was led away to be interrogated, but had the misfortune to fall into the hands of the king's violent and impetuous half-brother Sir John Holland. Holland had him tortured to death, and anything useful he might have said on the matter of who exactly had persuaded him to accuse the duke of Lancaster of plotting treason and murder was lost forever. According to Thomas Walsingham, Holland killed Latimer out of love for the duke of Lancaster, and it is certainly true that Gaunt and Holland had travelled to the Continent together on a couple of recent occasions.[7] The Salisbury Parliament was also the scene of a furious row between King Richard and the hawkish Richard Fitzalan, earl of Arundel, after the earl declared that England was suffering from bad governance and was 'at present almost in a state of decay'. The seventeen-year-old king was so furious he went white, and yelled at Arundel: 'You lie in your teeth! You can go to the devil!' John of Gaunt rose from his seat and managed to calm the situation down.[8]

Despite John's mediation on this occasion, matters between the king and his powerful uncle did not much improve throughout 1384, and in fact became worse. A few months later in August 1384, John of Northampton, a draper and former mayor of London, was put on trial at a meeting of the royal council in Reading, accused of inciting disorder in London after losing an election the previous autumn. When Richard II proposed that the council should move to judgement on John of Northampton, the former mayor declared that he hoped the king would not proceed further in the absence of the duke of Lancaster. Talking to King Richard in this manner was a red rag to a bull, and Richard angrily stated that if he wished, he would not only sit in judgement on Northampton, but on the duke of Lancaster as well. On this occasion, it was the queen, Anne of Bohemia, who interceded with her husband and persuaded him to spare Northampton's life.[9]

John and his brother Thomas of Woodstock spent part of the summer of 1384 in France, attempting to extend the short-term truce that John had negotiated at the start of the year. Eventually they and the French agreed to another one, to last until 1 May 1385. Despite his successes as a mediator, in the winter of 1384/85 the hostile relations between John and his nephew the king began to threaten the peace of the entire realm. Shortly after Christmas 1384, Richard held a meeting of the royal council probably at Windsor, and one chronicler claims that John of Gaunt was invited but was warned beforehand that some of the king's councillors (not named) were plotting to kill him. He therefore invented a pretext to stay away, but a furious Richard told him that he must attend, and therefore John went to the meeting with a large armed force. The king told John, whether truthfully or not, that he knew nothing of the threats against his life.[10]

45

A Catalogue of Strange Names

Another uneventful Parliament took place at Westminster from 12 November to 14 December 1384, when John of Gaunt took an opportunity to humiliate Henry Percy, earl of Northumberland, whom he had evidently not yet forgiven after their massive quarrel more than three years before. Northumberland was custodian of the important port of Berwick-on-Tweed on the far north-east coast, and a Scottish force had recently seized it, as John pointed out to him in public. The earl hastily headed back north and managed to recapture Berwick.[1]

On 31 December 1384, the religious reformer John Wycliffe died. He had remained unmolested by ecclesiastical authorities for the previous few years since his trial in St Paul's, which probably speaks to some ongoing protection of him by the powerful Gaunt. Wycliffe was buried in his churchyard of Lutterworth in Leicestershire, though many years later, in 1437, his remains were dug up and burnt, and the ashes were scattered into the River Swift.[2] Thomas Walsingham says, oddly, that although there was a good harvest of grain and fruit in 1384, 'there was a lot of suspicion that the fruits of the various trees such as apples, pears etc were infected because of the various unhealthy mists and noisome vapours in the atmosphere.' He also claims that a lot of people died or were seriously ill after eating these fruits.[3]

At another meeting of the royal council probably in February 1385, despite John's ongoing attempts to extend the truce with France, he and his brothers spoke in favour of a pre-emptive English expedition to France to forestall a French invasion of England. This was rejected, and John and his brothers walked out of the meeting in disgust. The Westminster chronicler states that afterwards, on the night of 24 February, John took an armed force to the royal manor house of Sheen on the Thames, where he berated the king for keeping evil counsellors around him, for acting lawlessly, and for countenancing vengeful murder. Although the king's mother Joan of Kent managed to bring about a temporary reconciliation between Richard and his uncle early in March 1385, following the apparent threats against the duke of Lancaster's life shortly before Christmas 1384, there is no doubt that the royal court had become a dangerous place by the mid-1380s.[4] The next time Parliament was held, in October 1385, tension between uncle and nephew was almost at breaking point, though the two were probably in each other's company on 9 June 1385 when John witnessed a grant to the king by the abbot of Bardney in Lincolnshire.[5]

John's two younger brothers received dukedoms on 6 August 1385. Edmund of Langley, earl of Cambridge, became the first duke of York, and Thomas of Woodstock, earl of Buckingham, became the first duke of Gloucester.[6] To raise Edward III's youngest sons to the same title as their older brothers was entirely conventional and expected and aroused no criticism whatsoever, but Richard II created a furore in October 1386 by granting his beloved Robert de Vere, earl of Oxford, the unprecedented dukedom of Ireland, having already made him marquess of Dublin in late 1385.[7]

A military campaign did take place in 1385, but to Scotland, not France. The eighteen-year-old king, leading his first major expedition, and his army entered Scotland on 6 August, the day Richard's uncles were elevated to dukedoms, and reached Edinburgh on 12 August. John of Gaunt wanted to continue farther north past the Firth of Forth, but Richard said that he preferred to turn back. The two managed to avert a huge row after John 'sufficiently humbled himself in the face of the king's violent anger,' but relations remained hostile, especially as the king's ally Michael de la Pole supposedly told Richard that 'the duke of Lancaster wishes for nothing more earnestly than your death, that he may be king.'[8] This is another indication that John was considered heir presumptive to the throne, rather than his great-nephew Roger Mortimer, earl of March (still only eleven years old in 1385).

During the Scottish campaign, Sir John Holland, the king's violent half-brother who had tortured the friar John Latimer to death the year before, killed a young nobleman named Ralph Stafford in a rage after a fight between members of Holland's retinue and Stafford's. Ralph, little more than twenty when he was murdered, was the eldest son and heir of Hugh, earl of Stafford, and a friend of King Richard. Richard was utterly furious, and – understandably – refused to pardon John Holland even though their mother the dowager princess of Wales begged him to do so. A few months later after Joan of Kent's death, Richard did grudgingly pardon John Holland, but very pointedly refused to acknowledge him as his brother, as he did on every other occasion throughout his reign, instead calling him 'John Holland, knight of the [royal] household.'[9]

At the Battle of Aljubarrota fought on 14 August 1385, Portuguese forces won a decisive victory against King Juan of Castile, whose wife Beatriz was the only surviving legitimate child of the late King Fernando of Portugal. Fernando's half-brother João of Aviz, born illegitimate in 1357, succeeded as king of Portugal, and the two-year interregnum came to an end. Beatriz and her claims to the throne of Portugal were set aside, and although she was the queen consort of Castile, she was to die in obscurity in *c.* 1420. One source states that when John of Gaunt heard the list of the casualties at Aljubarrota, he burst out laughing, and when asked why, exclaimed, 'Why, have I not sufficient cause? For I never in my life heard such a catalogue of strange names as you are repeating.'[10] According to the *Chronica d'El Rei D. João*, on hearing of the victory at Aljubarrota, Duchess Constanza took the opportunity to plead with her husband to champion her rights and to avenge her murdered father Pedro. Leading their daughter Catalina by the hand, Constanza fell to her knees in front of John of Gaunt and passionately entreated him to help her recover her lost homeland.[11] John wished nothing more than to do so, but was dependent on receiving funds from Parliament, which had never appeared.

John's sister-in-law Joan of Kent, dowager princess of Wales and Aquitaine, and countess of Kent and Lady Wake in her own right, died on the same day as the Portuguese victory at Aljubarrota. In her will of 7 August, she had requested burial next to her previous husband Sir Thomas Holland (d. 1360) in Stamford, Lincolnshire, rather than with her royal husband the prince of Wales, a request that reveals much about her strong feelings for the long-dead Holland. Whether Richard II was happy about this or not, he complied with her wishes, and duly buried his mother in Stamford. Sir Thomas Holland the younger (b. 1350/51) became earl of Kent and Lord Wake; as Joan's eldest son, he, rather than his much younger half-brother the king, was her heir. John of Gaunt's registers do not survive after 1383, but it seems virtually certain that he had Masses sung for the soul of his sister-in-law, a relative and friend whom he must have known for most of his life and for whom he had good reasons to feel affection and gratitude.

Parliament was held at Westminster between 20 October and 6 December 1385, and Henry of Lancaster, earl of Derby, now eighteen, was summoned for the first time. In late 1384, Henry had become a sizeable landowner by right of his wife Mary, who had turned fourteen and had come into her inheritance from her late father. John of Gaunt, finally, after trying for years, managed to secure funding for his expedition to Spain and Portugal during this Parliament, and in the coming summer he could at last travel to the Iberian Peninsula and attempt to claim the Castilian throne. It was probably the Portuguese victory over the Castilians at Aljubarrota a few months before that convinced English people that there was a realistic prospect of John's victory.

An important person arrived in England in late December 1385: King Levon of Cilician Armenia in modern-day Turkey, came for a visit, and was met at Dover by Edmund of Langley and Thomas of Woodstock. He spent the festive season at Eltham in Kent with King Richard and Queen Anne, who perhaps found his visit sorely trying as Levon spoke little French, little Latin and of course no English. The 1392 will of Isabel of Castile, duchess of York and countess of Cambridge, reveals that Levon gave her a 'tablet of jasper' during this visit, which she bequeathed to John of Gaunt.

46

Frightened Hares and Timid Mice

John of Gaunt was in Lincoln on 19 February 1386 when his son Henry was admitted into the fraternity of the cathedral, as Gaunt himself had been as an infant in 1343. One of the knights attending the duke of Lancaster on this occasion was Katherine Swynford's son Sir Thomas Swynford, and Thomas's aunt, Philippa Chaucer, was admitted to the fraternity on the same occasion. This surely means that Katherine herself was present (especially given that she lived in Lincoln part of the time and that her own manor of Kettlethorpe was only a few miles away), perhaps with her and John's four Beaufort children. John Beaufort was now perhaps thirteen, Henry eleven, Joan about nine, and Thomas about six.

By 16 March, the duke of Lancaster had returned south and was at Hertford Castle.[1] King Richard confirmed his grandfather's 1373 treaty with the kingdom of Portugal on 12 April 1386, and at the end of that month, he and his uncle made a treaty of perpetual alliance in their respective roles as king of England and king of Castile; John confirmed the treaty on 20 June that year before he set off for Spain and Portugal. Richard presented John and Duchess Constanza with gold crowns on Easter Sunday, 22 April, and John took the crowns with him to Spain to be used in his and his wife's intended coronation.[2]

In the summer of 1386, despite endless efforts over the previous few years by John and others to negotiate a peace settlement with the French, Charles VI and his uncles raised a large force and a fleet of ships, and came very close to invading England. Nicholas Brembre, mayor of London, made preparations in the city 'in view of an expected attack by the enemy,' and the ever-spiteful Thomas Walsingham in St Albans mocked the Londoners: 'they grew very fearful, and like frightened hares and timid mice they scurried hither and thither, looking for places in which to hide ... as if the city was now about to be captured.' Ultimately, however, the French, 'weakened by hunger and other miseries,' abandoned the whole idea.[3]

John, meanwhile, was ready to set off to Portugal and Spain at last. He was in Plymouth, Devon, on 18 June 1386 and at the wealthy Augustinian house of Plympton Priory near Plymouth two days later. In April that year before his departure, Pope Urban VI issued a papal bull in Rome 'granting indulgences to those serving in the expedition of the duke of Lancaster against John Henry [i.e. Juan, son of Enrique], pretending to [the throne of] Castile'. The kingdom of Castile, like its ally France, supported the pope or antipope in

Avignon, Clement VII (born Robert of Geneva), and therefore the Rome pope, Urban, stood firmly on England's side in the matter.[4]

According to the Leicester chronicler Henry Knighton, John of Gaunt departed from England on 8 July 1386 with the earl of Northumberland's younger brother Thomas Percy, Sir John Holland, Sir Richard Burley, Sir John Marmion and Lords FitzWalter and Poynings. Sir Hugh Hastings, Gaunt's former ward, also went to Portugal with him and would be killed there, and another young knight who travelled to Portugal was Sir John Cornwaille or Cornwall, who a few years later would marry the duke's daughter Elizabeth as her third husband. The duke and his retinue sailed in ships called the *Marie*, the *Maudeleyn* and the *Margarete* of London, and King Richard ordered three of his sergeants-at-arms on 20 April 1386 to ensure that the ships were sent from London to John in Plymouth as soon as possible.[5]

John was also accompanied by his daughters Philippa, Elizabeth and Catalina, and of course by Constanza, perhaps delighted to be returning to her homeland at last after nearly a decade and a half in the chilly north. As far as is known, she had not set foot in Castile since she was twelve in 1366, when her father sent her and her sisters as hostages to the prince of Wales in Aquitaine, and now she was in her early thirties. A scandal struck the Lancaster family that summer, probably shortly before their departure for the Iberian Peninsula. The six-year marriage of the duke's second daughter Elizabeth and the earl of Pembroke, still only thirteen years old, was annulled, and Elizabeth subsequently remarried Sir John Holland, constable of Gaunt's army. On the face of it, Holland made a perfectly acceptable husband for the duke of Lancaster's daughter: he was a great-grandson of Edward I, an older half-brother of Richard II, stepson of Gaunt's late brother the prince of Wales, and the younger brother of the earl of Kent (b. 1350/51). John's father Thomas Holland (d. 1360) had been a knight from a fairly humble background in Lancashire who was not even his father Robert's eldest son and heir, and made an excellent marriage to Joan of Kent, granddaughter of a king and ultimately the heir to her father's earldom of Kent, though not when Thomas married her. Their second son John Holland was most probably born in 1353, when Edward of Woodstock sent two expensive silver basins to an unnamed 'son of Sir Thomas Holland.' The basins seem likely to have been a christening gift for John, and John apparently accompanied Elizabeth of Lancaster's uncle Lionel of Antwerp to Italy in the spring of 1368 when he was fourteen or fifteen (unless the 'John Holland' who was part of Lionel's retinue was another man who shared John's rather common name). He was about a decade older than Elizabeth, and probably thirty-three when he married her.[6]

There remained two major issues. The first and more important was, of course, that Elizabeth was already married, and the second was John Holland's character. His older brother Thomas, the earl of Kent, was a much steadier and more stable individual, but John himself was violent and impetuous, the man who had murdered the earl of Stafford's eldest son Ralph in 1385 and who had tortured a friar to death. It seems almost certain that Elizabeth was already pregnant by John Holland, and given John Hastings' youth, the infant could not be his or passed off as his. Her father would never have agreed to the annulment of her Hastings marriage and her new marriage unless there had been some exceedingly pressing reason for him to do so; simply because Elizabeth desired Holland and wished to marry and sleep with him would under no circumstances have been sufficient grounds. Annulling a marriage was not only scandalous, it might destroy Gaunt's carefully built relations with the influential Hastings/Norfolk family, and he would only have permitted it if Elizabeth's remaining within her Hastings marriage would have been an even greater scandal than ending it. It would also have been impossible to obtain papal permission to end the marriage without a compelling reason.[7] If Holland had truly had an affair with his new wife's aunt-in-law Isabel of Castile, duchess of York, he apparently made a habit of seducing royal, married women. If he had perhaps even fathered Richard of Conisbrough, who was born in *c.* July 1385, the affair with Isabel had taken place not too long before he married Elizabeth. Holland had spent time in sanctuary in Beverly Minster, Yorkshire after killing Ralph Stafford in July or early August 1385, and was only pardoned for this murder on 8 February 1386, mere months before his wedding to the duke of Lancaster's daughter.

John Hastings' grandmother Margaret, countess of Norfolk, presented a petition at an unknown date. On 16 June 1384, a few weeks after the death of Margaret's younger daughter and co-heir, Hastings' mother Anne Manny, Margaret and John of Gaunt had been granted joint custody of Anne's lands during the minority of her son and heir. As the marriage of Gaunt's daughter and Margaret's grandson 'has since been terminated,' Margaret requested in her petition that the lands be given solely into her custody, and that she would pay the king £100 more for them than Gaunt was currently paying.[8] As for young John Hastings, the rejected pubescent husband who had done nothing wrong except to be born too late for Elizabeth of Lancaster's liking, he later married John of Gaunt's great-niece Philippa Mortimer, the younger daughter of Lionel of Antwerp's late daughter Philippa of Clarence, countess of March and Ulster. Born in 1375, she was much closer to his own age.

Gaunt's fifteen-year-old daughter-in-law Mary de Bohun, countess of Derby, was a few months pregnant when Gaunt departed from England, and on 16 September 1386 gave birth to a boy who immediately became the Lancastrian heir after his nineteen-year-old father.[9] He was also named Henry, and was born in Monmouth, a Lancastrian lordship in Wales. Later King Henry V, Henry of Monmouth was the second of three kings of England born in Wales.[10] Gaunt must have been overjoyed when the news finally reached him in distant Portugal. Henry of Monmouth was probably the duke's first grandchild – John was now forty-six – though it is not clear precisely when Elizabeth of Lancaster's first child was born. She gave birth to Constance Holland (or 'Custance', as the name was usually spelt in the late fourteenth century), future countess of Norfolk and Lady Grey, probably sometime in the second half of 1386 or in 1387.[11]

47

A Portuguese Son-in-law

For the campaign in Spain and Portugal in 1386/87, Gaunt raised a force of about 2,000 men-at-arms and 2,000 archers, as he had told Parliament on several occasions that he would.[1] Various chroniclers comment on the large numbers of Englishmen who fell while fighting for John of Gaunt in Spain and Portugal, and perhaps more than a third of his force were killed. One of them was Gaunt's former ward Sir Hugh Hastings, aged thirty-two, who died at Villanueva de Arosa on 6 November 1386.[2]

John, his wife and daughters landed at La Coruña in Galicia on 25 July 1386, and took the opportunity to travel to Santiago de Compostela on pilgrimage. The next few months would be spent in the town of Orense. The duke evidently learnt some Spanish, either from Constanza or members of her entourage before his departure from England or while he was in Castile, or both. Jean Froissart states that King Juan sent his confessor to John and Constanza as an ambassador, but the duke could not follow all that the man said (*'ne les avoit toutes entendues'*), which is interesting for revealing that John could actually follow some of the man's Spanish speech. John's biographer Anthony Goodman considers, however, that the duke took rather a dim view of Spain in general and perhaps felt a certain distaste for most things Spanish – though might have been aware of the exploits of his and Constanza's mutual ancestor Fernando III of Castile and Leon, who recaptured a great deal of Spanish territory from the Almohad caliphate between the 1220s and 1240s during the Reconquista of Spain.[3] (Fernando III was canonised as San Fernando, but not until 1671, and is now the patron saint of Seville, where Constanza probably grew up.)

On the feast day of St Valentine, 14 February 1387, John's daughter Philippa of Lancaster married King João of Portugal in the cathedral of Porto in Portugal (they had first been married by proxy twelve days earlier, before the necessary papal dispensation for the marriage arrived). John and Dom João agreed to take part in a joint military campaign against Castile, and sealed the deal with the marriage. In exchange for the Portuguese king's aid, John stated that he would give his daughter and new son-in-law a narrow but long line of Castilian territory, along the Portuguese border, once he was firmly ensconced as king of Castile in more than name only.[4] At almost twenty-seven, Philippa was far beyond the usual age when royal fourteenth-century women married, her aunt Isabella of Woodstock in 1365 being a notable exception.

Dom João was thirty and had already fathered several illegitimate children, including Beatriz (*c.* 1380/85–1439), who in 1405 married the English nobleman Thomas, earl of Arundel (1381–1415). After more than seventeen years of widowhood, in the early 1430s Countess Beatriz married John of Gaunt's grandson, John Holland the younger, earl of Huntingdon and later duke of Exeter, who was born in 1395 and was much her junior. Beatriz, who had no children, was buried with her first husband in Arundel, Sussex, in 1439, and her tomb and effigy can still be seen; she wears a horned headdress of quite remarkable width.

Queen Philippa became pregnant very soon after her wedding, but miscarried in July 1387 while visiting João in Curval, where he lay seriously ill.[5] Again, she became pregnant quickly, and gave birth to her eldest child in July 1388, naming her Branca after her mother Blanche of Lancaster. Sadly, little Branca of Portugal died when she was a few months old, and Philippa's second child and first son Alfonso, born in 1390, also died young – in 1400 when he was ten. Of the seven younger children whom Philippa bore between 1391 and 1402, six lived into adulthood: five boys and one girl. They are known to Portuguese historians as the 'Illustrious Generation'.

John of Gaunt sent letters on 22 July 1387 that reveal the names of some of the members of his council with him in Portugal: Robert Swillington, Thomas Hungerford, John Pole, John Scarle and Thomas Hesulden. In the letters he spoke of his 'present journey on the conquest of our kingdom of Castile'. He was in Coimbra on 23 and 24 July.[6] A member of his retinue in Portugal was named John Croft, and Croft married a Portuguese woman whose name is not recorded. After the duke's return to England, Croft was imprisoned in Windsor Castle and also in Winchester (for reasons that were not explained), and his Portuguese wife pleaded for his release, stating that he was a good and loyal liege of King Richard II and had done good service to the duke of Lancaster.[7] John was still in Porto on 7 and 20 September 1387, set sail for Bayonne in the duchy of Aquitaine in late September with a Portuguese fleet of fourteen galleys, and by 15 January 1388 had arrived in Bordeaux.[8]

The duke's eldest daughter Philippa was now married to the king of Portugal, and his second, Elizabeth, far less satisfactorily as far as Gaunt was concerned, to John Holland. There remained his third daughter Catalina of Lancaster, who was the heir of her mother Constanza and also of her grandfather King Pedro; although two of Pedro's sons, Juan and Diego, were still alive, they had never been legitimised as Constanza and her siblings had, and had been held in captivity by their Trastámara kin since Pedro's death almost twenty years before. As noted above, the duke of Lancaster had most probably long foreseen a role for his half-Castilian daughter in Spain, and conveniently, King Juan of Castile and his late first wife Leonor of Aragon had a son, named Enrique after his Trastámara grandfather, who was born in October 1379. This made him at least six and a half years younger than Catalina, perhaps more than seven, but this was not an insurmountable age gap.

According to Jean Froissart, however, the French duke of Berry (uncle of Charles VI) wished to have Catalina's marriage, and negotiations were ongoing between Berry and Gaunt, news of which reached the ears of King Juan and many others in Castile. On the other hand, several modern historians are sceptical that this was indeed the case, given that Catalina's marriage into Castile was the linchpin of Gaunt's Iberian policy.[9] Froissart may be correct that the duke of Berry wished to have Catalina's marriage, although perhaps not that John of Gaunt ever seriously entertained the idea. Froissart says that the duke of Berry's envoy, Sir Hélyon de Lignach, travelled to see John of Gaunt in Bayonne to discuss the possible marriage, and stayed there with him for over a month. Hélyon met the duke of Lancaster in his hall and bowed low to him, whereupon Gaunt courteously embraced him and took him into his chamber.[10]

Froissart here makes a point of commenting on John of Gaunt's polite and courtly treatment of the duke of Berry's envoy; whatever his other faults may have been, and although English people generally may have found it difficult to warm to him, John knew exactly how to behave in public and never lacked good manners. John's biographer Anthony Goodman has remarked on the duke's ability to put people at ease, telling the story of how on one occasion in 1370, John was aiding his brother the prince of Wales to bring down part of the city wall of Limoges, and supervised the mining operations. He encountered one man there who apologised for being a poor and undistinguished knight, and reassured him that he was in fact delighted to prove himself against such a good knight.[11]

Meanwhile, in London Gaunt's daughter-in-law, Mary de Bohun, countess of Derby, gave birth to her second son, Thomas of Lancaster, probably in early August 1387, under eleven months after her first son, Henry of Monmouth, was born.[12] At some point between September 1387 and September 1388, Mary and her two infant sons were living at Gaunt's castle of Kenilworth, and at Christmas 1387 Mary sent or gave cloth to Katherine Swynford and Katherine's daughter Joan Beaufort, so clearly the women kept in touch. Henry of Lancaster was at Kenilworth on 17 and 18 October 1388 and on 12 June and 1 July 1389 when he made grants there to a servant named Thomas Totty and to a retainer named Walter Blount; evidently he and Mary were welcome to make their home at his father's largest castle whenever they wished during John of Gaunt's absence. John and his son-in-law the king of Portugal both kept in touch with Countess Mary in 1388.[13]

A third Lancastrian son, named John after his paternal grandfather the duke, followed in June 1389, and a fourth, named Humphrey after Mary's late father the earl of Hereford, probably in September 1390.[14] Earlier in the century, there had been a dearth of male Lancastrian heirs: Duke Henry had six sisters but no brothers, and he himself had two daughters (plus another daughter who died in infancy and an illegitimate daughter) but no sons. John of Gaunt and Blanche of Lancaster lost two and perhaps even three sons in infancy, and for many years their youngest son Henry was the only male Lancastrian. Henry and Mary had now well and truly resolved this issue.

48

Forty-seven Mules Carrying Money

After many years of hoping and planning to take the kingdom of Castile, John's expedition there proved ultimately unsuccessful. The high death toll of the Anglo-Portuguese forces, the diseases including dysentery which ran rampant among his men, and the duke's inability to defeat the Castilians, forced John to come to terms with King Juan of Castile, and he eventually had to deal with the fact that he would never take the kingdom and would never rule in his wife's homeland. Used to the cooler, damper English climate, John grew listless in the heat, unwell, and dispirited (his brother Edward had also become ill while in Spain twenty years earlier).[1] Thomas Walsingham says that a large number of the duke's soldiers deserted to the French army and were well treated and given good food and medical aid, whereupon Walsingham makes the surprising comment that, for all their hostility to each other at home, the English and French treated each other as brothers when they met in foreign lands and showed 'an unbreakable loyalty' to each other.[2]

On 12 June 1387, John of Gaunt and King Juan came to a preliminary agreement in the Portuguese town of Trancoso, which was finally ratified in the Gascon city of Bayonne in July 1388 and is therefore generally known as the Treaty of Bayonne. The treaty stipulated that in exchange for renouncing all claims to the kingdom of Castile, John would receive a payment of £100,000 plus a pension of £6,600 every year for life. The money was to be transported to England on the backs of forty-seven mules, and John was to use part of it to finance his son Henry's expeditions to Prussia and the Holy Land in the early 1390s (he gave Henry over £3,500). John had already been exceedingly wealthy anyway, and thanks to this Castilian agreement, he became one of the richest men in Europe.

The Treaty of Bayonne also provided for the release from prison of Constanza's half-brothers Juan and Diego, illegitimate sons of King Pedro, who had been incarcerated by their uncle King Enrique in 1369 although they were children. A third half-brother, Sancho, had died in captivity in 1370 at the age of about seven. Forty years after his death in 1410, Sancho's niece Catalina of Lancaster, then the dowager queen consort of Castile, wrote to the prioress of Santo Domingo el Real in Toledo, Teresa de Ayala, herself a former lover of Catalina's grandfather King Pedro and mother of his daughter María de Ayala, who also became the prioress of Santo Domingo el Real. Queen Catalina asked Teresa to take charge of reburying Sancho's remains. Unfortunately for Catalina's other uncles Juan and Diego, they were not released from captivity in the late 1380s as their cousin King Juan I had promised. King Juan II, Catalina's son and John of Gaunt's grandson, finally set his great-uncle Diego free in 1424 after he had spent a staggering fifty-five years in captivity. Juan, born in early 1355 about six months after his half-sister Duchess Constanza, died still in prison in 1405, though in the meantime had married his warder's daughter Elvira and fathered several children.[3]

Both John of Gaunt and Constanza swore on the Gospels in 1387/88 that their daughter Catalina would marry King Juan I's son Enrique, and Juan in turn promised that the wedding would go ahead within two months of Catalina being handed over into his custody. The king also promised that Catalina would be looked after 'in seemly and secure conditions', at his own expense, by people whom her father would appoint, until Enrique was old enough for the marriage to be consummated. As was the case with Catalina's older half-sister Elizabeth and John Hastings, there was an age gap of a few years between bride and groom, and Constanza would be over twenty by the time Enrique became physically mature. If anything happened to young Enrique before he married Catalina, she would marry his younger brother Don Fernando (b. November 1380, a future king of Aragon and Majorca) instead. Finally, if Catalina and Enrique failed to have children together, the kingdom of Castile would fall to Edward of York, as the elder son of Constanza's sister Isabel and John's brother Edmund.

The fifth article of the treaty was an important one, stating that when Enrique was recognised as king after his father's death Catalina would be 'received and recognised' as queen. As it turned out, Enrique died in his twenties, leaving his and Catalina's infant son, Juan II, as king and Catalina thereafter ruled Castile as joint regent with her brother-in-law Don Fernando. On 5 August 1388, Catalina declared herself bound by the treaty and that she would freely enter into her Castilian marriage, and on 26 August, King Juan delivered sixty hostages to Gaunt. That same month, the king of Aragon addressed a letter to young Enrique of Castile as prince of Asturias, duke of Soria and lord of Molina, titles that, as his wife, Catalina of Lancaster would share.[4] John of Gaunt's daughter and son-in-law would rule one day in Castile and Leon, but his own long-term dream of becoming the ruler of two Spanish kingdoms was over.

During John's extended sojourn in southern Europe, dramatic events took place in England. His brother Thomas of Woodstock, son Henry of Lancaster, and the earls of Arundel, Warwick and Nottingham formed a group who called themselves the Lords Appellant because they wished to appeal the king's chief supporters for treason. In February 1388 at the so-called Merciless Parliament, a number of Richard II's chief supporters, including his former tutor and chamberlain Sir Simon Burley and his friend Sir James Berners, were executed. The king's beloved friend, or lover, Robert de Vere, earl of Oxford, fled to the Continent after falling into a brilliant trap at Radcot Bridge over the River Thames prepared for him by Gaunt's son, Henry; Robert would die in exile in 1392. It is even possible that King Richard was deposed for a few days and that his uncle Thomas of Woodstock tried to claim the throne, until Henry of Lancaster pointed out that his father was Thomas's older brother and therefore had precedence. John of Gaunt was surely kept informed of these dramatic events by letters and oral messages, and it cannot be a coincidence that the greatest political crisis of Richard II's reign so far took place during his long absence overseas.

Also while John was far away in the south of Europe, his servant Robert de Whiteby entrusted a counterpane (i.e. a bedspread) of expensive ermine fur, which belonged to John, to a Peter Mildenhale. Peter in turn pledged it as security to the executor of two skinners to whom he owed a debt, and soon afterwards was arrested and imprisoned in Nottingham Castle for various felonies he had committed. When John of Gaunt's servant Robert de Whiteby asked for John's counterpane to be given to him, the executor refused to deliver it, and Richard II had to intervene and send letters to the mayor and sheriffs of London on 16 January 1389 to demand the return of the counterpane to Whiteby.[5]

Gaunt's son-in-law John Holland travelled back to England with Elizabeth of Lancaster, and was made earl of Huntingdon by his half-brother the king on 2 June 1388.[6] As Elizabeth was now a countess, Gaunt perhaps became somewhat less disgruntled about the marriage. Elizabeth named her first daughter Constance Holland (b. *c.* 1386/87) after her stepmother; Constanza was almost certainly the little girl's godmother, which probably means that Constance Holland was born in Portugal or Spain while the Lancaster family were together there, before Elizabeth's return to England. Her first son, who died young in 1400, was named Richard Holland, which implies that Richard II was the boy's godfather and that he was born after Holland and Elizabeth returned to England. After John Holland's murder of the king's friend Ralph Stafford in 1385 and Richard's fury over it, Holland and the king reconciled to the point where John was one of his half-brother's most loyal followers for the rest of his reign. He would play a leading role in Richard's long-awaited revenge in 1397 against the Lords Appellant of 1388, and would die attempting to restore Richard to his lost throne.

Gaunt's four Beaufort children remained in England during his long sojourn in southern Europe, and his and Katherine's second son Henry began studying at Peterhouse College at the University of Cambridge in 1388, when he was probably thirteen. A couple of years later, Henry moved to the University of Oxford and resided at Queen's, a college founded by his grandmother Queen Philippa and her almoner in 1341, where he completed his Bachelor of Arts degree and began studying theology.[7]

Around New Year 1389, Jean Froissart was personally present in Bordeaux when five members of Gaunt's household jousted against five men of

Charles VI's allegiance, who were members of the marshal of France's household, over three days in the square in front of the cathedral. Gaunt himself watched the events with Constanza and Catalina, and they were joined by ladies and young ladies of the region. The competitors were: Petiton de Pelagrue, a 'Gascon Englishman', fighting against Morisse Movynet on the French side; Raymond of Aragon, on the English side, against the Bastard of Chauvigny; Loys or Louis de Malepue against Janequin Corne-de-Cherf (which means 'stag's horn'); Arcembault de Villers, a Frenchman, against the lord of Chaumont's son, also described as a 'Gascon Englishman'; and Guillemme Foulcaut, French, against the lord of Chaumont's brother, who fought on the English side. The duke of Lancaster became angry when Sir Raymond of Aragon, one of the knights on the English side, pointed his lance too low and killed the Bastard of Chauvigny's horse. Gaunt presented the Bastard with one of his own horses as compensation, evidence that chivalric rules of engagement were important to him and evidence also of his scrupulous fairness.[8]

49

Constanza and Catalina
Grandly Received

After the jousts in Bordeaux, Jean Froissart says, Duchess Constanza began preparing to travel to Castile to arrange and attend the wedding of her and Gaunt's daughter, which the couple had been planning all winter, to Catalina's second cousin Don Enrique. By March, when the days started getting longer and the weather was better, Constanza was ready. She, Gaunt and Catalina travelled from Bordeaux to Bayonne, then Constanza and Catalina went on to Dax, while Gaunt himself returned to Bordeaux. Mother and daughter spent two days at Dax, then travelled through the Basque country, over the Pyrenees via the pass at Roncesvalles and on to Pamplona. Here, the king and queen of Navarre 'received them grandly and honourably' because Queen Leonor of Navarre was the sister of the king of Castile, and thus was both Constanza's first cousin and the aunt of the young bridegroom-to-be.[1]

Constanza and Catalina stayed for over a month in the kingdom of Navarre with the king and queen, and finally crossed the border into Castile, or 'Spain' as Froissart and most other people of the era rather confusingly called it. All the important people of Castile, Galicia, Seville, Cordoba and Toledo came to watch them enter the kingdom, in order to see the young half-Castilian, half-English girl who would marry their king's son and would one day become their queen. King Juan himself met them in Burgos.

Constanza then went to Montiel, where her father Pedro had lost the battle against her uncle Enrique of Trastámara in 1369. Pedro was buried in Montiel after Trastámara stabbed him to death in the aftermath of the battle; Constanza exhumed his remains and took his body south to Seville where she had him 'richly and honourably' reinterred. King Juan attended the funeral of his uncle, the man his father had killed, as did his son Enrique and his soon-to-be daughter-in-law Catalina. Afterwards, Constanza went to Medina del Campo (or 'Medine-de-Camp' as Froissart calls it, a 'beautiful and large city of which she was lady') 30 miles from Valladolid, and stayed there for a while with her retinue.

Froissart, unfortunately, gives no details of the subsequent wedding of young Enrique of Castile and Catalina of Lancaster in the cathedral of Palencia in northern Spain in September (apparently in September 1388 though Froissart seems to state that it took place in 1389). Enrique was only nine when he married, and Catalina was probably sixteen. Their first child or at least their first surviving child, María of Castile, later queen of Aragon and Naples, was not born until 1401, though the young couple became king and queen of Castile much sooner than anybody had expected, in October 1390 when King Juan died in his early thirties. According to Froissart, Catalina and young Enrique received the entire land of Galicia and Enrique was known as 'prince of Galicia' until his accession, though other evidence indicates that he was titled 'prince of Asturias'.[2]

After his return to England from the Iberian Peninsula later in the year, as far as is known, John of Gaunt never saw his daughters Philippa and Catalina again, though he left them items in his will and must have kept in touch with them. Some of Queen Philippa of Portugal's letters still exist and reveal that she kept herself well informed of events in England, and took a keen interest in them and in her relatives there. She and the bishop of Norwich, Henry Despenser, exchanged correspondence, and the queen of Portugal held Bishop Despenser in far higher regard than her father did. Several of their amicable letters in French to each other survive, and reveal that Philippa addressed Henry as 'Reverend father in God, my dearest and most entirely beloved cousin' and that he addressed her as 'Very excellent and very dread, very gracious, and my sovereign lady'. Henry sent Philippa expensive cloth on two occasions, for which she thanked him, and at another time told her that he had been 'a little ill' ('*un poy malade*') but that God's mercy and Philippa's lovely letters containing good news of herself had 'cured him completely'.[3]

John was in Bayonne on 26 March 1389, where he made an indenture with Katherine Swynford's nephew Thomas Chaucer, who was the son of Geoffrey and Philippa and who a few years later became the father of Alice, duchess of Suffolk and countess of Salisbury. Thomas was retained for life to serve John 'in peace and war' in exchange for a payment of £10 a year.[4] By 6 April the duke had moved onto Orthez, and made another indenture with Gaston, count of Foix, which provided for mutual support against the count of Armagnac and the lord of Albret. Two days later, John granted the count 30,000 gold francs as a reward for his loyal service to the king of England. He had now given up calling himself 'king of Castile and Leon,' and referred to himself as 'We, Johan, by the grace of God, son of the king of England, duke of Lancaster, earl of Leicester, Lincoln and Derby, steward of England, and lieutenant in the duchy of Aquitaine.'[5] On 18 April, John was back in Bayonne and made yet another indenture with a minstrel called Claus Nakerer, who was to receive 100s (£5) a year for performing for him. A nakerer played a kind of drum, and Claus's first name implies that he was German.[6]

50

The King and the Livery Collar

John and Constanza were together in Bordeaux on 22 October 1389, when the duchess requested her husband to issue letters patent on behalf of a clerk named Bertrand Gerveys, and John did.[1] John, and presumably Constanza, finally returned to England on 19 November 1389, landing at Plymouth; he had been planning their return since at least 11 August, when a sergeant-at-arms named Thomas Sayvill was ordered to prepare six ships and one barge for the duke and his retinue. By 30 October, however, John had still made no real preparations for his departure, and his nephew Richard II sent him a letter requesting that he sail to England as soon as possible.

After the duke's landing at Plymouth, the king did him great honour by riding out to meet him on John's way to London. Richard publicly continued to show his uncle favour after John's long absence by taking the duke's livery collar from his neck and placing it around his own; the earl of Arundel complained about it. The king made a dignified speech pointing out that he had worn his other uncles' mottos on occasion, and thus the quarrelsome Arundel was silenced. Chronicler Thomas Walsingham, now much friendlier to John than he had been before, states that John hurried to a meeting of the royal council held at Reading on 9 December 1389, and adds that the duke 'graciously brought peace to the heart of the king and the minds of the nobles'. The Westminster chronicler says that John was given a semi-regal reception in London after his long sojourn away from England, and that he gave out alms at Westminster Abbey church before riding to St Paul's (where he presumably took the time to pray at Duchess Blanche's tomb).[2]

Possibly John's livery collar worn by the king in and after the late 1380s was designed with the famous Lancastrian S symbol, though this is uncertain. Although the S is more usually associated with Henry of Lancaster than with his father – the poet John Gower referred to Henry as 'He who wears the S' at the end of the fourteenth century – it may have been John of Gaunt himself who introduced the motto. In 1375, six livery collars belonging to the duke are mentioned in an account of the mercer William Caly, and these may have had an S design. In a drawing of Gaunt's tomb made in c. 1605, stained glass with a design of the S collar can be seen. In the early 1390s a few years after Gaunt's return to England, there is a reference in his son Henry's account to a 'collar of gold of Henry [of] Lancaster, earl of Derby, with seventeen letters of S in the form of feathers,' so the concept certainly dates to Gaunt's own lifetime.[3] His mother Queen Philippa had owned wall hangings stamped with the letter S and a cloak 'powdered with gold roses of eight petals and bordered with white pearls, in the middle of each rose an S of large pearls' as early as 1348.

In the three years and a few months that John had been away from England, his daughter-in-law Mary de Bohun had given birth to three sons (and bore her fourth a few months later), and John saw them all for the first time. He must have been delighted that the male succession to Blanche's inheritance was well and truly secure. The eldest and third Lancaster sons, Henry of Monmouth and John, were the only ones of Gaunt's many grandchildren to whom he left items in his will a few years later, so he might have been particularly fond of them. Also while John was away, in May 1389, Richard II had finally taken over the governance of his own realm, now aged twenty-two.

Sometime around October 1389, though the date is unclear, John and his nephew Richard worked together to petition Pope Urban VI (who died on 15 October 1389 and was succeeded by Pietro Tomacelli as Boniface IX) in Rome, regarding the Benedictine abbey of St Peter in Gloucester.[4] The abbey, which became Gloucester Cathedral in the sixteenth century, was the burial site of Edward II, Gaunt's grandfather and Richard's much-revered great-grandfather. The duke and the king pointed out that 'the possessions and lands of the monastery had been in great part submerged by unwonted and stormy floods of diverse waters and devastated by pestilences and other calamities which had long afflicted those parts,' an interesting indication both of awful weather and of the outbreaks of plague that devastated England (and other countries) in the fourteenth century. John and Richard also informed the pope that the abbey endured intolerable financial burdens and was unable to support its forty-four monks and 200 lay servants, and asked the pope to provide help.

A few days after Christmas 1389, Gaunt's former son-in-law John Hastings, earl of Pembroke, was killed while jousting, during the festivities over which King Richard and Queen Anne were presiding at the palace of Woodstock. Hastings was just seventeen. Sir John St John was pardoned in July 1391 for killing the young nobleman and for his subsequent outlawry, which implies that he had fled, terrified of the consequences of what he had done.[5] The young earl left his fourteen-year-old widow, Gaunt's great-niece Philippa Mortimer, who a few months later married the widowed earl of Arundel, a man almost thirty years her senior. John Hastings had no children and neither he, his father John nor his grandfather Laurence (d. 1348) had any siblings; his heir therefore was a rather distant cousin, Reynold, Lord Grey of Ruthin. John of Gaunt might not have been present during the royal festive season at the palace of Woodstock, as he was at Hertford Castle, over 60 miles away, on 1 January 1390.[6]

Parliament was held in Westminster from 17 January to 2 March 1390. John and Constanza's nephew Edward of York, now about sixteen and the elder son of Edmund of Langley and Isabel of Castile, was made earl of Rutland on 25 February, John's palatinate powers in the duchy of Lancaster, previously held only for John's life, were made hereditary, and his son-in-law John Holland, earl of Huntingdon, was made chamberlain of his half-brother the king's household.[7] A remarkable appointment came on 2 March, the last day of Parliament, when John of Gaunt was made duke of Aquitaine on account of 'his excellent and virtuous deeds.'[8] The duchy of Aquitaine had previously been held by the kings of England in person or by their direct heirs: Edward I gave it to his son the future Edward II in 1306, Edward II gave it to his son the future Edward III in 1325, and Edward III gave it to his son the prince of Wales, heir to the throne, in 1362. This would seem to be more evidence that John was considered Richard II's heir presumptive, and by March 1390, the month of his fiftieth birthday, he was once again acting as a member of the royal council.

At St Inglevert, near Calais in northern France, jousts were held from 20 March until 24 April 1390, which were perhaps attended by the twenty-one-year-old King Charles VI himself in disguise.[9] In Jean Froissart's detailed account of this tournament, four men are grouped together as the knights who took part in the jousts on 20 April, near the end of the tournament: Henry of Lancaster, earl of Derby ('le conte d'Erby'); Henry's half-brother, Gaunt's eldest illegitimate son Sir John Beaufort, 'bastard of Lancaster' ('Monseigneur Jehan de Biaufort, bastart de Lanclastre'); a man Froissart names as 'Sir Thomas Subincorde', which presumably is a garbled rendering of the name Swynford, identifying this man as Katherine and Hugh Swynford's son Thomas, who, like Henry of Lancaster, was John Beaufort's older half-brother; and Sir Robert Ferrers, a young English nobleman who would marry Gaunt and Katherine's daughter Joan Beaufort a couple of years later.

Ferrers' inclusion in this family group strongly implies that his marriage to Joan was already under discussion, and he seems to have been placed in Gaunt's wardship after the death of his father in 1381.[10] John Beaufort was evidently, assuming Froissart can be trusted on this point, already a knight, though the first certain reference to him as such in English records dates to 6 December 1391.[11] These young men were obviously close and spent much time together, and shortly after the St Inglevert jousts, both John Beaufort and Thomas Swynford went on crusade to Prussia in Henry of Lancaster's company. They departed on 6 May 1390, and the wealthy John of Gaunt paid all the expenses of his two sons and his beloved Katherine's son, using some of the money he received regularly from King Juan of Castile.[12]

51

England Is in a Bad State

The duke of Lancaster arranged a hunt at Leicester for 'the great men of the realm' between 24 July and 1 August 1390. King Richard and Queen Anne were there, as were John's brothers Edmund of Langley and Thomas of Woodstock, and his son-in-law John Holland, earl of Huntingdon. Richard II had recently visited the tomb of Edward II in St Peter's Abbey, Gloucester, and was endlessly interested in promoting his great-grandfather's canonisation as a saint.

King Richard held a spectacular jousting tournament at Smithfield in October 1390, and the duke of Lancaster held a lavish banquet for two important visitors to England, the count of St Pol (who was married to the king's half-sister Maud Holland) and for Wilhelm, count of Ostrevant, son of John's German cousin Duke Albrecht of Bavaria. Both men took part in the great tournament, and Richard II was doing his utmost to court Ostrevant as an ally, though according to Jean Froissart, Duke Albrecht tried to dissuade his son from visiting England and told him that he was too closely tied to the royal family of France and therefore had no need to seek allies in England. John Holland, earl of Huntingdon, won a prize on the first day of the tournament as the best defender, while his brother-in-law the count of St Pol won one as the best challenger.

There was, apparently, yet another outbreak of plague in England in 1390, a 'mighty pestilence' that disproportionately affected boys and young men, 'who died in all the towns and villages in incredibly huge numbers.' The following year, it returned, and supposedly 11,000 people died in York alone, though this must be a huge exaggeration, as that figure represents approximately the entire population of the city.[1] John of Gaunt must have been relieved that his four sons remained healthy, as well as Katherine's son Thomas Swynford. Henry of Lancaster turned twenty-three in 1390 not long before his departure overseas, and Thomas Swyford was the same age, while the Beaufort boys were about seventeen, fifteen and ten or eleven that year. King Juan of Castile died on 9 October 1390 at the age of only thirty-two, though not of plague; he passed away from injuries he suffered after he fell from his horse at Alcalá in central Spain. Catalina, now seventeen or eighteen, became queen consort of Castile, and her husband Enrique turned eleven years old five days before his father's death. He took over the rule of his own kingdom three years later at age fourteen.

Gaunt was at Hertford Castle on 16 December 1390 and 6 February 1391, and Constanza was at court with the king at Westminster on 9 January 1391. John was, for once, in the company of his son-in-law the earl of Huntingdon on 17 December 1390, when the men jointly asked Richard II to grant a favour to the Benedictine abbey of St Faith's, Norfolk.[2] The duchess of Lancaster requested of the king in early 1391 that a John Stapulton (or Stapleton) be given 'the office of the tronage of wools' in Kingston-upon-Hull. Stapleton was a servant of John of Gaunt's chamber, so Constanza requesting a favour for him of the king perhaps indicates that the duke and duchess were on reasonably good, or at least cordial, terms. There is little if anything to indicate, however, that their relationship was a particularly close one after their return to England from Spain. Their dream of reigning as king and queen of Castile and Leon was over, and this was the glue that had kept them together; whether they spent much time together after their return is difficult to determine for certain, but on the whole it seems they did not.

John and Katherine Swynford's second son Henry Beaufort was still almost certainly only sixteen years old, but on 17 April 1391, his cousin the king granted him 'the prebend of Sutton and Buckingham in the cathedral church of Lincoln'.[3] Both of Henry's parents had strong connections to the city of Lincoln and its cathedral; Katherine spent much of her time in the city and had given birth to at least one of her Swynford children (Thomas) there, while Gaunt himself had been admitted to the fraternity of the cathedral chapter of Lincoln Cathedral in 1343 and Katherine's son and sister were in 1386. For the young Henry Beaufort, still a student at the University of Oxford, this was an early step in what was to be a long and extremely successful career in the Church.

The year 1391 was a rather quiet and non-eventful year in England, and was also a quiet year in John of Gaunt's career. The author of the *Eulogium Historiarum* wrote 'Nothing is written here for the year of Our Lord 1391, because the kingdom of England was in a bad state.' Several chroniclers stated that there was a minor outbreak of the plague again in England in 1391, and that consequently the price of grain rose considerably.[4] On 9 July 1391, 'the sun was seen glowing red through a barrier of thick, evil-smelling clouds,' and from midday until sunset there was barely any light. For the next six weeks, there was a 'superabundance of clouds' which scarcely ever dispersed, though it hardly seems surprising that it was cloudy in England, even in summer.[5] Parliament was held at Westminster from 3 November to 2 December 1391. John of Gaunt was still at Hertford on 2 November, the day before it opened, but only had a few miles to travel from there to Westminster, and certainly attended on the first day.[6] On 6 December during this Parliament, Richard II sent a writ to the mayor and sheriffs of London regarding an ordinance for the slaughtering of animals in the city. John of Gaunt, Henry Percy, earl of Northumberland, the bishops of Ely and Lincoln, the abbot of Leicester, and a few others had complained about 'the nuisance caused by the slaughter of animals near Holbournbrigge', or Holborn Bridge. It was ordered that butchers must 'deposit filth' at least a mile from the city and its suburbs, and failure to comply would result in a staggeringly large fine of £1,000.[7]

This was the latest in a long series of ordinances made throughout the fourteenth century as the authorities sought to make the city of London cleaner and less smelly. This was evidently a subject close to John of Gaunt's heart, and efforts continued. At another Parliament held in early 1393, it was ordered that a dunghill on the banks of the Thames in London must be removed, and King Richard proclaimed that 'all the dung, filth, muck and rubbish' between the palace of Westminster and the Tower of London must also be removed and that the banks of the river must be kept clean, on threat of a large fine.[8]

Throughout 1391, arrangements had been made for a summit between Richard II and Charles VI of France, each of whom would be attended by 400 knights and squires, in the hope of finding a permanent peace between the two kingdoms. It was due to take place on 24 June 1392, the Nativity of St John the Baptist. During the Parliament of November 1391, the Commons declared that as John of Gaunt 'was the most powerful person in the realm,' it seemed sensible that he should also be present at the summit. Gaunt agreed, and, perhaps surprisingly, so did King Richard. In the end, however, the planned meeting between the two kings did not take place until late 1396. The unfortunate King Charles, still only in his early twenties, suffered some kind of breakdown in August 1392 which proved to be the start of three decades of severe bouts of insanity, and which led to a long and bloody power struggle in France between the king's younger brother the duke of Orleans and their uncle the duke of Burgundy.[9]

52

A Tablet of Jasper

Perhaps in March 1392, John of Gaunt supervised the wedding of his and Katherine Swynford's daughter Joan Beaufort to the young nobleman Robert Ferrers.[1] Robert was born around 1371 or 1373 so was some years older than Joan, and his father Robert the elder, first Lord Ferrers of Wem (d. 1381), was the younger brother of John, Lord Ferrers of Chartley, killed fighting with Gaunt and his brother Edward of Woodstock at the Battle of Nájera in 1367. An entry in Gaunt's register in February 1382 indicates that the younger Robert Ferrers was in Gaunt's wardship after his father died, so it makes sense that the duke would have arranged his young ward's marriage to his daughter, and had perhaps planned the match for some years.[2] If Robert was still underage when he wed Joan, he might not have had much or any say in the matter, and it is impossible to know whether he was happy about marrying a young woman who, although she was the daughter of the wealthy, powerful and royal duke of Lancaster and a first cousin of King Richard, was illegitimate and had absolutely no prospects whatsoever of inheriting any lands.

Joan's new husband was heir to his father and was also heir to the larger inheritance of his mother Elizabeth Botiller or Boteler, though in the end Elizabeth outlived her son by many years. Robert Ferrers of Wem the elder and Elizabeth Botiller were landowners in Warwickshire, Shropshire, Staffordshire and Leicestershire.[3] Elizabeth survived her first, Ferrers husband by thirty years, and married another two husbands before her death in 1411. In early January 1379, she suffered a terribly distressing situation when she was attacked and robbed in her own home by a criminal called Hanekyn Fauconer, and he even stole the linen and woollen clothes, rings and necklaces she was wearing. Fauconer also 'ill-treated and abducted' the unfortunate Elizabeth.[4] Robert Ferrers was then a small child, and might have witnessed this horrible attack on his mother.

Joan Ferrers née Beaufort gave birth to two Ferrers daughters: Elizabeth, named after Joan's mother-in-law, and Mary, perhaps named in honour of the Virgin Mary or after a godmother (although this is only speculation, perhaps her godmother was Joan's sister-in-law Mary de Bohun, countess of Derby, who certainly kept in touch with her husband's Beaufort half-kin). Between 24 August and 3 September 1411 the two Ferrers sisters were named as the heirs of their paternal grandmother Elizabeth Botiller when her inquisition post-mortem was taken in various counties, and were said to be eighteen and seventeen years old at the time. These ages would place the elder daughter Elizabeth's birth sometime between August 1392 and August 1393, and the younger daughter Mary's sometime between August 1393 and August 1394.[5] Assuming Joan Beaufort and Robert Ferrers did marry in March 1392, the earliest possible birthdate for their first daughter is December 1392, so it is likely that Elizabeth Ferrers was born sometime between then and the following August. She was the first grandchild of John of Gaunt and Katherine Swynford.

It is most unlikely, therefore, that Joan Beaufort was the child who was probably born to Katherine Swynford at Kettlethorpe near the end of 1379, as this would mean that Joan married at twelve and gave birth to her eldest child when she was barely thirteen. As noted above regarding the possible age of Joan's mother Katherine, Joan was not an heiress and was, as an illegitimate child, not of the highest rank even though she was the king's first cousin. There was no reason why she would have been expected to give birth at the very start of her teens, and it is far more likely that she was at least fifteen or sixteen when she bore her first child. Even if Joan was born closer to the middle of the 1370s then the end of that decade, she was still under forty when she bore Cecily Neville, duchess of York, the youngest of her many children, in 1415. Joan was widowed young, when her two Ferrers daughters were merely infants, sometime before late 1396 when she married her second husband. Although the date of Robert Ferrers' death is not recorded, possibly he was still alive on 7 July 1396, when an entry on the Patent Roll talks of 'trespasses' committed against him and does not explicitly state that he was then dead.[6]

Joan's eldest brother John Beaufort was also on the rise in 1392: on 7 June that year, King Richard retained his cousin as one of his household knights, at a salary of 100 marks a year. John was with the king at Westminster on 28 October 1392, when Richard pardoned a John Cros of Northamptonshire for murder at Beaufort's request.[7] Joan and John's sister-in-law Mary de Bohun, meanwhile, after bearing four sons in four years, gave birth to two daughters in 1392 and 1394: Blanche, who was named after her late grandmother the duchess of Lancaster, and Philippa, who was probably named in honour of her paternal great-grandmother Philippa of Hainault, queen of England.[8]

John of Gaunt's sister-in-law Isabel of Castile, duchess of York and countess of Cambridge, died on 23 December 1392, at the young age of thirty-seven. In her will written in French, she asked her nephew-in-law the king to 'take and keep his humble godson to heart,' meaning her youngest child Richard of Conisbrough – who was only seven when she died – and left generous bequests to her other two, much older children, Edward, earl of Rutland, and Constance, Lady Despenser. Duchess Isabel also left several tablets of gold and a 'psalter with the arms of Northampton' to her sister-in-law Eleanor de

Bohun, duchess of Gloucester, though nothing to Eleanor's husband Thomas of Woodstock; a drinking-horn studded with pearls to Richard II; seven gold belts to the queen, Anne of Bohemia; and 'a tablet of jasper which the king of Armonie [King Levon of Armenia] gave me' to John of Gaunt, whom she called 'my very honoured brother of Lancaster,' though she gave nothing to her sister Constanza. Isabel's failure to leave anything at all to the woman who was her only close blood relative, apart from her three children in England and her half-siblings and her niece Catalina in distant Castile, is perhaps revealing.

To Edmund of Langley, her 'very honoured lord and husband of York,' Isabel left, among other items, all her horses, all her beds including the cushions, bedspreads, canopies and everything else that went with them, her best brooch and her best gold cup, and her 'large primer.' Perhaps, however, Isabel rather added fuel to the fire of allegations that she had once had an affair with Gaunt's son-in-law John Holland, by leaving Holland her Bibles and 'the best fillet that I have'. The meaning of 'fillet' in this context is rather obscure; it usually meant a decorative headband of interlaced wire or a string of jewels to be worn on the head, but this was not an item one would expect to see being bequeathed to a man. Other than the many servants to whom the duchess left items, all the people named in the will were near relatives of Isabel's either by blood or marriage, so there was certainly some close connection between her and Holland. The duchess also bequeathed to her son Edward a gold cup, a gold brooch with 'very large pearls and three sapphires' and a gold chaplet with white flowers, all of which 'the earl of Huntingdon gave me,' and there must have been some reason why John Holland gave her such valuable things and why she treasured them. It was certainly the norm for people of their rank to exchange gifts frequently and to pass them on to other members of the nobility in an endless round of regifting, but in her will Isabel did not not mention other gifts she had received from anyone else, and she cared enough about Holland's to keep them and give them to her son. The gold cup Holland had given her was engraved with Isabel's arms (presumably she meant the arms of Castile), so evidently he had had it especially made for her.

Finally and rather interestingly, Isabel left her best gown and her best cloak, furred with costly miniver, to Marie de St Hilaire. She was the former attendant of Philippa of Hainault stated by Jean Froissart to have been the mother of an illegitimate daughter named Blanche, married name Morieux, who was supposedly fathered by John of Gaunt. This must mean that Marie had gone on to serve in Duchess Isabel's household after Queen Philippa's death, and as noted above, Marie was still alive in 1413 so outlived Isabel by at least twenty-one years. She presumably found another position in a noble household after the duchess's death in late 1392.[9]

Isabel of Castile was buried at the Dominican priory in Langley, Hertfordshire, on 14 January 1393.[10] The priory was founded by her husband's grandfather Edward II in 1308, and Richard II had his older brother Edward of Angoulême re-interred there, so it was an important place for the English royal family in the fourteenth century. Her widower Edmund would be buried there with her in 1402, though in the meantime he had married his second wife, about eleven months after Isabel died. She was Joan Holland, second of the five daughters of the earl of Kent, and one of the nieces of the earl of Huntingdon. Born around 1375/80 and only in her teens in 1393, the new duchess of York was decades her husband's junior, but as the wife of the king's second eldest uncle, Joan became the third lady in the realm on her marriage, behind Queen Anne and Duchess Constanza and before Eleanor de Bohun, duchess of Gloucester.

53

Grievous Heaviness of Heart

John of Gaunt was in Leicester in early 1393, then travelled to Winchester, where a Parliament was held from 20 January to 10 February 1393.[1] He was in the port of Dover on 8 March, when he granted his household knight David Rouclyf £20 a year on his marriage to 'the duke's damsel' Margery Hesill, and by 20 March had sailed across the Channel and arrived in Calais.[2] With his brother Thomas of Woodstock, Thomas Mowbray, earl of Nottingham, and several others in his company, he rode to Paris, where the men were to attempt to negotiate a permanent peace between England and France with the dukes of Berry and Burgundy. John, Thomas and the others spent three months in France and sealed a draft treaty on 16 June, and were back in Westminster on 21 June 1393 to mark the anniversary of their father's death in 1377.[3]

Trouble arose in Cheshire and Lancashire in the spring and early summer of 1393, when large numbers of men assembled and declared their intention of killing John of Gaunt, his son Henry and his brother Thomas, apparently to protest against the Anglo-French settlement. John rode north to attempt to placate the mob, and Henry joined him after his return to England at the end of June 1393 from his years-long escapades around Europe. The leaders of the northern rebellion included Sir Thomas Talbot and Sir Nicholas Clifton, perhaps the knight of this name who had raped Eleanor West in the New Forest in the early 1380s. The rebels were still active in mid-September 1393, and the finalisation of the peace treaty with France was therefore postponed until the following year. Thomas Talbot was imprisoned in the Tower of London but escaped before 14 April 1395, and in 1397 was pardoned, to the great annoyance of John and his brother Woodstock, who had petitioned Parliament complaining of Talbot's 'terrible offence' against them.[4]

The festive season of 1393/94 was spent at Hertford Castle, and Henry of Lancaster joined his father there and paid for a suit of armour for his half-brother Thomas Beaufort, who was now perhaps fourteen or thereabouts, so that he could take part in the jousting. Henry received presents from his father and his stepmother Constanza, and gave a gift to, among others, Katherine Swynford.[5] John's Beaufort children were openly welcomed in his homes even when Constanza was there, and Katherine Swynford was apparently also present. Mary de Bohun, countess of Derby, pregnant for the sixth time, was also with the family at Hertford, and after her husband left for London in January 1394, Henry had a hamper of mussels, oysters and sprats sent back to Hertford for her.[6] Henry's brother-in-law John Holland, earl of Huntingdon, meanwhile, was planning an expedition to Hungary, ruled by King Richard's brother-in-law Zikmund, in *c*. January 1394.[7]

John of Gaunt was in London on 22 January 1394, when he made a grant to Katherine Swynford's nephew Thomas Chaucer. He gave Thomas an annuity of £10 on top of an annuity of the same amount he already paid him as the younger man's retainer for serving him 'in peace and war'. On 5 and 6 February the duke was in Westminster, where he made grants of properties in Calais and leased a grange near Boston, Lincolnshire to Philip and Peter Gernon of Boston; the place appears in the grant as 'la grange de la Vacherie called Erleshous.'[8]

Parliament was held in Westminster beginning on 27 January, and saw John quarrel with Richard Fitzalan, earl of Arundel, over the earl's failure to put down the recent revolt in the north. Arundel accused John of being too friendly with the king, complaining that Richard II wore the duke's livery collar, and stated that John often 'spoke such harsh and overbearing words in council' that Arundel himself and others did not dare to express their own opinions. John hit back by accusing the earl of disloyalty, and King Richard also spoke out on the duke's behalf and stated that he wore his uncle's livery collar as 'a sign of the great love and whole-heartedness between them' (he said it in French, '*en signe de bon amour et d'entier coer entre eux*'). Although Arundel 'made a very forceful speech justifying his actions,' John won the argument, and, as the earl of Northumberland had had to do in 1381, the earl of Arundel was forced to make a humiliatingly public apology to John, in English on this occasion:

> Sire, sith that hit semeth to the kyng and to the other lordes, and eke that yhe ben so mychel greved and displesed be my wordes, hit forthynketh me, and byseche yowe of your gode lordship to remyt me your mautalent.

> [Sir, since it seems to the king and the other lords that you are much grieved and displeased by my words, it beseems me to beseech you of your good lordship to stay your anger towards me.][9]

According to one chronicler, at this Parliament John raised the issue of his son's claim to the throne, stating that Henry was the rightful heir of Henry III (d. 1272) as the senior descendant of King Henry's second son Edmund of Lancaster. Edmund, so the story went, was in fact the king's elder son but had been set aside in favour of his brother Edward I on account of a physical disability (Edmund is often known to posterity as 'Crouchback', though this appears to be an appellation given to him in the late fourteenth century, almost a hundred years after his death in 1296). For John to claim such a thing seems very odd, and the chronicler even states that he forged a document in support of his claims on his son's behalf. Not only did John and everyone else know perfectly well, however, that Edward I (b. June 1239) was older than his brother Edmund of Lancaster (b. January 1245), this claim would have made all the subsequent kings of England usurpers, not least John's father Edward III. John's great-nephew Roger Mortimer, earl of March, supposedly then claimed that he was heir presumptive to the throne as the grandson of John's older brother Lionel, but Richard II ordered both men to leave the matter alone. When Henry took the throne in 1399, he did in fact assert his claim to it on the basis of his descent from Edmund of Lancaster.[10] The succession to the throne was a sensitive subject for Richard. He had no children and no siblings, and was the only legitimate descendant of Edward III's eldest son. Roger Mortimer was the descendant of Edward's second eldest surviving son but via a female line, while John of Gaunt was Edward's third eldest surviving son and was certainly Richard's male heir.

On 18 October 1393, Duchess Constanza had been at court with Richard II at Westminster, when 'at the supplication of the king's aunt the duchess of Lancaster,' Richard granted Constanza's clerk William Benge all the goods and chattels, worth 45s, which had been forfeited by his late father for committing murder. Constanza had subsequently spent Christmas and New Year with her husband and his children (and his mistress), and had travelled to a hunting party held by the bishop of London the previous July, so apparently was in good health and able to travel throughout 1393.[11] The duchess, however, did not have much longer to live, and died on 24 March 1394 about three or four months before her fortieth birthday. Unlike her younger sister Duchess Isabel fifteen months earlier, Constanza left no will, and it seems likely, therefore, that she died suddenly and unexpectedly.

The duchess had been something of a cipher in politics, and almost certainly in John of Gaunt's life, for the previous few years, but he honoured her by burying her at the Newarke in Leicester, founded in 1330 by Blanche of Lancaster's royally born grandfather Henry, earl of Lancaster and Leicester. Gaunt's biographer Anthony Goodman stated in the early 1990s that Gaunt buried his second wife in 'relative obscurity' at the Newarke, but this hardly seems fair to either John or Constanza, given the prestige of its foundation and given that a few of the royal Lancasters, including John and Duchess Blanche's infant sons, were also interred there.[12] John was honouring his second wife by burying her in the Newarke, not placing her somewhere obscure. As he was earl of Leicester, he buried his wife in one of his own towns, and he stayed in Leicester very often. John left generous bequests to the Newarke in his will, and paid for work to be completed on the collegiate church, begun by his father-in-law Duke Henry, after Constanza's death.[13] He was overseas at the time she passed away, so her funeral was put on hold until his return. Gaunt and his brother the duke of York concluded yet another truce between England and France, again at Leulinghem between

Calais and Boulogne, on 27 May 1394. This time it was to last for four years.[14]

Whether Constanza had ever had much of a happy life in England is debatable, and surely her and Gaunt's failure to win her late father's kingdoms, and the loss of their newborn son in 1375, both caused her much grief. Her only child Catalina was far away in Constanza's native Castile, and Constanza did not live long enough to see or receive news of any of her three Castilian grandchildren (her son-in-law King Enrique III was still only fourteen in March 1394). Her only sister the duchess of York was already dead, and as Isabel left Constanza nothing in her will, the daughters of King Pedro might not have been very close anyway. Constanza's only living relatives in England were Isabel's three children, Edward, earl of Rutland, Constance, Lady Despenser, and Richard of Conisbrough. One hopes that she had plenty of friends, guests and well-wishers in the last months and years of her life, and was not lonely or depressed. It may be that she and Gaunt had grown fond of each other over the years, and certainly the duchess seems to have been close to all three of her stepchildren from John's first marriage and perhaps to John's illegitimate children born during her marriage to him and even to his mistress Katherine, given that they all spent the last Christmas of Constanza's life together at Hertford. It is perhaps significant that Constanza's stepdaughter Elizabeth of Lancaster named her daughter from her third marriage, born in the early 1400s a few years after Constanza's death, Constance Cornwall.

Gaunt's son-in-law John Holland, earl of Huntingdon, was said by the pope to be 'going with some persons in his company against the Turks and other enemies of Christ' on 5 June 1394.[15] Not long afterwards, Gaunt's daughter-in-law Mary de Bohun died after giving birth to her sixth child and second daughter, Philippa of Lancaster, who survived the birth and who later became queen of Denmark, Sweden and Norway. Almost certainly Mary was only twenty-three and a half years old when she died, and she was, like her husband's stepmother Constanza, buried in the Newarke. In June 1404, her widower, then King Henry IV, talked of 'the king's mother Constance, sometime duchess of Lancaster, the king's consort Mary, late countess of Derby, and the king's brothers, whose bodies lie buried in the said church.'[16] Mary was only ever countess of Derby as she died before her husband received the dukedom of Hereford in September 1397, and of course she was never duchess of Lancaster or queen of England either, though she was the mother of King Henry V.

Henry marked the second anniversary of his wife's death in 1396 (and no doubt in other years as well) by hiring twenty-four 'poor men', for whom he bought clothes, who would have said prayers for her soul in the church of the Newarke. The number of poor men might refer to Mary being in her twenty-fourth year when she passed away. The exact date of Mary's death is unclear: in 1401, Henry stated that she died on 1 July, but in 1406 her anniversary was celebrated on 4 July. She perhaps died in or close to Leicester given that her funeral took place there, within days of her death, on 6 July, the day after Duchess Constanza's funeral. The Westminster chronicler states, however, that Mary died in Peterborough (40 miles from Leicester) in late June. Only twenty-seven himself when he lost his wife of thirteen years, Henry lived as a widower from July 1394 until February 1403 when, as king of England, he married Juana of Navarre, dowager duchess of Brittany. Rather curiously, on 25 September 1397, Pope Boniface IX granted Henry an indult for himself, his household servants present and future, and 'his wife for the time being.'[17]

John's nephew the king was also widowed in early June 1394 when Queen Anne died at the royal palace of Sheen, aged twenty-eight. The cause of her death is unknown, and Anne is, sadly, another fourteenth-century woman whose personality is something of a closed book to us; none of her accounts and few of her letters survive today. Richard, who adored his wife and who rarely let her leave his side, was devastated by his sudden loss. In April 1395 he ordered the entire palace complex of Sheen to be razed to the ground, and for a year after her death refused to enter any room where he had been with the queen, churches excepted.[18] A few weeks after Anne of Bohemia died, Richard made long and extremely detailed arrangements for the funeral and obsequies he wished to take place after his own death, a fact which reveals much about the morbid and depressed state of mind of a man who was, after all, still only twenty-seven.[19]

The king sent a letter to Philip, duke of Burgundy, remarking on his grievous heaviness of heart and how he could not cease to dwell on the sad loss of his beloved wife, and sent another letter to the duke of Guelders, postponing the duke's visit to England as Richard would not be able to welcome him with as much *humanitas* as he would like owing to Queen Anne's death.[20] Richard II had no children, and the issue of the succession to his throne remained as pressing a matter as ever. Whether John of Gaunt attended his niece-in-law the queen's funeral in Westminster Abbey is uncertain, but he certainly attended those of his wife and his daughter-in-law in Leicester in early July 1394, and paid out a great deal of money to give his royal Castilian wife a splendid send-off.[21]

54

I Know No Other News

More trouble arose in the duchy of Aquitaine in 1394, when, at a meeting of John of Gaunt's important vassals in Bordeaux, they declared that they would no longer recognise his authority as duke. At the time of his appointment, they had complained that they only wished their duke to be the king or the king's direct heir, and it was not entirely clear whether John was the childless Richard's heir or not. Gaunt therefore set off from England for the duchy with an army of 1,500 men to set the matter straight.[1] Both he and his son Henry were in the port of Plymouth on 13 and 16 October before his departure.[2] John was at Le Blavet in Brittany, on his way south, on 7 November 1394, when he sent a letter to Richard II in French. He told his nephew that he and his retinue were currently unable to continue their journey south because of strong winds (he described the situation as a 'great adversity of wind'), and that they would have to wait where they were until the winds were more favourable for sailing. Gaunt addressed the king as, 'My very honoured, very dread and very sovereign lord' – this was an entirely conventional and normal style of address in the fourteenth century and does not show the duke being unnecessarily obsequious – and told him how glad he was to hear that Richard had arrived safely in Ireland (the king spent a few months there in 1394/95) and that he hoped his affairs would go well. John then wrote, rather amusingly, 'And, my very dread lord, regarding other news, I do not know any,' except that earlier that day, a squire called Machin, who worked for the *alferez* of the kingdom of Navarre, Sir Carlos de Beaumont, had travelled to Le Blavet in a barge to bring John letters from Beaumont.[3]

Gaunt spent much of December 1394 in the *bastide* of Libourne, which he had first visited in 1370.[4] He was to spend almost a year in Aquitaine, and skilfully defused the crisis, though some modern writers have held the opinion that he precipitated it in the first place and had behaved arrogantly towards his vassals. On 29 March 1395, while he was in the duchy, Gaunt became a grandfather again when his second daughter Elizabeth gave birth to her second son, John Holland, future earl of Huntingdon and duke of Exeter, in Dartington, Devon. This boy would become his namesake father's heir after his elder brother Richard died in September 1400. Even though young John was not born as his father's heir, his parents held a very expensive and lavish celebration for his baptism and asked the abbot of Tavistock to be one of his godfathers. John Holland (the father) hired Isabel Hugh as his son's wet nurse and ordered Isabel not to have marital relations with her husband for the duration, whereupon the disgruntled husband set off for Guernsey in the Channel Islands and lived there for three years.[5]

In November 1395, Gaunt passed through Brittany again on his way back to England, a year after his previous journey through the duchy, and visited his former brother-in-law, Duke John IV. The two men discussed a possible marriage for John IV's daughter Marie, born in 1391 to his third wife Juana of Navarre, and Gaunt's grandson and heir Henry of Monmouth. This was done without Richard II's permission, and the king was furious with his uncle when he heard about it.[6] An undated letter from Gaunt's son-in-law the earl of Huntingdon reveals that John Holland also negotiated with Duke John IV of Brittany regarding a possible marriage between the duke's son (possibly his and Juana's eldest son and heir John, b. 1389) and Holland and Elizabeth of Lancaster's 'young daughter' ('*nostre joene fille*'), one of Gaunt's granddaughters.[7] The daughter is not identified by name, but was not Holland and Elizabeth's first daughter, Constance, who had been betrothed to the son and heir of Thomas Mowbray, earl of Nottingham, in 1391. Perhaps their second daughter, Alice Holland, later countess of Oxford, was meant.[8] Ultimately, though, nothing came either of the proposed Holland-Brittany marriage or the Lancastrian marriage for Marie of Brittany, though she was exactly the right age to have married Henry of Monmouth or another of Gaunt's Lancastrian grandsons.

A fascinating letter signed 'J. of Lancaster' ('J. de Lancastre' in the French original) was sent to Roger Walden and dated in Paris on 9 April in an uncertain year in the late fourteenth century. Walden became archbishop of Canterbury a few weeks after Richard II banished Thomas Arundel from England in September 1397, and as the letter does not refer to Walden as archbishop, it was surely sent before that date.[9] Whether the letter was sent by John of Gaunt is uncertain as it was written without using any of his many titles, and a knight named John de Lancastre appears on several occasions in the chancery rolls of the late 1390s; for example, being appointed as one of the two keepers of an abbey in Lancashire in February 1397. He had been pardoned at the Parliament of early 1393 as an adherent of the exiled and now deceased Robert de Vere, earl of Oxford (d. November 1392).[10] On another occasion when John of Gaunt wrote to Roger Walden, he named himself 'duke of Lancaster,' not 'J. of Lancaster,' though it is worth noting that Gaunt was almost certainly in Paris in April 1393 when he and his brother Thomas of Woodstock met the dukes of Berry and Burgundy, and the letter was written in Paris on 9 April in an unstated year.

The author of the letter addressed Walden as 'very honoured and puissant lord' and thanked him for his love and support, and talked of his certainty that he would again find consolation and comfort in him. He enclosed letters from John of Brittany, which presumably means Duke John IV, and told Walden that his messenger would be able to inform him more fully about the ongoing situation. The author asked Walden to believe what his messenger would tell him orally about 'the fact of the misery in which I am and my release from it, in which I place my trust in you above all others after God, and think well that, without your good efforts and help, I am in danger of remaining for a long time in this misery, where I have already been for a long time'. If it truly was John of Gaunt who dictated this letter, it is very revealing of his feelings, though perhaps the author was Sir John de Lancastre, yearning for his homeland after years in exile with the earl of Oxford.

John of Gaunt certainly sent a letter to Richard II in French, the language he always used in his correspondence to the king, on 26 August in an uncertain year. The letter is not specifically dated, but in it John mentions 'yesterday evening, Tuesday, 25 August', and 25 August fell on a Tuesday in 1395. The previous year when that date fell on a Tuesday was 1389, but this cannot be the correct year of the letter, as Gaunt refers to his 'nephew of Rutland,' and Edmund of Langley's son Edward of York was only created earl of Rutland in 1390. Gaunt mentioned to the king that his 'dearest brothers of York and Gloucester [and] my dearest nephew of Rutland' ('*mes treschiers freres d'Everwyk et de Gloucestre, mon treschier nepveu de Routelonde*') were currently visiting him at his castle of Pontefract in Yorkshire. The letter cannot, therefore, date to 1395 as it would appear, as John of Gaunt was in Aquitaine, France and Brittany for all of that year and not in Yorkshire, so it seems that he or his clerk made an error in referring to 'Tuesday 25 August'. As Gaunt refers to his brother Thomas of Woodstock, duke of Gloucester, as being alive and visiting him when he wrote the letter, and as Thomas was killed in September 1397, this provides a *terminus ad quem* for the date of the letter. John's son Henry is not mentioned, so the duke might have written the letter during one of Henry's long sojourns abroad.[11]

John began by speaking of the 'very great joy of my heart' on hearing from Richard's letters to him that the king's 'very honoured person' was in good health, and thanked his nephew for giving him a house in London, which had once belonged to the former mayor, William Walworth (d. 1385). John's letter is so hedged about with flowery, courtly and empty expressions and takes so long to reach its main point that much of its meaning is rather difficult to unpick, but he finally got round to saying how he had heard that a person of lowly status (*de simple estat*), whose identity John did not know, had gone to see the king and had publicly and openly told him things which were against John's honour. The duke assured his nephew, with God as his witness, that he, above all loyal creatures, would never intend or even think of doing anything against Richard's honour and status, and would never behave towards the king except in the way that a true vassal should towards his very sovereign liege lord. He added that he hoped Richard would draw on his long experience of John's loyalty and would not easily believe words spoken against the duke's honour.

There is perhaps more than a touch of exasperation, and perhaps apprehension, in John's letter that even now, with Richard close to thirty years old and nearly two decades into his reign, John had to make declarations of his loyalty. The king still paid heed to naysayers and any person of lowly status who decided to drip poison about John in his ear, even in public. Even in the mid-1390s, the duke of Lancaster's relations with his prickly nephew were not always easy and cordial, and Richard still required assurance that John remained loyal and would not act against him in any way. Beginning in early 1397, Richard II began referring to Edward of York as his 'brother', and it is not impossible that he had begun to think of his cousin as a possible successor to his throne. It is therefore probably significant that John's letter mentioned that his nephew Edward (who had a great deal of influence at Richard's court in the mid to late 1390s) and both of his royal brothers were with him at the time of dictating a letter protesting his innocence, as though to let the king know that the three men were on his side in the matter. He certainly made a point of remarking that he and they were 'together at Pontefract', and made a reference to 'all our hearts,' as though to emphasise the point.

55

Their Hearts Would Burst with Grief

John returned to England from Aquitaine and Brittany at the end of 1395 after an absence of over a year, and was in Canterbury (perhaps on pilgrimage at the shrine of St Thomas Becket) on 1 January 1396 with Henry of Lancaster, who gave him nineteen ells of velvet motley cloth as his New Year gift. John was in London on 7 and 13 January.[1] He made a special visit to the king at Langley in Hertfordshire in early 1396, but according to chronicler Thomas Walsingham, Richard received him with due respect but 'without love' on this occasion, in stark contrast to his warm and affectionate greeting of John in November 1389.[2] Perhaps the person of lowly status whom John mentioned in his letter had already spoken to Richard, and perhaps the king was still annoyed with his uncle for negotiating a possible marriage for his eldest Lancaster grandson into Brittany without royal permission.

On or around 13 February 1396, just a few weeks after returning to England, Gaunt took a momentous step, and married his long-term lover Katherine Swynford in Lincoln Cathedral. (Thomas Walsingham gives 'the octave of the Epiphany,' i.e. 13 January, as the wedding date.) It is almost impossible to overstate how incredibly unusual it was for an Englishman of royal birth to marry a knight's daughter who had been his lover for many years, but Gaunt deeply loved the remarkable Katherine and their children, and wished to make the four Beauforts legitimate and to increase their fortunes. He had been widowed from Constanza for twenty-three months and had probably been mulling over his marriage to Katherine for a good few months; he did not disrespect Constanza and her memory by marrying his mistress almost before her body was cold, but waited for nearly two years. There was also, of course, the fact that he had spent the period from early November 1394 until late December 1395 outside England.

Astonishingly, Duchess Katherine became the first lady in England on her marriage, as Queen Anne was dead and as the king had not yet married his second wife, and as John was the second highest ranking man in England after Richard. Several noble English ladies, chief among them Gaunt's sister-in-law Eleanor de Bohun, duchess of Gloucester, and his great-niece Philippa Mortimer, countess of Pembroke and Arundel, publicly demonstrated their horror that a woman they considered of low birth now outranked them. Jean Froissart states that they refused to acknowledge the new duchess and declared that their 'hearts would burst with grief' if they had to give her precedence. Eleanor's husband Thomas of Woodstock added his voice to the chorus, claiming that his brother was a 'doting fool.'[3] Richard II, in contrast to several of his relatives, treated Katherine with great respect and affection.

At the beginning of September 1396, Pope Boniface IX confirmed John of Gaunt and Katherine Swynford's marriage, rather curiously referring to Katherine as a 'damsel,' usually a word applied to women or girls not yet married or to women who were or had been married to men who were not knights. They were permitted to remain within their marriage, and, most significantly, their 'offspring past and future' were declared legitimate. The papal confirmation states that John was the godfather of Katherine's daughter, presumably Blanche Swynford, and that John had committed adultery with Katherine while married to Constanza but while Katherine herself was unmarried. During the Parliament of early 1397, Richard II confirmed the legitimacy of his Beaufort cousins.[4]

Now that she was the legitimate daughter of a royal duke, Joan Ferrers née Beaufort was in a position to make an excellent second marriage, and she wed Sir Ralph Neville, a powerful magnate in the north of England, on or before 29 November 1396 when an entry on the Patent Roll refers to them as a married couple.[5] They had both been widowed recently: Ralph's first wife Margaret Stafford, daughter of Hugh, late earl of Stafford, died on 9 June 1396, and Joan's first husband Robert Ferrers may still have been alive on 7 July 1396.[6] On 13 February 1397, John of Gaunt granted 'Lord Nevill and Joan his wife, the duke's daughter,' an income of 400 marks a year. He had previously given this amount to Joan and Robert Ferrers.[7] The Beaufort/Neville marriage was to produce as many as thirteen or fourteen children, though a number of them died in childhood. Their eldest daughter was Eleanor, Lady Despenser and countess of Northumberland, their second daughter was Katherine, duchess of Norfolk, who was old enough to give birth in 1415 yet lived long enough to attend her nephew Richard III's coronation in 1483, and the eldest son was Richard, who married Alice Montacute, heir to the earldom of Salisbury. Possibly all three eldest Neville children were born before 1400.[8]

Richard II departed from England in October 1396 with a large retinue, and married his second wife Isabelle de Valois in early November. Isabelle was the eldest daughter of Charles VI of France and his Bavarian queen, Isabeau, and was painfully young; she turned seven a few days after her wedding. The marriage was intended to cement a long truce between the kingdoms of England and France, though ultimately it did not. Richard, whose first wife Anne of Bohemia had been the daughter of an emperor, had insisted that he would marry no-one but a king's daughter, which necessarily limited the options severely; the only other plausible candidate was Yolande of Aragon (b. 1384), daughter of the king of Aragon and later queen consort of Naples. John of Gaunt, with his wife Katherine, his brother Thomas of Woodstock, his sister-in-law Eleanor de Bohun, his son Henry, his daughter

Elizabeth, his nephew Edward of York, and his nieces Anne of Gloucester and Philippa de Coucy, travelled to France with the king. John's other brother Edmund of Langley remained in England as regent, though Froissart says that his young wife Joan Holland (*la duchesse d'Iorch*, i.e. the duchess of York) attended the royal wedding

The duchess of Burgundy, Margarethe of Flanders, whose possible marriage to Gaunt had been discussed in late 1368, invited Duchess Katherine of Lancaster to a splendid dinner with 'an immense variety of different dishes and decorations on the tables.' Jean Froissart says that Katherine attended this dinner with 'her son and two daughters,' though it is not clear which of her children he is referring to, and also not clear whether her daughter Blanche Swynford was still alive. Unless she was the same person as Blanche Morieux, Blanche Swynford's fate is unknown, and she does not appear again on known record after John of Gaunt gave Katherine the marriage of Robert Deincourt for her at the beginning of 1375. As far as the record shows, Joan Neville née Beaufort was the only daughter of Katherine likely to have been present at Richard II and Isabelle de Valois's wedding; if Margaret Swynford, nun and future abbess of Barking Abbey, was Katherine's daughter from her first marriage, it is improbable that she would have been allowed to leave her abbey and travel to France with her mother and stepfather.

The English and French sides tried to outdo each other in competitive and costly gift-giving during the endless festivities held to mark this important royal wedding, and John of Gaunt received a gift of a tapestry from Duke Philip of Burgundy which he mentioned in his will some years later ('a piece of arras cloth which the duke of Burgundy gave me the last time I was in Calais').[9] Charles VI was thankfully going through one of his periods of lucidity, and was able to attend his daughter's wedding and to meet and spend time with Richard II and Richard's royal kinsmen for the first time.

Little Queen Isabelle would not be able to give her husband children for at least another eight years and perhaps more, by which time Richard would be close to forty, and the question of the rightful succession to the English throne remained as pressing as ever. She was crowned queen of England at Westminster Abbey on 7 January 1397, the day after Richard's thirtieth birthday, and thereafter lived in her own household and was treated affectionately by King Richard as his little sister. John of Gaunt was back in England and in London on 1 December 1396, and spent that Christmas, the first festive season where he could openly present Katherine as his wife and duchess, at Hertford Castle.[10] Parliament was held in London in early 1397, and John must have been delighted when King Richard, rather startlingly referring to himself as 'undoubted emperor in our realm of England,' legitimised John and Katherine's four Beaufort children. Richard also raised John Beaufort to the peerage by making him earl of Somerset. Henry of Lancaster must also have witnessed the legitimation of his

Beaufort half-siblings and John's promotion to earl, as he was in London on 18 February and must have attended this Parliament.[11]

On the first day of the Parliament, 22 January 1397, John of Gaunt was one of the men who presented a report to the king about a dispute in Tonbridge, Kent between the newly-appointed and nobly born archbishop of Canterbury, the earl of Arundel's brother Thomas Arundel, and the executors of the late and also nobly born archbishop, William Courtenay, who had died on 31 July 1396.[12] Gaunt worked with, among others, his son-in-law John Holland, earl of Huntingdon, and Thomas Mowbray, earl of Nottingham, who was confirmed as marshal of England during this Parliament. These two men were responsible for bringing John Beaufort into Parliament for his elevation as an earl, wearing 'clothes of honour' (*vesture de honur*) and with 'his sword carried before him, the hilt uppermost.'[13] The duke of Lancaster, who dearly loved his son and his other Beaufort children, must have watched with great pride. The records of this Parliament refer to John Beaufort as 'Monsire [Sir] Johan de Beauford', though the duke's youngest son Thomas Beaufort had not yet been knighted: on 6 July 1397, Richard II retained him for life on a generous income of 100 marks a year, and called him 'Thomas de Beaufort, esquire.' The process of the Beauforts' legitimisation refers to Thomas a *donsel*, i.e. a young man of noble birth not yet knighted.[14]

56

The Extermination of Rebels

John of Gaunt was at Hertford Castle on the last day of February in an uncertain year, most probably in 1397, when he sent a letter to Roger Walden, treasurer of England.[1] He thanked Walden for his good friendship and the kindliness with which Walden had always treated his affairs. This letter was sent from 'the duke of Lancaster' rather than 'J. of Lancaster' as another rather mysterious letter sent to Roger Walden was (see pages 220–21).

In March 1397, John's son-in-law the earl of Huntingdon intended to 'come shortly to Italy and other parts for the extermination of schismatics and rebels and usurpers of cities and lands of the pope and the Roman church,' according to the pope in Rome, Boniface IX. Boniface added approvingly that he 'commend[ed] the laudable purpose' of John Holland's planned actions against 'the insolence of the schismatic adherents of Robert ... of damned memory, and the son of perdition, Peter de Luna ... the late and the present anti-popes.' Boniface appointed Holland as *gonfalonier* (standard-bearer) of the Roman Church and captain-general of the papal forces in Italy.[2]

Apparently, however, Holland did not travel to Italy that year as he had intended, or only for a fairly short time, as he was certainly in England in September 1397 when he took part in his half-brother the king's machinations against the Lords Appellant of 1388. At some point between 1388 and 1397, John Holland's barge, the *Barge Seint Johan*, was seized and detained by the mayor and bailiffs of Kingston-on-Hull, because they believed that the vessel 'was bound on a piratical expedition to Denmark'.[3] If Holland was indeed involved in piracy, it would seem to fit quite well with what we know of his character. Holland's elder brother Thomas, earl of Kent, died on 25 April 1397, leaving his son Thomas Holland the younger (b. *c.* 1371/75) as his heir. The earl wrote his will in English, and rather movingly talked of the 'love and trust that hath been between' himself and his wife Alice, the earl of Arundel's sister (and probably the godmother of her niece, Gaunt's granddaughter Alice Holland).[4]

John of Gaunt was in London on 20 April 1397 and again on 10 June, when he made an indenture with a squire named Ivo de Wyram.[5] On 28 August 1397, Richard II issued licences for John, Henry of Lancaster and Edmund of Langley to assemble their men-at-arms and archers and to come to him, 'notwithstanding any statutes, proclamations or prohibitions to the contrary,' after they had petitioned him to be allowed to do so. Gaunt was to come with 300 men-at-arms and 600 archers, Edmund with 100 men-at-arms and 200 archers, and Henry with 200 and 400; i.e., the two Lancastrians had 500 men-at-arms and 1,000 archers in total. This was in reference to a proclamation the king had made in every English county 'prohibiting any persons under pain of forfeiture of life and limb and all else they can forfeit, and of being reputed traitor,' from holding assemblies of people unless specifically permitted by the king himself or by the men he considered his closest allies in 1397. These were his cousin Edward of York, Edmund of Langley's son; his half-brother the earl of Huntingdon and their nephew the new earl of Kent; Thomas Mowbray, earl of Nottingham; Thomas Despenser, lord of Glamorgan (married to Gaunt's niece, Edward of York's sister Constance); John Montacute, who succeeded his elderly uncle William Montacute as earl of Salisbury that summer; Gaunt's son John Beaufort, earl of Somerset; and William Scrope, royal under-chamberlain. Gaunt had assembled a retinue and mustered them for Richard at Nottingham.

The later testimony of Edward of York, Thomas Despenser, John Beaufort and John and Thomas Holland reveals that while they were at Nottingham Castle dining with the king on 5 August 1397, Richard ordered them to arm themselves and to go out of the castle gate, where they heard William Scrope reading out a list of charges against Thomas of Woodstock, duke of Gloucester. Edward of York claimed that he talked to his father Edmund of Langley and his uncle John of Gaunt, and told them that 'he was commanded to do that day a thing the doing of which made him sadder than he ever had been'.[6] This 'thing' was the arrest of his uncle Thomas of Woodstock, and Edward and the other men claimed later that they were all opposed to it but did not dare gainsay the king and refuse. Richard had long hated and resented his uncle and the other senior Lords Appellant of 1387/88, the earls of Arundel and Warwick, and was determined to get revenge for their actions against his friends at the Merciless Parliament of 1388.

Thomas Mowbray, earl of Nottingham, who like Henry of Lancaster had been an Appellant in 1387/88 and had helped to destroy the king's closest allies, was put in charge of taking Thomas of Woodstock to Calais after King Richard and his half-brother John Holland arrested Thomas at his Essex castle of Pleshey. Rather than putting Thomas on trial, Richard decided to go for the secret murder, most probably because John of Gaunt as steward of England would be responsible for pronouncing the sentence on Thomas in Parliament. John might never have been particularly close to his youngest brother, who was a full decade and a half his junior and thus almost young enough to be his son, but he would certainly balk at pronouncing the death sentence on him. Thomas of Woodstock was murdered in Calais around 8 or 9 September 1397. According to the later testimony of John Hall, a valet of the earl of Nottingham, he was smothered in an inn in the port on the earl's orders (Thomas Mowbray would shortly afterwards be rewarded for this murder of a king's son with the new dukedom of Norfolk by a grateful Richard II).[7]

On 21 September 1397, Richard Fitzalan, earl of Arundel, now fifty years old, was brought to trial before Parliament. He was wearing a robe with a scarlet hood (scarlet in the fourteenth century meant a type of cloth, not a colour), while King Richard and his allies, including John of Gaunt, were all dressed alike in red silk robes with white silk bands, powdered with gold lettering.[8] Gaunt, as steward of England, presided over the trial. Arundel defended himself with wit and passion, telling Gaunt, 'I see it clearly now; all those who accuse me of treason, you are all liars. Never was I a traitor.' The speaker of the Commons, Sir John Bushy, informed the earl that his pardon for his actions as Lord Appellant in 1388 has been revoked 'by the king, the lords, and us, the faithful commons'. Arundel retorted 'Where are those faithful commons? I know all about you and your crew, and how you got here – not to act faithfully, but to shed my blood.' Gaunt's son Henry of Lancaster rose to accuse Arundel of plotting to seize the king in 1387. Arundel cried out 'You, Henry, earl of Derby, you lie in your teeth. I never said anything to you or to anyone else about my lord king, except what was to his honour and welfare.'

Thomas Walsingham says that the eight lords who were the king's chief allies tried to provoke the earl of Arundel with obscene gestures and prancing around, foremost among them the young earl of Kent, who was Arundel's own nephew as well as the king's. John of Gaunt pronounced the death sentence on Arundel, and, there being no such thing as death row in fourteenth-century England, the earl was forced to walk through the streets of London to his execution, accompanied by his nephew Thomas Holland, earl of Kent, and his son-in-law Thomas Mowbray, both on horseback. At Tower Hill, Mowbray tied a blindfold around the eyes of the man who was his children's grandfather before Arundel's head was removed with an axe.[9] Thomas Beauchamp, earl of Warwick, the other senior Appellant of 1388, was exiled to the Isle of Man, and the earl of Arundel's brother Thomas Arundel, elected archbishop of Canterbury not long before, was also exiled from England and was replaced as archbishop by Roger Walden. A lighter note was struck amid the doom and gloom of the three chief Appellants' downfall when Elizabeth of Lancaster won a prize as the best dancer during a feast held to mark the end of the Parliament.[10]

There was soon to be a macabre postscript to the earl of Arundel's story. King Richard was plagued by vivid nightmares of the earl's execution and was haunted by ghostly visions of the dead Arundel to the point where he hardly dared to sleep any more. He also came to believe that Arundel's head had miraculously reattached itself to his body, and heard that miracles were being performed at his burial place at the house of the Austin Friars on Bread

Street, London. In the dead of night, supposedly at four in the morning, John of Gaunt was one of the men forced to accompany the king to Arundel's grave, and who watched the earl's remains being dug up ten days after he had been buried. His nephew Edward of York was also present during this grim event, as was his former nemesis Henry Percy, earl of Northumberland. Arundel's head had indeed been sewn back on, and the two parts of his body were once more separated and reburied in an unmarked grave on the king's orders.[11]

57

Caterpillars of the Commonwealth

At the Parliament of September 1397, Richard II rewarded his loyal allies with higher titles. John of Gaunt's son-in-law Ralph Neville was made first earl of Westmorland, which meant that Katherine Swynford's daughter Joan Beaufort was now a countess. The earl of Northumberland's younger brother, Thomas Percy, was made earl of Worcester; Thomas Despenser, lord of Glamorgan and Gaunt's nephew-in-law, was made earl of Gloucester; William Scrope became earl of Wiltshire; Gaunt's son-in-law John Holland, earl of Huntingdon, was made duke of Exeter, and Holland's nephew Thomas Holland, earl of Kent, was made duke of Surrey; Thomas Mowbray, earl of Nottingham, was made duke of Norfolk; and Gaunt's nephew Edward of York, earl of Rutland, was made duke of Albemarle (or Aumale or Aumerle). Gaunt's son Henry of Lancaster, earl of Derby, was made the first duke of Hereford; previously it had been an earldom held by his late wife Mary's father Humphrey de Bohun.

Finally, Gaunt's son John Beaufort, already earl of Somerset, was made marquis of Dorset, and married Margaret Holland before 28 September 1397. She was one of the sisters of the new duke of Surrey, and a niece of John Holland, duke of Exeter.[1] One woman was also promoted to a higher title: Margaret, countess of Norfolk, now probably seventy-five and the only surviving grandchild of Edward I since the death of her eighty-year-old cousin the countess of Devon in 1391, became duchess of Norfolk in her own right (and thus shared the title with her grandson Thomas Mowbray's wife Elizabeth Arundel). Previously, the title of duke had been a rare one, held only by Edward III's sons and the royal cousin Henry of Grosmont, and contemporaries sneered at the new *duketti* or 'little dukes'. Although John of Gaunt remained the second man in the kingdom, he now shared his ducal rank with a number of other men.

John's eldest child, Philippa of Lancaster, queen of Portugal, sent a letter to Richard II on 1 October in either 1397, 1398 or 1399, calling herself 'P. de Portugale' ('P. of Portugal').[2] Queen Philippa informed her cousin that she, her husband King João and their four sons (Alfonso, who was to die young in 1400, Duarte, Pedro, and Henrique) were in excellent health. For some reason she did not mention her daughter Isabel, future duchess of Burgundy, who was born in February 1397 and who would be the only one of King João and Queen Philippa's three daughters who survived childhood.

Philippa sent her chancellor, Master Adam Davenport, who she said would bring Richard II more news from Portugal by word of mouth, to England with her letters, and she informed the English king that Adam wished to retire after serving her as chancellor for eight or nine years and to return to his native England. She asked Richard, therefore, to grant Adam a benefice 'in your very noble land of England' that would sustain him.

Gaunt was at Hertford Castle on 2 and 3 October 1397, and still there on 1 November when he granted Everard Bonde an income of 5 marks a year for good service to Duchess Katherine. His son Henry was with them at Hertford on 6 November.[3] Although the political situation seemed to be settled, with the king's loathed enemies dead or in exile, Richard II was acting strangely, and seems to have become paranoid and frightened. He was certainly a lonely, isolated figure who surrounded himself with a private army of archers from Cheshire and who, according to one chronicler, sat on a high throne, speaking to no-one but making everyone who caught his eye kneel to him. Later writers have speculated a great deal about what happened to King Richard in the last few years of his reign and what might explain the cruelty and tyranny he began to demonstrate; whether he was perhaps demonstrating narcissistic tendencies or was suffering from some kind of mental disorder. It certainly seems that Richard developed a strong sense of his own grandiosity, though rather contradictorily, also allowed his bodyguard of Cheshire archers to address him by the familiar 'thou' and to call him 'Diccun', i.e. Dickon.

Three courtiers, Sir John Bushy or Bussy, Sir William Bagot and Sir Henry Green(e), wielded a great deal of influence over the king in the late 1390s. Shakespeare wrote about the three men, who come across as basically interchangeable and who seemed to come out of nowhere to be extremely prominent at court in and after 1397, in his play about Richard II two centuries later; Shakespeare has Gaunt's son Henry call them the 'caterpillars of the commonwealth'.

At the beginning of 1380, John of Gaunt had referred to William Bagot as 'our dearest and beloved squire,' and two years later the duke granted half of the manor of Willasham to Sir Henry Greene during the minority of Robert Ferrers of Wem, his future son-in-law. He also referred to Greene as 'our dearest and beloved bachelor,' i.e. a knight who served in another knight's or lord's retinue.[4] On 2 January 1392, Gaunt again retained Henry Greene to serve in his household and on this occasion talked of 'the said Henry, otherwise called Leycestre the herald,' and Greene appears in his register as early as March 1373. Sir John Bushy went overseas with Gaunt in 1378 and served in his retinue from 1382 to 1397.[5] All three of the 'caterpillars', therefore, had strong connections to John of Gaunt before becoming King Richard's detested favourites.

On 24 December 1397, Henry of Lancaster was at Leicester, and inspected and confirmed a grant by his father, so most probably the two spent the festive season together and with Duchess Katherine. Possibly some of the Beauforts were also there, though John Beaufort was now married to the new duke of Surrey's sister Margaret Holland and perhaps spent Christmas with her, while Joan Neville is likely to have been pregnant or had perhaps recently given birth to the first of her many children with the earl of Westmorland. John of Gaunt was appointed to 'redress violations of the truce with Scotland' on 5 February 1398, with several men including his frequent associate Thomas Percy, now earl of Worcester. Almost immediately, however, Richard II changed his mind and appointed John's nephew Edward of York in his place.[6] Momentous events were taking place, and John's son Henry was heavily involved.

58

Imprisoned in the Wardrobe

The conflict that arose in 1397/98 between the new dukes of Hereford and Norfolk was, like the three 'caterpillars,' made famous 200 years later by Shakespeare in his play about Richard II. Sometime in December 1397, Henry of Lancaster was riding between Brentford and London with his retinue when he encountered his kinsman Thomas Mowbray. The two men talked for a while, apparently in French, or at least the conversation was recorded in that language in the rolls of Parliament. Mowbray opened the conversation with a warning: 'We are about to be undone' ('*Nous sumes en point d'estre diffaitz*'). When Henry asked why, Mowbray replied that it was because of what the two of them had done at Radcot Bridge ten years earlier, when a trap was laid for the king's dearest friend Robert de Vere a few weeks before the Lords Appellant executed and exiled other friends of the king during the Merciless Parliament. Mowbray went on to claim that there had been a plan to seize and kill both Henry and his father when they went to Windsor after the Parliament of September 1397, but that he himself, Gaunt's nephew Edward of York, the new duke of Albemarle, Gaunt's son-in-law John Holland, the new duke of Exeter, and the duke of Lancaster's long-term associate the earl of Worcester (Thomas Percy) had prevented it because they had jointly sworn an oath that 'they would never assent to the ruin of any lord without just and reasonable cause'.

Thomas Mowbray claimed that the duke of Surrey (Thomas Holland), earl of Gloucester (Thomas Despenser), earl of Salisbury (John Montacute) and earl of Wiltshire (William Scrope) had sworn to destroy six lords: himself, John of Gaunt, Gaunt's sons Henry of Lancaster and John Beaufort, Edward of York, and John Holland. There might have been some truth to this; Richard II's court at the end of the 1390s was both highly factional and highly dangerous, and no man, however close he seemed to be to the king, could consider himself safe – though why the duke of Surrey would have plotted to kill his own uncle the duke of Exeter is unclear, especially as the two Hollands were to work together in 1399/1400 to restore their kinsman the king to his lost throne, along with Thomas Despenser and John Montacute. As John of Gaunt was to appoint William Scrope as one of the executors of his will in early 1399, and therefore evidently trusted and liked him, it seems most unlikely that Scrope ever plotted to destroy him. Something of the fevered atmosphere at the English court at this time, however, is revealed by the admission of the king's friend Sir William Bagot that he was planning to kill John of Gaunt, Duchess Katherine and John's children, or failing that, to disinherit them. Bagot acknowledged that if John, his wife or his children 'shall in time to come be by him slain' and his guilt were proved, he could be put to death without due process. This was recorded on the Close Roll on 3 March 1398, as though plotting to kill the king's uncle, the second man in the realm, and his family was normal government business.[1]

At Shrewsbury on 30 January 1398, Henry of Lancaster was summoned to the king, and was told that ten days before Richard had heard how Thomas Mowbray, duke of Norfolk, 'had spoken many dishonourable words in slander of his [Richard's] person' to Henry. Richard ordered Henry to tell him what Mowbray had said, and Henry wrote it down from memory. On 4 February, the king ordered all the sheriffs of England to proclaim that Mowbray must appear before him within fifteen days to answer Henry's charges of treason. Two weeks later, the constable of Windsor Castle was told to keep both Henry and Mowbray secure, and on Tuesday 23 April the mayor and sheriffs of London were ordered to keep Mowbray securely in the king's wardrobe, a building near the house of the Blackfriars.[2] A letter, in French, was sent sometime between 25 March and 23 April 1398; unfortunately the identities of neither the sender nor the recipient are known, though evidently, judging from the style of address, the recipient was a high-ranking nobleman. The letter confirms that '*monseignur de Lancastre*', i.e. John of Gaunt, and Henry of Lancaster were in the king's company at the time of composing the letter, and that the mayor of London was keeping Thomas Mowbray well guarded day and night in the king's wardrobe.[3]

The king ordered Henry and Thomas to settle their differences by a jousting duel, and on 31 August 1398 sent out numerous couriers and messengers to all the counties of England. The archbishop of Canterbury, sundry bishops, and numerous lords, knights, squires and others were told to 'assemble themselves in person, with all haste' in Coventry on 16 September 1398, where the duel would determine the truth of the matter in the king's own presence. An order to both Henry of Lancaster and Thomas Mowbray to come to Richard on 2 August with no more than twenty men in their company had been issued on 22 July, and the king's order shows that Mowbray had been moved to Windsor Castle by then and was still being held in captivity.[4]

After leaving Shrewsbury, John of Gaunt spent the next few months in Yorkshire and the Midlands, and visited Pontefract, Tutbury, Newcastle-under-Lyme, Leicester and Rothwell. He and Henry were together at Pontefract on 10 January and 9 June 1398, and probably spent much or most of that year together.[5] John's other son named Henry, Henry Beaufort, was elected bishop of Lincoln by Boniface IX on 27 February 1398, surely a proud moment for the parents of the twenty-three-year-old. This was merely the latest step in a glittering ecclesiastical career; Henry had already been appointed chancellor of the University of Oxford in April 1397, and was made a deacon that same month.[6]

In July 1398, came the shocking news from Ireland that John's great-nephew Roger Mortimer, earl of March and Ulster, Lionel of Antwerp's grandson and heir, had been killed during a skirmish. Roger was only twenty-four, and left as his heir his seven-year-old son Edmund Mortimer, as well as a younger son named Roger and an eight-year-old daughter named Anne (who, like Gaunt and Katherine's daughter Joan Beaufort, became the grandmother of Edward IV and Richard III). The earl of March had always been something of an outsider in English politics, and whether he or anyone else had considered him the heir to the childless king's throne seems debatable. His kinsman the king had replaced him as lieutenant of Ireland with Thomas Holland, duke of Surrey and earl of Kent, in the month of March's death, and one chronicler says that Richard had ordered Surrey to arrest his brother-in-law March and bring him back to England.[7] Young Edmund Mortimer was now the senior male descendant of Gaunt's older brother Lionel of Antwerp.

The long-awaited day of the duel between Henry of Lancaster and Thomas Mowbray finally arrived in the early autumn of 1398. Richard expressed his shocking decision to exile Thomas Mowbray for life – he was to die in Venice less than a year later, still only thirty-two years old – and Henry for ten years. According to Jean Froissart, the king reduced Henry's exile to six years, though whether he was correct on this point is unclear.[8] Richard had probably never much liked or trusted his Lancastrian cousin, but his uncle John had perhaps believed that he had enough influence over the king to be able to dissuade him. If so, John was swiftly disabused of the notion. Thomas Walsingham states that the king 'added the pitiless decree that nobody on pain of heavy punishment' should beg him to show any favour or mercy to the two exiled dukes.[9]

Although the possibility of Henry going to Portugal or Castile to visit his sisters Philippa and Catalina was discussed, as was the idea that he might go to Hainault and spend time with his kinsman the count of Ostrevant, in the end the duke of Hereford went to Paris, where he was welcomed with great honour by the French royal family. Jean Froissart says that more than 40,000 men and women lined the streets to watch Henry's departure from London, and cried piteously to see him go.[10] This number is surely a gross exaggeration, as medieval chroniclers' estimated numbers usually are, but does give an indication of Henry's popularity. Perhaps as some kind of sop to John of Gaunt, on 24 September 1398 Richard II granted the castle, town and lordship of Castle Acre in Norfolk, forfeited by Thomas Mowbray, to Gaunt's youngest son Thomas Beaufort. The grant was for life, and Thomas was to pay no rent for this generous gift, which came on top of the 100 marks annually also granted to him by the king.[11]

59

Severely Despondent

John of Gaunt retreated to Lilleshall Abbey in Shropshire with Duchess Katherine, suffering from a fever and, surely, intense grief and rage at the exile of his beloved son; one chronicler says that John was '*graviter desolatus*' about it.[1] Having briefly travelled to London with Henry before his son departed from the kingdom, he had moved to Leicester Castle by 24 October and was still there on 4 November, 3 and 28 December 1398 and on 2 and 23 January 1399. At some point, the duke was treated by a leech (i.e. a physician who used leeches to draw blood) named Master Lewis.[2] John seems to have been seriously ill even before Christmas, and was perhaps aware that he was coming to the end of his eventful life. Most probably his nephew the king visited him before his death, as Richard was certainly in the Midlands in early 1399, though it seems most unlikely that John ever made the long and patriotic speech that Shakespeare puts in his mouth on this occasion. A writer in the 1440s, Thomas Gascoigne, claimed that John showed his nephew the ulcerated and putrefied flesh around his genitals as a warning against lechery, a story one can only hope is untrue (and which almost certainly is).[3]

John made his long and detailed will on 3 February 1399, though it is misdated to 3 February 1397, presumably an error by one of the scribes who wrote the document.[4] Almost certainly he dictated the will at Leicester Castle, though the location is not given in it. John had probably been too ill for several months to move to any of his many other castles, and people generally only made their wills when they thought they might be dying. His statement 'in case I die outside London,' however, shows that even on the last day of his life, he believed that he might rally enough to be able to travel to the city.

The duke left items to his wife Katherine, his nephew the king, his only surviving sibling the duke of York, each of his eight living children (Philippa, Elizabeth, Henry, Catalina, and the four Beauforts), and two of his grandsons, twelve-year-old Henry of Monmouth and nine-year-old John of Lancaster, the first and third sons of his son Henry, and the future king of England and duke of Bedford respectively. The will made no reference to Henry of Lancaster's exile or to any possible difficulties he might face in trying to obtain his bequests from his father. John left nothing to any of his numerous other grandchildren, his sons-in-law, his nieces and nephews, his cousins, his sisters-in-law the duchess of York and the dowager duchess of Gloucester, or his niece-in-law the nine-year-old Queen Isabelle, though did leave gifts of money to a few favoured retainers, one of whom was his stepson Sir Thomas Swynford.

Duchess Katherine appeared first in the list of family members who received bequests, even before Richard II, which is surprising given that the king outranked everyone and should, given the strict hierarchical etiquette of fourteenth-century England, have been named first. John named his daughter Catalina before his daughter Elizabeth though Elizabeth was the elder, as Catalina was a queen and thus outranked her half-sister the duchess of Exeter, and named his brother the duke of York, a king's son, before his son the duke of Hereford, a king's grandson. The 1392 will of John's sister-in-law the duchess of York listed the recipients of Isabel's bequests in strict order of rank: King Richard; Queen Anne; John of Gaunt; Edmund of Langley; Edward, earl of Rutland, Constance Despenser and Richard, as the children of Edmund, the king's second uncle; Eleanor, duchess of Gloucester, as the wife of the king's third and youngest uncle; and finally the earl of Huntingdon, great-grandson of a king. John of Gaunt outranked his brother Edmund because, although they held the same ducal rank, he was older than Edmund, and hence Isabel named John before his younger brother even though Edmund was her husband. In this context, for John to name Katherine before King Richard was remarkable.

John gave Katherine many more items and far more valuable items than he gave to anyone else, even the son and heir he adored, Henry; his great love and respect for her could hardly be more obvious. As well as all the items he left Katherine, he gave her the huge sum of £2,000, and also left her son Sir Thomas Swynford 100 marks or £66. Katherine's daughter Blanche Swynford is not named, and had perhaps already died; neither is Blanche Morieux, who was perhaps John's illegitimate daughter, or was perhaps the same person as Blanche Swynford. John appointed his and Katherine's son-in-law Ralph Neville, earl of Westmorland, and his kinsman Thomas Percy, earl of Worcester, as two of his executors. Significantly, his only other English son-in-law, John Holland, earl of Huntingdon, who had seduced his married daughter Elizabeth in 1386, and Thomas Percy's elder brother Henry, earl of Northumberland, with whom Gaunt had quarrelled badly in 1381, were not asked to be executors or supervisors.

Although John requested burial next to his long-dead first wife, Blanche of Lancaster, in the will, his huge generosity both to Duchess Katherine herself and to her children clearly demonstrates that he did not turn away from her at the end of his life and did not intend to insult or hurt her. Blanche was partly royal and had brought John his fortune and many of his titles, which was surely a major factor, if not the major factor, in his decision to be buried with her. It is absolutely certain that John loved Katherine deeply, and highly likely that he had loved Blanche too and that he remembered her with great affection and admiration for the rest of his life. The two women were not in competition for John's affections; he was capable of loving both and surely did, and also of honouring the memory of his royal second wife Constanza, whom he perhaps did not love as much as his other two wives but who had been an important figure in his life and in his family for the twenty-two and a half years of their marriage. Constanza is named several times in the will, as John was keen to establish an obit to be held every year on the anniversary of her death, 24 March, and to ensure that enough money was made available to keep the obit in perpetuity.

John also left many generous bequests to charity and to religious houses, including a hundred pounds of silver to the Minoresses near the Tower of London, which had been founded by Blanche of Lancaster's great-grandparents Edmund of Lancaster and Blanche of Artois in 1293, and left a red vestment embroidered with suns to Blanche's father and grandfather's foundation of the Newarke in Leicester. Other items John owned which he mentioned in his will included a gold table in his chapel which he had bought at Amiens in France and called 'Domesday,' and a tapestry given to him by the duke of Burgundy at Calais. John also owned a 'cup of silver with a cover bordered with gold, and on it a knob of gold, with which cup the most noble prince John, duke of Lancaster was often served, and with which he used to drink so long as he lived,' which is not mentioned in his will, but which many years later ended up in the possession of Walter, Lord Hungerford (d. 1449). Hungerford left it to Lord Beaumont (d. 1460), a descendant of John's aunt-in-law Eleanor of Lancaster, countess of Arundel and Lady Beaumont.[5]

In a long codicil to the will, John stated that the lands and lordships which he had purchased over the years, and thus were not part of the Lancastrian patrimony, which would belong by right to Henry after he died, would pass to his Beaufort children. Sir William Croiser sometimes appears in Gaunt's register and the duke had known him since at least 1368, and his daughter Elizabeth Croiser married Sir Edward de Kendale. Edward's father Edward the elder died at the beginning of 1373 and Elizabeth's husband in 1375, and her brother-in-law Thomas de Kendale and her mother-in-law also died in 1375 (it seems likely that the Kendales were victims of the fourth outbreak of the Black Death in England that year; they died on 23 or 25 July, 7 September and 11 or 12 September 1375). John of Gaunt took the opportunity to purchase from Elizabeth de Kendale née Croiser the reversion of various lordships, manors, tenements once held by the Kendales and now in Elizabeth's hands, though in the end she outlived her husband by well over forty years and did not die until late 1420. Sometime before William Montacute, earl of Salisbury, died in June 1397, John had also purchased the reversion of several of the earl's manors in the west country from him to benefit his Beaufort sons.[6] Salisbury had tragically killed his only son in a joust in 1382, and was on hostile terms with his nephew and heir, John Montacute; he was therefore happy enough to sell off some of his own lands to the duke.

Gaunt and Katherine's first two Beaufort children were of course born in *c.* 1373 and *c.* 1375, at the time that Edward de Kendale and his sons Edward and Thomas de Kendale passed away, and therefore it appears that John was thinking of his illegitimate sons' futures and how he could provide for them from the very beginning of their lives. He held the Lancastrian lands for the term of his life not by hereditary right but by the 'courtesy of England' as the widower of the Lancastrian heiress Duchess Blanche and as the father of her children, and his and Blanche's son Henry, not John himself, was the Lancastrian heir. John had no right and no legal ability to sell or give away any part of the lands he owned for decades – assuming he would ever have wished to disinherit Henry anyway, which is exceedingly unlikely. Like anyone else, however, he could purchase other lands and manors and do whatever he liked with them, and he was anxious to provide for his Beaufort children.

John made a point of specifying in his will that his body should not be embalmed or buried until forty days after his death, and historian Michael Bennett has suggested that he may have feared being buried alive. Although his father-in-law Henry of Grosmont had also requested in 1361 that he should not be buried until three weeks after death, it seems that Richard II paid messengers on or soon after 8 January 1399 to carry the news of John's death around England to the magnates and clergy. This was almost a month before John really did pass away (as Michael Bennett points out, Richard 'had an unfortunate habit of anticipating the deaths of his uncles'), so he may have been very ill and perhaps unconscious in early January.[7] If he subsequently heard that his nephew had spread the news of his demise when he was still alive, this would certainly explain his fears and his request not to be embalmed or buried for forty days, to ensure that it was absolutely certain that he truly was dead and not merely unconscious. John perhaps also hoped that the delay between death and burial would give his nephew the king time to relent and to allow John's son to travel home from exile in Paris to attend the funeral.

The duke ordered that 50 marks of silver should be given to the poor on each of the forty days that his body would lie above ground, 300 marks on the eve of his burial, and another 500 marks on the day of the burial. This came to a total of 2,800 marks or £1,866 to be given out in alms, which in modern money is several million pounds. He mentioned in his will a goblet which Duchess Katherine gave him 'at New Year last past,' so at some point between 1 January 1399 and his dictating the will on 3 February was evidently lucid enough to be aware of the gift. John's will is startlingly long, to the point where one wonders how he brought to mind so many of his possessions and how he found the breath to dictate it all, mere hours or so before he died, especially given that he had been seriously ill perhaps to the point of being unconscious for several months. The printed version, published in the original French in 1780, runs to twenty-eight pages (an

English translation of it published in the first volume of *Testamenta Vetusta* in 1826 is highly abridged and barely five pages long). Despite its length, there are some notable omissions; John did not, for example, mention the many dozens or even hundreds of horses he must have owned and what was to happen to them or to all the saddles, tack and other items that went with them. Parts of the will, and most especially the codicil, are repetitive – John must have dictated the words 'lands, manors, lordships, tenements, rents and services' a dozen times, and he talked about the obits for his late wives Blanche and Constanza on several occasions – so possibly his mind was wandering somewhat.

John of Gaunt died, still in his town of Leicester, on 3 February 1399, the same day as he dictated his will, a month short of his fifty-ninth birthday. His death left his brother Edmund of Langley as the only surviving child of Edward III. The cause of John's death, unless we accept the story of the chronicler fifty years later who claimed he suffered from and died of venereal disease – and we almost certainly should not accept it– is unknown. It is almost always the case in the fourteenth century that we do not know how anyone died. John's father is one exception: Edward III's death mask still exists and shows his mouth turned down at one side, which almost certainly reveals that he had a massive stroke or a series of strokes. This is a fortunate happenstance. On the rare occasions when a person's death occurred in suspicious circumstances and was investigated and found to be a result of illness, and the record of this still survives, the cause of death was given as something like 'he was very ill in one side' or 'she fell down and suddenly died.' Accidents were recorded as, for example, 'he fell from a ladder and fatally broke his head.' Lack of medical knowledge in the fourteenth century makes it basically impossible for a modern author to determine the actual cause of a person's death without a great deal of speculation. John of Gaunt, despite being the second most important man in England, did not die in suspicious circumstances and there was therefore no particular reason for anyone to record the cause of his death. We are left simply with the hostile, gossipy and almost certainly untrue speculation of a chronicler writing half a century later, though it is perhaps surprising, given the duke's central role in English political life for so many years, that contemporary chroniclers paid scant attention to his passing. The account of Thomas Walsingham, so opinionated on all matters relating to the duke for so long, in his *Chronica Maiora* barely even counts as cursory: 'At this time, occurred the death of John, duke of Lancaster.' He was scarcely more informative in his *Annales Ricardi Secundi*: 'On the morrow of the Purification of the Blessed Virgin [the Purification is 2 February] died Duke John of Lancaster.'[8]

John's body remained at Leicester until late February, and his son Henry Beaufort, bishop of Lincoln, and Henry's mother Katherine accompanied his funeral cortege to London. John was buried next to Blanche in St Paul's Cathedral on 15 or 16 March 1399, either on Passion Sunday or the day before, in line with his wish not to be buried for forty days (15 March was exactly forty days after his death). The king was there, though Henry of Lancaster, in exile, was not able to attend the funeral. When Henry returned to England a few months later, he visited his father's tomb at the earliest opportunity and is said by a chronicler to have 'cried very much'. Relatives who were able to attend the funeral included John's nephew Edward of York, his son-in-law John Holland, Holland's nephew Thomas and niece Margaret, Margaret's husband John Beaufort, and Gaunt's niece Philippa de Coucy, dowager countess of Oxford.[9]

60

Aftermath

And so, one of the great Englishmen of the Middle Ages passed away, leaving his nephew King Richard with a huge dilemma. Henry, the cousin whom Richard seems never to have much liked or trusted, and whom he had exiled, was now the rightful owner of the dukedom of Lancaster and the earldoms of Richmond, Lincoln, Leicester and Derby, plus the third of the large de Bohun inheritance (the earldoms of Hereford, Essex and Northampton), which he held for life from his late wife Mary by the 'courtesy of England'.[1] Richard was all too aware of the problems his great-grandfather Edward II had had in the 1310s and early 1320s with his own troublesome Lancastrian first cousin Thomas, and how the vast Lancastrian wealth and estates made their owner almost like another king in England.

The king therefore took the momentous decision to confiscate Henry's entire inheritance, and to exile him from England permanently. Richard granted custody of some of Gaunt's castles, manors and lordships in Lancashire and the Midlands to his half-nephew Thomas Holland, duke of Surrey, on 1 March. On 20 March, Gaunt's son-in-law the duke of Exeter was given custody of all of Gaunt's castles, lordships and manors in Wales until Exeter's brother-in-law Henry 'shall have sued the same out of the king's hands according to the law of the land or have had another grant thereof from the king'. Other castles, lordships and manors went to Gaunt's nephew Edward of York and to John Montacute, the royalist earl of Salisbury.[2]

Under normal circumstances, an inquisition post-mortem would have been held for the duke, which would have listed all his lands in all the counties where he held them, would have specified that he held most of them by the courtesy of England as Blanche's widower, and would have named Henry as his heir. As Henry was in exile and as Richard seized the inheritance within a few weeks of his uncle's death, this did not happen (the royal kinswoman Margaret, duchess of Norfolk, died a few weeks after John did, and as her grandson and heir Thomas Mowbray was also in exile, no inquisition post-mortem was held for her either). In his will, John of Gaunt left all his armour and his swords to Henry of Lancaster, and they were believed to be in the possession of John's armourer, Henry Armurer, in London. King Richard told Drew Barentyn, mayor of London, to arrest and imprison Henry Armurer in the belief that he had refused to surrender the late duke's armour to royal officials, but ordered his release in early July 1399 when it turned out that in fact Henry did not have the items.[3]

Henry of Lancaster, not a man to accept such ill-treatment passively, returned to England in July 1399 with the exiled archbishop of Canterbury, Thomas Arundel, and Arundel's teenage nephew, the executed earl of Arundel's son, who had escaped from the custody of Gaunt's son-in-law John Holland and fled abroad to join them. Ostensibly Henry only wished to claim his confiscated inheritance, but perhaps he returned with the intention of eventually taking the throne from his cousin. After Henry captured the city of Bristol in late July 1399, he had Sir John Bushy, Sir Henry Greene and William Scrope, earl of Wiltshire, executed without a trial, despite the men's close association with his father. Gaunt had appointed Wiltshire as one of the executors of his will less than six months previously, Bushy served with Gaunt overseas as early as 1378 and joined his retinue in 1382, and Greene also served in Gaunt's retinue for many years before becoming one of King's Richard's grossly unpopular counsellors in the late 1390s. (The other member of the 'caterpillars of the commonwealth' triumvirate, Sir William Bagot, who had admitted to plotting to kill John of Gaunt and to disinherit his children not long before, managed to escape, and survived until 1407.)

Henry's chief supporters in the summer of 1399 included his mother's cousin Henry Percy, earl of Northumberland, and his own brother-in-law Ralph Neville, earl of Westmorland. Most of Richard II's support simply collapsed and he was forced to abdicate his throne to Henry, whose reign as King Henry IV began on 30 September 1399. The former king, now merely Sir Richard of Bordeaux, was sent to captivity at Pontefract Castle in Yorkshire, and died there on or around 14 February 1400 at the age of thirty-three, possibly by being starved to death. Henry IV's stepbrother, Sir Thomas Swynford, may have been constable of Pontefract Castle in 1400, and if so, may have had a hand in the former king's demise. Duchess Katherine herself outlived John of Gaunt by four years and died on 10 May 1403, aged about sixty or so. She had apparently been ill for some time, as Pope Boniface IX replied on 14 March 1403 to a petition she had sent him asking him to inhibit anyone from 'hindering the executors of her will, under pain of excommunication'.[4] People usually only made their wills when they felt there was an imminent danger of their death.

Born the son of a reigning king, uncle of another and father of a third, John of Gaunt was also the grandfather of three kings: Catalina's son Juan II became king of Castile as an infant in 1406; Henry of Lancaster's eldest son, Henry of Monmouth, succeeded his father as King Henry V of England in 1413; and Philippa's eldest surviving son succeeded his elderly father Dom João as King Duarte I of Portugal in 1433. As well as the three Lancastrian kings of England descended from Gaunt and his first wife Blanche, Gaunt and Katherine Swynford's Beaufort descendants were destined to play a vital role in the political life of fifteenth-century England. Their daughter

Joan Beaufort (d. 1440), via her youngest child Cecily Neville, duchess of York, was the grandmother of two English kings, Edward IV and his brother Richard III, while their eldest son John Beaufort was the great-grandfather of Henry VII, the first king of the Tudor dynasty, via his granddaughter and heir Margaret Beaufort. Gaunt and Katherine's granddaughter Joan Beaufort (d. 1445), daughter of their eldest son John, became queen consort of Scotland after James I fell in love with her around 1420 while he was in captivity in England, and she was the ancestor of later kings of Scotland and of Mary, Queen of Scots. Katherine de Valois, the royal French widow of Gaunt's grandson Henry V and mother of Henry VI, might have had a relationship with another of Gaunt's grandsons, John Beaufort's fourth and youngest son Edmund Beaufort (b. *c.* 1406, later earl of Dorset and duke of Somerset), in the 1420s before she began her famous relationship with the Welsh squire Owen Tudor that ultimately resulted in the Tudor dynasty. That John of Gaunt and Katherine Swynford's grandchildren persuaded a king and a queen to have relationships with them surely reveals much about the appeal and attractiveness of the Beaufort family, and Edmund Beaufort was also rumoured in his own lifetime (whether accurately or not) to have had an affair with Marguerite of Anjou, Henry VI's French queen.

John and Katherine's wealthy second son Henry Beaufort enjoyed an enormously successful career in the Church and became a cardinal, and died in April 1447 in his early seventies, the last surviving of Gaunt's many children. On 28 November 1437, Henry's widowed sister Joan Neville née Beaufort, dowager countess of Westmorland, received a licence to found a perpetual chantry of two chaplains to celebrate divine service daily in the place where their mother Katherine Swynford was buried in Lincoln Cathedral, who would pray for Joan herself, for her great-nephew Henry VI, and for 'Henry [Beaufort], cardinal of England' while alive, and for the souls of Henry IV, Henry V, John of Gaunt, Katherine Swynford and Ralph Neville, 'the said chantry to be called the Chantry of Katherine, late duchess of Lancaster.'[5] When Countess Joan died in November 1440, she chose to be buried with her mother in Lincoln Cathedral, a fact which reveals a great deal about her love and affection for the woman who had been born a herald's daughter and who captured the heart of the richest and most powerful man in England.

St Paul's Cathedral was destroyed during the Great Fire of London in 1666 (the cathedral that stands there now was built in the late seventeenth century), and sadly, John of Gaunt and Blanche of Lancaster's tombs were lost. The Newarke in Leicester, burial place of Duchess Constanza, John and Blanche's sons who died in infancy, and John's daughter-in-law Mary de Bohun, survived Henry VIII and the dissolution, but was closed down in the reign of Henry VIII's son Edward VI in the middle of the sixteenth century. Their tombs, and the tombs of Blanche of Lancaster's father Duke Henry and grandfather Henry, earl of Lancaster, were therefore also lost.

Gaunt's son Henry IV was buried in Canterbury Cathedral in 1413, and his tomb and effigy still exist, near to those of Gaunt's eldest brother Edward of Woodstock, prince of Wales. Henry's second wife Juana of Navarre, dowager duchess of Brittany, was buried with him in 1437, having survived imprisonment for alleged witchcraft on the orders of her stepson Henry V. The effigies of Gaunt's parents Edward III and Philippa of Hainault can also still be seen, in Westminster Abbey, as can the tomb of Gaunt's third wife Katherine Swynford and their daughter the countess of Westmorland in Lincoln Cathedral.

Appendix 1

John of Gaunt's Will[1]

The will is written in French and is dated 3 February 1397 ('*le tierz jour de feverer l'an du grace mil trois centz quatre vingtz dis e sept*'), in error for 3 February 1399, the day John died. In the will, John referred to his son John Beaufort as marquis of Dorset, a title Beaufort did not receive until September 1397, and to his son Henry Beaufort as bishop of Lincoln, a position to which Henry was elected in February 1398. Furthermore, he called his daughters Elizabeth of Lancaster and Joan Beaufort duchess of Exeter and countess of Westmorland respectively, and their husbands John Holland and Ralph Neville did not receive these titles until September 1397. The will cannot, therefore, date to February 1397, and it appears that either John himself dated it incorrectly or the clerk(s) to whom he was dictating it did.

I have retained the original and inconsistent spelling of all given names (e.g. Blanche appears as both Blanche and Blanch, Katherine as both Katerin and Katerine, and Henry as both Henri and Henry), though all place names have been modernised, e.g. Lincoln for Nicol, Saint Paul's for Seynt Poule, London for Loundres, York for Everwyk and Bury St Edmunds for Seint Esmon de Bury. I have translated the entire will except for one very long, highly legalistic and rather tedious section about debts, and have merely paraphrased the seven-page codicil, which is also long, rambling and repetitive.

*

In the name of God the Father, the Son, and the Holy Spirit, Amen.

I, Johan, son of the king of England, duke of Lancaster, of sound mind, on the third day of February in the year of grace one thousand three hundred and ninety-seven [*sic*], have made my will in the manner which follows.

First, I bequeath my soul to God and His very sweet mother Saint Marie and to the joy of heaven [*joi du ciel*], and my body to be interred in the cathedral church of Saint Paul's in London, near the main altar in the same church, next to my dearest late consort Blanch, interred there.

Item, I leave to the parish where I shall die all that my executors wish to give in the name of my mortuary payment, which by law should be given as mortuary.[2]

And in case I die outside London, I will and devise that the first night when my body shall be brought to London, that it should be carried straight away to the Carmelite friars on Fleet Street [*Fletstrete*] for that night, to have the exequies there, and the next day the high requiem Mass, after which Mass I wish my body to be removed and carried straight away to the aforesaid church of Saint Paul's, to have the exequies that night, and the next day the high requiem Mass and the burial.

And wherever I die, I will and devise that after my passing, my body shall remain above ground and shall not be buried for forty days, and I charge my executors that during these forty days no embalming of my body shall be done, or pretended, privately or publicly.

Item, I will and devise that on each day of the aforesaid forty days, fifty marks of silver shall be given to poor people, for my soul; and on the eve of my burial 300 marks of silver, and on the day of my burial 500 marks of silver. If it seems to my executors that this may not be done, considering the quantity of my goods and my other instructions and bequests, the said amounts may not all be given to poor people as stated above; in which case, my executors, at their discretion, may give similar amounts to the poor on each of the said forty days, bearing in mind the quantity of my goods and my other instructions and bequests.

Item, I request that ten large candles be burned around my body on the day of my burial, in the name of the ten commandments of our Lord God, against which I have wickedly trespassed, beseeching our same Lord God that this, my devotion, may remedy all that I have done so very often and most wickedly against the said commandments. And above these ten, seven large candles should be placed in memory of the seven works of charity which I have often neglected and also of the seven deadly sins. And above these seven, I wish five large candles to be placed, in honour of the five precious wounds of our Lord Jesu, and for my five senses, which I have very carelessly expended, for which I pray to God for mercy. And above all these candles, I wish there to be three candles in honour of the Holy Trinity, upon which I confess all the evils I have done, begging for the mercy and pity which He of His benign grace has given for the salvation of myself and of other sinners. And I wish that among the aforesaid candles, mortars of wax should be placed around my body, however many it shall please my executors to place there.[3]

Item, I will that my executors beseech my kinsmen and friends [*mes cosyns e amys*] to be present at my burial in order to pray for my soul, without making of my death any other entertainment or ceremony, unless it be for the poor people praying to God for my soul.

Item, I wish, ordain and devise that after my death, from all my goods and chattels that are left after my other wishes and bequests, that my executors pay all my debts which are due on the day of my passing, as reason demands; except that under no circumstances do I wish my executors to pay any of the debts of the expeditionary army which my dearest brother the duke of York once led to Portugal [in the early 1380s], of which I hold myself, before God and all the world, discharged of everything.

But of all my other debts, I will that reasonable settlement be made, and also I will, ordain and devise that if at some time in my life, I held any lands, tenements, rents, services, or gold or silver, or other moveables from any other person without just and due title, or if I have done wrong or injury to any other, though at present I know of none, if in the future it may be duly proved, my executors should make full restitution and amends from whatever they have of my goods and chattels, saving the necessary expenses for my tomb and concerning my body on the day of my passing, until the time when my interment is accomplished; and that they should also pay to my servants their salaries, according to my commands; and furthermore that my executors take from my goods an appropriate sum from which they may make and accomplish all the chantries and obits ordained in this, my will, for my soul and for the souls of my dearest late consorts Blanche and Constance, whom God absolve.

And after my executors have fulfilled all my bequests expressed above, and after all the expenses concerning my body after my passing, and when my tomb and my interment have been fully accomplished; and after every and all [*trestouts*, literally 'very all', a word John uses often in the will] of my debts are paid and full restitution has been made for wrongs and injuries as above, and the salaries to be paid to my servants as commanded by me; a sum should be kept back and taken into the hands of my executors and reserved for the chantries and obits aforesaid. If my goods and chattels then remaining in the hands of my executors do not entirely suffice to accomplish my bequests expressed below, then of each of my said bequests, a rebate may be made according to the discretion of my executors, except that in any event, the things below specified which are for my very sovereign lord the king, I wish to be delivered to him as property given to him in my lifetime.

Item, I bequeath to the aforesaid altar of St Paul's my great bed [*mon graunt lyt*] of cloth of gold, the field partly powdered with gold roses on gold stalks, and on each stalk two plumes of white ostrich feathers, the taffeta curtains of the same work, and thirteen matching hangings of woven tapestry; and to the same altar, my vestments of white satin embroidered with gold, of which the embroidered work is a stripe passing between gold crowns, which I bought from Courtenay, embroiderer of London; and the vestments contain two frontals for the altar, and on each, three great gold tabernacles and large images embroidered on them in gold, a chasuble, two tunics, 111 albs, eleven stoles, 111 maniples, 111 copes, a canopy for the catafalque, a vessel for the Host, eleven hangings, eleven cloths for the altar, one together with a little frontal; and my entire vestments of black camoca used for requiem Masses and embroidered with a gold crucifix with three matching vessels for the Host, and other pieces which belong to these vestments.[4] And

I will that every and all of the things bequeathed to the aforesaid main altar of St Paul's with every and all of their accessories remain on the said altar always, and remain around my tomb without being changed to another use, and should in no way be removed from there.

And I will that the executors of my goods purchase in London, or outside, wherever it can be most profitably done, as much land, or rent, or appropriation of churches, or other possessions, for my soul and for the soul of my said late consort Blanch always, that is, for my soul, an obit to be celebrated solemnly every year on the day of my passing, and for the soul of my said late consort Blanch, an obit to be celebrated solemnly every year on 12 September. And also I will, ordain and devise that from my goods and chattels, my executors ordain and establish a chantry with two chaplains in the aforesaid church of Saint Paul's to celebrate divine service within always for my soul and for the soul of my said late consort Blanch, and so that it is sustained perpetually, certain lands and tenements of which the reversion has been purchased for my use should be given and amortised, rendering twenty marks per year to the lady Katerine del Staple for the term of her life. I will that during her lifetime she should be paid from the issues of the manor of Barnoldswick in the county of Yorkshire, which issues should sustain the chantry during the said Katerine's life.

Item, for the extreme devotion which I have [*verb missing*] at the abbey of Bury St Edmunds in the county of Suffolk, I bequeath to the said abbey my rich vestment of beryl, that is, a chasuble with ornaments, an alb, an amice, a stole, and a maniple of red velvet embroidered with a fret of gold jewels, and on every other mesh a ring of beryl, and on every other mesh an escutcheon of beryl of the arms of Saint George; and an altar-cloth with a small ornamental border of green velvet embroidered with beryl, worked with the heads of the twelve apostles; and one of the two pieces of cloth for an altar embroidered with gold which I bought in Amiens, made of our Lord God and His very sweet mother Saint Marie and the twelve apostles; and every and all of my cloths of arms of gold in portions which are made of God and Our Lady, except those which have been bequeathed elsewhere in my will; and my red cloth-of-gold vestment, of which the field is satin and the work is angels of gold, with every and all of the offcuts and pieces which belong to this vestment to the abbot and convent of this abbey; and that for these things, they hold for me a perpetual obit every year on the day of my passing.

Item, I bequeath to the house of Our Lady in Lincoln my third gold chalice, made in Bordeaux, which has a crucifix engraved under the foot and a vernicle engraved in the paten; the gold table in my chapel, bought in Amiens, which table I named *Domesday* [in English in the original]; my biggest gold candlesticks made for my chapel; and my new vestments of cloth-of-gold, the field red, with gold falcons and two ornamental borders, eleven altar-cloths, a chasuble, two tunics, three albs, three amices, eleven stoles, 111 maniples, 111 copes, a cover for the catafalque, eleven hangings for the altar striped with silk; and one of the pieces of altar-cloth embroidered with gold which I bought in Amiens, made of our Lord God and His very sweet mother Saint Marie and the twelve apostles.[5]

Item, I bequeath to the new collegiate church of Our Lady in Leicester my red velvet vestments embroidered with golden suns with all the apparel belonging to it, and to the same, every and all of my missals and the other books of my chapel which are of the ordinance of the cathedral church of Salisbury, and which have not been bequeathed elsewhere in my lifetime.[6]

Item, I bequeath to the main altar of the Carmelite friars of London my old white vestments of cloth-of-gold called *Rakamas*, with everything that belongs to these vestments, and to the same, fifteen marks of silver in honour of the fifteen joys of Our Lady.

Item, I bequeath to the other three orders of friars in London, that is, the Preachers, the Minor and the Augustinians, to each order ten marks, of which five marks are in honour of the five precious wounds of our Lord Jesu, and the other five in honour of the five joys of Our Lady.[7]

Item, I bequeath to the convent of the Minoresses in London near the Tower of London £100 of silver, to be paid out among them.[8]

Item, I bequeath to every poor hermit and recluse having a house in London or in five places nearby, wherein he stays, three nobles, in honour of the blessed Trinity.[9]

Item, I bequeath to each of the [convent of] nuns within London and in the suburbs five marks, in honour of the five joys of Our Lady, and to the nuns of Clerkenwell, twenty marks of silver.

Item, I bequeath to each house of lepers in five places around London responsible for five sick people, five nobles, in honour of the five precious wounds of our Lord Jesu, and to those who have fewer patients, three nobles, in honour of the blessed Trinity.

Item, I bequeath to each house of *Charthous* in England twenty pounds.[10]

Item, I bequeath to the prisons of Newgate and Ludgate in London a hundred marks, to be distributed among them in the best manner and to benefit them the most profitably, according to the discretion of my executors.

Item, I bequeath to my dearest consort Katerin the two best brooches that I have, excepting the brooch that I have bequeathed to my very dread lord and nephew the king, and my largest gold goblet, which the earl of Wiltshire gave to the king my lord and he [the king] gave to me at my last journey to Aquitaine, together with all the gold goblets that she herself has given me up to now and which are in her possession on the day of my passing, together with every and all of the clasps, rings, diamonds, rubies, and all the other things which will be found in a little box of cypress wood that I have, of which I myself carry the key; and also what will be found after my death in the money-bag that I wear about me; and my entire set of vestments of cloth-of-gold, the matching bed and the [items for my] hall, with every and all of the copes, tapestries for the chamber, kitchens, closet, cushions, and the embroidered cloths for the sepulchre of Our Lord and all other matching pieces in whatever condition or shape they be in, which I bought from my dearest cousin the duchess of Norfolk, in their entirety without anything being removed from them as I had them from her, of which the field is red with black lattice work, and in each place where the fret joins, a gold rose, and on each mesh of the fret a black letter M and on every other mesh a black leopard.[11]

And to the same [i.e. to Duchess Katherine], I bequeath my great bed of black velvet embroidered with pairs of iron compasses, and a turtle-dove in the middle of the compasses, and every and all of the tapestries which belong to this bed in my chamber; and to the same, I bequeath every and all of my other beds made for my body, called in England trussing-beds [*trussynbeddes*, in English in the original], with the tapestries and other accessories; my best drinking-horn with the good ruby, my best collar together with all the diamonds, and my second best ermine blanket, and two of my best cloaks of ermine with the matching clothes; and I bequeath to my said consort every and all of the goods and chattels, of whatever state and condition they be in, which she had before the marriage celebrated between myself and her, with every and all of the other goods and jewels which I have given to her since the aforesaid marriage, and the goods and jewels which are in her keeping and which are not set down in the inventory of my goods.

Item, I bequeath to my very dread lord and nephew the king the best brooch I own on the day of my passing, and my best goblet covered with gold, which my dearest consort Katerin gave me at New Year last past; and my gold salt cellar with the garter and on the ornamental border fashioned around the salt cellar, a turtle-dove; and to the same, twelve cloths-of-gold of which the field is red satin striped with gold, which cloths I ordered to be made into a bed, which has not yet been started; and an ermine blanket, the best that I have, together with the matching coverlet, and the piece of arras cloth which the duke of Burgundy gave me the last time I was in Calais.[12]

Item, I bequeath to my dearest brother the duke of York a goblet covered with gold.

Item, I bequeath to my dearest son Henri, duke of Hereford, earl of Derby, the two best pieces of arras cloth that I have, except those which I have especially bequeathed elsewhere in my will, of which one was given to me by my very dread lord and nephew the king and my beloved brother the duke of Gloucester, whom God absolve, and the other the last time I returned from Spain; and my great bed of white and red checked camaca, embroidered with a gold tree and a turtle-dove sitting on the tree, with fourteen tapestries.

And to the same [Henry], my great bed of cloth-of-gold, the field partly worked with gold trees, and next to each tree a black alaunt tied to the same tree, with the matching garments and all the tapestries made for it; and furthermore, I bequeath to him every and all of the armour, swords and daggers which will be mine on the day of my passing except for those which have been bequeathed or given elsewhere; and furthermore, I bequeath him four chargers, two dozen bowls, and six silver saucers; and I bequeath him a gold fastening of the old kind, with the name of God written in each part of the same fastening, which my very honoured lady and mother the queen [Philippa of Hainault], whom God absolve, gave to me, commanding me to keep it, with her blessing, and I wish him to keep it, with the blessing of God and mine.[13]

Item, I bequeath to my dearest daughter Phylypp, queen of Portugal, my second best gold drinking-horn, and a goblet covered with gold.

Item, I bequeath to my dearest daughter Katerin, queen of Castile and Leon [*roigne de Chastill et de Lyon*], a goblet covered with gold.

Item, I bequeath to my dearest daughter Elizabeth, duchess of Exeter, my white silk bed worked with blue eagles with outstretched wings, the curtains of matching decorated white taffeta and fourteen tapestries, and my best brooch that I have after those that have already been bequeathed.

Item, I bequeath to my dearest son Johan Beaufort, marquis of Dorset, two dozen bowls, two silver half-gallon jugs for wine, a gilded silver cup, eleven basins and eleven silver ewers.

Item, I bequeath to the reverend father in God and my beloved son the bishop of Lincoln [Henry Beaufort] a dozen bowls, a dozen saucers, two silver gallon jugs for wine, a gilded silver cup with a basin, and one silver ewer, and my entire vestment of yellow velvet with all the things belonging to this vestment, and my missal and my breviary [*portheus*] which belonged to my lord my brother the prince of Wales, whom God absolve.[14]

Item, I bequeath to my dearest son Thomas Beaufort, their brother, a dozen bowls, a dozen saucers, two silver half-gallon jugs for wine, and six silver cups.

Item, I bequeath to my dearest daughter, their sister, countess of Westmorland and Lady Nevyll, a bed of silk and a golden goblet, uncovered, with a ewer.

Item, I bequeath to my dearest Henry, eldest son of my dearest son the duke of Hereford, a golden goblet. And to my beloved [grand]son John, brother of the said Henry, son of my said son, a golden goblet.

Item, I will and bequeath that if after the costs concerning my body after my death and about my tomb, and my debts paid entirely and in full and full restitution made for any wrongs and injuries done by me or by my officials on my behalf, and the costs of my executors in fulfilling this my testament, and my servants also looked after and their rewards delivered to them, and the rightful sum kept in the hands of the executors for the foundation of the said chantries and obits as above; then my executors shall pay to the aforesaid abbey of Bury St Edmunds £1,000, and to my aforesaid consort Katerine £2,000, to my said son the duke of Hereford £1,000, to my said son the marquis [of Dorset] £1,000, to my said son Thomas Beaufort 1,000 marks [£666], to my dearest bachelor Sir Thomas Swynneford 100 marks, to Sir Waut' [Walter] Blount [*amount missing, presumably 100 marks*], to

Sir [*first name missing*] Chamblayn 100 marks, to Sir Hugh Shireley 100 marks, to Sir Ric[hard] Aburbury the son fifty marks, to Sir Wyllyam Par fifty marks of my bequest.[15]

Item, I will, ordain, and bequeath that from my goods and chattels, my executors make and establish in the new church of Our Lady of Leicester [the Newarke] a chantry with two chaplains to celebrate divine service therein forever for my soul and for the soul of my late beloved consort Lady Constances [*sic*] buried there, and to keep in the said church an obit for the soul of my said late consort on the 24th day of March annually forever. And to do this and sustain it perpetually, my said executors, on the advice of people of law, should ensure that my goods suffice to endow the aforesaid church for the sustenance of the chantries and obits aforesaid.

[There follows an extremely long section where John talks about debts owing to him, about his wish for his executors to put right any wrongs he has done to others, and about the annuity of 40,000 francs owed to him by his son-in-law the king of Castile and Leon. This is referring to the Treaty of Bayonne established in the late 1380s between John and Constanza 'of famous memory, during her lifetime my consort, daughter and heir of Petre [Pedro] of famous memory, late king of Castile and Leon, for the term of my life and the life of the said Constance then my consort,' and King Enrique's father King Juan]

And of my will and final wishes, to execute them well and faithfully, I make, ordain and appoint as my executors the reverend fathers in God Richard [Mitford], bishop of Salisbury, and Johan [Green], bishop of Worcester; my dearest and beloved cousins and companions Thomas [Percy], earl of Worcester, steward of the household of my very dread lord the king, and Wyllyam [Scrope], earl of Wiltshire, treasurer of England; my beloved son[-in-law] Rauf [Neville], earl of Westmorland; Sir Waltier Blownt, Sir Johan Dabruggecourt, Sir Wyllyam Par, Sir Hugh War'ton, Sir Thomas Skelton; and Johan Cokeyn, chief steward of my lands and possessions, Sir Rob't Qwytby, my attorney general, Piers Melburn, Willyam Keteryng, Robert Haytfield, controller of my household, Sir Johan Legburn, my receiver general, and Thomas Longley, clerk.

I give to them and each of them full power and authority to administer every and all of my goods and chattels and to carry out everything as good executors in a reasonable and justifiable way as seems befitting, and particularly in the manner which I have laid out above; and in other matters they should act with their very wise discretion and good conscience as seems best to them in order to carry out my affairs and in the service of God and His very sweet mother Marie; and for their actions they will have to answer before God on Judgement Day [*le haut jour de justice*, literally 'the high day of justice.' John then expanded on this idea at great length, explaining how his executors must act according to their consciences and must avoid acting fraudulently so as not to inperil their souls. To supervise them and to ensure that the executors complied with his final wishes, John beseeched his nephew Richard, 'my very dread lord, my king and sovereign earthly lord,' to be his good lord one last time and to act as the 'sovereign supervisor' of his will].

And after him [King Richard], I appoint as supervisors my dearest and most entirely well beloved brother Esmon, duke of York; my dearest and most entirely well beloved nephew Edward, duke of Aumerle; the very reverend fathers in God Roger [Walden], archbishop of Canterbury, and Richard [Scrope], archbishop of York; and the reverend father in God [Henry Beaufort] the bishop of Lincoln, my beloved son.

Praying to my aforesaid brother and nephew, who are related by blood and who by reason and nature should be the closest of friends, and to the said very reverend fathers in God and my beloved son, that they, with my very dread lord the king aforesaid, saving his honour above all, should be good supervisors of my will, and occupy themselves for the betterment of myself and the comfort of my aforesaid executors, so that neither by negligence, nonchalance, anger or other error, may these my said wishes and ordinances be set aside; nor may they in any other way alter what is written above, or they may have to answer for it to Him who is King of Kings [*luy qu'est roy des toutz roys*] and has the oversight of all earthly deeds and thoughts, for which he will render a reward to everyone according to his desserts.

In faith and in testimony of every and all of these things written above in this, my will, I have had the seal of my arms set, and for greater recognition and affirmation of my own deed, I have myself set on the dorse my signet which I carry myself at all times, the year and day aforesaid; and the people written below, I have requested to witness these things: that is, Master Johan Kynyngham, doctor of theology; Sire Johan Neuton, parson of the church of Burbach; Sire Wautier Piers, parson of the church of Wymondham; Wyllyam Harpeden and Robert Symeon, squires.'

*

After this long will, John dictated a seven-page codicil to it in which he discussed lands, manors, lordships, tenements, rents and services that he had purchased at various times throughout his life. He meant lands that did not belong to the Lancastrian patrimony and which therefore did not automatically fall to Henry of Lancaster. John stated that he had given certain of these lands, tenements and so on to Duchess Katherine to hold for the rest of her life, and others to their son John Beaufort, to be held by John for the rest of his life and thereafter by the heirs of his body. The lands held by Katherine would, after her death, pass to their third son Thomas Beaufort, and were specified as lands which had once belonged to Edward de Kendale (d. 1373) and his son Edward (d. 1375). John of Gaunt had purchased the reversion of the lands from Lady Elizabeth Croiser or Croyser, the younger Edward de Kendale's widow, though in the end, Elizabeth did not die until December 1420.[16] If John or Thomas Beaufort had no heirs of their body, the lands would fall to Gaunt's 'beloved daughter Johane, their sister, countess of Westm'land, and to the heirs of her body; and failing the issue of the said Johane, the remainder to my right heirs,' that is, if Gaunt's Beaufort children failed to have any children of their own or if the children did not survive, the lands would pass to his Lancastrian descendants.

John then went on to specify, again, that a chantry with two chaplains should be established in St Paul's Cathedral to celebrate divine service on 12 September for Duchess Blanche's soul, and for his own soul on the anniversary of his death. He talked, again, of 'two chaplains celebrating divine service in the new collegiate church of Our Lady of Leicester, for my soul and the soul of my dearest late consort Lady Constance buried there, and for an obit to be celebrated there for the soul of my said late consort Constance on the twenty-fourth day of March every year'. The next item was three wapentakes in Richmondshire (a wapentake was a division of a county in the north of England, called 'hundreds' elsewhere) which John had given to his daughter Joan Beaufort and her husband the earl of Westmorland for their lives, which he now made hereditary to their male issue. If Joan and Ralph Neville had no surviving sons, the wapentakes would pass to Joan's brother John, then to their brother Thomas, or failing any male issue born to the Beauforts, to the duke's Lancastrian heirs. John's final wish was that 'all other lordships, manors, lands, tenements, rents, services, possessions, reversions and advowsons, with their appurtenances purchased for my use,' should pass to Thomas Beaufort and then his male issue, or failing such, to John Beaufort and his male issue, then to Countess Joan.

Appendix 2

John of Gaunt's Children

John had eight children who survived infancy (and a few who did not):

1. Philippa of Lancaster, queen of Portugal (31 March 1360 – 19 July 1415)
John of Gaunt and Blanche of Lancaster's eldest child, named after her paternal grandmother Philippa of Hainault, queen of England, who may also have been her godmother. She married King João I of Portugal in February 1387, and bore nine children between 1388 and 1402, of whom six survived infancy and are known to historians as the 'Illustrious Generation'. Philippa was buried in Batalha Monastery in 1415, where her tomb and effigy can still be seen, and her widower João was buried next to her eighteen years later in 1433. Her many grandchildren included an archbishop of Lisbon, a titular prince of Antioch, a duke of Burgundy, and a Holy Roman Empress. Like her younger half-sister Catalina, Philippa was an ancestor of Philip II, king of Spain, and of Henry VIII's first wife Katherine of Aragon (1485–1536), queen of England, the first of the six wives of Henry VIII and the mother of Mary I of England.

2. Elizabeth of Lancaster, duchess of Exeter, countess of Pembroke and Huntingdon (*c.* 21 February 1363 – 24 November 1425)
Elizabeth's second husband, Sir John Holland, was the father of the eldest four of her children; his heir was their second son John, born 1395, after their first son, Richard, died in childhood a few months after John Holland was executed. Their elder daughter Constance married Thomas Mowbray, earl of Norfolk (b. 1385), who was executed by Elizabeth's brother Henry IV in 1405, and their younger daughter Alice married Richard de Vere, earl of Oxford, but died young and childless.

Elizabeth was widowed on *c.* 9 or 15 January 1400 when John Holland was beheaded in Essex after taking part in the Epiphany Rising to restore the deposed Richard II to the throne taken from him the previous September by Elizabeth's brother. (Joan de Bohun, dowager countess of Hereford and the mother-in-law of Elizabeth's brother, was responsible for Holland's execution.) Elizabeth almost certainly married her third husband Sir John Cornewaille or Cornwall sometime before 6 April 1400, only a few weeks after Holland's death. On that date, her brother Henry IV ordered Cornwall to be imprisoned in the Tower of London, presumably because he and Elizabeth had married without his permission.[1] Cornwall was soon freed, and he and Elizabeth had two children, Constance, countess of Arundel (d. *c.* 1427) and John (d. 1421), neither of whom had children of their own. Elizabeth died at the age of sixty-two in November 1425, and John Cornwall outlived her by eighteen years and was made Baron Fanhope by John of Gaunt's great-grandson Henry VI. Elizabeth's grandson Henry Holland, duke of Exeter (1430–75) married Anne of York, eldest sister of Edward IV and Richard III.

3. Henry of Lancaster, third duke of Lancaster, first duke of Hereford, earl of Derby, King Henry IV (15 April 1367 – 20 March 1413)
Henry became Henry IV of England on 30 September 1399, and died a few weeks before his forty-sixth birthday in 1413, having survived numerous rebellions against his rule. His throne passed to his eldest son Henry V. Henry's legitimate line came to an end with the death of Henry VI's only child Edward of Lancaster in 1471, though there were also several illegitimate lines of descent. Henry himself had an illegitimate son, Edmund Lebourde, and although he married Juana of Navarre, dowager duchess of Brittany, in 1403, they had no surviving children together.

4. Catalina (or Katherine) **of Lancaster,** queen of Castile and Leon (before 31 March 1373 – 2 June 1418)
Catalina's eldest child María of Castile (1401–58) became queen consort of Aragon, Naples, Majorca, Sardinia and Corsica by marriage to her cousin Alfonso V, and her third and youngest child, and her only son, was Juan II, king of Castile (b. 1405, r. 1406–54). Juan succeeded his father Enrique as king of Castile when he was an infant under two years old, and Catalina acted as co-regent for her son with her brother-in-law Don Fernando. She was the grandmother of Isabel the Catholic (1451–1504), queen regnant of Castile, and the great-grandmother of Katherine of Aragon, queen of England; Queen Katherine was probably named after her great-grandmother. Queen Catalina was buried with her husband Enrique III in Toledo Cathedral, where her tomb and effigy can still be seen, in 1418.

5. John Beaufort, marquis of Dorset, earl of Somerset (*c.* 1373 – 16 March 1410)
John Beaufort and Margaret Holland, daughter of the earl of Kent, had two daughters and four sons. Their elder daughter Joan Beaufort married James I, king of Scotland, and their younger daughter Margaret married Thomas Courtenay, earl of Devon. John Beaufort and Margaret Holland's eldest son Henry, earl of Somerset, and their third son Thomas, count of Perche, both died childless. Their second son John, duke of Somerset (*c.* 1404–44) was the father of Margaret Beaufort (*c.* 1442/43–1509), who was the mother of Henry VII (1457–1509) and the grandmother of Henry VIII. John and Margaret's fourth and youngest son Edmund Beaufort (*c.* 1406–55) was the grandfather of Henry Stafford, duke of Buckingham, executed by Richard III

in 1483. None of Edmund's sons left any legitimate children and the legitimate male Beaufort line ended in 1471, but Edmund's eldest son Henry Beaufort, duke of Somerset (1436–64) had an illegitimate son called Charles Somerset, earl of Worcester, who had and has descendants. There were and are also many descendants of Edmund Beaufort's daughters.

John Beaufort died on 16 March 1410, and his widow Margaret Holland subsequently married his half-nephew Thomas of Lancaster, duke of Clarence, second son of Henry IV and brother of Henry V; they received a papal dispensation to marry on 16 August 1410 and again on 10 November 1411.[2] Margaret had no children with Clarence, and died in 1439.

6. Henry Beaufort, bishop of Lincoln 1398, bishop of Winchester 1404, cardinal 1426, chancellor of England 1403 (*c.* 1375 – 11 April 1447)
Most probably the second child of Gaunt and Katherine Swynford, perhaps born around 14 January 1375 in Kettlethorpe. Henry enjoyed a hugely successful career in the Church for many years, and lived the longest of all of John of Gaunt's children. His heir on his death in 1447 was his great-niece Margaret Tudor née Beaufort (d. 1509), granddaughter of his older brother John Beaufort.[3] He usually appears in contemporary records as 'Henry the cardinal of England'.

7. Joan Neville née Beaufort, countess of Westmorland, Lady Ferrers and Neville (*c.* 1376/7 – 13 November 1440)
Joan was a formidable character who persuaded her second husband Ralph Neville to favour her own children over his children from his first marriage to Margaret Stafford. Joan was buried in Lincoln Cathedral next to her mother Katherine Swynford, and there is also an effigy of her in St Mary's Church, Staindrop, County Durham, next to Ralph Neville; an effigy of Margaret Stafford lies on his other side. Joan was the mother of the duchesses of Norfolk, Buckingham and York, among many others, and the grandmother of two kings.

8. Thomas Beaufort, duke of Exeter (c. 1379 – 31 December 1426)
Probably John and Katherine's youngest child, perhaps born in late 1379. Thomas's half-nephew Henry V made him duke of Exeter in 1416. Sometime before 15 February 1404, he married Margaret Neville of Hornby, an heiress in Lincolnshire and Yorkshire, who was born *c.* 1384/85; she was 'aged 28 and more' in May 1413. They had no surviving children; they did have a son named Henry, but he died childless in his father's lifetime.[4] At Thomas's inquisition post-mortem held between March and May 1427, his heir was named as his nephew John Beaufort (*c.* 1404–1444), earl and later duke of Somerset.[5] The dukedom of Exeter was subsequently given to John of Gaunt's grandson John Holland (1395–1447), whose father the elder John Holland, earl of Huntingdon, had held it between 1397 and 1399. Thomas was buried with his wife at the abbey of St Edmunds in Suffolk, and his remains were discovered and examined on 20 February 1772; his hair was said to be 'of a fine brown colour'.[6]

Appendix 3

John of Gaunt's Grandchildren

Gaunt had just under forty grandchildren who lived into adulthood (plus a sizeable number of others who died young and are not listed here):

Children of Philippa, Queen of Portugal
Duarte I, king of Portugal (d. 1438)
Pedro, duke of Coimbra (d. 1449)
Henrique 'the Navigator', duke of Viseu (d. 1460)
Isabel, duchess of Burgundy (d. 1471)
João, constable of Portugal (d. 1442)
Fernando, 'the Saint-Prince' (d. 1433)

Children of Elizabeth, Duchess of Exeter, Countess of Huntingdon
Constance Holland, countess of Norfolk, Lady Grey (d. 1437)
Alice Holland, countess of Oxford (d. c. 1406)
Richard Holland (d. 1400)
John Holland, duke of Exeter (1395–1447)
Constance Cornwall, countess of Arundel (d. c. 1427)
John Cornwall (d. 1421)

Children of Henry IV, King of England
Henry V, king of England (1386–1422)
Thomas of Lancaster, duke of Clarence (1387–1421)
John of Lancaster, duke of Bedford (1389–1435)
Humphrey of Lancaster, duke of Gloucester (1390–1447)
Blanche of Lancaster, electress-palatine of the Rhine (1392–1409)
Philippa of Lancaster, queen of Denmark, Norway and Sweden (1394–1430)
Edmund Lebourde, illegitimate

Children of Catalina, Queen of Castile
María of Castile, queen of Aragon, Naples, Majorca, Sardinia and Corsica (d. 1458)
Catalina of Castile, duchess of Villena, countess of Albuquerque and Asturias (d. 1439)
Juan II, king of Castile (1405–54)

Children of John Beaufort, Marquess of Somerset and Dorset
Henry Beaufort, earl of Somerset (1401–18)
John Beaufort, duke of Somerset (d. 1444)
Thomas Beaufort, count of Perche (d. 1431)
Edmund Beaufort, count of Mortain, duke of Somerset (d. 1455)
Joan Beaufort, queen of Scotland (d. 1445)
Margaret Beaufort, countess of Devon (d. 1449)

Children of Joan Beaufort, Lady Ferrers and Countess of Westmorland
Elizabeth Ferrers, Lady Greystoke (*c.* 1393–1434)
Mary Ferrers, Lady Neville (*c.* 1394–1458)
Eleanor Neville, Lady Despenser, countess of Northumberland (d. 1473)
Katherine Neville, duchess of Norfolk (d. 1483)
Anne Neville, duchess of Buckingham (d. 1480)
Cecily Neville, duchess of York (d. 1495)
Richard Neville, earl of Salisbury (d. 1460)
William Neville, earl of Kent (d. 1463)
Robert Neville, bishop of Durham and Salisbury (d. 1457)
George Neville, Lord Latimer (d. 1469)
Edward Neville, Lord Abergavenny (d. 1476)

Endnotes

Abbreviations

C	Chancery (National Archives)
CCR	Calendar of Close Rolls
CChR	Calendar of Charter Rolls
CFR	Calendar of Fine Rolls
CIPM	Calendar of Inquisitions Post Mortem
CPR	Calendar of Patent Rolls
DL	Duchy of Lancaster (National Archives)
E	Exchequer (National Archives)
ODNB	Oxford Dictionary of National Biography
PROME	Parliament Rolls of Medieval England
TNA	The National Archives
Register 1371–75	John of Gaunt's Register, Vol. 1, 1371–1375, ed. Sydney Armitage-Smith
Register 1379–83	John of Gaunt's Register, Vol. 2, 1379–1383, ed. Eleanor C. Lodge and Robert Somerville

Introduction

1. *Chronicque de la Traison et Mort de Richart Deux Roy Dengleterre,* ed. Benjamin Williams (London: S. and J. Bentley, Wilson and Fley, 1846), p. 18; Chris Given-Wilson, *Chronicles of the Revolution, 1397–1400: The Reign of Richard II* (Manchester: Manchester University Press, 1993), p. 132.
2. *Chonicque de la Traison*, p. 18.
3. *Chonicque de la Traison*, p. 21; Nigel Saul, *Richard II* (New Haven and London: Yale University Press, 1997), pp. 400–01.
4. Given-Wilson, *Chronicles of the Revolution*, pp. 23–31, 68–9, 75–76, 90–93, 97–98, 105–06.
5. For Richard of Cornwall, see the biographies of him by N. Denholm-Young and T.W. E. Roche. One major difference between the two men is that Richard had only two legitimate sons who lived into adulthood and no legitimate grandchildren, whereas Gaunt had more than forty grandchildren and was an ancestor of the royal houses of Portugal and Spain as well as that of England.

1. Birth in St Bavo, Ghent

1. Ian Mortimer, *The Perfect King: The Life of Edward III, Father of the English Nation* (London: Vintage, 2006), p. 149; W. Mark Ormrod, *Edward III,* (New Haven and London: Yale University Press, 2011), p. 201; B. C. Hardy, *Philippa of Hainault and her Times* (London: John Long Limited, 1910), p. 104.
2. Hardy, *Philippa of Hainault*, p. 104. The county of Guelders was upgraded to a dukedom a few years later.

3. *Calendar of Patent Rolls 1340–43*, p. 569; *CPR 1343–45*, p. 42; *Oeuvres de Froissart*, ed. Kervyn de Lettenhove, Vol. 7, pp. 246–47; *The Brut or the Chronicles of England*, ed. F. W. D. Brie, part 2, pp. 306, 309.

4. Henry Stephen Lucas, *The Low Countries and the Hundred Years' War, 1326–1347* (Ann Arbor: University of Michigan, 1929), p. 364.

5. Ormrod, *Edward III*, pp. 212, 225, 618.

6. Lucas, *The Low Countries and the Hundred Years' War*, p. 364.

7. Duke Jan's mother Margaret (1275–c. 1333) was a daughter of Edward I of England and older sister of Edward III's father Edward II. Jan's eldest child Johanna of Brabant (1322–1406), later duchess of Brabant in her own right after her three younger brothers died, was Queen Philippa's sister-in-law, wife of her brother Willem, count of Hainault and Holland.

8. Lucas, *Low Countries and the Hundred Years' War*, p. 377.

9. Charles de Valois's older brother Philip IV of France (d. 1314) was the father of Isabella of France, queen of England, who was Edward III's mother. Philippa of Hainault's mother Jeanne de Valois was the second, though eldest surviving, daughter of Charles de Valois; her eldest sister Isabelle, who married the heir to the duchy of Brittany, died at age seventeen in 1309.

10. Queen Philippa's date of birth is often given as 24 June 1314, but in fact we do not know her birthday for certain. Her eldest sister Margaretha, Holy Roman Empress, was almost certainly born on 24 June 1310, and her birthday has often erroneously been given to Philippa. Philippa was at least the third and perhaps even fourth daughter of her parents, not the second, as Froissart wrongly implies when he lists her and her sisters as 'Margaretha, Philippa, Johanna and Isabella'; it is certain that Johanna was older than Philippa. Philippa also had a younger sister called Agnes (d. *c.* 1325/27) whom Froissart does not mention, and perhaps another older sister named Sibilla, though this is not certain. See my *Philippa of Hainault: Mother of the English Nation* (Stroud: Amberley, 2019), pp. 25–29.

11. Via his mother Queen Philippa, John of Gaunt was descended from Queen Erzsébet in the female line: Erzsébet the Cuman, queen of Hungary and Croatia (d. 1290) – Marie of Hungary, queen of Naples and Albania (*c.* 1255–1323) – Marguerite of Anjou-Naples, countess of Valois (1272/73–99) – Jeanne de Valois, countess of Hainault and Holland (*c.* 1294/95–1352) – Philippa of Hainault, queen of England (*c.* 1314–69). Erzsébet's father Seyhan or Köten (or Kötöny) was the Cumans' chieftain, and Erzsébet converted to Christianity before her marriage to the future king of Hungary and Croatia, István V, and took a Christian name. Her previous name is not known, and neither, sadly, is the identity of her mother, whose mtDNA passed into the royal families of England, France, Hungary, Serbia, Byzantium, Aragon and Sicily.

12. *Calendar of Close Rolls 1341–43*, p. 467.

13. Ormrod, *Edward III*, pp. 212, 225, 618.

14. *CPR 1345–48*, p. 55.

15. Ormrod, *Edward III*, p. 130.

16. Walsingham's story goes that Queen Philippa confessed to the bishop of Winchester on her deathbed in 1369 that she had borne a daughter in Ghent in 1340, but was too afraid to tell King Edward that their child was a girl. Therefore, she persuaded a local woman to give up her newborn son to her, and raised him as her own child. There seems to be no reason to give this tale any credence whatsoever. Walsingham does not explain the reason for the queen's fear at bearing a girl, and it seems highly improbable, given that in 1340 the royal couple had two healthy male children and that Edward III was a loving father to his daughters as well as to his sons.

17. For this paragraph, see W. M. Ormrod, 'The Royal Nursery: A Household for the Younger Children of Edward III', *English Historical Review*, 120 (2005), especially pp. 402–05, 414; *CPR 1343–45*, pp. 28, 107; *CPR 1345–48*, p. 55; Anthony Goodman, *John of Gaunt: The Exercise of Princely Power in Fourteenth-Century Europe* (Harlow: Longman Group, 1992), p. 29. The gift from the mayor and aldermen is in *Calendar of Select Plea and Memoranda Rolls for the City of London*, Vol. 1, 1323–64, ed. A. H. Thomas (London: HMSO, 1926), p. 131. Goodman suggests that Gaunt was 'probably in the nursery' with his sisters Isabella and Joan, though the age difference of eight and six years makes it unlikely that Gaunt was educated with the girls or that they were particularly close playmates. The death of the third royal child, William of Hatfield, soon after he was born in January 1337, and the fact that Queen Philippa had a three-year break from childbearing between early 1334 and early 1337, meant there was a large age gap between the three eldest children, Edward, Isabella and Joan, and the next three, Lionel, John and Edmund. Joan, the third child, born at the end of 1333 or beginning of 1334, was almost five years older than Lionel, the fourth surviving child. After Blanche of the Tower (b. 1342) died soon after she was born, the next 'group' of royal children was formed by Mary of Waltham (b. October 1344), Margaret of Windsor (b. July 1346) and William of Windsor (b. May 1348, who died the year of his birth).

18. The twelfth and youngest royal sibling, Thomas of Woodstock, who would be the only one of the king and queen's children after Edmund of Langley to live past his teens, was not born until early 1355. As far as is known, this was Queen Philippa's first pregnancy since William of Windsor in 1347/48. A son often ascribed to Philippa, called 'Thomas of Windsor', supposedly born in the summer of 1347 and a victim of the Black Death the following year, did not in fact exist. His entire existence appears to be based on the false claim by two chroniclers (Jean Froissart and Jean le Bel) that the queen was pregnant when she pleaded with her husband to spare the lives of the burghers of Calais at the beginning of August 1347. From the evidence that we have, Queen Philippa gave birth to seven (not eight) sons and five daughters, and certainly she outlived four of her daughters and three of her sons.

19. *CPR 1350–54*, p. 287; *CPR 1358–61*, p. 117.

20. Lisa Benz, 'Queen Consort, Queen Mother: The Power and Authority of Fourteenth-Century Plantagenet Queens', University of York PhD thesis (2009), p. 168.

2. The Infant's Earldom

1. *Calendar of Charter Rolls 1341–1417*, pp. 9, 12.

2. John de Montfort's (b. *c.* 1295) namesake son (b. 1339) released all claims to the earldom of Richmond to John 'de Gaudano', i.e. John of Gaunt, in 1360: The National Archives DL 27/325. Duke John III's childless uncle John of Brittany (b. *c.* 1266), earl of Richmond, a son of Henry III of England's second daughter Beatrice, who spent most of his life in his mother's homeland, died in 1334, and the duke was his heir and received the earldom of Richmond. John of Gaunt had another family connection to the War of the Breton Succession: his mother's uncle-in-law Robert of Artois (b. 1287), count of Beaumont-le-Roger, abandoned the cause of his brother-in-law Philip VI of France and offered his support to the English king, and was killed fighting in the duchy of Brittany in late 1342. Philip VI imprisoned Artois's wife Jeanne de Valois, his own half-sister, and their children, after Artois defected and moved to England, and the unfortunate

woman was to remain in prison until she finally died in 1363. Confusingly, Queen Philippa's mother was also Jeanne de Valois, born *c.* 1294/95 as the second daughter of Charles de Valois (d. 1325), and Jeanne had a younger half-sister also called Jeanne de Valois, born in 1304 and married to Robert of Artois.

3. Malcolm Vale, *The Princely Court: Medieval Courts and Culture in North-West Europe* (Oxford: Oxford University Press, 2001), pp. 272–73, 368–69.

4. Mortimer, *The Perfect King*, p. 67; W. M. Ormrod, 'The Personal Religion of Edward III', *Speculum*, 64 (1989), p. 857; Michael A. Michael, 'A Manuscript Wedding Gift from Philippa of Hainault to Edward III', *The Burlington Magazine*, Vol. 127, No. 990 (September 1985).

5. *Calendar of Inquisitions Post Mortem 1361–65*, No. 118, is Henry of Grosmont's inquisition post-mortem, which gives the ages and dates of birth of Blanche and her sister Maud in 1361; most jurors in the dozens of counties where inquisitions were held merely guessed the women's ages, but the Derbyshire and Staffordshire jurors gave the exact dates. As Henry of Grosmont was only earl of Derby at the time of his daughters' births and had not yet come into the large Lancastrian inheritance of his father, it is probably significant that it was the Derbyshire jurors who specified their dates of birth, and the information is likely to be reliable. Henry IV's biographer Chris Given-Wilson in his *Henry IV* (pp. 16, 24) states rather implausibly and without citing a source that Blanche of Lancaster was born in 1347 and only twenty-one when she died in September 1368, which would make her barely thirteen when she gave birth to her eldest child Philippa of Lancaster, queen of Portugal, on 31 March 1360. Chronicler Jean Froissart believed that Blanche was about twenty-two at the time of her death, which is also almost impossibly young. None of the jurors who took part in Duke Henry's IPM in 1361 estimated Blanche's age at only fourteen or fifteen; the youngest estimate was sixteen, and the oldest was twenty-one. On the other hand, it is perhaps odd that Blanche did not marry John of Gaunt until 1359 when she was as old as seventeen, given that her elder sister Maud married for the first time at age four and for the second time before she turned twelve, and given that very early marriage was the norm in the English royal family in the fourteenth century, both for girls and boys. Another daughter of Henry of Grosmont, Isabella, is mentioned in the records of the borough of Leicester in 1338/39, but must have died young; this is the only known reference to her. See Mary Bateson, ed., *Records of the Borough of Leicester*, Vol. 2, 1327–1509 (London: C. J. Clay and Sons Ltd, 1901), p. 46. If Isabella of Lancaster had not died young, she would have shared the vast Lancastrian inheritance equally with her younger sisters Maud and Blanche after their father's death. Henry of Grosmont (b. *c.* 1310/12) was the only son of Henry of Lancaster (*c.* 1280/81–1345), whose father Edmund of Lancaster (1245–96) was the second son of Henry III and brother of Edward I. Henry of Lancaster's mother Blanche of Artois (*c.* 1245/48–1302), queen of Navarre by her first marriage and countess of Lancaster by her second, was the mother of Queen Jeanne I of Navarre (1274–1305), the mother-in-law of King Philip IV of France, and the maternal grandmother of Edward III's mother Isabella of France. Henry of Grosmont was therefore both a first cousin once removed of King Edward III, and his second cousin.

6. Henry Beaumont's father Louis Brienne (Henry and several of his siblings adopted the name of their mother, Agnes, viscountess of Beaumont-au-Maine) was the youngest child of John Brienne (d. 1237), king of Jerusalem by marriage, elected Latin Emperor of Constantinople, and claimant to the throne of Cilician Armenia. Henry Beaumont's wife Alice Comyn (*c.* late 1290s–1349), mother of Isabella Beaumont and grandmother of Blanche of Lancaster, was co-heir,

with her younger sister Margaret, to the Scottish earldom of Buchan. Isabella Beaumont's date of birth is uncertain but was probably around 1315, and she married Henry of Grosmont in 1330.

7. Mortimer, *Perfect King*, p. 199, gives March 1342; Ormrod, *Edward III*, p. 130, gives June 1342.

8. Blanche of Artois was also the great-grandmother of Blanche of Lancaster, via her second marriage to Edward I's brother Edmund of Lancaster.

9. E. Déprez, 'La Mort de Robert d'Artois', *Revue Historique*, 94 (1907), pp. 65–66.

10. *The True Chronicles of Jean le Bel, 1290–1360*, ed. and trans. Nigel Bryant (Woodbridge: Boydell and Brewer, 2011), p. 147; Ormrod, *Edward III*, pp. 130, 140; Ormrod, 'Royal Nursery', p. 411 note 74; *Plea and Memoranda Rolls for the City of London*, Vol. 1, 1323–64, p. 153; Richard Rastall, 'Secular Musicians in Late Medieval England', Manchester University PhD thesis (1968), p. 92. Elizabeth de Burgh's mother was Maud of Lancaster (b. *c.* 1310/12), dowager countess of Ulster, third of the six daughters of Henry of Lancaster and Leicester and most probably the sister closest in age to Henry of Grosmont, earl of Derby. Elizabeth's paternal grandmother Elizabeth de Burgh née de Clare (1295–1360), after whom she was named, was a granddaughter of Edward I and was thus Edward III's first cousin, and the young Elizabeth was related to the king's children on both sides of her family.

11. Ormrod, 'Royal Nursery', p. 402; *CPR 1340–43*, p. 569; *CPR 1343–45*, pp. 42–43.

12. *CPR 1345–48*, p. 431.

13. *Calendar of Charter Rolls 1341–1417*, p. 14. It had previously belonged to the duke of Brittany and earl of Richmond, *CCR 1341–43*, p. 622.

14. Goodman, *John of Gaunt*, p. 30.

15. Edward III himself had never held the title of prince of Wales, though his father the future Edward II received the principality from his own father Edward I in February 1301 when he was sixteen; he was the first heir to the English throne to be granted the title.

3. The Two Leonors

1. *Foedera, Conventiones, Litterae et Cujuscunque Acta Publica*, ed. Thomas Rymer, 1344–61, p. 46.

2. *CPR 1345–48*, pp. 12, 357; Richard Barber, *Edward, Prince of Wales and Aquitaine: A Biography of the Black Prince* (Woodbridge: The Boydell Press, 1978, reprinted 1996), p. 82. Leonor had no children with King Pere of Aragon, and died of the plague in 1348 the year after her wedding. Medieval Spain was divided into the kingdoms of Castile, Leon, Navarre and Aragon. Pere IV ruled Aragon from 1336 to 1387, and the king of Navarre from 1349 to 1387 was Carlos II 'the Bad' (b. 1332), son of Edward III's first cousin Queen Jeanne II (b. 1312). The king of both Castile and Leon was Alfonso XI, born 1311 and just fifteen months older than his distant kinsman Edward III, who reigned from 1312 to 1350.

3. *Foedera 1344–61*, pp. 59, 74.

4. *Foedera 1344–61*, p. 61; *CPR 1343–45*, p. 555; *CPR 1345–48*, pp. 26, 70–71, 150; Ormrod, *Edward III*, p. 288 and note 72; Lucas, *Low Countries and the Hundred Years' War*, pp. 539–40. Philippa's older sisters were Margaretha (d. 1356) and Johanna (d. 1374), and her younger sister was Isabella (d. 1361). Her other sister, Agnes, had died young in *c.* 1326, and her other three brothers, Jan I, Lodewijk and Jan II, also died young.

5. *Register of the Black Prince Preserved in the Public Record Office*, ed. M. C. B. Dawes, Vol. 4 (London: HMSO, 1933), p. 73.

6. *CPR 1345–48*, pp. 310–12, 318–19, 344, 427, 436, 460, 543–44.

7. *Calendar of Charter Rolls 1341–1417*, p. 63.

8. The younger Ludwig was named 'the Roman' because he was born in Rome in 1328, some months after his parents were crowned emperor and empress there. Elisabeth of Jülich was a daughter of Queen Philippa's older sister Johanna of Hainault; John, earl of Kent (b. 7 April 1330) was the posthumous son and heir of Edward III's uncle Edmund of Woodstock, earl of Kent (1301–30). Elisabeth and John had no children, and John's heir was his older sister Joan, later princess of Wales and John of Gaunt's sister-in-law. Elisabeth died in England in 1411, having outlived her first husband by almost six decades.

9. *Issues of the Exchequer; Being a Collection of Payments Made Out of His Majesty's Revenue, From King Henry III to King Henry VI Inclusive*, ed. Frederick Devon (London: John Murray, 1837), pp. 153–54; C. M. Woolgar, *The Great Household in Late Medieval England* (New Haven and London: Yale University Press, 1999), p. 100; Arthur P. Purey-Cust, *The Collar of SS: A History and Conjecture* (Leeds: Richard Jackson, 1910), p. 199; Matthew Ward, *The Livery Collar in Late Medieval England and Wales: Politics, Identity and Affinity* (Woodbridge: Boydell and Brewer, 2016), pp. 19, 21; Doris Fletcher, 'The Lancastrian Collar of Esses: Its Origins and Transformations Down the Ages', *The Age of Richard II*, ed. James L. Gillespie (Stroud: Sutton Publishing, 1997), pp. 191–92.

10. C. M. Woolgar, *The Great Household in late Medieval England* (New Haven and London: Yale University Press, 1999), p. 100, and Stella Mary Newton, *Fashion in the Age of the Black Prince: A Study of the Years 1340–1365* (Woodbridge: The Boydell Press, 1980), p. 34, for Philippa and her sons' clothes; *Register of Edward the Black Prince*, Vol. 4, p. 67, for the horse; Ormrod, *Edward III*, p. 316, and Mortimer, *Perfect King*, p. 259, for the tournament and motto; Kathleen Pribyl, *Farming, Famine and Plague: The Impact of Climate in Late Medieval England* (Springer International Publishing, 2017), p. 131, for the weather in 1348.

11. *Register of Edward the Black Prince*, Vol. 4, pp. 72, 150.

12. Mortimer, *Perfect King*, p. 434.

13. Devon, *Issues of the Exchequer*, p. 153; Woolgar, *Great Household*, p. 100.

4. Spaniards on the Sea

1. *Foedera 1344–61*, p. 155; *CPR 1348–50*, p. 40.

2. *Register of Edward the Black Prince*, Vol. 4, p. 68.

3. *Register of Edward*, Vol. 4, p. 69.

4. *Foedera 1344–61*, p. 171, cited and translated by Rosemary Horrox, *The Black Death* (Manchester: Manchester University Press, 1994), p. 250.

5. Goodman, *John of Gaunt*, p. 29.

6. *Oeuvres de Froissart*, Vol. 5, p. 258, cited in Goodman, *Gaunt*, p. 31.

7. Kenneth Fowler, 'Henry of Grosmont, First Duke of Lancaster 1310–1361', University of Leeds PhD thesis (1961), pp. 393–94.

8. Goodman, *Gaunt*, p. 31; quotation from *Oeuvres de Froissart*, ed. Lettenhove, Vol. 5, pp. 264–65, Goodman's translation.

9. *CIPM 1347–52*, No. 415.

10. *CPR 1350–54*, p. 64.

11. *The Brut or the Chronicles of England*, ed. F. W. D. Brie, part 2, p. 304, modernised spelling.

12. *Vita Edwardi Secundi Monachi Cuiusdam Malmesberiensis*, ed. No. Denholm-Young (London: Thomas Nelson and Sons Ltd, 1957), p. 70.
13. *Register of Edward the Black Prince*, Vol. 4, p. 10.
14. *Foedera 1307–27*, p. 204 ('Saracen face'); *CCR 1307–13*, p. 537 (Dover).
15. *Register of Edward*, Vol. 4, pp. 34, 66, 90, 164.
16. *Register of Edward*, Vol. 4, p. 54. *CPR 1307–13*, p. 487, shows that Byfleet was in Edward II's hands by 1312, though how it had come to him is obscure; in 1305 it was held by Sir Henry Leybourne, from a noble family of Kent. *CIPM 1300–07*, No. 263.

5. No Pleasure in the Company of Ladies

1. Kenneth Fowler, *The King's Lieutenant: Henry of Grosmont*, pp. 106–09.
2. *Foedera 1344–61*, pp. 235, 241; *Knighton's Chronicle 1337–1396*, ed. Martin, Vol. 2, p. 69.
3. Her brother-in-law John of Gaunt referred to her in later years as 'our dearest and beloved sister, the lady of Hainault': *Register 1371–75*, No. 1577 (*nostre tres cher[e] e bien ame soer la dame de Henaud*).
4. *True Chronicles of Jean le Bel*, pp. 107–08.
5. *Foedera 1344–61*, p. 263.
6. See Catherine Batt's translation of the Book of Holy Medicines, and the text of it is also available in the original French on the anglo-norman.net website.
7. For example, *Foedera 1361–77*, p. 947; Michaela Bleicher, 'Das Herzogtum Niederbayern-Straubing in den Hussitenkriegen. Kriegsalltag und Kriegsführung im Spiegel der Landschreiberrechnungen', PhD thesis, Universität Regensburg (2004), p. 40 note 211.
8. Brad Verity, 'The First English Duchess: Isabel de Beaumont, Duchess of Lancaster (c. 1318–c. 1359)', *Foundations*, Vol. 1.5 (2004), p. 319; Bleicher, 'Das Herzogtum Niederbayern-Straubing', p. 40.
9. *Calendar of Inquisitions Post Mortem 1365–69*, No. 385. Edward of Woodstock had a son also named Edward, who was old enough for the prince to buy him a pony in 1349: Beltz, *Memorials of the Garter*, p. 385; *Register of Edward*, Vol. 4, p. 71. The prince was only nineteen in 1349, a young age to have fathered a child already old enough to ride a horse that year. Some writers have speculated that the child Edward was the prince's godson, though the purchase of a horse for him states that he was the prince's son.
10. Goodman, *John of Gaunt*, p. 32.
11. *CPR 1354–58*, pp. 345, 543, 562. Blanche of Lancaster, Lady Wake, born c. 1302/05, was the eldest of the six sisters of Henry of Grosmont, duke of Lancaster, and was the aunt and possibly the godmother of Gaunt's future wife, also called Blanche of Lancaster. The heir of the late Thomas, Lord Wake was his sister Margaret's daughter Joan of Kent, granddaughter of Edward I, and future princess of Wales as the wife of Edward of Woodstock.
12. *CPR 1354–58*, p. 458. Men came of age at twenty-one in the fourteenth century, women at fourteen if married or sixteen if not.

6. A Damsel and a Daughter

1. Michael Bennett, 'Isabelle of France, Anglo-French Diplomacy and Cultural Exchange in the 1350s', *The Age of Edward III*, ed. James Bothwell (York: York Medieval Press, 2001), p. 217.

2. Isabella and Henry were both grandchildren of Blanche of Artois (c. 1245/48–1302), queen of Navarre and countess of Lancaster, Isabella from Blanche's first marriage and Henry from her second.

3. F. D. Blackley, 'Isabella of France, Queen of England (1308–1358) and the Late Medieval Cult of the Dead', *Canadian Journal of History*, 14 (1980), pp. 26–31.

4. W. M. Ormrod, 'Edward III and his Family', *Journal of British Studies*, 26 (1987), p. 410 note 46, gives the wedding date. Edmund Mortimer was born on 1 February 1352: *CIPM 1370–73*, No. 293.

5. Bridget Wells-Furby, 'Marriage and Inheritance: The Element of Chance in the Development of Lay Estates in the Fourteenth Century', *Fourteenth Century England X*, ed. Gwilym Dodd (Woodbridge: Boydell and Brewer, 2018), p. 125.

6. *Oeuvres de Froissart*, ed. Lettenhove, Vol. 11, p. 326.

7. *Life-Records of Chaucer*, pp. 163, 170, 172; *CPR 1358–61*, p. 488; *CPR 1377–81*, p. 180.

8. Register 1379–83, No. 558; Judy Perry, 'Katherine Roet's Swynfords: A Re-Examination of Interfamily Relationships and Descent', part 1, *Foundations*, 1.2 (2003), p. 128; Nicholas Harris Nicolas, *The Controversy between Sir Richard Scrope and Sir Robert Grosvenor in the Court of Chivalry*, Vol. 2 (London: Samuel Bentley, 1833), p. 185. I owe the Harris Nicolas reference to Judy Perry's article.

9. *Register 1379–83*, Nos 982, 1009, 1010, 1039.

10. Harris Nicolas, *Controversy between Sir Richard Scrope*, Vol. 2, p. 185 note 1; CPR 1396–99, p. 517, CPR 1399–1405, p. 74, CPR 1413–16, p. 48, CCR 1396–99, p. 463 ('Mary de Sancto Hillario').

11. Perry, 'Katherine Roet's Swynfords', part 1, pp. 128–30. In 1375, Gaunt gave the marriage rights of the young nobleman Robert Deincourt or Deyncourt to Katherine Swynford with the intention that she would arrange Robert's marriage to her daughter Blanche, but for whatever reason, the two did not marry; see also below.

12. Harris Nicholas, *Controversy*, p. 185.

13. *Petitions to the Pope 1342–1419*, p. 337. This dispensation was absolutely correct to state that the couple were related in both the 'third and fourth degrees'. John and Blanche were second cousins once removed: they were both descendants of Blanche of Artois (d. 1302), queen of Navarre by her first marriage and countess of Lancaster by her second, hence were related in the third degree of kindred. They were also third cousins via common descent from Henry III, king of England (d. 1272) and his queen Eleanor of Provence (d. 1291), a relationship in the fourth degree.

14. Goodman, *John of Gaunt*, pp. 34–35.

15. *Records of the Borough of Leicester*, ed. Bateson, Vol. 2, pp. 108–09.

16. *Issues of the Exchequer*, p. 172; TNA E 101/393/10.

7. Guileless, of Humble Manner

1. Froissart cited in the original and in English translation in Goodman, *John of Gaunt*, p. 34, though my translation is a little different; *The Book of the Duchess*, lines 948–59, available in full on various websites.

2. For Juliane, see Evelyn H. Martin, *History of the Manor of Westhope, Co. Salop* (Oswestry: Caxton Press, 1909), pp. 19, 33. She was still alive in the early 1400s, during the reign of her nephew, Blanche and Gaunt's son Henry IV. The identity of her mother is not known.

3. For Isabella, see Brad Verity's article 'The First English Duchess: Isabel de Beaumont, Duchess of Lancaster (c. 1318–c. 1359)', pp. 307–23. He points out

(p. 317) that Duke Henry often visited and kept in touch with his kinswoman the elder Elizabeth de Burgh (b. 1295), but his wife is never mentioned in Elizabeth's accounts, and although Elizabeth left Henry a piece of the True Cross in her will of 1355, she bequeathed nothing to Isabella.

4. *Calendar of Papal Letters 1342–62*, p. 607.

5. BCM/D/5/101/8 (Berkeley Castle Muniments), available on the National Archives website. John Segrave's mother Margaret, countess of Norfolk was the elder daughter and ultimate heir of Edward I's son Thomas of Brotherton, earl of Norfolk (1300–38).

6. *Calendar of Inquisitions Post Mortem 1352–60*, No. 116: young John was already dead when his father John, Lord Segrave's inquisition post-mortem was held in April 1353. Elizabeth Segrave married John, Lord Mowbray (1340–68) and was the mother of John Mowbray, earl of Nottingham (1365–83) and his younger brother and heir Thomas, earl of Nottingham and first duke of Norfolk (b. 1367).

7. *Calendar of Inquisitions Post Mortem 1347–52*, No. 56, is Hugh Audley's IPM of late November 1347, and reveals that he and his son-in-law had granted various manors to his grandson Ralph Stafford and Ralph's wife Maud of Lancaster, but that little Ralph was already dead. For the Lancaster/Stafford marriage, see *Knighton's Chronicle 1337–1396*, Vol. 2, ed. G. H. Martin (Oxford, 1995), p. 30; *CPR 1343–45*, pp. 366, 384; *CCR 1346–49*, pp. 344–45; TNA DL 25/2184. Young Ralph Stafford's grandmother Margaret de Clare (d. 1342), countess of Cornwall and Gloucester, was a granddaughter of Edward I, and Edward III's first cousin.

8. *Issues of the Exchequer*, p. 172; Ormrod, 'Edward III and his Family', p. 410 note 46.

9. *Calendar of Inquisitions Post Mortem 1347–52*, No. 118; *Calendar of Inquisitions Post Mortem 1365–69*, No. 266. Via his mother Agnes Mortimer, John Hastings was a grandson of Roger Mortimer, first earl of March, executed by Edward III in November 1330.

10. *Issues of the Exchequer*, p. 171; *The Brut or the Chronicles of England*, ed. F. W. D. Brie, p. 309; Barber, *Edward, Prince of Wales and Aquitaine*, p. 155, for the 'fields and towns' quotation; Simon Walker, *The Lancastrian Affinity 1361–1399* (Oxford: Clarendon Press, 1990), p. 57, for all comers.

11. Goodman, *John of Gaunt*, p. 35; TNA SC 1/50/124.

12. See for example *Register 1379–83*, No. 811.

8. The Departure of Duke Henry's Soul

1. *CPR 1358–61*, pp. 375, 428.

2. Henry's date of birth is not known, but usually estimated as around 1310; his parents married in early 1297 or a little before, and he had six sisters, probably three older and three younger. The siblings were born between *c.* 1302/05 and *c.* 1320. He was born in Grosmont Castle in Wales, and his father was there on 29 September 1312: TNA DL 25/1193. Henry first appears on record as 'Sir Henry de Grosemound' in 1323/24: *Records of the Borough of Leicester, ed. Bateson*, Vol. 1, p. 345. The 'Sir' here is a courtesy title given to a nobleman, and he had probably not yet been knighted.

3. *A Collection of All the Wills Now Known to be Extant of the Kings and Queens of England, Princes and Princesses of Wales, and Every Branch of the Blood Royal* (London: J. Nichols, 1780), p. 83.

4. *Calendar of Inquisitions Post Mortem 1361–65*, No. 118.

5. *CFR 1356–68*, pp. 157–59, 163–66, 194; *CCR 1360–64*, pp. 201–11; *CPR 1361–64*, pp. 50, 114, 118; *Register 1371–75*, No. 1800.

6. Maud Chaworth, born *c.* 2 February 1282, married Henry of Lancaster in or soon before early 1297, and was the mother of Duke Henry and his six sisters. She was the heir of her father Patrick Chaworth (d. 1283) and his brother Payn (d. 1279), and their mother Hawise of London. Alice de Lacy, born on Christmas Day 1281, was the heir of her father Henry de Lacy, earl of Lincoln (d. 1311) and her mother Margaret Longespee, countess of Salisbury (d. *c.* 1308/09). John of Lancaster was the third son of Edmund of Lancaster and Blanche of Artois, and the brother of Thomas and Henry. He spent most of his life in France and married there, and died childless sometime before 12 June 1317; Henry was his heir to his French lordships. *Foedera 1307–27*, p. 334; *CPR 1317–21*, pp. 145–46, 153, 217.

7. As note 5, above; *CFR 1356–68*, p. 163, for the quotation.

8. *CPR 1361–64*, p. 171.

9. *CIPM 1352–60*, No. 46, the inquisition post-mortem of John, earl of Kent in early 1353, states that his sister and heir Joan had turned either twenty-five or twenty-six at the last feast of St Michael, placing her date of birth around 29 September 1326 or 29 September 1327. Richard Barber, *Edward, Prince of Wales and Aquitaine: A Biography of the Black Prince* (Woodbridge: The Boydell Press, 1978, reprinted 1996), p. 173, for the wedding. John, earl of Kent (b. April 1330), was married to Elisabeth of Jülich (d. 1411), a daughter of Queen Philippa's older sister Johanna of Hainault and thus John of Gaunt's first cousin, but they had no children.

10. A. K. McHardy, 'A Personal Portrait of Richard II', *The Reign of Richard II*, ed. Gwilym Dodd (Stroud: Tempus Publishing, 2000), p. 11.

11. *Memorials of the Order of the Garter from Its Foundation to the Present Time*, ed. George Frederick Beltz (London: W. Pickering, 1841), p. 385.

12. The *Polychronicon*, vol 8, p. 360, cited in Edward of Woodstock's entry in the *Oxford Dictionary of National Biography* and in Barber, *Edward, Prince of Wales and Aquitaine*, pp. 173–74.

13. Cited in the original French in G. A. Holmes, *The Estates of the Higher Nobility in Fourteenth-Century England* (Cambridge: Cambridge University Press, 1957), pp. 124–26. John was at his and Blanche's castle of Kenilworth on 21 February 1362, *CPR 1370–73*, p. 284.

9. Great Wonders and Signs

1. Cited in *Genealogie des Erlauchten Stammhauses Wittelsbach von dessen Wiedereinsetzung in das Herzogthum Bayern bis herab auf Unsere Tage*, ed. Christian Häutle (Munich: Hermann Manz'sche Hofkunsthandlung und Buchhandlung, 1870), p. 117.

2. *True Chronicles of Jean le Bel*, p. 108.

3. *CPR 1364–67*, p. 90; *Calendar of Charter Rolls 1341–1417*, pp. 172–73. In early June 1365, John demised the castles of Beaufort and Nogent-sur-Marne in Champagne, formerly held by Maud, to a John Wyn for a period of ten years. TNA DL 25/962.

4. *CIPM 1361–65*, No. 299 (Maud's IPM); *Register 1371–75*, Nos 998–99. Duke Henry spent about £35,000 on the Savoy: Fowler, *King's Lieutenant*, p. 214. Maud of Lancaster had also held four manors in Northamptonshire jointly with her child-husband Ralph Stafford, and these reverted by right to Ralph's father Ralph the elder, earl of Stafford.

5. *CPR 1292–1301*, p. 30 ('his house called Sauvey').

6. Verity, 'Isabel de Beaumont', p. 319, says that Maud bore a daughter in 1356 who died shortly after birth, though no source is cited. The Devon jurors at Maud's IPM (p. 236) stated that she and Wilhelm had had no child, but given that some of the jurors at Duke Henry's IPM the year before did not even remember Maud's name or know if she was alive, they might not be the most reliable source.

7. Wilhelm died in the castle of Le Quesnoy on 17 April 1388, the month before his fifty-eighth birthday, and was buried at the conventual church in Valenciennes, chief town of the county of Hainault which he had inherited from his mother Margaretha; *Genealogie des Erlauchten Stammhauses Wittelsbach*, ed. Häutle, p. 17.

8. *Knighton's Chronicle*, ed. Martin, Vol. 2, p. 116. In later years, John of Gaunt referred to Maud of Lancaster as 'our dearest and beloved sister, the lady of Hainault, whom God absolve.' *Register 1371–75*, Nos 1538, 1577.

9. Anna of Bavaria (b. 1326/27) was the second daughter of Empress Margaretha and a nun at the abbey of Fontenelle, and was an older sister of Maud of Lancaster's widower Wilhelm.

10. *The Brut or the Chronicles of England*, ed. Brie, part 2, pp. 313–14.

11. *Register 1371–75*, No. 623; *CPR 1361–64*, p. 202. On 5 August 1362 he was at Ravensdale in Derbyshire, *Register 1371–75*, No. 748.

10. Almost the King of Scotland

1. *Calendar of Charter Rolls 1341–1417*, p. 174; *CPR 1361–64*, p. 290. Edward III must have planned to give his sons titles for a while before doing so, as Pope Urban V in Avignon referred to 'Lionel duke of Clarence and John de Gandavo, duke of Lancaster' as early as 7 November 1362 (unless this letter is dated incorrectly): *Calendar of Papal Letters 1362–1404*, p. 1. *Testamenta Vetusta*, Vol. 1, ed. Nicholas Harris Nicolas, pp. 70–71: Lionel's will refers to 'a circle of gold with which my brother and lord [Edward of Woodstock] was created Prince [of Wales]', and 'the circle with which I was created duke.'

2. Blanche of Lancaster's great-uncle Thomas of Lancaster employed an astonishing 708 people in his household in the 1310s and early 1320s, and had over 400 horses: Woolgar, *Great Household in Later Medieval England*, p. 12. John's income is given in Goodman, *John of Gaunt*, p. 341 and Goodman's entry about John in the *ODNB*, and Fowler, *King's Lieutenant*, p. 226; his retinue is in Simon Walker, *The Lancastrian Affinity 1361–1399* (Oxford: Oxford University Press, 1990), pp. 14–22, and Given-Wilson, *Henry IV*, p. 19.

3. In the same letter, Gaunt also referred to a chaplain of Tutbury named Rauf Brouster who had died during 'the first pestilence,' i.e. the first great outbreak of the Black Death in 1348/49. *Register 1371–75*, No. 415.

4. *The Brut*, ed. Brie, part 2, p. 315.

5. TNA E 40/11046. The grantor was Sir Thomas Despenser, a young nobleman who was descended from Edward I and was the same age as Gaunt himself, and whose brother Edward, Lord Despenser also witnessed the grant.

6. *Foedera 1361–77*, p. 715, dated 27 November 1363.

7. *Foedera 1361–77*, pp. 723, 839; *Register 1371–75*, No. 1810.

8. TNA E 40/167 and CCA-DCc-ChAnt/C/103, Canterbury Cathedral Archives and Library.

9. *Issues of the Exchequer*, p. 183. 6s and 8d was half a mark, or one noble.

10. TNA Fa/1/4, Kent History and Library Centre.

11. *CCR 1364–68*, pp. 112–13. Gaunt was at Bolingbroke Castle in Lincolnshire on 1 and 18 April and in Leicester on 6 June 1365: TNA DD/FJ/9/7/13,

Nottinghamshire Archives; Register 1371–75, No. 748; TNA DL 25/962/748. He was in London on 12 and 16 May 1366, Leicester on 1 June 1366, and at the Savoy on 1 October 1366: TNA DL 25/2096/1777; Walker, *Lancastrian Affinity* (an indenture John made with Sir Hugh Hastings. d. 1369), p. 294; *CPR 1370–73*, p. 297; *Register 1371–75*, No. 748.

12. See Jessica Lutkin, 'Isabella de Coucy, Daughter of Edward III: The Exception Who Proves the Rule', *Fourteenth Century England VI*, ed. Chris Given-Wilson and Nigel Saul.

13. *Issues of the Exchequer*, p. 187; TNA E 101/314/32; *Foedera 1361–77*, pp. 744, 750, 758; *Calendar of Papal Letters 1362–1404*, p. 19.

14. *CPR 1281–92*, p. 343; *CCR 1323–27*, p. 136; *CPR 1317–21*, p. 341.

15. *CPR 1364–67*, p. 330, and see also *CPR 1334–38*, p. 124. Edward II's letters patent of 1319 are at *CPR 1317–21*, p. 341.

16. Queen Giovanna's mother Marie de Valois was a younger half-sister of Queen Philippa's mother Jeanne de Valois. For the Flanders theory, see Goodman, *John of Gaunt*, p. 177.

17. TNA SC 7/34/16; *Calendar of Papal Letters 1362–1404*, pp. 99, 169.

11. Defeating Enrique and Claiming Provence

1. *CPR 1401–05*, p. 397; *CChR 1341–1417*, pp. 432, 451.

2. *Complete Peerage*, Vol. 7, p. 415 note g; Goodman, *John of Gaunt*, pp. 46–47. A book called *Feudal Manuals of English History* published in 1872 states that John and Blanche had three sons who died young, two called John and one called Edward, but neither this book nor the *Complete Peerage* cites a source for the boys' names (though it is highly likely that the couple would have named a son after John's father Edward III and another after John himself, and highly likely that they would have named a daughter after Blanche's mother Isabella Beaumont). See Thomas Wright, *Feudal Manuals of English History*, p. 151. *Feudal Manuals* states, wrongly, that Gaunt's second sister Joan of Woodstock was queen of Castile and that his fourth sister Mary of Waltham was duchess of Brittany when in fact both of them died as teenagers before their husbands received these titles, and misses the existence of Gaunt's niece Constance of York, daughter of Edmund of Langley and Isabel of Castile, so is perhaps not the most reliable source. It also states that John and Blanche's eldest child Philippa of Lancaster was their third child after John and Edward, who both died young. As Philippa was born ten months and twelve days after her parents' wedding, it is impossible that she had older siblings.

3. *CPR 1377–81*, pp. 194–95. Walter de Urswyk or Ursewyk was one of Gaunt's squires: *CPR 1367–70*, pp. 77–78.

4. *Foedera 1361–77*, pp. 800, 805. Carlos II of Navarre (1332–87) was the son of Jeanne II, queen regnant of Navarre (1312–49), herself the only surviving child of Louis X of France and Navarre (1289–1316) and a first cousin of Edward III of England. As the grandson of Philip IV's eldest son Louis X, Carlos II had a reasonable claim to the French throne, but Navarre was a small kingdom and Carlos did not have sufficient influence to be able to push his claims against Philip VI and his successors, or against Edward III.

5. Goodman, *Gaunt*, pp. 45–46. Richard was born on 6 January 1367.

6. *Foedera 1361–77*, pp. 810, 812, for Gaunt's preparations; p. 824 for Enrique's letters, in Spanish and Latin. Nazare/Nazery: *Issues of the Exchequer*, p. 191; *CPR 1367–70*, pp. 78, 297; A. E. Prince, 'A Letter of Edward the Black Prince Describing the Battle of Nájera', *English Historical Review*, 11 (1926), p. 418.

7. *CPR 1367–70*, p. 78; Prince, 'Letter of Edward', p. 418.
8. *Calendar of Papal Letters 1362–1404*, p. 99; *Foedera 1361–77*, p. 830.
9. See for example TNA SC 8/332/15718A, B and C.
10. Devon, *Issues of the Exchequer*, pp. 190–91. Ingelram Falconer had previously served in the household of Blanche's father Duke Henry, and was still in John of Gaunt's service with his wife Amye in April 1372: Kenneth Fowler, 'Henry of Grosmont', PhD thesis, Appendix J; *Register 1371–75*, No. 938. Gaunt granted Ingelram and Amye £10 a year for life for 'good service' to him a little before 1 July 1366: *CPR 1364–67*, p. 260.
11. *Register 1371–75*, Nos 965, 1368. Bolingbroke lies about 35 miles from the manor of Kettlethorpe and thirty from Coleby, the two Lincolnshire manors which belonged to the Swynfords, the family into which John of Gaunt's future mistress Katherine Roet married in or around the early 1360s.
12. Goodman, *John of Gaunt*, p. 46; *Register 1371–75*, No. 748; *CPR 1370–74*, pp. 297, 351.
13. TNA E 40/2489. Henry Beaumont, b. late 1339, was a first cousin of Blanche of Lancaster, being the only child of Eleanor of Lancaster, countess of Arundel, by her first marriage to John Beaumont. The cross at Charing had been built as one of a series by Edward III's grandfather Edward I after losing his wife Leonor of Castile in November 1290.
14. Albert Stanburrough Cook, *The Last Months of Chaucer's Earliest Patron* (New Haven, Connecticut, 1916), pp. 30ff; *Foedera 1361–77*, pp. 842–44.

12. Lady Blanche, Our Late Consort

1. TNA DL 25/2292/1988. Leicester to Tutbury, where Blanche died a few weeks later, is about 40 miles.
2. J. J. N. Palmer, 'The Historical Context of the "Book of the Duchess": A Revision', *The Chaucer Review*, Vol. 8 (1974).
3. *John of Gaunt's Register*, ed. Armitage-Smith, part 1, 1371–75, Nos 620–21. Gaunt was at the Savoy (*nostre manoir de la Sauuoie*) on 1 October 1368, when he demised one of his Lincolnshire manors to his clerk John de Nesfeld for ten years: TNA DL 25/1817.
4. *Register 1371–75*, Nos 918, 943, 1091, 1417, 1585, etc. Tutbury was where Blanche died, and was also where alabaster was frequently purchased: in July 1362, for example, Gaunt's mother Queen Philippa had six carts of *alebaustre* taken from Tutbury to London. *CPR 1361–64*, p. 232.
5. *Oeuvres de Froissart*, ed. Lettenhove, vol 7, p. 251; *Calendar of Papal Letters 1362–1404*, p. 27.
6. *Testamenta Vetusta*, Vol. 1, ed. Nicholas Harris Nicolas, pp. 70–71.
7. Philippa's letter is cited in full in Palmer, 'Historical Context of the "Book of the Duchess": A Revision', pp. 253–55. A membrane of the envoy Richard de Stury's expenses travelling to Flanders: TNA E 101/315/26. See also Léon Mirot and Eugène Dupréz, 'Les ambassades anglaises pendant la guerre de Cent Ans. Catalogue chronologique (1327–1450)', part 2, *Bibliothèque de l'école des chartes* (Paris: A. Picard, 1899), tome 60, p. 185. Young though she was, Margarethe was already a widow; her first husband Philippe de Rouvres, duke of Burgundy, her second cousin, died in 1361 when she was only eleven and he fifteen.
8. *Life-Records of Chaucer*, p. 162.
9. Oxford's son and heir Robert, who was six years old in 1368, would become the notorious and hated favourite of Edward III and Queen Philippa's grandson

Richard II in the 1380s. Oxford's wife Maud Ufford was the much younger half-sister of the late Elizabeth de Burgh, duchess of Clarence and was thus Lionel of Antwerp's sister-in-law, and may, as a member of the extended royal family, also have been present. Robert de Vere was named after his godfather and maternal great-uncle, Robert Ufford, earl of Suffolk (1298–1369): *CIPM 1377–84*, No. 889.

13. My Very Honoured Mother, Whom God Absolve

1. *Oxford Dictionary of National Biography*, entry for Edmund of Langley; *Foedera 1361–77*, p. 871.
2. *Register 1371–75*, No. 960.
3. Many of her grants in the 1360s include the wording 'if the queen predecease' the grantee or 'if he survive the queen'. See for example *CPR 1361–64*, p. 102; *CPR 1364–67*, pp. 109, 114, 235, 300, 383, 396, 421.
4. *Oeuvres de Froissart*, ed. Lettenhove, Vol. 7, p. 429.
5. *Testamenta Eboracensia, Or Wills Registered at York*, part 1, ed. James Raine (London: J. B. Nichols and Son, 1836), p. 231 (John's will and the gold fastening); *Register 1371–75*, No. 1090, p. 93 (gold cup).
6. Elisabeth of Holland wrote her will in England in September 1375, and probably died not long afterwards. She called herself 'sister of the lady Queen Philippa' and left a gold ring to Philippa's youngest child Thomas of Woodstock and a silver ring to Edward III's cousin Margaret, countess of Norfolk. In August 1367, Edward III granted £20 a year to the queen's 'bastard sister' Elisabeth, and also acknowledged her as 'sister of our said consort' in his letter purchasing black cloth and fur for those who attended Philippa's funeral. *CPR 1367–70*, p. 6; *Excerpta Historica, Or, Illustrations of English History*, ed. Samuel Bentley (London: printed by and for Samuel Bentley, 1831), pp. 23–25. Queen Philippa also had at least six illegitimate half-brothers and one or perhaps two other half-sisters, some of whom were probably known to their nephew John of Gaunt. See my *Philippa of Hainault*, pp. 30–31.
7. *Life-Records of Chaucer*, pp. 172–75.
8. TNA E 30/256; *Foedera 1361–77*, pp. 881–83; Goodman, *Gaunt*, p. 47.
9. *Life-Records of Chaucer*, pp. 172–75; Blanche Swynford is mentioned on pp. 172–73, and the *souzdamoiselles* on p. 173.

14. Feasts and Celebrations in Aquitaine

1. Walker, *Lancastrian Affinity*, p. 295; TNA DD/FJ/9/7/15, Nottinghamshire Archives.
2. Blanche Wake also had the care of her great-nephews John and Thomas Mowbray, both of them future earls of Nottingham, in 1372. *Register 1371–75*, Nos 940, 1241; TNA SC 8/163/8116; *CPR 1370–74*, p. 370; *ODNB* entry for Henry IV; Mortimer, *The Fears of Henry IV*, p. 26. The Mowbray brothers' paternal grandmother was Joan of Lancaster (d. 1349), fourth of Duke Henry's six sisters. Her eldest sister Blanche of Lancaster, Lady Wake, had no children from her marriage of thirty-three years to the late Thomas, Lord Wake (1298–1349), whom she outlived by more than three decades. Wake's heir was his sister Margaret's daughter Joan of Kent, princess of Wales, Gaunt's sister-in-law.
3. *Register 1371–75*, Nos 773–74, 783.

4. *Calendar of Papal Letters 1362–1404*, p. 94; *Oeuvres de Froissart*, Vol. 8, pp. 60–61. John's chamberlain at this time was John Newmarche, *Calendar of Papal Letters*, p. 95.

5. Goodman, *John of Gaunt*, p. 48; *Register 1371–75*, No. 780.

6. *Register 1371–75*, Nos 167, 941, 1668. Arundel's father Edmund, earl of Arundel, was executed in November 1326 by Gaunt's grandmother Queen Isabella and her ally Roger Mortimer, during the revolution which swept Edward II from his throne. Gaunt borrowed another 2,000 marks from the earl of Arundel in July 1372, and 3,000 and 4,000 marks on other occasions; see below.

7. *Oeuvres de Froissart*, ed. Lettenhove, Vol. 8, pp. 43, 105–07.

8. Clara Estow, *Pedro the Cruel of Castile 1350–1369* (New York: E. J. Brill, 1996), pp. 131–32, 139–40, 211–12. Pedro was born in Burgos in northern Spain: Estow, p. 22. John of Gaunt's great-grandparents the future King Edward I of England, then the fifteen-year-old heir to the throne, and Leonor of Castile married in the monastery of Santa María la Real near Burgos in 1254. Jean Froissart states (see below, Chapter 49) that Constanza re-buried her father in Seville in 1389, though according to Estow (p. xxxiii, note 57) Pedro was re-buried in Madrid in 1446 and only moved to Seville in 1877. Blanche de Bourbon was born *c.* 1337/39 and was close in age to her sister Queen Jeanne of France (wife of Charles V and mother of Charles VI). Her mother was Isabelle de Valois, duchess of Bourbon (d. 1383), a younger half-sister of John of Gaunt's maternal grandmother Jeanne de Valois, countess of Hainault and Holland. Clara Estow (p. 211) discusses the possibility that Pedro had Blanche killed, and states that it is impossible to come to a firm conclusion based on the available evidence; some contemporary Castilian chronicles thought he was guilty of poisoning her, others believed she died naturally. For Pedro's relationships and children, see *Memorias de las Reynas Catholicas: Historia Genealogica de la Casa Real de Castilla y de León*, Vol. 2 (Madrid: Antonio Marin, 1770), pp. 635ff. Constanza's and her siblings' dates of birth and birthplaces are given on pp. 654–55.

15. My Lord of Spain

1. *Register 1371–75*, Nos 215, 878 (the *Gaynpayn* and salt); Goodman, *John of Gaunt*, p. 48 (short of money and pawning items).

2. *Register 1371–75*, Nos 879–82, 895, 940, 1090. *Calendar of Inquisitions Post Mortem 1370–73*, No. 204, is Hugh Swynford's IPM of April/June 1372, which says that he died 'beyond seas on Thursday after St Martin in the Winter last' (the feast of St Martin is 11 November). *CFR 1369–77*, p. 153, is the writ for his IPM, and the order to hold it was repeated on 8 April 1372: *Ibid.*, p. 200. For Hugh Despenser, see *CIPM 1374–77*, No. 56. Pieres Genlichshein's name also appears as 'Petre Galesheyn' and Piers Gaynlesheyn' in Gaunt's register: Nos 1089, 1091. Gaunt called Elizabeth Montacute's husband William Montacute, earl of Salisbury, 'our dearest and beloved companion' in September 1375: *Register 1371–75*, No. 375. The earl of Salisbury was born in June 1328 and had once been married to John's sister-in-law Joan of Kent, a bigamous marriage as Joan also wed Sir Thomas Holland, and the pope annulled her Montacute marriage in 1349. Salisbury married secondly Elizabeth Mohun, and the couple suffered an awful tragedy in 1382 when the earl accidentally killed their only son William the younger during a joust.

3. *Register 1371–75*, Nos 213, 876–77, 883–88, 915, 973, 1090.

4. *Register 1371–75*, No. 1056.

5. *Register 1371–75*, Nos 473, 1124, 1343; *Life-Records of Chaucer*, pp. 172–73.
6. *Register 1371–75*, Nos 931, 1133.
7. *The Anonimalle Chronicle 1333–81*, ed. Vivian Hunter Galbraith (Manchester: Manchester University Press, 1927; reprinted with minor corrections, 1970), p. 69; Barber, *Edward, Prince of Wales and Aquitaine*, pp. 227–28.
8. *Register 1371–75*, No. 927. John was at the Savoy on 23 January 1372: *CPR 1396–99*, p. 571.
9. Before he married Constanza, Gaunt's letters began 'Johan, son of the king of England and France, duke of Lancaster, earl of Richmond, Derby, Lincoln and Leicester, steward of England.' For example, *Register 1371–75*, No. 317.

16. A Woman of Great Beauty

1. Clara Estow, 'Royal Madness in the Crónica del Rey Don Pedro', *Mediterranean Studies*, 6 (1996), p. 19; Estow, *Pedro the Cruel of Castile*, pp. 30, 134; John Pohl and Garry Embleton, *Armies of Castile and Aragon 1370–1516* (Oxford: Osprey Publishing, 2015), p. 44; Margaretta Jolly, ed., *Encyclopedia of Life Writing: Autobiographical and Biographical Forms* (London: Routledge, 2013), p. 698; Robert Folger, *Generaciones Y Semblanzas: Memory and Genealogy in Medieval Iberian Historiography* (Tübingen: Günter Narr, 2003), p. 187; Fernán Pérez de Guzmán, *Pen Portraits of Illustrious Castilians* (The Catholic University of America Press, 2003), p. 12.
2. *Anonimalle 1333 to 1381*, pp. 69, 153, for Constanza. For Pedro's reputation, see Bretton Rodriguez, 'Competing Images of Pedro I: López de Ayala and the Formation of Historical Memory', *La Corónica: A Journal of Medieval Hispoanic Languages, Literatures, and Cultures*, 45 (2017), and Clara Estow's biography *Pedro the Cruel* and her article 'Royal Madness in the Crónica del Rey'. Pero López de Ayala was the uncle of Teresa de Ayala, who had an affair with King Pedro which resulted in a daughter, María.
3. This is how Constanza is depicted in Anya Seton's enormously popular and influential 1950s novel about Katherine Swynford. Apart from the near-saintly Blanche of Lancaster, John of Gaunt and of course Katherine herself, other characters fare little better in the novel. Isabel of Castile is 'frivolous and empty-headed,' Eleanor de Bohun is 'a high-nosed girl with a mouth like a haddock' and a 'fish mouth,' Joan of Kent is 'an enormous mound of periwinkle blue surmounted by an orange blob of hair' and Anne of Bohemia is 'lumpish and brown as a nut.' While Gaunt is depicted as physically attractive, his brother Edmund of Langley has a 'weak, foolish face' and another brother, Lionel of Antwerp, is 'good-natured' but also 'stupid.' Sir Hugh Swynford is an ugly, 'scowling lout' for whom his future wife Katherine feels 'repulsion' when she first meets him, and who attempts to rape her before Gaunt rescues her.
4. *Register 1371–75*, No. 321, *l'entier amour et affectione lesqueux nous avons a nostre tres chiere et tres amee compaigne la Royne dame Constance.*
5. See for example Sydney Armitage-Smith, *John of Gaunt, King of Castile and Leon, Duke of Aquitaine and Lancaster, Earl of Derby, Lincoln, and Leicester, Seneschal of England* (New York: Charles Scribner, 1904), p. 357.
6. *Records of the Borough of Leicester*, ed. Mary Bateson, Vol. 2, p. 170; Goodman, *John of Gaunt*, pp. 361–62.
7. See chapter below for a discussion of Katherine's probable age; it is impossible that she was ten years younger than John, as often stated.

17. Dame Katherine de Roet, Lady Swynford

1. *Calendar of Inquisitions Post Mortem 1361–65*, No. 197; *CFR 1356–68*, pp. 200, 206.
2. Anthony Goodman, *Katherine Swynford* (Lincoln: The Honywood Press, 1994), p. 10.
3. *Register 1371–75*, No. 1342. In a Latin entry in his register in 1382, John of Gaunt referred to Katherine as his two daughters' *nuper* [former] *magistrisse*.
4. *Chaucer Life-Records*, pp. 172–73; Blanche Swynford, Agneys Fauconer and Eleyne Gerberge (who later worked as a damsel of Duchess Constanza as well) are called *damoiselles a les dites deux filles de Lancastre*, 'damsels to the said two daughters of Lancaster', in a letter of Edward III dated 1 September 1369.
5. *CIPM 1392–99*, No. 576, is Thomas's proof of age; *CIPM 1370–73*, No. 204, is Hugh's inquisition post-mortem. When landowners died when their heir was underage, when the heir came of age (twenty-one for men but only fourteen for women if married or sixteen if unmarried), he or she had to prove their date of birth and to demonstrate that they were now old enough to enter the lands they had inherited. The proof of age was held in the heir's birthplace, and a dozen or so male jurors stated his or her date of birth and the reasons why they remembered the date.
6. R. E. G. Cole, 'The Manor and Rectory of Kettlethorpe', *Architectural Societies Reports*, 31, report 66 (1911), pp. 58–9, gives 21 September 1368 as Thomas's date of birth. The author seems to have confused St Matthias with St Matthew the Evangelist, whose feast day is 21 September.
7. *CPR 1408–13*, pp. 323–24.
8. *CPR 1370–74*, p. 325 (John of Worksop); *Foedera 1361–77*, p. 812.
9. *CPR 1396–99*, p. 493, and see also below.
10. *Calendar of Papal Letters 1362–1404*, p. 545.
11. Katherine Swynford's Wikipedia page, accessed 5 February 2020, currently states that her daughter Blanche was born on 1 May 1367, but as she was named as a damsel of Gaunt's daughters on 1 September 1369, this is impossible, and no source is cited. Chris Given-Wilson and Alice Curteis's *Royal Bastards of Medieval England* (London: Routledge and Kegan Paul, 1984), p. 48, says that Blanche was born *c.* 1370, which is of course also impossible.
12. *Life-Records of Chaucer*, pp. 172–73.
13. Judy Perry, 'Katherine Roet's Swynfords: A Re-Examination of Interfamily Relationships and Descent', part 1, *Foundations*, 1.2 (2003), pp. 125–27.
14. *CPR 1377–81*, p. 20; *CPR 1416–22*, p. 214.
15. *Register 1379–83*, No. 524.
16. See british-history.ac.uk/vch/essex/vol2/pp115-122, accessed 4 February 2020.
17. Jeannette Lucraft, *Katherine Swynford: The History of a Medieval Mistress* (Stroud: Sutton Publishing, 2006) p. 6.
18. In Anya Seton's novel, Katherine is just fifteen when she first meets the twenty-six-year-old John of Gaunt in 1366, which is also impossible, and in reality Katherine had been married to Hugh for a few years and had borne two daughters by then. Weir, *Katherine Swynford*, pp. 9, 68, points out correctly that Katherine's daughter Blanche cannot have been born later than 1363, yet still claims that Katherine was born around 1350 and almost certainly no earlier than 1349.
19. The reigning king of England in 1457 was Henry VI (b. 1421), great-grandson of John of Gaunt and Blanche of Lancaster, and his half-brother was Edmund Tudor (b. *c.* 1430). Margaret Beaufort, usually assumed to have been born on 31 May 1443, was possibly slightly older than that: the inquisition post-mortem of her

father John Beaufort states that she was either one or two or 'two and more' years old in October/November 1444 and 'three and more' in January/February 1446, and the IPM of her great-uncle Cardinal Beaufort says that she was seven in November 1448. *CIPM 1442–47*, Nos 178–94, 582.

18. A Barrel of Relics and a Flying Dragon

1. *Calendar of Inquisitions Post Mortem 1361–65*, No. 197; *Calendar of Inquisitions Post Mortem 1370–73*, No. 204.
2. Weir, *Katherine Swynford*, p. 62, claims that Kettlethorpe was 'stony and out of cultivation', but has mixed up the references; it was Coleby, not Kettlethorpe, that was said to be sandy, stony and uncultivated in the inquisitions post-mortem of Hugh and his father Thomas in 1361 and 1372. In July 2019, Sarah Hogg published the book *Katherine's House* about the village of Kettlethorpe.
3. Cited in John Fenn, ed., *The Paston Letters. Original Letters Written During the Reigns of Henry VI, Edward IV, and Richard III*, new edition, Vol. 1 (London: Charles Knight and Co., 1840), pp. 152–53.
4. *Oeuvres de Froissart*, ed. Lettenhove, Vol. 15, p. 239.
5. Rodriguez, 'Competing Images of Pedro I', pp. 88, 100–01.
6. *Register 1371–75*, Nos 1123–24.

19. The Midwife of Leicester

1. *Register 1371–75*, Nos 983–84, 1728.
2. *Issues of the Exchequer*, p. 195. John of Gaunt was at the Savoy on 31 March 1373: *Register 1371–75*, No. 1196. There was often a delay of weeks or even several months between the king making payments and the payments being recorded in his accounts; John's son Henry was born on *c.* 15 April 1367, and the payment to Duchess Blanche's messenger appears on 1 June 1367.
3. *Register 1371–75*, No. 988.
4. *ODNB*; *Complete Peerage*, Vol. 12A, pp. 39–40. John's Wikipedia page (accessed 23 March 2020) also gives *c.* 1371 as his year of birth.
5. *Oeuvres de Froissart*, ed. Lettenhove, Vol. 15, p. 239; *Vita Edwardi Secundi*, ed. Noel Denholm-Young, p. 62.
6. *CPR 1391–96*, p. 15 (John named as a knight).
7. *Complete Peerage*, Vol. 12A, p. 40 note d; *CPR 1391–96*, p. 63.
8. Weir, *Katherine Swynford*, p. 104, following the *Complete Peerage*, is one of the writers who claims that 'in his twenty-first year' means that John Beaufort was in his twenty-first year on 7 June 1392 and who was therefore (according to this evidence) born between June 1371 and June 1372. As she herself points out, these dates are problematic given that Hugh Swynford died in November 1371. The memorandum added to the Patent Roll entry (*CPR 1391–96*, p. 63) states perfectly clearly, however, that Richard II granted Beaufort 100 marks from the issues of the royal castle of Wallingford 'on 10 September in his twenty-first [regnal] year,' i.e. on 10 September 1397, so it is hard to see how it can have been misunderstood as referring to Beaufort's age in June 1392. The grant to Beaufort on 10 September 1397 is also recorded on the Patent Roll, *CPR 1396–99*, p. 205: 'Grant for life or until further order to the king's knight John de Beaufort of 100 marks a year from the issues of the castle and lordship of Walyngford, co. Berks [Wallingford, Berkshire], instead of at the Exchequer, as granted to him by letters patent dated 7 June in the fifteenth year [of Richard II's reign, i.e. 1392], now surrendered.'

Michael K. Jones and Malcolm G. Underwood's book *The King's Mother: Lady Margaret Beaufort, Countess of Richmond and Derby* (Cambridge: Cambridge University Press, 1992), pp. 20–21, claims that John Beaufort was born in 1372 and was therefore probably conceived in Hugh Swynford's lifetime, 'in double adultery' (as Gaunt married Constanza in September 1371). The reason cited for this statement is that Beaufort's 'date of birth in 1372 is confirmed by the grant of an annuity to him as king's knight twenty years later.' Why Beaufort being a king's knight in 1392 is proof that he was born in 1372 is not explained, and as noted, his half-brother Thomas Swynford, born 1367/68, was already a knight on 1 March 1383.

9. *Register 1371–75*, Nos 408–10, 1289.
10. *Register 1371–75*, No. 446.
11. *CCR 1369–74*, p. 382.
12. *CIPM 1370–73*, No. 204.
13. *CCR 1369–74*, pp. 388, 403; *CPR 1370–74*, pp. 202–03.

20. Victory over Your Enemies

1. Given-Wilson, *Henry IV*, p. 31 and note 38.
2. Elizabeth's daughters were Constance Holland, born *c.* 1387, and Constance Cornwall, born in the early 1400s. Duchess Constanza was almost certainly Constance Holland's godmother, and Elizabeth perhaps named her Cornwall daughter in memory of Constanza or perhaps because Constanza's niece Constance of York, Lady Despenser (herself almost certainly Constanza's goddaughter as well) was the girl's godmother.
3. See for example *CPR 1401–05*, pp. 397, 408, and *CPR 1408–13*, p. 419, where Henry refers to 'the king's mother Constance' (on p. 408, there is also a reference to 'the king's mother Katherine [Swynford]'). One exception to the usual rule is that John of Gaunt always referred to Henry of Grosmont and King Pedro of Castile as *nostre trescher piere en ley*, literally 'our dearest father in law'. This is highly unusual. For 'parents', see *Calendar of Papal Letters 1398–1404*, p. 472.
4. TNA SC 8/181/9045; *CPR 1399–1405*, p. 408. Henry gave Katherine a gift of £100 during the first year of his reign: TNA E 42/536.
5. TNA SC 1/43/81; the letter is also printed in the original French in *Recueil de Lettres Anglo-Francaises, 1265–1399*, ed. F. J. Tanqueray (Paris: Librairie Ancienne Honoré Champion, 1916), No. 163, and in John of Gaunt's *Register 1371–75*, No. 1809. The National Archives website dates the letter to *c.* 1376/78 without explanation, and Tanqueray to the period 1389–99, as a man named John Hill escaped from the bishop of London's prison in 1392.
6. *Register 1371–75*, Nos 982, 1290, 1292, 1563. Elizabeth Ferrers (b. late 1330s or 1340s) was one of the daughters of Ralph, earl of Stafford (d. 1372) and sister of Hugh, earl of Stafford (d. 1386); her brother Ralph, who died as a child in or before 1347, had once been married to Gaunt's sister-in-law Maud of Lancaster. The mother of Blanche Mowbray, Lady Poynings, was Joan of Lancaster (d. 1349), fourth of Duke Henry's six sisters. Gaunt was still at the Savoy on 28 June 1372: *Register 1371–75*, No. 1797.
7. *Register 1371–75*, No. 1012. North Cotes and Tetney are now inland.
8. TNA SC 1/56/73 and 74.
9. Walsingham: *Chronica Maiora*, trans. Preest, pp. 291–92; Froissart cited in the *Oxford Dictionary of National Biography* entry for Edmund of Langley. For the *Compleynt of Mars*, see Gervase Mathew, *The Court of Richard II* (London: John Murray, 1968), pp. 64–65, and for John Shirley, see his entry in the *ODNB*.

10. TNA SC 8/103/5145.
11. *CPR 1374–77*, p. 347; *CPR 1377–81*, pp. 440–41; *CPR 1381–85*, p. 574.
12. *ODNB*, entry for Richard of Conisbrough.
13. See below, Chapter 52, for Isabel's will. T. B. Pugh, *Henry V and the Southampton Plot* (Southampton: Alan Sutton, 1988), p. 90, suggests that Isabel's 'ruffianly lover' John Holland might have fathered her son Richard, as does Richard's entry in the *ODNB*.

21. To Resist and Withstand Malice

1. *Register 1371–75*, No. 244. He also appointed John Bradley to teach in the grammar schools of Crofton in August 1372, No. 259.
2. *Register 1371–75*, Nos 245, 1147, 1167, 1263. The letters about Philippa's marriage talk of the *aide a nous ottroiez pur nostre eisne fille marier*. In October 1375, Gaunt gave William Nesfeld permission to live in Knaresborough Castle, Yorkshire: *Register 1371–75*, No. 371. See Philippa's entry in the *ODNB* for the Foix marriage.
3. *Register 1371–75*, Nos 63, 250, 1005. Gaunt was at the Savoy on 14 July 1372: TNA SC 1/56/72. Edward III would turn sixty on 13 November 1372.
4. CPR 1370–74, p. 195; *Calendar of Inquisitions Miscellaneous 1348–77*, No. 850; CCR 1369–74, pp. 456, 462, 466; Ormrod, *Edward III*, pp. 411–13; Mortimer, Perfect King, pp. 376–77; Jonathan Sumption, *Divided Houses: The Hundred Years War*, Vol. 3 (London, 2009), pp. 135–56. Sir Michael de la Pole, later earl of Suffolk, went to France with John, and received war wages of more than £416 for doing so: *Register 1371–75*, No. 1107.
5. Gaunt was at Langdon Abbey in Kent from 20 to 27 August 1372. *Register 1371–75*, Nos 63, 494–6, 500–05, 509, 511, 513, 1032, 1041, 1056; CCR 1369–74, p. 461, for the *Grace Dieu*; Life-Records of Chaucer, p. 181 (No. 67) for Philippa Chaucer (*le bon et agreable service que nostre bien ame damoysele Philippe Chause ad fait et ferra en temps auenir a nostre treschere et tresame compaigne la Reine*).
6. *Register 1371–75*, Nos 253, 1027, 1032, 1135.
7. *Register 1371–75*, Nos 299, 524, 535.
8. CPR 1370–74, p. 242. John was at the Savoy on 4 November 1372: *CPR 1381–85*, p. 384.
9. *Register 1371–75*, No. 1133.
10. *Register 1371–75*, No. 1112; Nos 1103, 1126, 1133 for Hertford. The duke made a similar gift on 3 August 1375 when he was at Leicester, and ordered a dozen fat stags to be hunted and delivered to 'knights, ladies, squires and others of the area' in his Derbyshire lordship of High Peak, or *Haut Peek* as his clerk wrote it, half in French and half in English. *Register 1371–75*, No. 1740.

22. The King of Cambridge and Agnes Bonsergeant

1. *Register 1371–75*, No. 1342.
2. Anthony Goodman, in his pamphlet about Katherine Swynford (p. 12), missed the word *fille*, and wrongly assumed that Gaunt was making a payment to Katherine Swynford's former nurse. The error is perpetuated and extended by Alison Weir in her book about Katherine Swynford, on pp. 11 and 129, who takes this entry as evidence that Katherine must have been placed in Philippa of Hainault's household as an infant and that Queen Philippa appointed Agnes Bonsergeant to look after her (and makes the 'virtually unheard of' point). Nathen Amin's *The House of Beaufort: The Bastard Line That Captured the Crown*

(Stroud: Amberley, 2017), p. 24, also repeats the claim that Agnes was Katherine Swynford's former nurse, and suggests that the annuity to her in July 1375 might indicate that Katherine was then pregnant with one of her Beaufort children. As Agnes Bonsergeant had until recently taken care of Gaunt and Constanza's little daughter in Melbourne near Derby, it seems unlikely that she was looking after Katherine Swynford during a pregnancy, and there is no reason to suppose that Agnes even knew Katherine. The entry in Gaunt's account (*Register 1371–75*, No. 718) states '*pour le bon e aggreable service que nostre bien amee Agneys femme jadys a Johan Bonsergeant ad fait a nostre tres chere e tres amee fille Katerine au temps quelle estoit sa nurice*', 'for the good and agreeable service that our beloved Agnes, formerly wife of John Bonsergeant, did for our dearest and well-loved daughter Katerine at the time when she was her nurse.'

3. *Register 1371–75*, Nos 670, 699, 718, 1171, 1456, 1458, 1597, 1611, 1727, 1737, 1781. Gaunt had addressed another letter to Johane Martyns a couple of years earlier. One of the 'young ladies of Spain' was called 'Maiour Roderic' (No. 1456). *CIPM 1361–65*, No. 118, for the Melbourne details. The servants in great households usually received their new clothes twice a year, at Christmas and either at the moveable feast of Pentecost or at the Nativity of St John the Baptist (24 June), and at Christmas 1372 Gaunt made a point of purchasing new shoes for the men who worked in his stables and looked after his coursers, palfreys and packhorses.

4. *ODNB*, entry for Catalina; for Lady Mohun, see below.

5. *Register 1371–75*, No. 1242. In the early 1380s, Gaunt employed Walter Lorchon as his chief bargeman, with eight other bargemen: *Register 1379–83*, Nos 771–2. Humphrey de Bohun was born on 24 March 1342 and was exactly Blanche of Lancaster's age: *CIPM 1361–65*, No. 543.

6. *Register 1371–75*, Nos 298, 1242. John was at the Savoy on 1 March 1373, *CPR 1399–1405*, p. 155.

7. Devon, *Issues of the Exchequer*, p. 195.

8. *Register 1371–75*, No. 1242. Scrope, *c.* 1327–1403, served Gaunt for decades: see 'Sir Richard Scrope – 1st Baron Scrope of Bolton' at thehistoryjar.com, accessed 23 February 2020.

9. *Register 1371–75*, Nos 832, 836.

10. *Register 1371–75*, No. 1343; *CPR 1361–64*, p. 241; *CPR 1364–67*, p. 155; *CPR 1367–70*, p. 223; *CPR 1370–74*, pp. 89, 100, 225; *CPR 1374–77*, pp. 128, 211, 286. Gaunt paid 12*s* and 8*d* on having 500 Masses sung for 'the soul of our beloved companion Sir Wauter de Manny, one of the Knights of the Garter' sometime before 1 May 1372: *Register 1371–75*, No. 973.

11. *Register 1371–75*, No. 1343. Gaunt had sent messengers to 'the parts of Portugal' sometime before 10 January 1373: *Register 1371–75*, No. 1143. 'Nunye Fernandz, messenger of the king of Portugal' was still in England on 19 July 1374, No. 1446.

23. Smelts, Bumbepiper and Frysh

1. *Register 1371–75*, Nos 297, 949; *Register 1379–83*, No. 722; *Petitions to the Pope 1342–1419*, p. 271. In the early 1380s, the town of Pontefract had a road called *Monkhull*, which had a pond on it, and another road called Newgate. A John Knottyng rented a tenement with a garden on Monkhull from Gaunt. *Register 1379–83*, No. 1139.

2. *Register 1371–75*, Nos 859–62, 1416, 1660, 1675, and *Register 1379–83*, Nos 959, 1003.

3. *Register 1371–75*, No. 1344; *CPL 1398–1404*, p. 285; *CPR 1399–1405*, p. 310. A few years later, Gaunt appointed William Tuttebury 'under-steward of all the *Engliscerie*,' i.e. Englishry, in his lordships of Kidwelly and Llanelli, and also referred to the *Gallessherie*, i.e. the Welshry: *Register 1379–83*, Nos 1093, 1131. Gaunt was with his father at Westminster on or a little before 10 June 1373, when he requested a pardon for a John de Thorlay of Barton-upon-Humber: *CPR 1370–74*, p. 295.

4. *Register 1371–75*, Nos 1356–57.

5. Or 'murrain' (*morine* in the French original). *Register 1371–75*, Nos 111, 1302, 1368–9, 1383, 1550, 1637, 1735. John was at the Savoy on 1 July 1373, No. 1776.

6. *Register 1371–75*, No. 321.

7. *Register 1371–75*, Nos 1200, 1202–05, 1208, 1223–24, 1228, 1243–46.

8. *Register 1371–75*, Nos 310–12, 1226. On 28 April 1373, two sailors were ordered to provide sailors for Gaunt's passage, and on 12 June, he was appointed Edward III's lieutenant and captain-general in France and Aquitaine; *Foedera 1361–77*, pp. 975, 982.

9. *Register 1371–75*, Nos 973, 1334.

10. See David Nicholle, *The Great Chevauchée: John of Gaunt's Raid on France 1373* (Oxford: Osprey Publishing, 2012). On 3 August 1373, place not given, Gaunt demised a hotel in Calais called the 'Hotel of Our Lord' to a William de Foxton of Calais, for twenty years: TNA DL 25/2191. According to his register, John was staying at the Savoy on 30 September 1373 when he spent 400 marks on (unspecified) work he was having done at Kenilworth Castle and put his chief mason Henry Spenser in charge, but this must be misdated. *Register 1371–75*, No. 1156. His register (No. 1766) places him in Bordeaux on 26 March 1373, but this must also be misdated.

24. The Lady of Woodstock

1. *CPR 1370–74*, p. 384.

2. *CPR 1370–74*, p. 447; *CPR 1374–77*, p. 22.

3. *Register 1371–75*, No. 1449.

4. *Register 1371–75*, Nos 667–68, 1430.

5. *Register 1371–75*, Nos 608, 865–7, 869–70, 1394–1400, 1404–5, 1450–51. On 31 May 1374 or a little before, Gaunt rode to see his father in Westminster, and the king pardoned John Blakebourne for outlawry at his request. Gaunt also complained on 8 July at Westminster that a group of men had hunted without licence in one of his chases in Yorkshire, and as well as taking his deer had assaulted some of his servants. *CPR 1370–74*, pp. 446, 487–88.

6. *Register 1371–75*, No. 608; *Life-Records of Chaucer*, p. 192, No. 83.

7. *Register 1371–75*, No. 1429.

8. *Register 1371–75*, No. 1431. In the same letter, John ordered that gifts should be sent from him to the archbishop of Ravenna, Pietro Pileo di Prata (d. 1400): a matching silver goblet and ewer given to him by his sister-in-law Joan of Kent, and a gold ring with a large sapphire.

9. : *CPR 1377–81*, p. 502; *CCR 1377–81*, pp. 390–95. An inquisition taken in Essex on 9 April 1380 (*CIPM 1377–84*, No. 201), says that Eleanor was 'aged 14 years on the feast of St Barnabas last,' which if accurate would give her a date of birth around 11 June 1365, though in that case it is not clear why she and Thomas did not receive her lands until June 1380. Eleanor is called Thomas of Woodstock's wife on the Patent Roll on 24 August 1376: *CPR 1374–77*, p. 337. She was then

still in her 'nonage', and must therefore have been born after 24 August 1362. Eleanor's younger sister and co-heir Mary, who would marry John of Gaunt's son Henry of Lancaster in 1381, was probably born in late 1370, and was certainly born after 5 February 1367, as Gaunt promised to pay her mother the countess of Hereford an annuity of 100 marks until Mary turned fourteen, beginning on 5 February 1381 (the entry in the duke's register states 1382, but this is probably an error by one of Gaunt's clerks for 1381; see also below). *Register 1379–83*, No. 996: *tanque la dite Marie soit de xiiij ans pleinement accompliez*. It is likely that Mary was born not too long before 22 December 1370, as on 22 December 1384 she and Henry of Lancaster were given her share of her late father's lands as she had come of age: *CCR 1381–85*, pp. 511–16, 548. The Essex inquisition of 9 April 1380 mentioned above states that she was then nine years old, which fits well with the other evidence. In 1380, the jurors of Calais, where the earl of Hereford had owned an inn, stated that they knew the earl had left two daughters as his heirs, 'but as to their ages or names the jurors are ignorant.' *CIPM 1370–73*, No. 167; *CIPM 1377–84*, No. 208. At their father's inquisition post-mortem in early 1373 which gives rather vague estimates of the girls' ages, Eleanor was said to be seven and Mary either three or 'aged four years and more,' though it seems probable that she was in fact born in or a little before December 1370, and therefore was only two years old when her father died in January 1373.

25. Floods and High Winds

1. *Register 1371–75*, Nos 1441, 1664, 1666, 1674; *CCR 1377–81*, p. 277, for Frances (Richard II released her on account of his 'compassion for her long imprisonment, being based upon suspicion only'). The clerk of John of Gaunt's great wardrobe was John de Yerdebergh. Confusingly, John de Yerdebergh's brother was also named John, and they worked together, *Register 1371–75*, No. 1740.
2. *Register 1371–75*, No. 1803.
3. *Register 1371–75*, Nos 1475, 1509–10, 1514, 1524, 1538, 1547, 1566, 1571, 1639, 1724–25. Gaunt's clerk called Newcastle-under-Lyme 'Novel Chastel souz Lyne', No. 613.
4. *Register 1371–75*, No. 1635; Society of Antiquaries of London, Manuscript No. 122, p. 61; *Calendar of Memoranda Rolls Michaelmas 1326-Michaelmas 1327 (Exchequer)* (1968), No. 2264. Kenilworth, Pickering and Pontefract were all in Edward II's hands between 1322 and 1326, after he executed his cousin Thomas, earl of Lancaster.
5. TNA SC 8/102/5059.
6. *Register 1371–75*, No. 1585.

26. Your Lusts Torture You

1. *Register 1371–75*, Nos 181, 1607, 1661. The same grammatical error appears in a letter of Gaunt's in March 1372 relating to Elizabeth Chandos, where Gaunt's clerk wrote *au dit Elizabeth* for 'to the said Elizabeth' instead of the correct *a la dite Elizabeth*; in another letter about Margery Brompton in November 1372; and in a third about Duchess Constanza's damsel Blanche Notton in March 1373 (*Register 1371–75*, Nos 929, 1105, 1145). At least one of Gaunt's clerks seem to have been rather uncomfortable with French grammar and on many occasions wrote *avoir*, the infinitive verb meaning 'to have', rather than *avons*, as in 'we have', when this was the correct form required.

Calendar of Inquisitions Post Mortem 1384–92, Nos 847–50, states that Robert Deincourt was twenty-six or twenty-eight at the start of 1391, though the Lincolnshire jurors claimed that he was then 'thirty-nine and more'. This cannot be correct, as he would have been over twenty-one years old and therefore of age in early 1375, and Gaunt could not have given his lands, wardship and marriage rights to Katherine Swynford. For some reason, Robert Deyncourt and Blanche Swynford never married, and possibly she married Sir Thomas Morieux instead.

2. *Register 1371–75*, Nos 1604, 1661.
3. *Register 1371–75*, No. 351; this letter is misdated by the editor to 11 January 1374, but John was still in France then, and he himself dated it to 11 January in the forty-eighth year of his father's reign, which ran from 25 January 1374 to 24 January 1375.
4. *Register 1371–75*, No. 1608.
5. Amin, *House of Beaufort*, p. 24.
6. *Register 1371–75*, Nos 80, 142–3, 203–4, 352, 355, 360, 364, 373, 675, 684, 686, 690, 692–3, 696–7, 770, 1646–59, 1764, 1778, 1780–82.
7. *Register 1371–75*, Nos 364, 374, 712, 1683.
8. *Register 1371–75*, No. 1711; *CPR 1374–77*, pp. 433, 435. Richard II, or rather someone acting in the ten-year-old king's name, confirmed John's grant to Katherine of these two manors on 20 July 1377, at the start of his reign: *CPR 1377–81*, p. 7. Earlier in the 1370s, Gaunt's steward of Gringley and Wheatley was William Fyncheden, the manors' receiver was Robert Morton, and the guardian of the parks within the manors was Richard of Lancaster: *Register 1371–75*, Nos 263–64, 586–87.
9. Translated by Lucraft, *Katherine Swynford*, pp. 57–58.
10. Lucraft, pp. 78–81.
11. *Chronicon Angliae, ab Anno Domini 1328 usque ad Annum 1388*, ed. Edward Maunde Thompson (Cambridge: Cambridge University Press, 1874), p. 196.

27. Making Merry with Anjou

1. *Calendar of Inquisitions Post Mortem 1374–77*, No. 105.
2. *Register 1371–75*, Nos 1659, 1661.
3. *Register 1371–75*, Nos 1143, 1283, 1295, 1720; *Register 1379–83*, Nos 876, 887, 1012.
4. *Register 1371–75*, Nos 162, 167, 1241, 1659. Gaunt also borrowed 1,000 marks from John Neville, lord of Raby, in July 1372 (Nos 163, 167). The duke borrowed at least 11,000 marks from Arundel between 1372 and 1374: Chris Given-Wilson, 'Wealth and Credit, Public and Private: The Earls of Arundel 1306–1397', *English Historical Review*, 106 (1991), p. 6.
5. *Register 1371–75*, Nos 1554, 1649.
6. *Register 1371–75*, No. 1675.
7. *Anonimalle 1333–81*, p. 79, '*fist graunt despens e graunt riot al count de Aungeoy, fitz al roy de Frauns, qare chescun iour a poy furount ensemble pur reveler et daunser*'. The chronicler dates the visit to 1374, though Gaunt's register makes it apparent that he travelled in 1375; he was in Bruges on 18, 22 and 25 May 1375 and in Dover on 8 and 9 March that year before departure, and was appointed by his father to 'treat for peace with France' and to make a truce on 20 February 1375 (*Foedera 1361–77*, pp. 1024–25; another man empowered to conduct the negotiations with Gaunt was William Montacute, earl of Salisbury). King Charles V empowered his brother Anjou to treat for peace with Gaunt

on 14 October 1373, and Pope Gregory mentioned Gaunt and Anjou's mutual 'hostilities' on 10 March 1374: TNA C 47/30/8/11; *Calendar of Papal Letters 1362–1404*, pp. 108, 131. Anjou had been in England as a hostage, and on 20 November 1364 Edward III declared that he had left the country without permission: *Foedera 1361–77*, p. 756.

8. *Register 1371–75*, No. 1696, *le peril que pourroit avenir de ceste pestilence q'ore est.*

9. *Register 1371–75*, No. 1786.

10. *Oeuvres de Froissart*, ed. Lettenhove, Vol. 8, pp. 466–67. The town of Grammont, its French name, is called Geraadsbergen in Dutch, and lies in the modern Belgian province of East Flanders. The abbey of St Adrian is now a museum.

28. A Great Need for Money

1. *Register 1371–75*, Nos 173, 1757–60, 1773.

2. *Register 1371–75*, Nos 389, 1707, 1713. TNA 44'28/62, Leicester and Rutland Record Office, is a quitclaim of September 1381 which reveals that Leicester had a 'fraternity of the Assumption of St Mary' in the south and a hospital dedicated to St John in the north, roads called Bernegate, Sorelane and Gosselyncrofte, and a meadow with the curious name of Gerinndeswong. John of Gaunt's letter stated firmly 'We order that you do not suffer any person living in the said town of Tutbury to keep any hounds or bitches in the same town in any way whatsoever.' In February 1372, John referred to an area of his town of Boston, Lincolnshire, called *Pynsonlane*, and called Boston itself 'the town of Saint Botulph'. *Register 1371–75*, Nos 391–92, 412.

3. *Register 1371–75*, No. 1730.

4. TNA amsg/AMS5592/2, East Sussex Record Office; *Register 1371–75*, No. 1689.

5. *Register 1371–75*, No. 1805.

6. *Register 1371–75*, Nos 749, 1362–3, 1761, 1790–91, 1794–6, 1805: Letters dictated by Gaunt on 25 November, 7 and 11 December 1375 and 20 January 1376 were dated at Bruges. He had arrived in Dover on or a little before 21 October, No. 749. John, his brother Edmund of Langley, William Montacute, earl of Salisbury, and others were empowered to prorogue the truce with France on 20 September 1375: *Foedera 1361–77*, pp. 1039–40.

7. *Register 1371–75*, No. 1802, p. 358, wrongly dating the letter to 1374; also TNA SC 1/41/168.

29. His Exact Image and True Likeness

1. *PROME*; Goodman, *Gaunt*, p. 55; *Anonimalle 1333–1381*, pp. 79–94. John had already arrived in London by 1 April 1376, *CPR 1396–99*, p. 496.

2. *Anonimalle*, p. 87; Walsingham cited in Saul, *Richard II*, p. 20; Goodman, *Gaunt*, p. 56.

3. *Chronicon Angliae*, p. 105; Saul, *Richard II*, p. 20.

4. Goodman, *Gaunt*, p. 57.

5. Cited in *English Historical Documents*, Vol. 4, no, 47, and in *PROME*.

6. Goodman, *Gaunt*, p. 30.

7. Michael Bennett, 'Edward III's Entail and the Succession to the Crown, 1376–1471', *English Historical Review*, 113 (1998), p. 585; Ormrod, 'Edward III and his Family', p. 418, pointing out that it was remarkable how little was done to try to guarantee the safety of Richard's succession.

30. The Heirs Male of his Body

1. *CPR 1374–77*, p. 299; TNA SC 1/41/52, SC 1/63/244, SC 1/40/199; *CPR 1396–99*, p. 518.
2. *Foedera 1361–77*, p. 1080.
3. See Ian Mortimer, 'Richard II and the Succession to the Crown' in his *Medieval Intrigue: Decoding Royal Conspiracies* (London: Continuum, 2010), pp. 259–78, and Michael Bennett, 'Edward III's Entail and the Succession to the Crown, 1376–1471', *English Historical Review*, 113 (1998), pp. 580–609, who points out (p. 583) that the list of witnesses to the entail is very similar to the witnesses to and the executors of the king's will.
4. Ormrod, 'Edward III and his Family', pp. 419–20.
5. *PROME*; *Foedera 1361–77*, pp. 1070, 1073; *English Historical Documents*, Vol. 4, p. 9. Nigel Saul, *Richard II*, p. 21, says that John was by now anxious to promote the young heir as the symbol of unity.
6. *CPR 1374–77*, pp. 437–38, 457; *CIPM 1374–77*, No. 173. The Lestrange lands and Elizabeth's marriage rights had been given to Richard, earl of Arundel, on 8 August 1375, but he died the following January; *CFR 1369–77*, p. 293.
7. Gaunt's nephew Richard II arranged Elizabeth Lestrange's marriage to Thomas Mowbray, earl of Nottingham in February 1383, but she died on 23 August that year (her heir was her aunt Ankaret Talbot). *CPR 1381–85*, p. 229; *CPR 1389–92*, p. 16; *CIPM 1374–77*, Nos 105, 173; *CIPM 1377–84*, Nos 1022–27.
8. *English Historical Documents*, Vol. 4, 1327–1485, ed. A. R. Myers (London: Eyre and Spottiswoode, 1969; reprinted by Routledge, 1996), pp. 9–10.

31. Alice and the Rings

1. See *Register 1379–83*, No. 803 for an example.
2. Laura Tompkins, 'Mary Percy and John de Southeray: Wardship, Marriage and Divorce in Fourteenth-Century England, *Fourteenth Century England X*, ed. Gwilym Dodd (Woodbridge: The Boydell Press, 2018), pp. 141–43; *CCR 1374–77*, p. 48.
3. *Foedera 1373–97*, p. 490; *CIPM 1384–92*, Nos 847–50; *CIPM 1399–1405*, No. 335; *CPL 1362–1404*, pp. 96, 135–36, 146.
4. Chris Given-Wilson, 'The Exequies of Edward III and the Royal Funeral Ceremony', *English Historical Review*, 124 (2009), p. 260.
5. See Goodman, *John of Gaunt*, p. 356.
6. *CCR 1377–81*, p. 74; Saul, *Richard II*, p. 469; Chris Given-Wilson, 'Exequies of Edward III', p. 263.
7. *CCR 1377–81*, pp. 74–5.
8. *Register 1379–83*, No. 1183; his clerk wrote by mistake that Winchelsea was 'in the dioceses of Chester,' an error for Chichester. Gaunt was appointed, or appointed himself, to the custody of St Frideswide's Priory in Oxford on 22 July 1377; the priory was said to be 'intolerably burdened with debts beyond seas and within seas', and John was to 'rule it and dispose of its resources to the best advantage.' *CPR 1377–81*, p. 8.
9. For Edward III's funeral, see Ormrod, *Edward III*, pp. 578–81; Mortimer, *Perfect King*, p. 392; Saul, *Richard II*, pp. 22–23.

32. The Coronation and Curtana

1. *CPR 1377–81*, pp. 2, 4, 5.
2. *CCR 1377–81*, pp. 1–5.

3. *Chronicon Angliae 1328–1388*, ed. Maunde Thompson, p. 154; *Anonimalle*, pp. 107–114; Westminster Chronicle *1381–1394*, ed. L. C. Hector and B. F. Harvey, pp. 414–16; *The Chronica Maiora of Thomas Walsingham, 1376–1422*, translated by David Preest (Woodbridge: The Boydell Press, 2005), pp. 38–39.
4. *Anonimalle*, p. 114; Mortimer, *Fears of Henry IV*, p. 35; Given-Wilson, *Henry IV*, p. 25.
5. *CPR 1377–81*, pp. 294–95.
6. Thomas was also a good, solid Lancastrian name, having been borne by Duchess Blanche's royal great-uncle Thomas, earl of Lancaster and Leicester, born in 1277 or 1278 and executed by his cousin Edward II in 1322. A few years later, Gaunt's son and heir Henry would also choose the name Thomas for the second of his four sons. Why John of Gaunt and Katherine Swynford chose the name 'Joan' for their only daughter is unclear; perhaps John intended to honour his late sister Joan of Woodstock (d. 1348), or perhaps Joan Beaufort was named for Joan de Bohun, dowager countess of Hereford, Essex and Northampton. Joan de Bohun was a woman for whom Gaunt clearly felt great affection and respect, and her daughter Mary would marry his son and heir Henry in 1381. It is also possible that Joan Beaufort was named in honour of one of her godmothers.
7. *Register 1371–75*, No. 1807.

33. Wasted and Ruinous

1. *Calendar of Letter-Books of London*, Letter-Book H, 1375-99, p. 80.
2. *PROME*.
3. *CCR 1369–74*, p. 484; *CPR 1377–81*, pp. 24–25, 69–70; *Register 1371–75*, Nos 13, 24. Duke John of Brittany was the widower of John of Gaunt's sister Mary of Waltham; Joan Holland was one of Joan of Kent's two daughters from her marriage to Thomas Holland, and was the sister of Gaunt's future son-in-law John Holland. Chris Given-Wilson (*Henry IV*, p. 16) points out that Gaunt agreed to surrender his earldom in 1372 so that it could be used as 'diplomatic bait for the duke of Brittany'.
4. TNA SC 8/94/4678; SC 8/223/11132. The first petition refers to *le roy v[ost]re ayel*, 'the king your [Richard's] grandfather'.
5. *CPR 1377–81*, pp. 105, 343. John was at the Savoy on 26 February and 26 March 1378, *CPR 1396–99*, pp. 548, 561.
6. *Records of the Borough of Leicester*, ed. Bateson, Vol. 2, pp. 155, 170–71.
7. *Foedera 1377–83*, pp. 15, 23, 100, 110, 124; Saul, *Richard II*, pp. 36–37; Tuck, *Richard II and the English Nobility*, pp. 41–42; McHardy, *Reign of Richard II*, pp. 38–43.

34. Abusive Words Touching the Duke

1. *CPR 1377–81*, p. 456; Goodman, *John of Gaunt*, p. 280; Rees R. Davies, ed. Brendan Smith, *Lords and Lordship in the British Isles in the Late Middle Ages* (Oxford: Oxford University Press, 2009), p. 151; *Register 1379–83*, Nos 68, 88, 175–6, 297, 310, 452, and p. 941. A petition presented by Edward III and Alice Perrers' daughter Joan, Gaunt's half-sister, probably in January 1393 (or a few months after that) states that Edward III had granted her the earl of Nottingham's marriage rights and that John de Wyndesore owed her 2,000 marks from the sale of them. TNA SC 8/22/1060; *PROME*, January 1394 Parliament; *CCR 1392–96*, pp. 48–9.
2. *Register 1371–75*, No. 1778; *CFR 1391–99*, p. 16; Anthony Goodman, 'The Military Subcontracts of Sir Hugh Hastings, 1380', *English Historical Review*,

95 (1980), p. 115 note 9. Hastings was the son of Hugh Hastings the elder (d. 1369), with whom Gaunt had made an indenture in 1366, and they were a cadet branch of the Hastings family who were earls of Pembroke.

3. *Register 1379–83*, No. 953, *nostre tres seint pier le pape Urban vj.*
4. *Register 1379–83*, No. 1070.
5. *Chronicon Angliae*, Vol. 1, p. 211, cited in *PROME*.
6. *CPR 1377–81*, p. 284; *PROME*.
7. TNA SC 8/134/6670, SC 8/41/2011 (Isabella's petition dates to before June 1378 as it refers to her father's death as having occurred at the feast of St John the Baptist, i.e. 24 June, 'last'.
8. *Calendar of Letter-Books of London*, Letter-Book H, 1375–99, p. 107; *Memorials of London and London Life in the XIIIth, XIVth and XVth Centuries*, ed. H. T. Riley (London: Longmans, Green, 1868), p. 425.
9. *Register 1379–83*, No. 963; the editor of Gaunt's register has dated the letter to 1376, but it ends *le xxv. jour de Juill lan etc tierz*, 'the 25th day of July, the third year etc.' This must mean Richard II's third regnal year, which ran from 22 June 1379 to 21 June 1380. On 12 June 1379, John appointed king's lieutenant in France and Aquitaine, Foedera 1377–83, p. 63.
10. Walker, *Lancastrian Affinity*, p. 90.
11. *Register 1379–83*, Nos 1051–9, 1142, 1149, 1158.
12. *Register 1379–83*, Nos 108–15, 1060.
13. *Register 1379–83*, p. 50.
14. *Register 1379–83*, Nos 1062–63, 1172.

35. Elizabeth's Seven-year-old Bridegroom

1. Gaunt's clerk ended the entry with *le xix. jour de Janver lan du grace selonc le cours et computacion de leglise de l'Engleterre milles troiscentz septante et noef*, probably in error for 1380, as the next entry in the register is the men acknowledging that they owed Gaunt £2,100 on 21 January 1380. *Register 1379–83*, Nos 925–26.
2. See also *Register 1379–83*, Nos 950–52; *Issues of the Exchequer*, pp. 224–25.
3. *CPR 1377–81*, p. 313.
4. *PROME*, Introduction to the January 1380 Parliament.
5. *Register 1379–83*, Nos 927–28, 1150.
6. *Register 1379–83*, No. 1203.
7. *Register 1379–83*, Nos 738a, 921. John was at Kenilworth on 15 and 17 April and 5 June 1380, Nos 1017–18, 1067–68.
8. *Register 1379–83*, Nos 723, 903, 922–23. Dunstanburgh Castle was built by Duchess Blanche's great-uncle Thomas, earl of Lancaster, in the 1310s and early 1320s; he began to build it without first gaining the necessary permission of his hated cousin Edward II.
9. *Complete Peerage*, Vol. 10, p. 395; *Knighton's Chronicle*, Vol. 2, p. 208; *Register 1379–83*, No. 463; *CPR 1374–77*, p. 340.
10. Margaret of Norfolk's younger daughter Anne Manny, John Hastings' mother, was to die in 1384; her elder daughter, John and Thomas Mowbray's mother Elizabeth Segrave, had died in 1367 or 1368. Elizabeth of Lancaster's future second husband Sir John Holland was one of her wedding guests, *Register 1379–83*, No. 463.
11. John was 'aged two on the feast of St Martin last' in May/July 1375 and 'aged eleven years on the feast of St Martin in the Winter last' in June 1384: *CIPM 1370–73*, No. 148 (his father's IPM); *CIPM 1384–92*, Nos 12, 13, 20

(his mother's IPM). He was knighted by Richard II on 15 August 1381, aged eight: *Complete Peerage*, Vol. 10, p. 395.

12. *Register 1379–83*, Nos 803, 890, 898 etc. After her marriage, Elizabeth's servants included Agneys Sallowe and Nicholas de la Pyne: *Register 1379–83*, Nos 971–72.

13. *CPR 1381–85*, p. 437; TNA SC 8/125/6209–6211, SC 8/129/6440. John of Gaunt was at the Savoy on 27 June and 10 July 1380 and at Tutbury in Staffordshire on 22 August; Register *1379–83*, Nos 1075–77.

36. Mutiny in Portugal

1. TNA E 30/1282.
2. *Foedera 1377–83*, pp. 86, 93, 94, 156. For the campaign, see Sumption, *Divided Houses*, pp. 379–87, 431–8, 462–69, and for John's will, Appendix 1 below.
3. Tompkins, 'Mary Percy and John de Southeray', pp. 149–50.
4. Tompkins, 'Mary Percy and John de Southeray', p. 150 note 79.
5. *Anonimalle*, p. 132; *Register 1379–83*, No. 1080; *Foedera 1377–83*, p. 97. John was in Ravensdale, Derbyshire on 15 September and in York on 28 September, *Register 1379–83*, Nos 1078–79.
6. *Register 1379–83*, Nos 922, 1185; *Foedera 1377–83*, pp. 99–100. The port of Berwick-on-Tweed often changed hands between England and Scotland in the Middle Ages, and was currently held by England.
7. *CPR 1377–81*, p. 557.
8. *Register 1379–83*, No. 983. Elys's name also appears in Gaunt's register as Elys North de Thoresby: *Register 1371–75*, No. 1012.
9. TNA SC 1/58/43.

37. He Never after Loved the Duke

1. *CPR 1377–81*, p. 537; Given-Wilson, *Henry IV*, p. 27 note 17. Henry and Mary's marriage is mentioned on the Close Roll on 10 February 1381, *CCR 1377–81*, pp. 439–40. They were both great-grandchildren of Henry, earl of Lancaster (d. 1345) and Maud Chaworth (d. 1322) – Mary's maternal grandmother Eleanor of Lancaster, Lady Beaumont and countess of Arundel (d. 1372), was Henry and Maud's fifth daughter – and hence were second cousins.
2. Given-Wilson, *Henry IV*, pp. 27–28.
3. *CCR 1381–85*, pp. 511–16, 548.
4. *CPR 1377–81*, p. 452; *CPR 1381–85*, p. 95; *Register 1379–83*, No. 996. This says that the payments to Joan would commence *de le quint jour de Feverer lan du regne nostre tres redoute seignur le roy Richard second puis le Conquest quint, tanque la dite Marie soit de xiiij ans pleinement accompliez*. This reference to 'the fifth year of the reign of our very dread lord King Richard, second [of that name] since the Conquest' should probably say 'the fourth year'; Gaunt's scribe may have mistakenly repeated *quint* (fifth) from 'the fifth day of February' earlier in the sentence. Richard II's fourth regnal year ran from 22 June 1380 to 21 June 1381. Given that Henry and Mary married on *c.* 5 February 1381, it seems far more likely that Gaunt promised the payment for her maintenance to her mother on the day of the wedding, rather than exactly one year later.
5. Holmes, Estates of the Higher Nobility, p. 24; Given-Wilson, *Henry IV*, pp. 26–27; Mortimer, *Fears of Henry IV*, pp. 39–40. Thomas of Woodstock had been granted custody of Mary's half of the de Bohun inheritance until she came of age on 8 May 1380 (*CPR 1377–81*, p. 502), but the payments to her mother Joan for her sustenance made by Gaunt and Richard II strongly suggest that she lived with

her mother rather than with her sister and brother-in-law, as Froissart implies. Perhaps she was staying with them when Gaunt allegedly took her away, however.

6. Cited in Given-Wilson, *Henry IV*, p. 28.

7. Mortimer, *Fears of Henry IV*, pp. 370–71. Weir, *Katherine Swynford*, p. 186, claims that the infant was born at Rochford Hall on 24 April 1382, was named Edward, and only lived for four days. She also states that Mary de Bohun turned fourteen on 15 February 1382, but no sources are cited for any of these statements, and if Mary was born in February 1368 it is difficult to understand why she did not prove her age and receive her lands until December 1384.

8. *CPR 1377–81*, p. 600; *CCR 1381–85*, pp. 30, 33; TNA SC 8/104/5168, SC 8/111/5517.

9. *Register 1379–83*, No. 1088.

10. *Register 1379–83*, Nos 744, 976.

11. *Register 1379–83*, No. 943.

12. *Oeuvres de Froissart*, ed. Lettenhove, Vol. 10, pp. 312–14, and see Anthony Tuck, 'Richard II and the House of Luxembourg', *Richard II: The Art of Kingship*, eds. Anthony Goodman and James Gillespie (Oxford: Clarendon Press, 1999), pp. 224, 227.

38. An Almost Infinite Variety of Objects

1. *Register 1379–83*, Nos 981, 1095; *Foedera 1377–83*, pp 124–25.

2. In modern Britain, a person's chances of being murdered are roughly one in 100,000 in any year. In fourteenth-century England, it was more like one in 1,000.

3. McHardy, *Reign of Richard II*, pp. 65–67; *Chronica Maiora*, pp. 123–24.

4. *Register 1371–75*, No. 743. Gaunt put a value of £11, 6 and a halfpence on the wax and 115s on the carts of hay.

5. *CCR 1381–85*, p. 7; McHardy, *Reign of Richard II*, pp. 79–83.

6. CPR 1381–85, p. 23; *Calendar of Select Plea and Memoranda Rolls of the City of London*, ed. A. H. Thomas, Vol. 3, 1381–1412 (London: HMSO, 1932), p. 37; *Foedera 1361–77*, p. 130.

7. Cited in *ODNB*.

8. *Register 1379–83*, No. 1096.

39. Of Very Noble and Royal Blood

1. Henry Percy's apology is printed in the original French and in English translation in Armitage-Smith, *John of Gaunt*, pp. 257–58, and in French in Gaunt's *Register 1379–83*, No. 1243, pp. 410–11. See also PROME, November 1381 Parliament, and Kris Towson, 'Hearts Warped by Passion: The Percy-Gaunt Dispute of 1381', *Fourteenth Century England III*, ed. W. M. Ormrod (Woodbridge: Boydell and Brewer, 2004), especially pp. 143, 150. For Gaunt's description of Percy, which appeared in a letter where the duke gave Percy permission to hunt 'two or three' beasts in Gaunt's forests and chases whenever he happened to pass through the duke's manors and lordships, see *Register 1371–75*, No. 414. The gift of wine (in November 1380) is in *Register 1379–83*, No. 415, and the Douglas episode is in *Foedera 1377–83*, p. 20. Northumberland was born in 1341 so was almost exactly Gaunt's age, and was a first cousin of the late Blanche of Lancaster via his mother Mary of Lancaster, Lady Percy (d. 1362), youngest of Duke Henry's six sisters.

2. For example, Henry Beaumont (b. late 1339), son of Grosmont's fifth sister Eleanor, later countess of Arundel, from her first marriage, called himself 'nephew and donsel of the duke of Lancaster' in 1355: *Petitions to the Pope 1342–1419*, p. 282.

3. *Register 1379–83*, Nos 1105, 1109, 1192; *CPR 1396–99*, p. 492.

4. James Hamilton Wylie, *History of England Under Henry the Fourth*, Vol. 4 (London: Longmans, Green and Co., 1898), p. 166; Given-Wilson, *Henry IV*, p. 31.

5. Cited in McHardy, *Reign of Richard II*, p. 93, and Saul, *Richard II*, p. 455; *Foedera 1377–83*, p. 60. As late as June 1380, Richard's marriage to a 'daughter of the late emperor Louis' was under discussion: Foedera 1377–83, p. 90. As John of Gaunt's uncle-in-law Ludwig of Bavaria had died as far back as 1347, any daughter of his would be a good twenty years older than Richard, so it was a peculiar choice.

40. A Wicked Life

1. *Register 1379–83*, Nos 984, 1146. The space he granted for the construction of the new chapel was 600 feet long and 500 feet wide.

2. *Register 1379–83*, No. 1157; Weir, *Katherine Swynford*, pp. 184–86.

3. *Anonimalle 1333–1381*, pp. 153–54; Lucraft, *Katherine Swynford*, p. 59 for Walsingham.

4. *The Diplomatic Correspondence of Richard II*, ed. Edouard Perroy (London: Camden third series, volume 48, 1933), Nos 32, 40, pp. 19–20, 192–95.

5. TNA DD/FJ/9/7/18, Nottinghamshire Archives.

6. Wylie, *History of England Under Henry the Fourth*, Vol. 4, pp. 162, 165; ODNB, 'Katherine, Duchess of Lancaster'.

7. *Life-Records of Chaucer*, p. xxxiii; Walter, *Lancastrian Affinity*, p. 82; Given-Wilson, *Henry IV*, p. 77.

8. *CPR 1381–85*, pp. 371, 501, 504.

9. Beltz, *Memorials of the Order of the Garter*, p. 250.

41. Petitions and the Countess

1. Wylie, *History of England Under Henry the Fourth*, pp. 166–67. Romney or Rumney wine was a kind of Greek wine popular in England in the fourteenth century.

2. Wylie, *History of England*, p. 166; Mortimer, *Fears of Henry IV*, pp. 370–71.

3. *Register 1379–83*, No. 744.

4. *Register 1379–83*, No. 1198, and see british-history.ac.uk/vch/yorks/vol3/pp267-270, accessed 22 December 2019.

5. *CPR 1381–85*, pp. 138–39; TNA KB [King's Bench] 9/1069. John was also appointed to head the commissions in Hertfordshire and Derbyshire.

6. *Register 1379–83*, No. 739.

7. TNA SC 8/146/7252; SC 8/147/7347; *CPR 1381–85*, pp. 197, 236. Malwood Castle is a Bronze Age hill fort in the New Forest.

8. TNA SC 8/103/5111.

9. Jessica Lutkin has shown that Isabella died in 1382, not in 1379 as usually stated: see 'Isabella de Coucy, Daughter of Edward III: The Exception Who Proves the Rule', pp. 132–33. Entries in the chancery rolls prove that Isabella was still alive on 22 March and 25 June 1382: *CPR 1381–85*, pp. 105, 149, and see also *CCR 1377–81*, p. 265, which shows that she was still alive in August 1379. *CCR 1381–85*, p. 186, dated 8 December 1382, states '…from 5 October last, when the countess [of Bedford] died'. As Lutkin points out, the Westminster Chronicle, pp. 28–29, confirms the date and gives Isabella's places of death and burial ('*obiit London*' … *que apud Fratres Minores London' sepulta est*'). Edward I's widow Marguerite of France (d. 1318), stepmother of Edward II and grandmother of Joan of Kent, princess of Wales, was also buried in the London Greyfriars.

10. TNA SC 8/249/12442; CPR 1381–85, pp. 204–05. Isabella's will does not survive. Pembroke's Inn had perhaps been sold or given to her by John Hastings, earl of Pembroke (d. 1375), widower of her youngest sister Margaret of Windsor. The earl still owned his London inn in February 1369 and April 1372: CPR 1374–77, pp. 78, 287. Pembroke's Inn later belonged to William Beauchamp, Lord Abergavenny (d. 1411) a cousin of Pembroke to whom the earl left some of his lands and manors, and William's widow Joan (d. 1435), daughter of the earl of Arundel: *CIPM 1405–13*, No. 850; *CIPM 1432–37*, No. 500.

42. The Commons in a Ferment

1. *Register 1379–83*, Nos 747, 750.
2. *Early Lincoln Wills: An Abstract of All the Wills and Administrations Recorded in the Episcopal Registers of the Old Diocese of Lincoln, 1280–1547*, ed. Alfred Gibbons (Lincoln: James Williamson, 1888), p. 78; CPR 1327–30, pp. 13, 38, 442. Simon also often appears on record as a servant of Edward III, and by 1350 was lord of the manor of Surfleet in Lincolnshire: CPR 1348–50, p. 589.
3. Simon was still active at Gaunt's steward of Bolingbroke in April 1383: *Register 1379–83*, No. 1129. Walker, *Lancastrian Affinity*, p. 97 for the tower.
4. *Register 1379–83*, Nos 775, 786.
5. *Register 1379–83*, Nos 794–96.
6. Henry Despenser was born in 1341 or early 1342, so was just slightly Gaunt's junior. His paternal grandmother Eleanor de Clare (1292–1337), who married Hugh Despenser the younger in 1306, was Edward I's eldest granddaughter, and was thus a first cousin of Gaunt's father Edward III.
7. *PROME*.
8. CPR 1396–99, p. 493: 'Thomas de Swynford, knight, and Joan Croppehull, his wife ... dated at London, 1 March in the sixth year [of Richard II's reign]'; *Early Lincoln Wills*, p. 42. For the Crophills, see *CIPM 1377–84*, Nos 478, 958–63; *CIPM 1384–92*, No. 337; CPR 1381–85, pp. 232, 308; CCR 1381–85, p. 324. Agnes Crophill was born in 'Chabbenore' near Dilwyn, Herefordshire, and married Walter Devereux. Joan's father John Crophill was '60 and more' in late 1381, and his wife was named Margery: CPR 1358–61, pp. 116, 302.
9. CPR 1381–85, p. 232.
10. *Register 1379–83*, Nos 811, 815, 835–36.
11. *Calendar of Papal Letters 1362–1404*, p. 265.

43. Corpus Christi and a Christening

1. *Register 1379–83*, No. 856.
2. *PROME*, November 1381 Parliament; CPR 1381–85, p. 143. In 1383, John Kenne appears on record as 'master of Corpus Christi, Cambridge, alias master of the scholars of St Benedict': CPR 1381–85, p. 315.
3. *Register 1379–83*, Nos 934–35.
4. TNA SC 8/20/990. After Thomas Stafford died in 1392, Anne married his younger brother Edmund, the father of several of her children, including Humphrey Stafford, first duke of Buckingham. Thomas, the earl of Stafford's second son and heir, was born *c*. 25 March 1369 ('aged 18 years on the feast of the Annunciation, 10 Richard II'): *CIPM 1384–92*, Nos 423–54.
5. *Register 1379–83*, No. 803, pp. 258–59. Thomas of Woodstock and Eleanor de Bohun had a second daughter, Joan, b. *c*. 1384/85, who died on 16 August 1400, and a third, Isabel, born 23 April 1386 or 23 April 1387, who was professed as a nun at the Minoresses' convent in London. Their son Humphrey died aged

seventeen in 1399, and Anne was their heir. *CIPM 1399–1405*, Nos 126–89; *Testamenta Vetusta*, Vol. 1, p. 148.

6. Register 1379–83, No. 803, p. 259. Lady Mohun was about sixty years old in 1383; she was born Joan Burghersh in the early or mid-1320s, probably when her parents Bartholomew, Lord Burghersh and Elizabeth de Verdon were imprisoned in the Tower of London by Gaunt's grandfather Edward II. Lady Mohun's eldest daughter Elizabeth married William Montacute, earl of Salisbury, after the annulment of Salisbury's marriage to Joan of Kent, and her third and youngest daughter, Philippa, would marry Gaunt's nephew Edward of York in the late 1390s, as her third husband. On 24 December 1372, Gaunt gave Lady Mohun forty large pearls for her fret: *Register 1371–75*, No. 1133.

7. *Register 1379–83*, No. 803, pp. 259–60; *CPR 1381–85*, p. 336.

8. *Register 1379–83*, No. 1141, *nostre tresamee compaigne la roygne et nostre tresamee fille Phellipe.*

9. GLY/3469, East Sussex Record Office, available on the National Archives website.

10. *Register 1379–83*, No. 905. On 25 June 1383, Gaunt was in Durham: Register 1379–83, Nos 1134–36. The earl of Carrick was John, eldest son of Robert II, king of Scotland from 1371 to 1390.

11. *PROME*.

44. A State of Decay

1. *Register 1379–83*, Nos 910–13. The items were probably for Elys to use in John's household, rather than being gifts which Gaunt intended him to keep.

2. TNA CCA-DCc-ChAnt/C/92 and 94, Canterbury Cathedral Archives and Library.

3. *Register 1379–83*, No. 919. This entry and the one before it show that Yerdebergh retired at this time.

4. *PROME*, October 1383 Parliament.

5. *PROME*; *Calendar of Letter-Books of London*, Letter-Book H, p. 252; *Foedera 1373–97*, pp. 412–13; Goodman, *Gaunt*, pp. 98–99.

6. *Anglo-Norman Letters and Petitions*, ed. Mary Dominica Legge (Oxford: Basil Blackwell, 1941), No. 269, p. 329.

7. McHardy, *Reign of Richard II*, pp. 116–17, 124; Saul, *Richard II*, p. 131; *PROME*, Introduction to the 1384 Parliament; *ODNB*, entries for Thomas of Woodstock and John Holland.

8. *PROME*.

9. Saul, *Richard II*, pp. 132–33.

10. *PROME*; McHardy, *Reign of Richard II*, p. 124, citing the *Historia Vitae et Regni Ricardi Secundi* and pointing out that the chronicler gives Waltham, but that Richard was at Windsor from 28 December 1384 until 3 February 1385.

45. A Catalogue of Strange Names

1. *PROME*; *Chronica Maiora*, pp. 219–20.

2. *ODNB*, entry for Wyclif(fe).

3. *Chronica Maiora*, p. 213.

4. Goodman, *Gaunt*, pp. 102–03; *Chronica Maiora*, pp. 225–36; *Westminster Chronicle*, pp. 114–15; Saul, *Richard II*, pp. 133–34; *PROME*.

5. TNA E 326/2677. Gaunt was at Rothwell in Northamptonshire on 30 April 1385, when he made an indenture with his squire Richard Ryxton. Walker, *Lancastrian Affinity*, p. 296; *English Historical Documents*, Vol. 4, ed. Myers, No. 653.

6. *CChR 1341–1417*, pp. 300, 323. Michael de la Pole was made earl of Suffolk on the same day. See *PROME*; it is possible that at first Edmund and Thomas received the new dukedoms of Canterbury and Aumale respectively.

7. *CChR 1341–1417*, pp. 301, 307.

8. *Chronica Maiora*, pp. 229–30 ('humbled' quotation); Mortimer, 'Richard II and the Succession to the Crown' in his *Medieval Intrigue*, p. 262, citing Jean Froissart ('earnestly' quotation); Saul, *Richard II*, p. 145; Tuck, *Richard II and the English Nobility*, pp. 97–98.

9. *CPR 1385–89*, pp. 99, 122, dated 8 February and 17 March 1386. On 18 February, the earl of Stafford came to an agreement with Holland that the latter should establish a chantry of three chaplains to sing for Ralph's soul. *CPR 1385–89*, pp. 114, 386; TNA SC 8/254/12673. Stafford died on 26 or 27 September 1386, leaving his second son Thomas, later the husband of Gaunt's young niece Anne of Gloucester, as his heir.

10. Cited in Goodman, *John of Gaunt*, pp. 356–57.

11. Cited in Armitage-Smith, *John of Gaunt*, Chapter 13, location 4179.

46. Frightened Hares and Timid Mice

1. *Life-Records of Chaucer*, p. xxxiii (Lincoln); TNA SC 1/51/26 (Hertford).

2. TNA E 30/1087; *Foedera 1373–97*, pp. 510, 525; McHardy, *Reign of Richard II*, pp. 143–44; Goodman, *Gaunt*, p. 118.

3. *Chronica Maiora of Thomas Walsingham*, trans. Preest, p. 240; McHardy, *Reign of Richard II*, pp. 144–49.

4. *Foedera 1373–97*, p. 507 (papal bulls); Goodman, 'Military Subcontracts of Hugh Hastings', p. 115 note 9; TNA E 30/1254 (John's location); see also *Chronica Maiora*, p. 238.

5. *Foedera 1373–97*, pp. 504, 509, 524 (ships); *Knighton's Chronicle*, Vol. 2, pp. 207–08, gives the names of Gaunt's officials, and see also *Foedera*, p. 583. John Holland appointed attorneys prior to accompanying Gaunt to Spain on 5 April 1386: *CPR 1385–89*, p. 213; medievalsoldier.org, accessed 11 March 2020.

6. *Register of the Black Prince*, Vol. 4, p. 87; *Foedera 1361–77*, p. 844. Thomas Holland the younger served in Gaunt's retinue in the early 1370s: *Register 1371–75*, No. 1784.

7. There are, perhaps rather curiously, no references to the matter in the *Calendar of Papal Letters 1362–1404* or in *Petitions to the Pope 1342–1419*, and Gaunt's registers do not survive past 1383. The date of Elizabeth's wedding to Holland is uncertain.

8. TNA SC 8/224/11176; *CPR 1381–85*, p. 437.

9. Mortimer, *Fears of Henry IV*, p. 371, for the date.

10. The others were Edward II, born in Caernarfon in 1284, and Henry VII, born in Pembroke in 1457.

11. On 18 September 1391, Pope Boniface IX stated that Constance Holland was then in her fourth year, meaning that she was three years old (*Calendar of Papal Letters 1362–1404*, p. 396). However, young Thomas Mowbray, the namesake elder son and heir of the earl of Nottingham, whose future marriage to Constance was then being arranged, was said to be in his fifth year (i.e. four years old) in September 1391, when in fact he turned six that month. Constance Holland therefore may have been somewhat older than the pope's letter suggests, born in 1386/87. As Elizabeth's Pembroke marriage was annulled in 1386 and she hastily remarried John Holland, it seems virtually certain that she was then pregnant, perhaps with Constance. *CIPM 1399–1405*, Nos 264, 269–70, says that Thomas Mowbray was '14 on 17 September last' in January 1400, so he was born on 17 September 1385.

47. A Portuguese Son-in-law

1. Goodman, *John of Gaunt*, p. 115; Graham St John, 'Dying Beyond Seas: Testamentary Preparation for Campaigning during the Hundred Years War', *Fourteenth Century England VII*, ed. W. Mark Ormrod (Woodbridge: Boydell and Brewer, 2012), p. 192.

2. St John, 'Dying Beyond Seas', p. 93; Goodman, 'Military Subcontracts of Sir Hugh Hastings', p. 115.

3. *Oeuvres de Froissart*, Vol. 13, p. 134; Goodman, *Gaunt*, pp. 120–23, 136–37. Gaunt was in 'Caracedo', Portugal on 12 January 1387, *CPR 1396–99*, p. 496, giving 12 January 1386, which cannot be correct as he was certainly still in England then. *CPR 1399–1405*, p. 110, says he was in Quitenla, Portugal on 16 March 1386.

4. Manuela Santos Silva, 'The Marriage of Philippa of Lancaster and João I of Portugal', *Royal and Elite Households in Medieval and Early Modern Europe, More Than Just a Castle*, ed. Theresa Earenfight (Leiden/Boston: Brill, Explorations in Medieval Culture, Vol. 6, 2018), p. 272.

5. Goodman, *Gaunt*, p. 130.

6. *Register 1379–83*, Nos 1235–39.

7. TNA SC 8/224/11175; *CCR 1392–96*, p. 314.

8. Goodman, *Gaunt*, p. 130; *CPR 1396–99*, pp. 526, 534, 547, 553. He was in Dax on 14 March 1388.

9. *Oeuvres de Froissart*, ed. Lettenhove, Vol. 13, pp. 127–31. See Goodman, *Gaunt*, pp. 193–4 and note 98 on p. 208. Duke John of Berry (1340–1416) was the third son of John II, brother of Charles V and uncle of Charles VI, and was just a few months younger than Gaunt. Berry remained a hostage in England until 1369 after his father died there in 1364. Presumably, if Froissart is correct on this point, Berry wished Catalina to marry his son Jean de Valois, who was born in 1375 or 1376 and was a little Catalina's junior, and who was count of Montpensier from 1386, the year he married his first cousin, Charles V's daughter Catherine de Valois.

10. *Oeuvres de Froissart*, Vol. 13, pp. 126–27.

11. Goodman, *John of Gaunt*, pp. 226, 356.

12. Mortimer, *Fears of Henry IV*, p. 372. Thomas appears on record in the Lancastrian accounts of 30 September 1387 to 30 September 1388, and was born in London: Wylie, *England Under Henry the Fourth*, pp. 157–59.

13. Wylie, *England Under Henry the Fourth*, pp. 158–59; *CPR 1396–99*, pp. 122, 518, 547; Given-Wilson, *Henry IV*, pp. 77–78.

14. Mortimer, *Fears of Henry IV*, p. 372; Given-Wilson, *Henry IV*, p. 77; *Complete Peerage*, Vol. 2, p. 70.

48. Forty-seven Mules Carrying Money

1. Goodman, *Gaunt*, p. 125.

2. *Chronica Maiora*, p. 276.

3. *Chronica Maiora*, p. 276; McHardy, *Reign of Richard II*, pp. 172–74; Given-Wilson, *Henry IV*, pp. 61, 71, 76; Goodman, *John of Gaunt*, 345; Lucy Toulmin Smith, ed., *Expeditions to Prussia and the Holy Land Made by Henry, Earl of Derby (Afterwards King Henry IV) in the Years 1390–1 and 1392–3, Being the Accounts Kept by his Treasurer for Two Years* (London: Camden Society, 1894), p. xlvii; Francisco de Paula Cañas Gálvez, ed., *Colección Diplomática de Santo Domingo el Real de Toledo I: Documentos Reales (1249–1473)* (Madrid: Sílex Ediciones, 2010), pp. 148–50.

4. *ODNB*; *Foedera 1373–97*, p. 603; Goodman, *Gaunt*, pp. 128, 131. Enrique of Castile was King Juan's son from his first marriage to Leonor of Aragon and was the stepson of Beatriz of Portugal, the only legitimate child of the late King Fernando of Portugal, once betrothed to Gaunt's nephew Edward of York. Fernando of Castile's (b. 1380) son Alfonso (b. 1396) married his cousin, Enrique and Catalina's daughter María (b. 1401), and his daughter, also María, married Enrique and Catalina's son Juan II of Castile.

5. *Calendar of Plea and Memoranda Rolls of the City of London*, Vol. 3, p. 151.

6. *CChR 1341–1417*, p. 309.

7. *ODNB*, Henry Beaufort's entry.

8 *Oeuvres de Froissart*, ed. Lettenhove, Vol. 13, pp. 301–02; Goodman, *John of Gaunt*, p. 360.

49. Constanza and Catalina Grandly Received

1. Leonor of Castile, daughter of Enrique of Trastámara and sister of King Juan, was married to Carlos III of Navarre, son of Carlos II 'the Bad' (d. 1387).

2. *Oeuvres de Froissart*, ed. Lettenhove, Vol. 13, pp. 301–04. Anthony Goodman's *ODNB* entry for Catalina dates her wedding to 17 September 1388.

3. *Anglo-Norman Letters and Petitions*, ed. Legge, Nos 297, 307, pp. 360–61, 372–73.

4. *CPR 1396–99*, pp. 490, 499.

5. TNA E 30/314, E 30/1356; *Foedera 1373–97*, pp. 615–16.

6. *CPR 1396–99*, p. 558.

50. The King and the Livery Collar

1. *CPR 1389–92*, p. 203. John was also in Bordeaux on 22 September 1389, *CPR 1396–99*, p. 576.

2. *Foedera 1373–97*, pp. 641, 648 (ships and Richard's letter); Goodman, *Gaunt*, pp. 144–45; *PROME*; *Chronica Maiora*, p. 276.

3. Matthew Ward, *Livery Collar in Late Medieval England and Wales*, p. 21; Fletcher, 'The Lancastrian Collar of Esses', *The Age of Richard II*, ed. Gillespie, p. 192.

4. *CPL 1398–1404*, pp. 598–600.

5. *CPR 1389–92*, p. 469; *Complete Peerage*, Vol. 10, p. 395.

6. *CIPM 1384–92*, Nos 885–923; *CPR 1396–99*, p. 566 (Gaunt's location). Grey of Ruthin was a grandson of Elizabeth Hastings, sister of John's great-grandfather (d. 1325). The jurors at the young earl's inquisition post-mortem were, however, hopelessly confused as to who his correct heirs were, and to confuse matters even further, the earl who died in 1375 had left some of his lordships to his cousin William Beauchamp, the earl of Warwick's brother. *CCR 1389–92*, pp. 411–15; *CCR 1396–99*, pp. 83–84.

7. *CChR 1341–1417*, p. 318; *PROME*. John was in London on 10 March and back at Hertford on 18 April, *CPR 1396–99*, pp. 542, 568.

8. *PROME*.

9. Juliet Barker, *The Tournament in England, 1100–1400* (Woodbridge: The Boydell Press, 1996), p. 37.

10. *Oeuvres de Froissart*, ed. Lettenhove, Vol. 14, p. 416, and see also below.

11. *CPR 1391–96*, p. 15.

12. Toulmin Smith, *Expeditions to Prussia and the Holy Land*, pp. xxxv, xxxviii, xxxix, lxxxi, 301. John was in London on 22 February and 24 May 1390 and at Hertford on 18 April, *CPR 1396–99*, pp. 539, 548, 557–58.

51. England Is in a Bad State

1. *Chronica Maiora*, p. 278.
2. TNA SC 1/40/178; *CPR 1389–92*, pp. 360, 366; *CPR 1396–99*, p. 522. Gaunt was in Leicester on 12 March and at Hertford Castle again on 7 and 31 August 1391, *CPR 1396–99*, pp. 478, 532; Walker, *Lancastrian Affinity*, pp. 297–98.
3. *CPR 1389–92*, p. 409.
4. Cited in *PROME*, Introduction to the November 1391 Parliament.
5. *Chronica Maiora*, p. 282.
6. *CPR 1396–99*, p. 544; *PROME*. He was in London on 12 November, Walker, *Lancastrian Affinity*, p. 298.
7. *Calendar of Letter-Books of London*, Letter-Book H, p. 372.
8. *PROME*.
9. Duke John of Berry, who lived until 1416 and was the longest-living of King John II and Bonne of Bohemia's four sons, did his best to reconcile the warring factions. Duke Louis of Anjou, second son of John II, had died in 1384.

52. A Tablet of Jasper

1. According to Douglas Richardson's *Plantagenet Ancestry: A Study in Colonial and Medieval Familie*s (2004), p. 334, Joan and Robert married before 30 September 1390, but it is impossible to follow Richardson's source for this statement. The National Archives website says the couple married in March 1392, and G. L. Harriss's *Cardinal Beaufort: A Study of Lancastrian Ascendancy and Decline* (Oxford: Clarendon Press, 1988), p. 6, says they were betrothed in 1386 and married in 1392. Joan Beaufort's entry in the *Oxford Dictionary of National Biography* also states that she married in 1392.
2. *Register 1379–83*, No. 1029.
3. *CFR 1377–83*, p. 260; *CIPM 1377–84*, Nos 346–49.
4. *CPR 1381–85*, p. 99.
5. *CIPM 1405–13*, Nos 821–24.
6. *CPR 1396–99*, p. 127. There is no extant inquisition post-mortem for Robert Ferrers, which would give at least an approximate date of death. Both of Joan Beaufort's Ferrers daughters married and had offspring; Elizabeth married John, Lord Greystoke (b. *c*. 1389/90) and had twelve children, and Mary married her stepbrother Ralph Neville, one of the sons of Joan Beaufort's second husband from his first marriage, and also had children of her own.
7. *CPR 1391–96*, p. 63, 196, 205.
8. Gaunt's whereabouts and actions are not too easy to follow in 1392, but he probably attended his granddaughter Blanche's baptism, and was in Leicester on 2 and July 1392 and in Hertford on 16 August, in London on 20 April 1392, and in Stamford, Lincolnshire on 27 May: *CPR 1396–99*, pp. 122, 499, 501, 524, 561.
9. Isabel's will is now in the National Archives in London, PROB 11/1/53, and a greatly abridged version of it is printed in *Testamenta Vetusta*, Vol. 1, pp. 134–35. Isabel's entry in the *ODNB* by Anthony Tuck states that she left nothing to her husband, and indeed the highly abbreviated (and rather misleading) version of her will in *Testamenta Vetusta* fails to mention any of her bequests to him. I have also previously stated, incorrectly, that Isabel left nothing to Edmund.
10. *Complete Peerage*, Vol. 12B, p. 898.

53. Grievous Heaviness of Heart

1. *CPR 1396–99*, pp. 534, 537; Walker, *Lancastrian Affinity*, p. 299; *PROME*.
2. *CPR 1396–99*, pp. 499–501.
3. *Foedera 1373–97*, p. 738; *PROME*; Goodman, *Gaunt*, p. 152.
4. *PROME*; Goodman, *Gaunt*, pp. 152–53; Mortimer, *Fears of Henry IV*, pp. 116–17; *CPR 1391–96*, p. 560; *CCR 1392–96*, p. 294. On 2 October 1393, Gaunt made a grant to the mayor of King's Lynn, TNA DL 25/2034/1696, and was at Plympton on 12 October 1393, *CPR 1396–99*, p. 571.
5. Mortimer, *Fears*, pp. 117–18. Henry inspected and confirmed letters patent of his father in favour of one of John's servants at Hertford on 26 December 1393: *CPR 1396–99*, p. 561.
6. Goodman, *Gaunt*, p. 153.
7. *Diplomatic Correspondence of Richard II*, ed. Perroy, No. 199, pp. 144–45.
8. *CPR 1396–99*, p. 490; TNA DL 25/3487, DL 25/2192/1875, DL 25/2194/1879, DL 25/2194/1881, DL 25/3487/3041 and 3042.
9. *PROME*; Goodman, *Gaunt*, p. 153. John was in London on 4 March 1394, two days before Parliament ended, *CPR 1396–99*, p. 547.
10. *Eulogium Historiarum*, cited in *PROME*; Given-Wilson, *Henry IV*, pp. 96–97.
11. *CPR 1391–96*, p. 322, for Benge; Goodman, *Gaunt*, p. 155, for the hunting party.
12. Goodman, *Gaunt*, p. 361.
13. *CPR 1396–99*, p. 74.
14. Goodman, *Gaunt*, p. 155; Armitage-Smith, *John of Gaunt*, p. 449; *Calendar of Letter-Books of London*, Letter-Book H, p. 414.
15. *CPL 1362–1404*, p. 489.
16. *CPR 1401–05*, p. 397.
17. Wylie, *England Under Henry the Fourth*, Vol. 4, p. 168 (poor men); *Calendar of Papal Letters*, Vol. 5, 1398–1404, p. 152 (indult); *CPR 1399–1405*, p. 457, for the date of 1 July; *ODNB*, entry for Henry IV, for 4 July; Westminster chronicler, pp. 520–21, cited in Given-Wilson, *Henry IV*, p. 86, for Peterborough; Goodman, *Gaunt*, p. 155, for the dates of the funerals.
18. *CPR 1391–96*, p. 448; *Foedera 1373–97*, p. 527; Saul, *Richard II*, p. 448. Walsingham's *Chronica Maiora*, p. 220, states that Richard 'rarely if ever allowed [Anne] to be away from his side.'
19. *CChR 1341–1417*, pp. 375–80.
20. *Anglo-Norman Letters and Petitions*, ed. Legge, No. 3, pp. 47–48; Christopher Fletcher, *Richard II, Manhood, Youth and Politics 1377–1399* (Oxford: Oxford University Press, 2008), p. 48, citing *Diplomatic Correspondence of Richard II*, ed. Perroy, No. 204.
21. Goodman, *Gaunt*, pp. 155, 172 note 53. John was still in Leicester on 10 July 1394 a few days after the two funerals, *CPR 1396–99*, pp. 533–34.

54. I Know No Other News

1. Goodman, *Gaunt*, p. 196; Given-Wilson, *Henry IV*, p. 97.
2. *CPR 1396–99*, p. 542.
3. *Anglo-Norman Letters and Petitions*, ed. Legge, No. 19, pp. 63–64; my translation. King Carlos III sent an undated letter to Richard II stating that Carlos de Beaumont would travel to Richard to discuss certain matters with him, and also mentions John of Gaunt: *Anglo-Norman Letters and Petitions*, No. 21, pp. 64–65. Thomas Walsingham says that Gaunt had suffered a lack of wind while attempting to sail to Portugal in 1386, but finally managed to cross the Channel to Brest: *Chronica Maiora*, p. 238.

4. Goodman, *Gaunt*, p. 196; *CPR 1396–99*, p. 499.

5. Goodman, *Gaunt*, pp. 197–98. Gaunt was at Saint-Seurin a few miles from Bordeaux on 12 March 1395. He was in Bordeaux on 20 March, 1, 3 and 22 April, 2 May 1395 and again much later that year, on 2 October. TNA WARD 2/60/234/53; *CPR 1396–99*, pp. 478, 499, 537, 547, 549, 558; Walter, *Lancastrian Affinity*, pp. 299–300. For John Holland, *CIPM 1418–22*, No. 149.

6. Goodman, *Gaunt*, p. 187; Given-Wilson, *Henry IV*, p. 92.

7. *Anglo-Norman Letters and Petitions*, No. 268, p. 328. John Holland's *ODNB* entry states that Holland and his father-in-law Gaunt had 'rival marital plans involving the duke of Brittany's children'.

8. John Holland was also a former brother-in-law of Duke John of Brittany, who had married firstly Gaunt's sister Mary of Waltham (d. 1361/62), secondly Holland's sister Joan Holland (d. 1384), and thirdly Juana of Navarre (d. 1437), mother of all his children. Juana would later marry Gaunt's son Henry IV and become queen of England.

9. *ODNB* for the date of Walden's appointment; the letter is printed in *Anglo-Norman Letters and Petitions*, No. 22, pp. 66–67.

10. *CFR 1391–99*, p. 209. John was the son and heir of William de Lancastre, who died before 1 May 1399: *CFR 1391–99*, p. 290. See *PROME* for the pardon.

11. *Anglo-Norman Letters and Petitions*, No. 29, pp. 74–76. Goodman, *Gaunt*, p. 155, dates the letter to 1394 before John's departure to the south.

55. Their Hearts Would Burst with Grief

1. Wylie, *England Under Henry the Fourth*, p. 168; Walker, *Lancastrian Affinity*, p. 301. An ell was forty-five inches.

2. *Chronica Maiora of Thomas Walsingham*, p. 295; Given-Wilson, *Henry IV*, p. 91.

3. Cited in McHardy, *Reign of Richard II*, p. 310. Froissart states that the countess of Derby was one of the ladies, but Mary de Bohun had died eighteen months previously.

4. *CPL 1362–1404*, p. 545; *CPR 1396–99*, p. 86, and see also below.

5. *CPR 1396–99*, p. 39.

6. *ODNB* for Margaret Stafford's date of death; *CPR 1396–99*, p. 127, for Robert Ferrers.

7. *CPR 1396–99*, p. 548.

8. Eleanor Neville – said by the chronicler of Tewkesbury Abbey in Gloucestershire to be the eldest daughter of Joan and Ralph – married her first husband and second cousin Richard, Lord Despenser (November 1396 – c. October 1413) in July 1411, and Katherine Neville married John Mowbray in January 1412 and was old enough to give birth in September 1415. Richard Neville's name might imply that he was born before the downfall of King Richard II in September 1399, unless he was named after a godfather.

9. McHardy, *Reign of Richard II*, pp. 310–15; *CPR 1396–99*, p. 29; *Oeuvres de Froissart*, ed. Lettenhove, Vol. 15, p. 306.

10. *CPR 1396–99*, pp. 542, 561.

11. *PROME*; *CPR 1396–99*, p. 532. Gaunt himself was in London on 6 January, 13 February and 20 February 1397, *CPR 1396–99*, pp. 514, 535, 548.

12. TNA CC-DCc-ChAnt/T/33, Canterbury Cathedral Archives and Library; *CPR 1396–99*, p. 92. Thomas Arundel was also a brother of Joan de Bohun, dowager countess of Hereford, Henry of Lancaster's mother-in-law.

13. *PROME*.

14. *CPR 1396–99*, p. 171; *Foedera 1373–97*, pp. 849–50.

56. The Extermination of Rebels

1. *Anglo-Norman Letters and Petitions*, No. 283, p. 343.
2. *CPL 1362–1404*, pp. 294–95, 300. Boniface was referring to Robert of Geneva or Clement VII (d. 1394) and Pedro Martínez de Luna y Pérez de Gotor or Benedict XIII (d. 1423), the Avignon popes, later recognised by the Catholic Church as antipopes.
3. TNA C 1/68/40.
4. *CIPM 1392–99*, Nos 798–849; *Testamenta Vetusta*, Vol. 1, p. 139.
5. *CPR 1396–99*, pp. 12, 527, 556.
6. *CPR 1396–99*, pp. 190–91, 193; TNA SC 8/221/11038; *PROME*, October 1399 Parliament. John was certainly in Nottingham at the time, *CPR 1396–99*, p. 557.
7. An inquisition held on 19 September 1413 states that he died on 9 September 1397: *CIPM 1413–18*, No. 2, and see Thomas's *ODNB* entry, Given-Wilson, *Chronicles of the Revolution*, pp. 219–21, and Saul, *Richard II*, p. 379. Perhaps coincidentally, the duke of Gloucester's father-in-law the earl of Hereford (d. 1373) had once owned an inn in Calais. In 1380, it was said to be 'on the south-west corner of the market-place, between the lane wherein John Bouchecourt now dwells on the west, the great street leading from 'Milkyate' to 'le Wachehous' on the south, a cottage of Agnes Crabbe on the north and the great market on the east.' However, 'about Mid-Lent, 46 Edward III [i.e. in March 1372], it fell to the ground through lack of repair, and since then has been worth nothing.' On the site of the inn, there also stood a cottage and an 'old ruinous stable.' *CIPM 1377–84*, No. 208.
8. *Chronicles of the Revolution*, pp. 58–60; Michael Bennett, *Richard II and the Revolution of 1399* (Stroud: Sutton Publishing, 1999), pp. 101–02.
9. *ODNB*; Bennett, *Richard II and the Revolution*, pp. 102–03.
10: *Chonicque de la Traison et Mort*, p. 11: *ot le pris pour la mieulx dancant*.
11. *Chronica Maiora*, p. 301; *ODNB*; Bennett, *Richard II and the Revolution*, pp. 103, 112.

57. Caterpillars of the Commonwealth

1. *CChR 1341–1417*, p. 369; *CPR 1396–99*, p. 211. Confusingly, Margaret's second sister Joan was married to Gaunt's brother the duke of York, and their eldest sister Eleanor or Alianore was married to Gaunt's nephew Roger Mortimer, earl of March. The fourth sister, Elizabeth, later married Joan Beaufort's stepson John Neville.
2. *Anglo-Norman Letters and Petitions*, ed. Legge, No. 28, pp. 73–74.
3. Walker, *Lancastrian Affinity*, p. 302; *CPR 1396–99*, pp. 553, 564.
4. *Register 1379–83*, Nos 1029, 1113 (Greene), 1172 (Bagot).
5. *CPR 1396–99*, p. 544; *Register 1371–75*, No. 49; Walker, *Lancastrian Affinity*, p. 266.
6. *CPR 1396–99*, p. 535; *Foedera 1397–1413*, pp. 32–33.

58. Imprisoned in the Wardrobe

1. *CCR 1396–99*, pp. 291–92. The conversation between Thomas Mowbray and Henry of Lancaster is recorded in *PROME* and in Given-Wilson, *Chronicles of the Revolution*, pp. 86–87.
2. *CCR 1396–99*, pp. 281–82; *Foedera 1373–97*, p. 532.
3. *Anglo-Norman Letters and Petitions*, ed. Legge, No. 56, p. 104.

4. *Issues of the Exchequer*, ed. Devon, pp. 267–68; CCR 1396–99, p. 324.
5. *CPR 1396–99*, pp. 499, 522, 542, 547, 571, 582, 593; Walker, *Lancastrian Affinity*, p. 302. Henry was in London on 7 and 10 October 1398, a few days before the joust with Mowbray: *CPR 1396–99*, p. 534.
6. Henry's entry in the *ODNB*.
7. *CCR 1396–99*, p. 325; *CPR 1396–99*, pp. 379, 390, 402; Alastair Dunn, 'Richard II and the Mortimer Inheritance', *Fourteenth Century England II*, ed. Chris Given-Wilson (Woodbridge: The Boydell Press, 2002), p. 166.
8. *Oeuvres de Froissart*, ed. Lettenhove, Vol. 16, p. 110.
9. *Chronica Maiora*, trans. Preest, p. 303. Thomas Mowbray's inquisition post-mortem states that he was thirty-three years and twenty-six weeks old when he died in September 1399, which would place his date of birth in March 1366, but as his brother John was born in August 1365 and his sister Eleanor in March 1364, this is impossible. *CPR 1367–70*, p. 237; *CIPM 1365–69*, No. 397; *CIPM 1399–1405*, No. 268.
10. *Oeuvres de Froissart*, ed. Lettenhove, Vol. 16, p. 111.
11. *CPR 1396–99*, p. 414.

59. Severely Despondent

1. Goodman, *John of Gaunt*, pp. 166, 174 note 106; Walker, *Lancastrian Affinity*, p. 82.
2. *CPR 1396–99*, pp. 380, 469–70, 478, 489, 499, 500, 524.
3. Bennett, *Richard II and the Revolution*, p. 141; Goodman, *Gaunt*, p. 167.
4. I have translated the will in Appendix 1.
5. *Testamenta Vetusta*, Vol. 1, pp. 257–59.
6. *CIPM 1370–73*, No. 241; *CIPM 1374–77*, Nos 152–54; *CIPM 1418–22*, Nos 797–99; CFR 1369–77, pp. 202, 207, 293, 319, 324–25; *CPR 1374–77*, p. 208; CCR 1419–22, pp. 180–81; CCR 1422–29, pp. 230–31; TNA C 146/1047, C 146/2001; and see Appendix 1, below. William Croiser was the sheriff of Bedfordshire and Buckinghamshire in the late 1340s and named as the coroner of Edward III's household in 1354: *CPR 1348–50*, p. 237; *CPR 1354–58*, p. 161.
7. Bennett, *Richard II and the Revolution*, pp. 141, 143.
8. *Chronica Maiora of Thomas Walsingham*, trans. Preest, p. 305; Given-Wilson, *Chronicles of the Revolution*, p. 75.
9. *Chronicque de la Traison et Mort de Richart Deux Roy Dengleterre*, ed. Williams, pp. 63, 214; Bennett, *Revolution*, pp. 143–44. John of Gaunt's former retainer Thomas Fog petitioned the archbishop of Canterbury sometime after John's death, complaining that John had not paid him the fees he was owed and claiming, most improbably, that he had expended 10,000 marks (£6,666) in Gaunt's service which was also still owing: *Anglo-Norman Letters and Petitions*, ed. Legge, No. 309, p. 375.

60. Aftermath

1. Mary's mother Joan de Bohun, dowager countess of Hereford, who outlived Henry by six years and died in 1419 when she was well past seventy, held a third of her late husband's lands in dower, and the other third was held by her elder daughter Eleanor de Bohun, duchess of Gloucester, who died on 3 October 1399. On Joan's death in 1419, her lands were shared out between her two heirs: her and John of Gaunt's mutual grandson Henry V, as Mary's eldest son, and Anne of Gloucester, countess of Stafford, as Eleanor's only surviving, secular child. *CIPM 1418–22*, Nos 278–80.

2. *CFR 1391–99*, pp. 293–97. Richard II also benefited from the death of his kinswoman Margaret, duchess of Norfolk, on 24 March 1399, aged about seventy-six or seventy-seven: her heir was her grandson Thomas Mowbray, who was in exile and who died in Venice in September 1399.

3. *CCR 1396–99*, pp. 517–18.

4. *CPL 1398–1404*, p. 527.

5. *CPR 1436–41*, p. 137.

Appendix 1. John of Gaunt's Will

1. John's will is printed in full, in the original French, in *A Collection of All the Wills Now Known to be Extant of the Kings and Queens of England, Princes and Princesses of Wales, and Every Branch of the Blood Royal* (London: J. Nichols, 1780), pp. 145–73, and also in *Testamenta Eboracensia, Or Wills Registered at York*, part 1, ed. James Raine (London: J. B. Nichols and Son, 1836), pp. 223–39. A highly abridged English translation is printed in *Testamenta Vetusta: Being Illustrations from Wills*, ed. Nicholas Harris Nicolas, Vol. 1, pp. 140–45. The *Testamenta Eboracensia* version gives *l'an du grace mil trois centz quatre vintz dis et eyt*, i.e. 1398, rather than 1397 as in *Collection of All the Wills*.

2. Mortuary: a gift to a parish from a deceased parishioner.

3. Mortars: bowls of wax with floating wicks.

4. Camoca or camaca: a type of rich silk cloth.

5. 'The house of Our Lady in Lincoln': Lincoln Cathedral.

6. The collegiate church of Our Lady in Leicester: better known as the Newarke, a hospital founded by Blanche of Lancaster's grandfather Henry, earl of Lancaster and Leicester, in 1330, and much extended by her father Duke Henry.

7. The Friars Preacher were the Dominicans or Blackfriars, founded by St Dominic in 1216; the Friars Minor were the Franciscans or Greyfriars, founded by St Francis of Assisi in 1209; and the Augustinians, also sometimes called the Austin Friars, were founded in 1244 and followed the Rule of St Augustine.

8. The London convent of Minoresses was founded in 1293 by Blanche of Lancaster's great-grandparents Edmund of Lancaster, earl of Lancaster and Leicester (1245–96) and Blanche of Artois, dowager queen of Navarre (*c.* 1245/48–1302), and stood near the Tower of London. It was also sometimes called the Minories, and was dissolved in 1539; the road where it stood is still called the Minories.

9. A noble was half a mark, i.e. 6*s* and 8*d*, or 80p.

10. *Charthous*: Charterhouse, the Carthusian order of monks and nuns, also sometimes called the Order of St Bruno, founded by Bruno of Cologne in 1084.

11. The duchess of Norfolk meant Margaret Marshal, b. *c.* 1322, d. 24 March 1399, daughter and heir of Edward I's son Thomas of Brotherton (1300–38) and a first cousin of Edward III. A fret was an interlaced network or an ornament of jewels.

12. The duke of Burgundy was Philip 'the Bold', b. 1342, youngest son of John II and brother of Charles V, and Gaunt's second cousin. Philip died in 1404 and was succeeded by his son from his marriage to Margarethe of Flanders, John the Fearless (*Jean sans Peur*).

13. An alaunt was a breed of hunting dog, now extinct; a charger meant a flat dish.

14. The 'Testament du Prince Noir', printed as an appendix in J. Moisant, *Le Prince Noir en Aquitaine* (Paris: Imprimerie D. Dumoulin, 1894), p. 228, mentions the missal and the breviary (*portehors*), which Edward gave to 'our chapel of our said Lady Undercrofte' in Canterbury Cathedral. Edward of Woodstock's will is also printed in the original French in *A Collection of All the Wills*, pp. 66–77.

15. 'Bachelor' meant a knight serving in a lord's retinue and did not have anything to do with his marital status.
16. *CIPM 1374–77*, Nos 152–54; *CIPM 1418–22*, Nos 797–99; *CPR 1374–77*, p. 208; *CCR 1419–22*, pp. 180–81.

Appendix 2. John of Gaunt's Children

1. *CCR 1399–1402*, p. 78.
2. *CPL 1404–15*, pp. 212–13, 249.
3. *CIPM 1442–47*, No. 582.
4. *Calendar of Papal Letters 1398–1404*, pp. 621, 626, 627; *CIPM 1413–18*, No. 30; *CFR 1430–37*, p. 138.
5. *CIPM 1422–27*, Nos 791–804.
6. *Complete Peerage*, Vol. 5, p. 204 note c.

Bibliography

Primary Sources

Adae Murimuth Continuatio Chronicarum, ed. E. M. Thompson (London: Eyre and Spottiswoode, 1889)

Anglo-Norman Letters and Petitions from All Souls MS 182, ed. Mary Dominica Legge (Oxford: Basil Blackwell, 1941)

Annales Paulini 1307–1340, in. W. Stubbs, ed., *Chronicles of the Reigns of Edward I and Edward II*, Vol. 1 (London: Rolls Series, 1882)

The Anonimalle Chronicle 1307 to 1334, from Brotherton Collection MS 29, ed. W. R. Childs and J. Taylor (Yorkshire Archaeological Society Records Series 147, 1991)

The Anonimalle Chronicle 1333–81, ed. Vivian Hunter Galbraith (Manchester: Manchester University Press, 1927; reprinted with minor corrections, 1970)

The Antient Kalenders and Inventories of the Treasury of His Majesty's Exchequer, three vols, ed. Francis Palgrave (London, 1836)

The Brut or the Chronicles of England, parts 1 and 2, ed. F. W. D. Brie (London: Early English Text Society, 1906–08)

Calendar of Ancient Petitions Relating to Wales, ed. William Rees (Cardiff: University of Wales Press, 1975)

Calendar of the Charter Rolls, one vol., 1341–1417 (London: His Majesty's Stationery Office, 1916)

Calendar of the Close Rolls, twenty-one vols, 1330–1402 (London: HMSO, 1898–1927)

Calendar of Documents Relating to Scotland, two vols, 1307–1509, ed. Joseph Bain (Edinburgh: H. M. General Register House, 1887)

Calendar of Entries in the Papal Registers Relating to Great Britain and Ireland: Papal Letters, three vols, 1305–1404, ed. W. H. Bliss and J. A. Twemlow (London: HMSO, 1895–1902)

Calendar of Entries in the Papal Registers Relating to Great Britain and Ireland: Petitions to the Pope, one vol., 1342–1419, ed. W. H. Bliss (London: HMSO, 1896)

Calendar of the Fine Rolls, seven vols, 1337–99 (London: HMSO, 1915–29)

Calendar of Inquisitions Miscellaneous (Chancery), two vols, 1308–77 (London: HMSO, 1916)

Calendar of Inquisitions Post Mortem, twelve vols, 1327–1399 (London: HMSO, 1909–88)

Calendar of Letter-Books Preserved Among the Archives of the Corporation of the City of London, Letter-Books E, F, G, H, 1314–99, ed. Reginald R. Sharpe (London: John Edward Francis for HMSO, 1903–07)

Calendar of the Patent Rolls, twenty-three vols, 1330–1401 (London: HMSO, 1893–1903)

John of Gaunt

Calendar of Select Plea and Memoranda Rolls of the City of London, three vols, 1323–1412, ed. A. H. Thomas (London: HMSO, 1926–32)

The Chronica Maiora of Thomas Walsingham, 1376–1422, ed. Richard Barber, translated David Preest (Woodbridge: The Boydell Press, 2005)

The Chronicle of Adam Usk, 1377–1421, ed. Chris Given-Wilson (Oxford: Clarendon Press, 1997)

The Chronicle of Geoffrey le Baker of Swinbrook, ed. Richard Barber, trans. David Preest (Woodbridge: Boydell and Brewer, 2012)

Chronicles of the Revolution, 1397–1400: The Reign of Richard II, ed. Chris Given-Wilson (Manchester: Manchester University Press, 1993)

Chronicon Angliae, ab Anno Domini 1328 usque ad Annum 1388, ed. Edward Maunde Thompson (Cambridge: Cambridge University Press, 1874)

Chronicon Galfridi le Baker de Swynebroke, ed. Edward Maunde Thompson (Oxford: Clarendon Press, 1889)

Chronicon Henrici Knighton, vel Cnitthon, monachi Leycestrensis, two vols, ed. J. R. Lumby (London: Eyre and Spottiswoode for HMSO, 1889–95)

Chronicque de la Traison et Mort de Richart Deux Roy Dengleterre, ed. Benjamin Williams (London: S. and J. Bentley, Wilson and Fley, 1846)

Chroniques de London, ed. J. G. Aungier (London: Camden Society, 1844)

Colección Diplomática de Santo Domingo el Real de Toledo I: Documentos Reales (1249–1473), ed. Francisco de Paula Cañas Gálvez (Madrid: Sílex Ediciones, 2010)

A Collection of All the Wills Now Known to be Extant of the Kings and Queens of England, Princes and Princesses of Wales, and Every Branch of the Blood Royal (London: J. Nichols, 1780)

The Diplomatic Correspondence of Richard II, ed. Edouard Perroy (London: Camden third series, volume 48, 1933)

Early Lincoln Wills: An Abstract of All the Wills and Administrations Recorded in the Episcopal Registers of the Old Diocese of Lincoln, 1280–1547, ed. Alfred Gibbons (Lincoln: James Williamson, 1888)

English Historical Documents, Vol. 4, 1327–1485, ed. A. R. Myers (London: Eyre and Spottiswoode, 1969; reprinted by Routledge, 1996)

Eulogium Historiarum Sive Temporis, Vol. 3, ed. Frank Scott Haydon (London: Longman Green, 1863)

Excerpta Historica, Or, Illustrations of English History, ed. Samuel Bentley (London: printed by and for Samuel Bentley, 1831)

Expeditions to Prussia and the Holy Land Made by Henry, Earl of Derby (Afterwards King Henry IV) in the Years 1390–1 and 1392–3, Being the Accounts Kept by his Treasurer for Two Years, ed. Lucy Toulmin Smith (London: Camden Society, 1894)

Foedera, Conventiones, Litterae et Cujuscunque Acta Publica, eight vols, 1327–1413, ed. Thomas Rymer (London, 1821–29)

The Gascon Rolls Project (1317–1468), at www.gasconrolls.org

Henry of Grosmont, First Duke of Lancaster, *Le Livre de Seyntz Medicines: The Book of Holy Medicines*, translated with notes and introduction by Catherine Batt (Tempe, Arizona: Medieval and Renaissance Texts, Vol. 419, 2014)

Historia Vitae et Regni Ricardi Secundi, ed. George B. Stow (Philadelphia: University of Pennsylvania Press, 1977)

Issues of the Exchequer; Being a Collection of Payments Made Out of His Majesty's Revenue, From King Henry III to King Henry VI Inclusive, ed. Frederick Devon (London: John Murray, 1837)

Jean Froissart: Chronicles, translated and edited Geoffrey Brereton (London: Penguin, 1968, reprinted with minor corrections 1978)

John of Gaunt's Register, Vol. 1, 1371–1375, ed. Sydney Armitage-Smith (London: Camden third series, volume 20, 1911)

John of Gaunt's Register, Vol. 2, 1379–1383, ed. Eleanor C. Lodge and Robert Somerville (London: Camden third series, volume 56, 1937)

Knighton's Chronicle 1337–1396, ed. Geoffrey Haward Martin (Oxford: Clarendon Press, 1995)

Life-Records of Chaucer, Parts I–IV, ed. Walford D. Selby, F. J. Furnivall, Edward A. Bond and R. E. G. Kirk (London: Chaucer Society, 1900)

Memorials of London and London Life in the XIIIth, XIVth and XVth Centuries, ed. H. T. Riley, (London: Longmans, Green, 1868)

Memorials of the Order of the Garter from Its Foundation to the Present Time, ed. George Frederick Beltz (London: W. Pickering, 1841)

The National Archives: C (Chancery), DL (Duchy of Lancaster), E (Exchequer), SC (Special Collections)

Oeuvres de Froissart, ed. Kervyn de Lettenhove, twenty-five vols (Brussels, 1867–77)

The Parliament Rolls of Medieval England, ed. Brand, Curry, Given-Wilson, Horrox, Martin, Ormrod and Phillips (Scholarly Editions, 2005)

Records of the Borough of Leicester, Vols 1 and 2, ed. Mary Bateson (London: C. J. Clay and Sons, 1899–1901)

Recueil de Lettres Anglo-Francaises, 1265–1399, ed. F. J. Tanqueray (Paris: Librairie Ancienne Honoré Champion, 1916).

The Reign of Richard II from Majority to Tyranny 1377–1397, ed. A. K. McHardy (Manchester: Manchester University Press, 2012)

Register of Edward the Black Prince Preserved in the Public Record Office, ed. M. C. B. Dawes, parts I–IV (London: HMSO, 1930–33)

Testamenta Eboracensia, Or Wills Registered at York, part 1, ed. James Raine (London: J. B. Nichols and Son, 1836)

Testamenta Vetusta: Being Illustrations from Wills, Vol. 1, ed. Nicholas Harris Nicolas (London: Nichols and Son, 1826)

Thomae Walsingham, Quondam Monachi S. Albani, Historia Anglicana, ed. Henry Thomas Riley, Vol. 2 (London: Longman Green, 1864)

The True Chronicles of Jean le Bel, 1290–1360, ed. and trans. Nigel Bryant (Woodbridge: Boydell and Brewer, 2011)

The Westminster Chronicle 1381–1394, ed. L. C. Hector and B. F. Harvey (Oxford Medieval Texts, Clarendon Press, 1982)

Selected Secondary Sources

Ambühl, Rémy, James Bothwell, and Laura Tompkins, eds., *Ruling Fourteenth-Century England: Essays in Honour of Christopher Given-Wilson* (Woodbridge: The Boydell Press, 2019)

Amin, Nathen, *The House of Beaufort: The Bastard Line That Captured the Crown* (Stroud: Amberley, 2017)

Armitage-Smith, Sydney, *John of Gaunt, King of Castile and Leon, Duke of Aquitaine and Lancaster, Earl of Derby, Lincoln, and Leicester, Seneschal of England* (New York: Charles Scribner, 1904)

Arvanigian, Mark, 'A Lancastrian Polity? John of Gaunt, John Neville, and the War with France, 1368–88', *Fourteenth Century England III*, ed. WM. Ormrod (Woodbridge: Boydell and Brewer, 2004)

Ball, Patrick, "Mercy Gramercy': A Study of Henry of Grosmont', BA thesis, Univ. of Tasmania (2007)

Barber, Richard, *Edward, Prince of Wales and Aquitaine: A Biography of the Black Prince* (Woodbridge: The Boydell Press, 1978, reprinted 1996)

Barker, Juliet, *The Tournament in England, 1100–1400* (Woodbridge: The Boydell Press, 1996)

Barker, Juliet, *England, Arise: The People, the King and the Great Revolt of 1381* (London: Little, Brown, 2014)

Beltz, George Frederick, *Memorials of the Most Noble Order of the Garter from its Foundations to the Present Time* (London: William Pickering, 1841)

Bennett, Michael, 'Edward III's Entail and the Succession to the Crown, 1376–1471', *English Historical Review*, 113 (1998).

Bennett, Michael, *Richard II and the Revolution of 1399* (Stroud: Sutton Publishing, 1999)

Bennett, Michael, '*Honi soit qui mal y pense*: Adultery and Anxieties about Paternity in Late Medieval England', *The Medieval Python: The Purposive and Provocative Work of Terry Jones*, ed. R. F. Yeager and Toshiyuki Takamiya (London: Palgrave MacMillan, 2012)

Blackley, F. D., 'Isabella of France, Queen of England (1308–1358) and the Late Medieval Cult of the Dead', *Canadian Journal of History*, 14 (1980)

Bleicher, Michaela, 'Das Herzogtum Niederbayern-Straubing in den Hussitenkriegen. Kriegsalltag und Kriegsführung im Spiegel der Landschreiberrechnungen', PhD thesis, Universität Regensburg (2004)

Cantor, Norman F., *The Last Knight: The Twilight of the Middle Ages and the Birth of the Modern Era* (New York: Harper Perennial, 2004)

Cole, R. E. G., 'The Manor and Rectory of Kettlethorpe', *Architectural Societies Reports*, 31, report 66 (1911)

Déprez, E., 'La Mort de Robert d'Artois', *Revue Historique*, 94 (1907)

DeVries, Kelly, 'The Reasons for the Bishop of Norwich's Attack of Flanders in 1383', *Fourteenth Century England III*, ed. W. M. Ormrod (Woodbridge: Boydell and Brewer, 2004)

Dodd, Gwilym, ed., *The Reign of Richard II* (Stroud: Tempus Publishing, 2000)

Dunn, Alastair, 'Richard II and the Mortimer Inheritance', *Fourteenth Century England II*, ed. Chris Given-Wilson (Woodbridge: The Boydell Press, 2002)

Emerson, Barbara, *The Black Prince* (London: Weidenfeld and Nicholson, 1976)

Estow, Clara, *Pedro the Cruel of Castile, 1350–1369* (The Medieval Mediterranean: Peoples, Economies and Cultures, 400–1453, number 6; New York: E. J. Brill, 1996)

Estow, Clara, 'Royal Madness in the Crónica del Rey Don Pedro', *Mediterranean Studies*, 6 (1996)

Fletcher, Christopher, 'Manhood and Politics in the Reign of Richard II', *Past and Present*, 89 (2005)

Folger, Robert, *Generaciones Y Semblanzas: Memory and Genealogy in Medieval Iberian Historiography* (Tübingen: Gunter Narr, 2003)

Fowler, Kenneth, 'Henry of Grosmont, First Duke of Lancaster 1310–1361', University of Leeds PhD thesis (1961)

Fowler, Kenneth, *The King's Lieutenant: Henry of Grosmont, First Duke of Lancaster 1310–1361* (London: Elek Books, 1969)

Gibbs, Vicary, *The Complete Peerage of England, Scotland, Ireland, Great Britain and the United Kingdom: Extant, Extinct, or Dormant, by G. E. C.*, 13 vols in 14 parts (second edition, London, 1910–59)

Gillespie, James L., ed., *The Age of Richard II* (Stroud: Sutton Publishing, 1997)

Given-Wilson, Chris, and Alice Curteis, *Royal Bastards of Medieval England* (London: Routledge and Kegan Paul, 1984)

Given-Wilson, Chris, 'Richard II and his Grandfather's Will', *English Historical Review*, 93 (1978)

Given-Wilson, Chris, 'Wealth and Credit, Public and Private: The Earls of Arundel 1306–1397', *English Historical Review*, 106 (1991)

Given-Wilson, Chris, 'The Exequies of Edward III and the Royal Funeral Ceremony', *English Historical Review*, 124 (2009)

Given-Wilson, Chris, *Henry IV* (New Haven and London: Yale University Press, 2016)

Goodman, Anthony, *John of Gaunt: The Exercise of Princely Power in Fourteenth-Century Europe* (Harlow: Longman Group, 1992)

Goodman, Anthony, *Katherine Swynford* (Lincoln: The Honywood Press, 1994)

Goodman, Anthony, *The Loyal Conspiracy: The Lords Appellant under Richard II* (Coral Gables, Florida: University of Miami Press, 1971)

Goodman, Anthony, 'The Military Subcontracts of Sir Hugh Hastings, 1380', *English Historical Review*, 95 (1980)

Goodman, Anthony, and James Gillespie, eds., *Richard II: The Art of Kingship* (Oxford: Clarendon Press, 1999)

Hardy, B. C. [Blanche Christabel], *Philippa of Hainault and her Times* (London: John Long Limited, 1910)

Harris Nicolas, Nicholas, *The Controversy between Sir Richard Scrope and Sir Robert Grosvenor in the Court of Chivalry*, Vol. 2 (London: Samuel Bentley, 1833)

Harvey, John, *The Black Prince and his Age* (London: B. T. Batsford, 1976)

Holmes, G. A., *The Estates of the Higher Nobility in Fourteenth-Century England* (Cambridge: Cambridge University Press, 1957)

Jolly, Margaretta, ed., *Encyclopedia of Life Writing: Autobiographical and Biographical Forms* (London: Routledge, 2013)

Jones, Michael, *The Black Prince: The King That Never Was* (London: Head of Zeus, 2017)

Lucas, Henry Stephen, *The Low Countries and the Hundred Years' War, 1326–1347* (Ann Arbor: University of Michigan, 1929)

Lucraft, Jeannette, *Katherine Swynford: The History of a Medieval Mistress* (Stroud: Sutton, 2006)

Lutkin, Jessica, 'Isabella de Coucy, Daughter of Edward III: The Exception Who Proves the Rule', *Fourteenth Century England VI*, ed. Chris Given-Wilson and Nigel Saul (Woodbridge: The Boydell Press, 2010)

Manly, John Matthews, *Some New Light on Chaucer: Lectures Delivered at the Lowell Institute* (Gloucester, Mass.: Peter Smith, 1959)

Martin, Evelyn H., *History of the Manor of Westhope, Co. Salop* (Oswestry: Caxton Press, 1909)

Mathew, Gervase, *The Court of Richard II* (London: John Murray, 1968).

Moisant, J., *Le Prince Noir en Aquitaine* (Paris: Imprimerie D. Dumoulin, 1894)

Mortimer, Ian, *The Perfect King: The Life of Edward III, Father of the English Nation* (London: Vintage, 2006)

Mortimer, Ian, *The Fears of Henry IV: The Life of England's Self-Made King* (London: Vintage, 2008)

Mortimer, Ian, 'Richard II and the Succession to the Crown' in his *Medieval Intrigue: Decoding Royal Conspiracies* (London: Continuum, 2010)

Munby, Julian, Richard Barber, and Richard Brown, *Edward III's Round Table at Windsor: The House of the Round Table and the Windsor Festival of 1344* (Woodbridge: The Boydell Press, 2007)

Nicolle, David, *The Great Chevauchée: John of Gaunt's Raid on France 1373* (Osprey, 2011)

Ormrod, W. Mark, *Edward III* (New Haven and London: Yale University Press, 2011)

Ormrod, W. M., 'Edward III and his Family', *Journal of British Studies*, 26 (1987)

Ormrod, W. M., 'The Personal Religion of Edward III', *Speculum*, 64 (1989)

Ormrod, W. M., 'The Royal Nursery: A Household for the Younger Children of Edward III', *English Historical Review*, 120 (2005)

Oxford Dictionary of National Biography, online edition: www.oxforddnb.com

Palmer, J. J. N., 'The Historical Context of the "Book of the Duchess": A Revision', *The Chaucer Review*, Vol. 8 (1974)

Perry, Judy, 'Katherine Roet's Swynfords: A Re-Examination of Interfamily Relationships and Descent', parts 1 and 2, *Foundations*, 1.2 and 1.3 (2003–4) [Journal of the Foundation for Medieval Genealogy]

Pohl, John, and Garry Embleton, *Armies of Castile and Aragon 1370–1516* (Oxford: Osprey Publishing, 2015)

Prince, A. E., 'A Letter of Edward the Black Prince Describing the Battle of Nájera', *English Historical Review*, 11 (1926)

Purey-Cust, Arthur P., *The Collar of SS: A History and Conjecture* (Leeds: Richard Jackson, 1910)

Rastall, Richard, 'Secular Musicians in Late Medieval England', Manchester University PhD thesis (1968)

Rodriguez, Bretton, 'Competing Images of Pedro I: López de Ayala and the Formation of Historical Memory', *La Corónica: A Journal of Medieval Hispoanic Languages, Literatures, and Cultures*, 45 (2017)

Sarpy, Julie, *Joanna of Flanders: Heroine and Exile* (Stroud: Amberley, 2019)

Saul, Nigel, *Richard II* (New Haven and London: Yale University Press, 1997)

Santos Silva, Manuela, 'The Marriage of Philippa of Lancaster and João I of Portugal', *Royal and Elite Households in Medieval and Early Modern Europe, More Than Just a Castle*, ed. Theresa Earenfight (Leiden/Boston: Brill, Explorations in Medieval Culture, Vol. 6, 2018)

Silva-Vigier, Anil, *This Moste Highe Prince: John of Gaunt, 1340–1399* (Edinburgh: Pentland, 1992)

Somerville, Robert, *History of the Duchy of Lancaster*, Vol. 1, 1265–1603 (Chancellor and Council of the Duchy of Lancaster, 1953)

St John, Graham, 'Dying Beyond Seas: Testamentary Preparation for Campaigning during the Hundred Years War', *Fourteenth Century England VII*, ed. W. Mark Ormrod (Woodbridge: Boydell and Brewer, 2012)

Stanborrough Cook, Albert, *The Last Months of Chaucer's Earliest Patron* (New Haven, Connecticut, 1916)

Sumption, Jonathan, *Divided Houses: The Hundred Years War*, Vol. 3 (London: Faber and Faber, 2009)

Sumption, Jonathan, *Cursed Kings: The Hundred Years War*, Vol. 4 (London: Faber and Faber, 2015)

Tompkins, Laura, 'Mary Percy and John de Southeray: Wardship, Marriage and Divorce in Fourteenth-Century England, *Fourteenth Century England X*, ed. Gwilym Dodd (Woodbridge: The Boydell Press, 2018)

Towson, Kris, 'Hearts Warped by Passion: The Percy-Gaunt Dispute of 1381', *Fourteenth Century England III*, ed. W. M. Ormrod (Woodbridge: Boydell and Brewer, 2004)

Towson, Kris, 'Henry Percy, Earl of Northumberland: Ambition, Conflict and Cooperation in Late Medieval England', PhD thesis, Univ. of St Andrews (2005)

Vale, Juliet, *Edward III and Chivalry: Chivalric Society and Its Context, 1270–1350* (Woodbridge: The Boydell Press, 1983)

Vale, Malcolm, *The Origins of the Hundred Years War: The Angevin Legacy 1250–1340* (Oxford: Clarendon Press, 1990, reprinted 2004)

Vale, Malcolm, *The Princely Court: Medieval Courts and Culture in North-West Europe* (Oxford: Oxford University Press, 2001)

Verity, Brad, 'The First English Duchess: Isabel de Beaumont, Duchess of Lancaster (*c.* 1318–*c.* 1359)', *Foundations*, Vol. 1.5 (2004)

Walker, Simon, *The Lancastrian Affinity 1361–1399* (Oxford: Oxford University Press, 1990)

Ward, Jennifer, *English Noblewomen in the Later Middle Ages* (London and New York: Longman, 1992)

Ward, Matthew, *The Livery Collar in Late Medieval England and Wales: Politics, Identity and Affinity* (Woodbridge: Boydell and Brewer, 2016)

Warner, Kathryn, *Isabella of France: The Rebel Queen* (Stroud: Amberley, 2016)

Warner, Kathryn, *Philippa of Hainault: Mother of the English Nation* (Stroud: Amberley, 2019)

Warner, Kathryn, *Richard II: A True King's Fall* (Stroud: Amberley, 2017)

Waugh, Scott, *England in the Reign of Edward III* (Cambridge: Cambridge University Press, 1991)

Weir, Alison, *Katherine Swynford: The Story of John of Gaunt and his Scandalous Duchess* (London: Vintage, 2007)

Wells-Furby, Bridget, 'Marriage and Inheritance: The Element of Chance in the Development of Lay Estates in the Fourteenth Century', *Fourteenth Century England X*, ed. Gwilym Dodd (Woodbridge: Boydell and Brewer, 2018)

Wylie, James Hamilton, *History of England Under Henry the Fourth*, Vol. 4 (London: Longmans, Green and Co., 1898)

Woolgar, C. M., *The Great Household in Late Medieval England* (New Haven and London: Yale University Press, 1999)

Woolgar, C. M., *The Senses in Late Medieval England* (New Haven and London: Yale University Press, 2006)

Index

Alfonso XI, queen of Castile   36, 41,
    42, 72, 85, 90, 91, 92
Anne of Bohemia, queen of England
    154, 158, 171, 176, 182, 187, 190,
    205, 207, 212, 213, 218, 223, 224,
    228
Anne of Gloucester, countess of Stafford
    182, 225, 302
Arundel, Thomas, archbishop of
    Canterbury   220, 226, 229, 244,
    300
Ayala, Teresa and María de   85, 198,
    277

Bagot, William   232, 235, 244
Beauchamp, Thomas, earl of Warwick
    (d. 1401)   120, 149, 183, 229
Beaufort, Henry, bishop of Lincoln
    101, 131, 132, 136, 181, 191, 200,
    208, 235-6, 241, 253, 255, 259
Beaufort, Joan, countess of Westmorland
    101, 149-50, 156, 191, 196, 206,
    210, 211, 224, 225, 231, 245, 253,
    256, 259
Beaufort, John, marquis of Dorset   101,
    105, 106, 107, 123, 132, 191, 206,
    211, 225, 226, 228, 231, 233, 234,
    245, 253, 255, 256, 258-9
Beaufort, Roger   144, 145
Beaufort, Thomas   90, 101, 150, 156,
    191, 214, 226, 236, 253, 255, 256,
    259
Beaumont, Isabella, duchess of
    Lancaster   33, 37, 45, 53, 56, 57,
    58, 68, 92
Benedict XII, antipope   154, 301
Blanche of Lancaster, duchess of
    Lancaster   23, 33, 34, 37, 51, 53,
    54, 55, 58, 59, 60, 61, 63, 68, 69,
    70, 72, 74, 76, 77, 78, 89, 95, 96,
    97, 98, 100, 104, 107, 109, 118,

    122, 129, 130, 146, 159, 173, 195,
    197, 204, 238, 239, 241, 247, 249,
    250, 257, 258
Blanche of the Tower   30, 33, 34, 35,
    40
Bohun, Eleanor de, duchess of
    Gloucester   126, 127, 163, 175,
    176, 211-12, 213, 223, 224, 277,
    293-4
Bohun, Humphrey de, earl of Hereford
    (d. 1373)   69, 101-2, 119, 231, 282
Bohun, Joan de, countess of Hereford
    109, 163, 257, 288, 290-1, 300, 302
Bohun, Mary de, countess of Derby
    126, 127, 163, 164, 173, 174, 193,
    196, 205, 210, 211, 214, 217, 243,
    245, 290-1, 300
Boniface IX, pope   109, 205, 218, 224,
    227, 235, 244
Bonne of Bohemia, duchess of
    Normandy   42, 69, 155
Bonsergeant, Agnes   118, 281-2
Bourbon, Blanche de, queen of Castile
    73, 84, 85, 86, 91, 161-2
Bourbon, Jeanne de, queen of France
    73, 75, 161
Burgh, Elizabeth de, duchess of Clarence
    34, 37, 40, 47, 50, 51, 54, 55, 68, 77
Burley, Simon   118, 158, 199
Bushy, John   22, 229, 232, 244

Catalina of Lancaster, queen of Castile
    52, 90, 104, 105, 106, 111, 118,
    119, 134, 136, 159, 172, 174, 183,
    190, 192, 195, 196, 198, 199, 201,
    202-3, 207, 212, 217, 236, 237, 238,
    244, 253, 258
Cerda, Carlos de la   42, 43
Charles V, king of France   69, 71, 73,
    74, 75, 78, 135, 155, 161

Charles VI, king of France   161, 185, 191, 196, 201, 206, 209, 224, 225

Chaucer, Geoffrey   24, 52, 55, 56, 80, 88, 94, 98, 112, 126, 203

Chaucer, Philippa   52, 88, 91, 94, 98, 115, 126, 174, 191, 203

Clement VII, antipope   154, 192, 301

Constanza of Castile, duchess of Lancaster   52, 73, 80, 87, 88, 89, 91, 92, 95, 101, 102, 109, 112, 113, 115, 117, 118, 119, 120, 123, 124, 125, 128, 133, 142, 146, 152, 156, 158, 162, 171, 172, 173, 174, 178, 183, 190, 192, 194, 195, 200, 201, 202, 204, 208, 212, 214

appearance   90, 92

birth, background and siblings   84-6, 195-6, 198-9

children   104, 105, 106, 111, 119, 125, 136

death and funeral   216-18

wedding   84

Coucy, Enguerrand de, earl of Bedford   70, 75, 79, 166, 177

Coucy, Philippa de, countess of Oxford   70, 79, 82, 174, 177, 185, 225, 242

Courtenay, William, archbishop of Canterbury   128-9, 143, 153, 170, 226

courtesy of England   64, 76, 77, 99, 148, 240, 243

Crophill, Joan   179, 180, 293

David II, king of Scotland   29, 38, 49, 53, 69

Deincourt, Robert   130, 144, 156, 225, 269

Despenser, Edward (d. 1375)   69, 75, 77, 78, 87, 157

Despenser, Henry, bishop of Norwich   87, 157, 179, 184, 203

Despenser, Hugh (d. 1374)   77, 78, 87, 145

Despenser, Thomas, earl of Gloucester   156-7, 228, 231, 234

Duarte I, king of Portugal   231, 244, 260

Edmund of Langley, duke of York   30, 33, 34, 39, 40, 41, 44, 47, 51, 69, 70, 75, 78, 79, 80, 88, 102, 111, 112, 113, 114, 117, 139, 141, 142,

147, 148, 149, 156, 161, 163, 177, 185, 189, 190, 207, 212, 213, 221, 225, 227, 228, 238, 241, 249, 252

Edward II, king of England   26, 27, 28, 33, 37, 44, 50, 155, 205, 213

Edward III, king of England   22, 25, 26, 27, 28, 29, 30, 31, 32, 33, 34, 35, 36, 37, 38, 39, 40, 41, 42, 43, 44, 45, 47, 49, 50, 51, 53, 57, 58, 59, 61, 67, 69, 70, 71, 74, 78, 79, 80, 81, 83, 88, 89, 104, 105, 107, 112, 114, 117, 119, 120, 121, 139, 140, 142, 144, 145, 146, 147

Edward of Woodstock, prince of Wales   25, 28, 29, 34, 35, 36, 37, 38, 39, 40, 41, 42, 43, 44, 47, 49, 51, 54, 61, 62, 67, 72, 73, 78, 79, 83, 89, 93, 114, 117, 126, 140, 141

Edward of York, duke of Aumerle   113, 149, 199, 205, 221, 222, 225, 228, 230, 231, 233, 234, 242

Elizabeth of Lancaster, duchess of Exeter   68, 82, 97, 109, 159, 160, 182, 183, 192, 193, 200, 217, 219, 220, 229, 247, 253, 257

Enrique II of Trastámara, king of Castile (d. 1379)   36, 72, 73, 80, 84, 85, 91, 102, 114, 156, 186, 196, 198

Enrique III, king of Castile (d. 1406)   196, 199, 202, 203, 207, 217, 254, 258

Fernando, king of Portugal   80, 121, 161, 185, 186, 189

Ferrers, Elizabeth   110, 111, 120, 134

Ferrers, Robert, of Wem (d. c. 1396)   206, 210, 211, 224

Fitzalan, Richard, earl of Arundel (d. 1376)   39, 69, 84, 126, 135

Fitzalan, Richard, earl of Arundel (d. 1397)   129, 149, 158, 184, 186, 199, 204, 205, 215, 226, 227, 228, 229, 230

Froissart, Jean   26, 27, 42, 51, 52, 55, 75, 76, 77, 81, 84, 101, 106, 112, 136, 145, 161, 163, 165, 194, 196, 200, 202, 203, 206, 212, 223, 225, 236

Giovanna I, queen of Naples   71, 73, 74, 135, 273

Great Schism   154, 155, 227

Great Uprising 64, 162, 166-8
Greene, Henry 232, 244
Gregory XI, pope 71, 144, 145
Guzmán, Leonor de 36, 72, 85, 91, 92

Hastings, John, earl of Pembroke (d. 1375) 57, 58, 79, 80, 114, 120, 159
Hastings, John, earl of Pembroke (d. 1389) 79, 120, 159, 160, 183, 192, 193, 199, 205
Henry of Grosmont, duke of Lancaster (d. 1361) 33, 34, 37, 38, 42, 45, 46, 49, 51, 53, 56, 57, 59, 60, 62, 63, 64, 68, 74, 77, 83, 118, 122, 131, 178, 197, 216, 245, 265, 270, 271
Henry of Lancaster, earl of Lancaster (d. 1345) 33, 35, 36, 60, 67, 68, 71, 178, 245
Henry of Lancaster, duke of Hereford, later Henry IV (d. 1413) 22, 24, 39, 52, 72, 74, 75, 81, 82, 105, 109, 115, 117, 119, 129, 144, 149, 150, 154, 157, 163, 168, 171, 172, 173, 175, 185, 190, 191, 196, 197, 198, 199, 200, 204, 206, 207, 214, 219, 221, 223, 224, 225, 227, 229, 231, 232, 234, 235, 236, 237, 240, 242, 243, 244, 246, 252-3, 258
Henry of Monmouth, later Henry V 24, 52, 98, 109, 164, 193, 196, 205, 217, 220, 237, 244, 245, 253, 260
Holland, John, duke of Exeter (d. 1400) 75, 112, 113, 185, 186, 189, 192, 193, 195, 200, 206, 207, 212, 215, 217, 219-20, 226, 227, 228, 231, 234, 238
Holland, John, later duke of Exeter (d. 1447) 195, 219
Holland, Thomas, earl of Kent (d. 1360) 61, 190, 192, 276
Holland, Thomas, earl of Kent (d. 1397) 190, 192, 227
Holland, Thomas, duke of Surrey (d. 1400) 227, 228, 229, 231, 234, 236, 243
Humphrey of Gloucester (d. 1399) 164, 175, 182
Humphrey of Lancaster (d. 1447) 197, 260

Isabel of Castile, duchess of York 85, 87, 88, 102, 103, 111, 112, 113, 117, 149, 156, 190, 193, 206, 211, 212, 213, 217
Isabelle de Valois, queen of England (d. 1409) 224, 225, 237
Isabella of France, queen of England (d. 1358) 27, 28, 33, 36, 37, 49, 50, 59, 67, 122, 177, 178
Isabella of Woodstock, countess of Bedford 25, 29, 30, 31, 34, 50, 51, 53, 65, 70, 78, 79, 103, 126, 134, 145, 155, 177

Jaime IV, king of Majorca 71, 73, 74
Jan III, duke of Brabant 26
Jeanne de Valois, countess of Hainault 26, 27, 28, 32
Joan of Kent, princess of Wales 61, 62, 67, 73, 79, 83, 88, 112, 117, 120, 125, 126, 130, 143, 146, 188, 189, 190
Joan of the Tower, queen of Scotland 27, 29, 49, 50, 53, 67
Joan of Woodstock 25, 30, 34, 36, 41, 42, 73
João, king of Portugal 22, 186, 189, 194, 195, 231, 244, 257
John, duke of Berry 74, 75, 161, 185, 196, 214, 220, 296
John of Gaunt
  background and relatives 25-9, 39, 45, 46-7, 49, 62, 65, 82, 88, 136, 150, 158, 165
  birth and childhood 26-44
  children 51, 52, 53, 56, 58, 59, 66, 68, 72, 74, 75, 76, 83, 95, 97, 104, 105-6, 115, 118-19, 136, 159-60, 165, 257-9
  claims Castile 89, 110, 170, 173, 176-7, 178, 180, 184, 190, 191, 192, 194, 195, 196, 198, 199
  claims Provence 70, 71, 74
  descendants 23, 244-5, 257-61
  final illness and death 237, 241-2
  gifts given and received 54, 88, 101-3, 105, 110-11, 115-16, 117-18, 120-21, 126, 130, 134, 136, 157, 163, 182, 223
  heir presumptive to the throne 140, 142, 189, 200, 206, 216

household, retinue and wards 29, 43, 44, 67, 83, 87, 120, 122, 154, 156, 157, 169-70, 175, 178, 180, 203, 227
in Castile and Portugal 191, 194-6, 198-9, 200
income and wealth 56, 67, 84, 87, 112, 166, 198
jousting, hunting and hawking 40, 57-8, 134, 182, 200-01, 214
lands and castles 32, 35, 48, 60, 61, 63-5, 68, 70, 74, 76-7, 88, 129, 159, 178
languages and education 32, 33, 129, 159, 179, 181
letters to and from 109-10, 114, 138, 184, 219-22, 227
made duke of Aquitaine in 1390 206
made duke of Lancaster in 1362 67
made earl of Richmond in 1342 32, 34
marries Blanche 51, 53, 54
marries Constanza 84
marries Katherine 223-4
military career 42, 43, 47, 48, 59, 73, 80, 82, 83, 114-15, 124, 170, 228
possessions 44, 137, 164, 167, 183, 184, 200
potential king of Scotland 69
potential marriages 36, 78
quarrel with Henry Percy 169, 188
relations with Blanche 37, 45, 55-6, 61, 76, 129
relations with Constanza 91-2, 104, 109, 112-13, 123-4, 125-6, 162, 173, 202, 204, 208, 216, 217, 218
relations with family 34, 41, 46, 59, 78-9, 81, 140-41, 144, 145-6, 164, 175, 177, 182, 203, 221, 225, 228
relations with son Henry 145, 175, 214, 232-3, 235, 236
relations with Katherine 91, 93, 98-9, 100, 101, 105, 107-8, 123, 125, 130-33, 149-50, 152, 156, 162, 172-4, 180, 191, 225
relations with Richard II 141, 151, 186-7, 188, 204, 205, 215, 221-2
religion 122-3, 124, 188
Savoy destroyed 167-8, 175
travels to Bruges 135-6, 137-8

travels to France 185, 187, 214, 224-5
travels to Scotland 162, 166, 183, 186, 189
will 237-41, 247-56
John of Kent, earl of Kent 39, 62
John of Lancaster (d. 1435) 197, 237, 253, 260
John II, king of France 42, 45, 46, 47, 49, 69, 78, 94
Juan I, king of Castile (d. 1390) 156, 161, 180, 186, 189, 191, 194, 196, 198, 199, 202, 206, 207, 254
Juan II, king of Castile (d. 1454) 90, 199, 244, 258
Juana of Navarre, queen of England 109, 218, 220, 246, 258, 300
Jülich, Elisabeth von, countess of Kent 39, 62, 267

Karl IV, Holy Roman Emperor 71, 74, 154-5, 171

Lacy, Alice de, countess of Lincoln 37, 60, 68, 74, 271
Lionel of Antwerp, duke of Clarence 25, 26, 30, 34, 35, 38, 39, 40, 43, 44, 47, 48, 49, 50, 51, 53, 54, 57, 59, 67, 68, 70, 75, 77, 78, 142, 157, 171, 192, 193
Lords Appellant 199, 200, 227, 228, 229
Louis, count of Flanders 70, 78, 134
Louis, duke of Anjou 71, 135, 161
Ludwig of Bavaria, Holy Roman Emperor 28-9, 37, 39, 57, 64

Małgorzata of Brzeg, duchess of Bavaria 45, 136
Manny, Anne, countess of Pembroke 79, 120, 160, 193, 289
Mare, Peter de la 139
Margaret of Norfolk, duchess of Norfolk 57, 79, 94, 111, 117, 120, 154, 159, 160, 193, 231, 243, 252
Margaret of Windsor 30, 47, 51, 54, 65, 103, 264
Margaretha of Hainault, Holy Roman Empress 28, 37, 39, 45, 46, 47, 263
Margarethe of Flanders, duchess of Burgundy 70, 71, 78, 112, 134, 165, 225

Maria of Portugal, queen of Castile 36, 41, 72, 85, 91, 102

Mary of Waltham 30, 35, 47, 51, 53-4, 65, 73, 103, 130, 264

Maud of Lancaster, duchess of Bavaria 33, 45, 46, 57, 61, 62, 63, 64, 65, 136

Merciless Parliament 199, 200, 228, 234

Mohun, Joan 111, 119, 120

Montacute, John, earl of Salisbury (d. 1400) 228, 234

Montacute, William, earl of Salisbury (d. 1397) 61, 70, 144, 228, 239

Montfort, John IV de, duke of Brittany 32, 73, 82, 151-2, 220

Montiel, battle of 73, 80, 202

Morieux, Blanche and Thomas 52, 53, 212, 225

Mortimer, Edmund, earl of March (d. 1381) 50, 53, 57, 77, 79, 82, 117, 139, 145, 171

Mortimer, Roger, earl of March (d. 1398) 50, 189, 216, 236

Mowbray, John (d. 1383) 120, 149, 154, 159, 185

Mowbray, Thomas, duke of Norfolk (d. 1399) 22, 154, 185, 214, 220, 226, 228, 229, 231, 234, 235, 236, 243

Nájera, battle of 73, 74, 75, 91, 152, 210

Neville, Ralph, earl of Westmorland 224, 231, 233, 238, 244, 245, 247, 254, 256, 259

Newarke, the 60, 72, 109, 178, 216, 217, 239, 245, 251

Padilla, María de 41, 73, 80, 84, 85, 86, 90, 112

parliament 35, 43, 94, 129, 139, 140, 142, 143, 151, 155, 156, 158, 162, 169, 170, 175, 176, 179, 182, 184, 185, 186, 188, 190, 199, 205, 208, 209, 214, 215, 220, 224, 225, 226, 229, 231, 234

Pedro I 'the Cruel', king of Castile 36, 41, 42, 72, 73, 80, 84, 85, 86, 88, 90, 91, 92, 102, 161, 190, 195, 198, 202, 217, 254

Percy, Henry, earl of Northumberland 139, 143, 144, 149, 154, 161, 169, 188, 192, 208, 230, 231, 238, 244

Percy, Thomas, earl of Worcester 192, 231, 233, 234, 238, 254

Perrers, Alice 81, 93, 120, 128, 132, 139, 144, 145, 152, 155, 161

Philip, duke of Burgundy 75, 78, 82, 161, 165, 185, 209, 214, 218, 220, 225, 239, 252

Philip VI, king of France 25, 26, 28, 37, 42, 46, 155

Philippa of Clarence, countess of March 47, 50, 77, 79, 82, 117, 142, 171, 193

Philippa of Hainault, queen of England 25, 26, 27, 28, 29, 30, 31, 32, 33, 34, 35, 36, 37, 38, 39, 40, 45, 47, 49, 50, 51, 52, 53, 54, 58, 59, 65, 70, 71, 78, 80, 81, 82, 88, 94, 95, 211, 212, 246, 253

Philippa of Lancaster, queen of Portugal 52, 58, 59, 82, 88, 114, 165, 194, 195, 203, 231, 244, 253

plague 40, 41, 42, 65, 69, 76, 124, 135-6, 166, 205, 207

Provence 70, 71, 74

Richard II, king of England 22, 33, 61, 62, 72, 83, 98, 106, 113, 114, 121, 140, 142, 144, 146, 147, 148, 149, 152, 153, 154, 155, 158, 161, 162, 163, 166, 167, 168, 169, 170, 171, 176, 183, 185, 186, 187, 188, 189, 190, 191, 192, 199, 200, 204, 205, 207, 208, 209, 211, 212, 215, 219, 221-2, 223, 224, 225, 228, 229, 232, 234, 236, 238, 243, 244, 252, 254-5

Robert II, king of Scotland 166, 183

Roet, Katherine: see Swynford

St Hilaire, Marie de 51, 52, 212

Savoy Palace 60, 62, 64, 66, 69, 75, 83, 89, 101, 104, 105, 107, 110, 111, 115, 119, 120, 122, 124, 125, 130, 131, 132, 134, 137, 142, 143, 149, 158, 164, 167, 168

Southeray, John de 81, 144, 161

Stafford, Hugh, earl of Stafford (d. 1386) 57, 119, 134, 182, 184, 189, 192, 224

Stafford, Ralph, earl of Stafford (d. 1372) 57, 83, 119
Stafford, Ralph (d. 1385) 189, 192, 193
Sudbury, Simon, archbishop of Canterbury 135, 168, 170, 176
Swynford, Blanche 52, 53, 82, 97, 98, 130, 224, 225, 238
Swynford, Hugh 53, 87, 88, 94, 95, 96, 97, 98, 99, 100, 101, 105, 106, 108, 180, 206
Swynford, Katherine, duchess of Lancaster 23, 38, 52, 53, 64, 82, 88, 91, 92, 93, 94, 95, 96, 97, 98, 99, 100, 101, 104, 105, 106, 107, 108, 109, 115, 118, 119, 121, 123, 125, 126, 130, 132, 133, 136, 144, 149, 152, 155, 156, 162, 165, 172, 173, 179, 180, 191, 196, 203, 208, 210, 211, 214, 215, 223, 224, 225, 231, 232, 233, 235, 237, 238, 240, 244, 251, 252, 255
Swynford, Thomas 95, 96, 97, 100, 106, 109, 150, 174, 179, 191, 206, 207, 238, 244, 253

Thomas of Lancaster, earl of Lancaster (d. 1322) 37, 60, 67, 68, 70, 122
Thomas of Lancaster (d. 1421) 77, 196, 259, 260
Thomas of Woodstock, duke of Gloucester 47, 51, 54, 58, 59, 67, 79, 81, 117, 119, 126, 141, 142, 144, 147, 148, 149, 156, 163, 164, 170, 175, 177, 182, 186, 187, 189, 190, 199, 200, 207, 212, 214, 220, 221, 224, 228, 229

truces with France 59, 135, 185, 187, 188, 216, 224, 285

Urban V, pope 71, 74, 77, 78, 84
Urban VI, pope 154, 180, 191, 192, 205

Vere, Robert de, earl of Oxford 70, 144, 177, 185, 189, 199-200, 220, 234
Visconti, Bernabo 171
Visconti, Galeazzo 75
Visconti, Gian Galeazzo 22
Visconti, Violante 75, 77

Walsingham, Thomas 29, 111, 132, 133, 139, 143, 145, 149, 155, 167, 171, 172, 185, 186, 188, 191, 198, 204, 223, 229, 236, 241
Wenzel, king of Germany and Bohemia 22, 154, 155, 158, 182
Wilhelm, duke of Jülich 29, 67
Willem, count of Hainault 26, 27, 28, 32, 39
William of Hatfield 25, 34, 264
William of Windsor 39, 40
Winchelsea, battle of 42-3
Wittelsbach, Albrecht von, duke of Bavaria 39, 45, 46, 63, 64, 136, 150, 158, 165, 175, 207
Wittelsbach, Wilhelm von, duke of Bavaria 39, 45-6, 57, 61, 63, 64, 65, 136
Wycliffe, John 143, 188
Wykeham, William, bishop of Winchester 158

About the Author

Kathryn Warner holds two degrees in medieval history from the University of Manchester. She is considered a foremost expert on Edward II and an article from her on the subject was published in the *English Historical Review*. She has run a website about him since 2005 and a Facebook page about him since 2010 and has carved out a strong online presence as an expert on Edward II and the fourteenth century in general. Kathryn teaches Business English as a foreign language and lives between Dusseldorf and Cumbria.